Troublemakers or Peacemakers?

Youth and Post-Accord Peace Building

EDITED BY SIOBHÁN MCEVOY-LEVY

FROM THE
**JOAN B. KROC INSTITUTE
FOR INTERNATIONAL PEACE STUDIES**

THE RIREC PROJECT ON POST-ACCORD PEACE BUILDING

■

THE RESEARCH INITIATIVE ON THE RESOLUTION OF ETHNIC CONFLICT

Troublemakers

or

Peacemakers?

YOUTH AND POST-ACCORD PEACE BUILDING

 EDITED BY SIOBHÁN McEVOY-LEVY

UNIVERSITY OF NOTRE DAME PRESS
NOTRE DAME, INDIANA

Library of Congress Cataloging-in-Publication Data

Troublemakers or peacemakers? : youth and post-accord peace building / editor,
Siobhán McEvoy-Levy.
p.   cm.
"From the Joan B. Kroc Institute for International Peace Studies, the RIREC
Project on Post-Accord Peace Building, the Research Initiative on the Resolution
of Ethnic Conflict."
Includes bibliographical references and index.
ISBN 0-268-03493-1 (cloth : alk. paper)
ISBN 0-268-03494-X (pbk. : alk. paper)

1. Youth and peace.   2. Children and peace.   3. Children and war.   4. Peace-
building.   5. Youth movement.   6. Youth—Political activity.   7. Child soldiers.
I. McEvoy-Levy, Siobhán, 1968–   II. Joan B. Kroc Institute for International Peace
Studies.   III. RIREC Project on Post-Accord Peace Building.   IV. Research Initiative
on the Resolution of Ethnic Conflict.

JZ5579.T76   2006
303.6'6—dc22

                                                        2005021223

CONTENTS

ACKNOWLEDGMENTS

This book was made possible through the generous support of the Joan B. Kroc Institute for International Peace Studies at the University of Notre Dame, its director Scott Appleby, and its Faculty Fellows. My time as a visiting fellow at the Kroc Institute provided the financial support and thinking space to begin this project. Thanks, in particular, to Scott Appleby and George Lopez for their guidance. Rashied Omar, the brilliant coordinator of the RIREC project, was an invaluable support both intellectually and logistically. Students in the MA Program in Peace Studies at Notre Dame also contributed useful comments on an early draft of the project proposal, as did Ellen Ambrosone and the students in my senior seminar at Butler University. Participants in the Catholic Relief Services Summer Peacebuilding Institute at Notre Dame also provided valuable feedback.

My RIREC co-directors Tristan Anne Borer and John Darby were good friends and challenging intellectual partners. Thanks to them for their camaraderie and commitment to the project during all its twists and turns and their careful and insightful comments on successive drafts of the introduction and conclusion to this book.

All of the chapter contributors to the book—many of them working under very difficult conditions in war zones and postwar situations around the world—are owed special acknowledgment. Each of them has produced a remarkably fresh, intense, and multidimensional analysis of the various roles of youth in war and peace building. They have presented new facts, theories, challenges, pleas, and hope. Thanks especially to Carolyn, Dan, Ed, Jaco, Jeff, Jessica, Johan, Marc, Mike, Namik, Neil, Nir, Sami, Sean, and Victoria, who were able to attend the RIREC workshops and/or conference and who created a very special community of discourse, encouragement, and constructive intellectual collaboration. Additional thanks to Jeffrey Helsing and the United States Institute of Peace (USIP) for sponsoring the visits of Namik, Neil, and Nir.

At my home institution of Butler University, great support was pro-vided by colleagues in the Political Science Department—Craig Auchter, Margaret Brabant, the late Dale Hathaway, Terri Jett, and David Mason. Special thanks to Craig Auchter for reading my specific chapters of this book and making many useful comments. Thanks too to Mary Kaiser, who provided administrative assistance. Others who have had a significant impact on the book include Christina Catanzarite, the University of Notre Dame Press's editor; Linda Ferreira and Annie Pruitt; and the two anonymous reviewers who provided very helpful suggestions and encouragement at a critical time.

Many other friends and family members supported me along the way. As always they are deeply appreciated. The book is dedicated with love to my husband Andy and to our son Aedan, who embody kindness and intelligence, unconditional and cheerful support, and who are always an inspiration.

Siobhán McEvoy-Levy
September 2004

Preface

This book is one of three edited volumes resulting from a three-year collaborative Research Initiative on the Resolution of Ethnic Conflict (RIREC) at the Joan B. Kroc Institute for International Peace Studies at the University of Notre Dame. From 2000 to 2003, the RIREC initiative examined the problems and challenges that develop after a peace accord has been reached between conflicting parties but before the agreement has been fully implemented. It focused on post-accord peacebuilding and the difficult but pressing question of how to create a sustainable just peace after a period of protracted conflict. The project set out to understand why so many recent peace accords have not been successfully implemented and to provide guidance from experience for those engaged in peace building.

The RIREC project identified and integrated the study of three key dimensions of the post-accord landscape: post-accord violence, the role of young people in violent conflict and peace building, and truth telling and peace building. A research cluster was developed for each dimension and brought together a team of interdisciplinary international scholars and practitioners for a series of workshops and an international conference at the University of Notre Dame in September 2003 on the theme of "Peacebuilding after Peace Accords."

Each research cluster resulted in an edited book. In addition to this book, the truth-telling and peace building-cluster, directed by Tristan Anne Borer, produced *Telling the Truths: Truth Telling and Peace Building in Post-Conflict Societies,* and the post-accord violence team, directed by John Darby, produced *Violence and Reconstruction.*

Separately, each of these dimensions combines conflict management and conflict transformation challenges and opportunities. The synergy between youth, truth telling and transitional justice, and post-accord violence, however, has not been conceptualized in this fashion, much less systematically studied as a dynamic process generating its own outcomes and patterns of behavior. Yet any peace process is doomed to failure if it lacks a realistic strategy to reduce levels of violence and counter violence; if it skirts the hard political, legal, and cultural choices that nurture genuine reconciliation; and if it fails to recognize and accommodate the central role of youth.

Together, the series of three books develops new perspectives on post-accord peace building, as well as on the intersections between different aspects of reconstruction that were once studied in isolation.

SIOBHÁN McEVOY-LEVY

Introduction

Youth and the Post-Accord Environment

We used to fear them [youth soldiers] and thought they would start fighting in our communities. When they came from the bush, we looked at them as animals.[1]

We have a lot of new buildings and reconstruction projects, but we are not seeing a bright future for ourselves. . . . Decisions are made for us by people who do not have an idea of what we are faced with on a daily basis.[2]

Most [male] youth are waiting for their parents to give them land. . . . Struggling for life and being patient is very, very difficult.[3]

Nobody knows what peace is. You could ask that question to any-body and nobody will know what peace is.

"Post-accord" does not mean "postwar" or "post-conflict." From a theoretical standpoint, it is important to make the differentiation. Practically speaking, the difference between an accord and an end to a war is even more relevant on the ground in former war zones. Political agreements establish ceasefires and mandate new institutions, but rarely do they completely end political violence, nor do they frequently produce solutions to all the small wars for survival that people face once political elites leave the negotiating table. But accords mark a turning point and create an opportunity for a new era. In such an environment, youth needs, perceptions, and roles are central to the project of peace building and to the attainment of a sustainable peace, yet they remain understudied. This volume attempts to address this neglect.

The distinct problems, needs, and dynamics of the post-accord phases of conflict are only beginning to be systematically studied (see Darby and Mac Ginty 2002; Darby 2001; Miall, Ramsbotham, and Woodhouse 1999; Stedman et al. 2002). And so far neither children nor youth appear as important variables in the scholarly literature on peace processes. The neglect of children in this literature is balanced by now extensive work on child soldiers, children displaced by war, and education in contexts of civil strife (see, for example, the following excellent works: Bonnerjea 1994; Brett and McCallin 1996; Cohn and Goodwin-Gill 1994; Machel 1996; McKay and Mazurana 2000; Smith and Vaux 2003; Sommers 2002, 2003; Thompson 1999; Wessells 1998, 2000; West 2000; Young 2002; Boothby and Knudsen 2000; Brett and Sprecht 2004; and Solomon 2004).

But even authors of important United Nations (UN) reports admit that adolescents have not been separately or well considered (Lowicki and Pillsbury 2000; Winnipeg 2000; International Tribunal 2000). The advocacy-oriented research on war-affected children prioritizes the most vulnerable in war and its aftermath. But many contemporary conflicts take their fuel and energy from adolescents and older young people in their early to mid-twenties, who are key actors in terms of post-accord violence and social reconstruction. Their experiences are very different from those of older adults who have not been central to the fighting or who can remember a time before war. In addition, the culturally influenced elasticity of the concept of "youth," as explored below, means that this population is not easily accommodated by advocacy paradigms that focus on the child. They are invisible in the adult political world, too. Although young people are often on the frontlines of combat, they are rarely included at the negotiation table and almost always become marginal players in the politics of the post-accord period.

In this volume the focus is particularly on adolescents and older young people and on the crucial post-accord phase, with its twin challenges of violence prevention/accord maintenance and societal reconstruction and reconciliation. Youth (defined in this volume as people between the ages of twelve and thirty) embody essential elements of both challenges, at once potential threats to peace and significant peace-building resources. From political activists and militarized youth, to criminal and bandit youth, to peace activist youth, they form crucial parts of the post-accord reconstruction puzzle. It is hoped the research in this volume will provide a useful complement to existing literature on war-affected children and contribute to the literature on peace processes.

Young people are a viable and important population for inclusion at the very earliest stages of a peace process and as it unfolds, and it is current UN policy to promote this inclusion. The chapters in this book demonstrate why this should be the case, but they particularly explore the relationship of youth to the sustainability of peace accords, to the quality and legitimacy of the peace produced, and to the prevention of cycles of violence. Given the number of accords reached in the last fifteen years—at least thirty-eight according to Darby and Mac Ginty (2000)—these concerns already form a pressing and extensive challenge.

This book explores the attitudes, needs, lived experiences, and social and political roles of young people in periods of transition in internal armed conflicts through a number of cases—Sierra Leone, Angola, Rwanda, Northern Ireland, Israel/Palestine, Bosnia, Guatemala, and Columbia.[5] The chapters variously look at youth combatants, their pathways into armed conflict, the costs and lessons of their involvement, and the reintegration challenges after accords. More generally, they examine young people's subjective understandings of war, peace, and peace processes. They examine specific activities of youth in support of peace and specific initiatives designed to engage youth in peace building. While one book can offer only a limited picture of all the places where youth have active roles in conflict, these chapters offer persuasive conclusions about how best to work with young people to help cement accords and build genuine, multigenerational, lasting peace. In doing so, they add a new dimension to our understanding of the nature of contemporary armed conflict and the challenges of conflict resolution.

WHO ARE YOUTH? DEFINITIONAL ISSUES

The labels "youth"and "child" are socially constructed, historically variable, and highly contestable categories.[6] Currently, legal and cultural differences abound in the definition process. The norm in studies of child soldiers is to focus on those under eighteen, in accordance with relevant international law, which defines children in terms of this universal standard. The recent Optional Protocol on the Involvement of Children in Armed Conflict (2002) to the Convention on the Rights of the Child (1989) raises the minimum age for compulsory recruitment into armed groups from fifteen to eighteen. The International Labor Organization Convention No. 182 (2000) defines "child soldiering" as one of the worst forms of child labor. And the African Charter of the Rights and Welfare of the Child (1999) makes eighteen the cutoff for both compulsory and voluntary recruitment. But the Rome Statute (2002) establishing the International Criminal Court only makes it a war crime to recruit children under fifteen into armed forces (*Guide* 2003). The CRC also acknowledges that legal differences exist with respect to age of majority in different countries. As Cohn and Goodwin-Gill have explained, the age of majority "is a social, religious, cultural or legal device by which societies acknowledge the transition to adulthood" (1994, 7). Even within a single society, different ages (and varying assumptions about competency) may apply to acquisition of different "adult" roles such as taking part in a religious ritual, marriage, voting, giving evidence in court, and joining the state military (Cohn and Goodwin-Gill 1994, 7).

If the distinction between child and adult is difficult, the designation of who is a youth is thornier still. In some cultures, a person may be considered an adult at age twelve or fourteen if married or having fulfilled certain rites of passage. However, he or she may remain a "youth" in the eyes and terminology of their community into their thirties or forties (see chapter 1 in this volume) if they do not cross these thresholds. In a similar vein, many industrialized countries now report a prolonged period of "youth" well into the twenties, which is marked by extended academic studies, inability to find employment, deferred earnings, protracted residency with parents, and late marriage (Coffield 1995; Cote and Allahar 1996).

If these differences reflect cultural norms and changing economic realities, a further complicating factor is the way in which the terms "youth" and "child" are conventionally used in media, criminal justice, and advocacy discourse. Following Western criminal justice models, it is common to talk of *youth* but not *child* gangs, *youth* but not *child* delinquency. Conversely, the advocacy community tends to highlight *child* labor and *child* soldiers, not working or warrior *youth*. The Western media reports riots and demonstrations by Palestinian "youth," but the plight of "children" displaced by war in Kosovo; "youth" militias in Liberia, but "child" poverty and hunger in Ethiopia. The tendency is to equate children with victimization and youth (usually defined as teens or adolescents) with perpetration. But often these classifications refer to the same age groups and to related if not identical pursuits (for example, a youth rioter may also be a child of poverty and war displacement) and reveal not empirical categories but assumptions about what is acceptable or unacceptable for "our" children and "their" children, assumptions that may be tied to foreign policy interests or gender stereotypes. Erica Burman argues that child-youth distinctions reveal "a gendered polarity around ideas of agency and responsibility. While the image of the 'child' is predominantly feminine, the term 'youth' has a masculine nuance. . . . So feminised children need to be saved, but bad boys need to be contained" (1994, 244, 245).

Viewing children as only victims ignores the other politically and socially relevant roles they may play, not just in soldiering but in maintaining families and communities, and ignores evidence that political involvement may have positive psychological effects for children in situations of political violence (see Barber 1999; Cairns 1996; Dawes 1994; Burman 1994; Straker et al. 1992). It also ignores that children as active agents in war can cause tremendous suffering and destabilization. Similarly, conceiving "youth" (defined as teens or adolescents) primarily as perpetrators limits their agency to the sphere of violence and is reductionist, missing the complexity of youth (teen) agency in war zones as well as excluding older young people who are at the center of war and essential to peace.

THE NEW YOUTH

In this book youth is not equated with adolescence. This volume works with an extended definition of youth (twelve to thirty years of age) for three reasons: first, as discussed, in many cultures youth is a similarly expanded category; second, the economic realities of globalization and the experience of war conspire to ensure that many who are children according to international law are in fact heads of households, sole economic providers, or soldiers while at the same time politically disenfranchised. De facto adults, but legal children, they may be better understood as a part of a new youth—rightless, voiceless, but practically central to reconstruction and peace building after war. Third, the twelve to thirty framework takes in a larger and politically and socially more significant cohort containing the militarized youth, who are at the center of political violence and war, and the peace activist youth (who may themselves be former child combatants), both of which are distinct from the general adult population in that they are often economically insecure and marginal from real power and political decision making but, at the same time, have the energy and idealism to devote to organization and agitation. Yet the lines are still somewhat arbitrary, as is inevitable given cultural and subcultural differences involved, and one or two of the authors in this volume stray beyond these lines in either direction. Focused policy development in the health, economic, political, and education spheres necessitates tighter boxes separating young children from adolescents, post-adolescent youth from young adults and so on, but this new youth lens is an analytical tool that may help us better understand the wider context of child soldiering and the cumulative effects of conflict as it unfolds in people's lives from childhood through middle age.

Some stark demographic evidence from several transitional situations illustrates the extent and relevance of the challenge of youth. In Kosovo, for example, half of the population is under 20 (Kosovar Youth Council 2000); in Bosnia 33.9 percent of the population is under 24 (UNICEF statistics 2002). In Northern Ireland 40 percent of the population is under 24 (NISRA 1998). In South Africa 54.7 percent is under 24 (United Nations 2000). In Gaza and the West Bank over 50 percent of the population is under 15 and 65 percent under 24 (UN 2000), while in the Middle East generally, more than 40 percent of the population is under 15 (Khayat 1994). In Sri Lanka those under 18 comprise 32 percent of the population (UNICEF statistics 2002). In Guatemala 20.3 percent of the population is 15–24 years old (UN 2000) and 51 percent is under 18 (UNICEF statistics 2002). Sierra Leone, Angola, and Mozambique also have large youth populations: in Angola, for example, 66.4 percent of the population is under 24 (UN 2000). In Afghanistan 17.3 percent of the population is between 15 and 24 years old (UN 2000) and 50 percent is under 18 years (UNICEF statistics 2002). UN population projections for 2010 predict decreases in the youth population in most of these countries by 1 or 2 percentage points, but the numbers remain enormous. Neither a policy of saving nor containing, to follow Erica Burman's 1994 critique, is a sufficient or practical response to the challenge that so many young people pose in postwar environments, if a sustainable peace is to be achieved.

The impact that youth so defined can have on the stability of peace accords and the prospect for a long-term peace is extensive. If they have been combatants they pose a major undertaking in terms of demobilization and rehabilitation. And as victims of violence during armed conflicts they have special and diverse needs—physical, economic, psychological, and political—in the post-accord period. Youth are also significant actors in terms of the production of violence after accords. They have been dissidents/rejectionists during peace processes (for example, the Young Unionists in Northern Ireland or the youth of the second Palestinian Intifada). In a post-accord period youth may shift identities and social roles from political activism to criminal activity and vigilantism (as is noticeable in South Africa), which, while not fatal to a peace process, can create an unstable or unjust peace. Youth are key actors in relation to (new) justice mechanisms and security forces (whether or not they are consulted in the new arrangements). They are significant actors in the activities of communal defense organizations, in vigilante and bandit groups, and in political demonstrations and street violence after accords. Youth are also the victims of much post-accord violence, both direct assaults and structural violence, which shapes attitudes and behavior over the long-term and can hardly be productive of a sustainable peace.

Although less well acknowledged, youth also play multiple peace-building roles. The role of the nonviolent youth movement Otpor (Resistance) in Serbia in undermining the Milosevic regime is just one celebrated contemporary case of such influence (Cohen 2000; USIP 2000). In most conflicts, youth may be found working at the grassroots in community development organizations, intergroup dialogue and peace groups, and progressive politics. Many will have direct experience of political imprisonment and/or as a perpetrator or victim of violence. They exist on, and work with, meager funds in stressful and often life-threatening conditions. They are also students and teachers. As such they are at the front lines of peace building: creating themselves while also creating each other. As Andoni has written (from the Palestinian perspective), "the younger generation" is "the most sensitive compass in any nation" (2001, 210).

In the longer term, a peace agreement's endurance depends on whether the next generations accept or reject it, how they are socialized during the peace process, their perceptions of what the peace process has achieved, and their tangible experiences of a better life. Youth dimensions are central to such structural issues of peace building as inequality, poverty, and unemployment. The next generation of leaders, facilitators, and stakeholders will emerge from among the current cohort of young people; thus, their engagement in the peace process/peace building and the shaping of their political attitudes and skills in the post-conflict period will have important long-term implications. These different aspects of the new youth challenge are explored in greater detail later in this introduction; but first, the literature on post-accord peace building is examined.

CONFLICT RESOLUTION, POST-ACCORD PEACE BUILDING, AND SUSTAINABLE PEACE

Post-accord peace building refers to a crucial and distinct phase in a conflict when both violence prevention and social reconstruction challenges co-exist and overlap, and conflict management, conflict resolution, and conflict transformation measures are required in an effort to construct a "sustainable peace." The definition here is adapted from Miall, Ramsbotham, and Woodhouse (1999), who define "post-settlement" peace building as involving "(a) the 'negative' task of preventing a relapse into overt violence and (b) the 'positive' tasks of aiding national recovery and expediting the eventual removal of underlying causes of internal war" (188). As this definition deftly identifies, post-accord peace building involves parallel and mutually supporting (but also sometimes antagonistic) challenges. Importantly, the definition emphasizes that, in reality, peace processes are not clean, linear, and able to be characterized solely in terms of a series of negotiation steps involving political parties and armies but rather involve many more actors in civil society. They entail not just demobilization of combatants, demilitarization, and holding parties to an agreement but also require wider attention to the building of new institutions and to root causes of conflict such as "inequity, poverty, racism, ineffective governance and impunity" (Winnipeg 2000). The conflict management and violence prevention phase is described by Miall et al. as dealing with "'Clausewitz in reverse'—the continuation of the politics of war into the ensuing peace" (1999, 188). In arguing for the importance of third-party involvement to keep peace processes on track, Hampson (1996b) underlines the problem: "Peace settlements, no matter how precise, are not refined road maps providing specific (let alone wise) answers to the hundreds of questions that arise each week. Rather, they set forth the expectations, goals, and compromises that the parties and mediators identified at a given point in time" (549). Those items and principles agreed upon "at a given point in time" may be later subject to dispute and renegotiation, and this occurs not only between the original negotiators but in the public domain. As Darby and Mac Ginty (2000) note, the parties in some negotiations may leave important issues unsettled because they are so contentious, agreeing instead to tackle them within a limited time frame after accords. But they then "risk timetabling a series of post-settlement crises" (Darby and Mac Ginty 2000, 250) as in Northern Ireland; or, as with the Oslo Accords, they may create an unacceptable peace that has little chance of garnering public legitimacy. Preventing a relapse into overt violence requires that parties to the settlement, and their constituencies, remain convinced that the accord continues to be in their best interests. However, such support is undermined by both perceived and objective losses and the dynamics unleashed by what Miall et al. call "the precarious and unpredictable jockeying for power that is post-agreement politics" (1999, 190). Intragroup tensions may increase with the development of splinters and new factions, and this occurs on top of already existing, deeply entrenched intergroup mistrust and antipathy.

The aim of violence prevention, if understood only to seek to avoid a return to the prior armed conflict, is too minimalist a reading of the violence inherent to a post-accord period. The signing of an agreement, while in the best-case scenarios preventing a return to the macro war, does not eliminate all overt violence: for example, dissident or so-called spoiler violence (Stedman 1997), criminal violence, politically motivated or sectarian/ethnic street fighting, assault and intimidation, as well as detainment, harassment, and excessive use of force and power by police and militaries, which continue and may even be exacerbated (Darby and Mac Ginty 2000; Darby 2006). In addition, the prevention of overt violence is necessary but not sufficient to create sustainable peace, which requires attention to the memories, attitudes, and values that support and sustain or justify violence (cultural violence) and the impoverishment, discrimination, institutionalized inequality, and militarization (structural violence) of society—all of which support, sustain, and provide legitimization for use of physical force.

In this way, the prevention of violence, as if it were not a difficult enough endeavor, is linked with another set of post-accord tasks under the rubric of reconstruction, and these entail conflict resolution and conflict transformation measures: "constitutional and institutional reform, social reconstruction, reconciliation, and the rebuilding of shattered polities, economies and communities" (Miall et al. 1999, 191). The establishment of an effective and legitimate government, the implementation of reforms to create new legal, political, and security institutions, and the beginning of social and economic revitalization and measures "consolidating civilian security" are the main areas of activity (Ball 1996). Complex tasks such as the return of refugees, removal of landmines, rebuilding infrastructure, stabilizing currencies, enabling renewed agricultural work, cleaning war-produced pollution, implementing trauma therapy programs, encouraging local healing initiatives, and devising mechanisms to deal with the past make perpetrators accountable, provide reparations to victims, and promote national reconciliation. All are expected to begin in the post-accord period. The massive destruction of war and the psychosocial effects of prolonged fear and violence work against this complicated and costly agenda. Moreover, it is clear that the tasks of violence prevention and reconstruction, while necessary in combination, also compete with each other. Mechanisms for dealing with the past, economic and electoral reforms, and development programs, for example, may spark new perceptions of grievance, new or renewed conflicts, and ultimately violence. Measures to achieve stability and violence prevention (such as amnesties for perpetrators) can work against goals of justice, equality, and restitution.

The recognition that conflict continues after peace accords and that conflicts are contained within the relationships of participants at all levels of society provides a rationale for the process-oriented conflict transformation approach that endeavors to enable conflict to be played out by means other than violence. While proponents of this approach accept that some conflicts may be impossible to resolve definitively, the conflict transformation model does more than emulate conflict management. As Lederach argues, genuine conflict transformation requires more than attention to "the technical task of transition" (1998, 186) but a shift "away from a concern with the resolution of issues and toward a frame of reference that focuses on the restoration and rebuilding of relationships" (Lederach 1997, 24).

> In more specific terms, a process-structure for peacebuilding transforms a *war-system* characterized by deeply divided, hostile, and violent relationships into a *peace-system* characterized by just and interdependent relationships with the capacity to find nonviolent

mechanisms for expressing and handling conflict. The goal is not stasis, but rather the generation of continuous, dynamic, self-regenerat-
ing processes that maintain form over time and are able to adapt to
environmental change. Such an infrastructure is made up of a web of
people, their relationships and activities, and the social mechanisms
necessary to sustain the change sought. This takes place at all levels
of society. (Lederach 1997, 84)

One interpretation of such an approach is to effect a shift in how people
see themselves in relation to others in order to stimulate a corresponding behavior
shift. For youth involved in armed struggle, for example, this may involve effecting
a shift from identities based on resistance and defense to those based on cooperation and reconciliation. This approach expands the view of who the peace builders
are in important ways. Viewed using Lederach's (1997) peace-building approach,
which involves the identification of representative individuals and groups at three
different levels of a society in conflict—the top leadership, middle-range leadership, and grassroots leadership—and locating different peace-building tasks within
each sector, youth are primarily the recipients of peace-building endeavors formulated at the grassroots level rather than producers and/or actors in other levels.
However, his framework does not specifically preclude youth leadership in any
of these areas. Moreover, those defined as "middle-range leadership"—such as respected sectoral figures, ethnic and religious leaders, academics and intellectuals,
and nongovernmental organization (NGO) heads—who can be empowered "to establish a relationship- and skill-based infrastructure for sustaining the peace building process" (1997, 152–153), are key actors and perform core activities in terms
of cultural reproduction[7] and, therefore, engage in important interactions with
youth and the perpetuation of conflict and cycles of violence.

But conflict transformation is also understood more broadly as an overarch-
ing term, sometimes competing with the term "conflict resolution," to describe
all the changes necessary to a variety of factors and relational processes that otherwise maintain cultures of war. Building on the tradition formed by Galtung,
Vayrynen (1991) conceives conflict transformation as multidimensional and
dynamic, involving many situational variables, actor learning experiences, and
adversary interactions that shift over time. Conflicts are located in local, regional,
and global environments (contexts) and within relational webs of overlapping
and competing actors, issues, and goals (structures), the transformation of any
of which may affect how a conflict unfolds. Changes in the actors involved—such
as the development of new parties or leaders or shifts in leaders' attitudes and
goals—or of the issues involved may also transform a conflict and/or allow a peace
process to begin (Miall et al. 1999). In the post-accord period such shifts can

help cement an agreement, but they can just as easily change the conditions under which the agreement was forged and affect a peace process negatively. Much of this may be unpredictable and difficult to control by the parties to the conflict.[8]

In addition, transformation of how people think and feel is influential in transforming conflicts (Curle 1971). A transformation of the heart seems integral to the tasks of psychosocial healing that are linked with the aim of effecting reconciliation in the post-accord period. The word "accord" has linguistic roots in the Latin word for "heart," and Sanford notes (following Galeano) that the root of the Spanish *recordar,* "to remember" (and the English "to record"), is the Latin *re-cordis,* meaning "to pass back through the heart" (Sanford 2003a, 70). In the testimony of Guatemalan Maya who had lost loved ones as a result of army massacres, healing or closure sought through information about the disappeared was described as "to feel good in the heart" (Sanford 2003a, 232). This language indicates an intimate connection between an accord (coming to an agreement), memory, and a transformation of heart. But the exact nature of this transaction in human experience is hard to determine. Personal and collective transformation through both changes in attitudes/values and reconciliation with the "other" are implied. The intuitive prescription—that an agreement and an end to overt violence triggers a process of remembering that eventually leads to a healing of hearts—seems too simplistic and linear given the complexity of the human psyche and the continued hurts and privations of the post-accord environment. Yet the formula—agreement, remembering, healing—is "at the heart" of most conceptions of a process of reconciliation and is effective in evoking the pain and hopes of victims of political violence. This formula is usually intersected with one additional element—"truth." On one level, truth contrasts with memory or remembering in that it purports to be objective or at the very least reflective of widely shared beliefs. However, truth is also subjective, and peace builders struggle with its implications for justice and reconciliation. Can a plurality of truths be accommodated in a reconciliation process, or must one shared truth be obtained? If the winners write the truth along with history, how can such processes ever lead to a just peace? Is there justice in a "win-win" configuration where no one is to blame? What is the relationship between truth and justice? Is the function of truth finding to attribute blame and reprisal, to acknowledge victims, or to create a national narrative? Is the effect of a search for the truth to stifle, create, transform, or resolve conflict? What is the relationship of healing to truth and to reconciliation (all of which are contested and contextual)?[9]

The ultimate aim of post-accord peace building is to lay strong foundations for the development of a sustainable peace. "The term sustainable peace," accord-

ing to Reychler, "refers to a situation characterized by the absence of physical violence; the elimination of unacceptable political, economic and cultural forms of
discrimination; a high level of internal and external legitimacy or support; self-
sustainability; and a propensity to enhance the constructive transformation of
conflicts" (2001, 12). While this definition raises difficult questions—such as how
much discrimination is "acceptable" and how a "propensity" to promote constructive conflict transformation can be measured—it does point to a significant
role for young people in achieving sustainable peace. The chapters in this volume show, as is argued in the conclusion, that youth are significant whether one
thinks in terms of conflict management (mitigation, containment) and violence
prevention; conflict resolution (long-term removal of root causes); conflict transformation (shifting to nonviolent conflict, changed relationships); or social reconstruction, reconciliation, and sustainable peace. The conclusion also proposes
that the crucial missing element of peace processes is the intentional, meaningful provision for youth political participation.

TROUBLEMAKERS AND PEACEMAKERS:
THE GLOBAL CHALLENGE

The second half of this introduction elaborates on the post-accord implications
of young people's involvement in armed conflict, the relationship between youth
and post-accord violence, the role of youth as peace resources, and the relationship of youth to processes for dealing with the past and promoting healing.
Along the way, it previews the key themes of the chapters in this volume in a
wider context of related research on both children and youth.

VICTIMS, PERPETRATORS, DISPLACED:
YOUTH INVOLVED IN ARMED CONFLICT

In the literature on children and young people in armed conflict (Brett and
Sprecht 2004; Brett and McCallin 1996; Cohn and Goodwin-Gill 1994; Klare
1999; Machel 1996; Wessells 2000, 1998), there is now extensive evidence of
their roles as fighters, cooks, spies, couriers, and providers of sexual services. But
the experiences and needs of young people in armed conflict are crucially
affected, for example, by whether or not they had minority or majority status in
a conflict, were refugees or internally displaced, were active combatants or
bystanders, fought by choice or under duress, experienced low-intensity conflict
or genocides, were from poor families or wealthy, or were male or female. Dif-

ferent challenges emerge where the youth combatant was an unwilling abductee, subject to enforced drug use or other forms of physical and psychological abuse and manipulation, than in cases where the youth in question was a politically motivated, willing recruit, carrying on a family or community tradition. Demobilization and reintegration programs have different requirements and urgency where child soldiers have been forcibly recruited, such as in Sierra Leone and Guatemala, than in other conflict contexts, where combatants have remained more tightly integrated into their communities, such as Palestine, Northern Ireland, or South Africa. And in any given case, not all young people experience the conflict in the same way. Some may be intimately involved, active agents in numerous ways, while others may be more or less bystanders. Examined longitudinally, the changing youth cohort of a given region may utilize different strategies and modes of involvement over time. For example, analysis of the Kosovo/a conflict finds decades-long youth activism first at the center of nonviolent and later armed struggle (Mertus 1999; Reitan 2000). The categories of victim and perpetrator may be indistinct, with individuals and groups fitting both at different times.

In this volume, the chapter by Mike Wessells and Davidson Jonah and that by Victoria Sanford examine ex-youth combatants in Sierra Leone, Colombia, and Guatemala. Wessells and Jonah provide a much more complex analysis than previously available of the differences between the recruitment strategies of various armed groups in Sierra Leone and the varied motivations and roles of youth involved, and they caution against "monolithic images" of youth soldiers. Wessells and Jonah's appraisal of the strengths and weaknesses of the reintegration project with which they work provides a model that will be a useful reference for others. Particularly important is their caution about privileging ex-combatants over others in the community. This is a theme emerging also from Marc Sommers's study of youth in a region of Rwanda that to this point has been neglected by scholars and aid agencies.

A second shared theme is the challenge of displacement. On a global scale, young people feature amongst those displaced and made homeless by warfare. According to the State of the World's Children (UNICEF 2002), 80 percent of the world's 35 million refugees are women and children, and half are believed to be children (Jones 2000). These displaced pose enormous humanitarian challenges. In conflicts where large movements of people have occurred, where families have splintered as a survival strategy (Bonnerjea 1994), or where children have been abducted to armed groups, the reunion of displaced children with their families is merely the initial challenge in reconstructing their shattered worlds (and in some cases may not be possible). Moreover, the socialization of new generations in misery in refugee camps or in exile contributes to the development of war-supporting diaspora, as illustrated by the Afghan youth educated in Pakistani Madrassas who later became Taliban recruits (Rashied 2000).

Sanford's study in this volume underscores the importance of acknowledging pre-recruitment trauma, particularly the trauma of displacement, in preventing cycles of political violence. Her studies of Guatemala and Colombia suggest that displaced and orphaned youth have very limited survival options—they can join one of the armed groups (army, paramilitaries, or guerrilla) or they can live almost permanently on the move to avoid recruitment or "social cleansing." In her cases, "rightlessness" associated with displacement is the original trauma leading to youth soldiering, and involvement in armed conflict is "post-traumatic play." In Sommers's chapter on Rwanda, the displaced from the 1994 war/genocide and earlier periods of ethnic violence, who returned to their communities in the shadow of the genocide, are among the rural youth experiencing "profound despair and frustration" because of their dire economic circumstances. But displacement is also an impetus for creative community building, as Sanford shows in her chapter with a groundbreaking section on the Guatemalan Communities of Population in Resistance and the Colombian Peace Communities; she demonstrates an alternative form of power rooted in "the moral imagination." Similarly, Carolyn Nordstrom's chapter on Angolan war orphans provides original and provocative evidence of the power of young people to create new subcultures and counter discourses to prevailing norms amid terrible conditions of adult neglect and abuse.

These studies also contribute to our knowledge about the relationship between gender and peace building. There is a growing recognition of "the special situation of girls" in war zones (Machel 1996; Brett and McCallin 1996). In El Salvador, Ethiopia, and Uganda, for example, girls have made up over 30 percent of the membership of armed groups (Coalition 2000 n.d.). Girls may need to be treated for the mental and physical symptoms of sexual abuse, including sexually transmitted diseases, war-rape pregnancies, feelings of worthlessness, and shunning by their families and communities. In turn, the product of war-rape pregnancies and displaced families are manifested in thousands of homeless and parentless children. In Africa the AIDS epidemic exacerbates this enormous tragedy of orphaned children. Girls in armed groups may be the last to be demobilized after accords because they perform useful post-accord functions as cooks, clothes washers, and providers of sexual services (McKay and Mazurana 2000). These special characteristics of young women's experiences in armed groups require active consideration during post-accord peace building.

In this volume, Wessells and Jonah report the use of sexual violence "as a tool of simultaneously violating women, demeaning the enemy, and asserting dominance through terror." At the same time, they show how some women subvert their expected roles (see the story of the "Mommy queen" in their chapter).

As Sanford's chapter notes, women may also be empowered by participation in armed conflict, which may provide the only means for women to perform as equals to men. In my study of Northern Ireland in this volume, the different narratives of the Protestant girls and the Catholic boys illustrate how gendered roles and gender stereotypes are mediated by ethnic and historical positions and may be broken down during armed conflict. In their chapter, Ed Cairns, Frances McLernon, Wendy Moore, and Ilse Hakvoort highlight the different conceptualizations of war and peace held by girls and boys globally, which adds support to Johan Galtung's innovative theorizing about age- and gender-related aptitude for creative peace building. Sommers shows that women are particularly vulnerable and marginalized in Rwanda but also highlights how much the plight of young men in Rwanda is related to gendered expectations.

The conflicts in Northern Ireland and Bosnia may not be comparable in terms of the levels of youth involvement to Rwanda or Sierra Leone, but as Kelly has argued, "the impact [on the young] may be harder to name and the damage, consequently, harder to repair" (2000, 35). The chapters on Bosnia and Northern Ireland in this volume examine a variety of youth perspectives, from those involved in violence, to those relatively insulated, to those actively involved in peace building. The longitudinal study by Cairns et al. of young people in Northern Ireland demonstrates the value of using a variety of methods over time to capture young people's changing war/peace conceptualizations; their study surveys young people from a variety of backgrounds and with different degrees of exposure to violence. They show how the Northern Ireland peace process has impacted only the war/peace perceptions of older children and adolescents and not consistently. In Northern Ireland civil society is highly functioning, as community organizations developed in parallel to the conflict and provide a basis for post-accord development. Schools have consistently been both havens from conflict and, because of educational segregation, means of conflict reproduction. Educational institutions and mechanisms have important roles in post-accord peace building. Post-accord educational transformation is the theme of Jaco Cillier's chapter on Bosnia, which is discussed in more detail below.

Criminals, Rejectionists, Marginals: Youth and Violence after Accords

Post-accord political violence can stall, derail, or collapse a peace process (Darby 2001). Criminal violence and its kin, structural violence, can severely reduce the quality of life for the population in question. All are barriers to genuine peace and an analysis of each of these kinds of violence finds youth to be significant actors. An example of the former may be found in the political activism of the youth of the second Palestinian Intifada. This is not to say that the role of youth in the Al-Aqsa Intifada is solely, or even chiefly, responsible for ending the peace process. Such violence may reflect perceptions of an unjust accord and is usually reflective of wider political and social crises related to the actions of political elites.[10] As Sami Adwan and Dan Bar-On's chapter suggests, the relationship between rejectionist Palestinian youth, the support or opposition of adults, and the violence they all experience is constitutive of and mediated through collective narratives of conflict.

Less severe dissident political violence and criminal violence may or may not reflect a wider societal or peace process crisis, but it does threaten sustainable peace by shaping the next generation's perceptions of the peace and attitudes toward law and order. In post-agreement Northern Ireland, for example, the young have experienced and are involved in violence at the micro level—random sectarian assaults, interface street fighting, and so-called recreational rioting (Jarman and O'Halloran 2001)—all of which hold the potential for escalation and legitimize the maintenance of exclusive sectarian communities for reasons of protection (McEvoy-Levy 2000, 2001a). These acts help create the experience of a peace process permanently in crisis that maintains popular insecurity, enhances frustration and cynicism about the prospects for peace, and undercuts peace-building programs.[11] In addition to continued political violence, whether in limited dissident form or as part of a complete rejection of a peace process, the post-accord period may also see increased blurring between the political and the criminal—as in guerrilla or paramilitary groups engaged in drug activities or the existence of alternative policing forces, corrupt official policing, and institutional corruption. As Cilliers and Jeffrey Helsing et al. show, in Bosnia this contributes to considerable cynicism among the young and apathy about politics.

Political violence can be recast in the post-accord period into parapolitical, economic, and criminal forms. When linked with liberation politics, nationalism, and defense of one's family, community, ethnic, or racial group, several generations' experience of deprivation and conflict can be potently combined in the post-accord period with new or continued privation to structure the meaning of violence as a salve for humiliation. A report by the Center for the Study of Violence and Reconciliation in Johannesburg refers to the "reparative" power of violence for the young and marginalized: "violence . . . is a way of building up and fortifying the self rather than a regressive breaking down. Violence is enlivening, restitutive and meaningful in the face of subjective experiences of smallness and vulnerability" (CSVR 1998).[12] Findings in the United States on the motivations among youth for gang involvement suggest that complicated reasons will persist for youth involvement in violence after conflicts shift into a post-accord phase even if (and this is a big if) earlier conflict identifications are somehow erased. Spergel finds U.S. gang involvement to be driven by the desire for physical protection, social support, and solidarity or a surrogate family; the need for cultural identification, moral education, self-esteem, and honor; and the pursuit of economic gain (Spergel 1995). The chapters in this volume show how youth soldiers and rioters share these motivations blended with complex narrations of an oppressive historical/political past, a combination that is not well understood nor addressed in the post-accord period. In my chapter, young people in Northern Ireland explain why they are involved in "recreational rioting," offering a portrait of violence structured but not dictated by the paramilitaries, security forces, and political elites; by collective memories of grievance; and by structural violence, including their own political marginalization. The chapter shows how local communities sustain, protect, and politicize youth during conflict, but after accords these same communities restrict young people's creative, political, and peace agency. While the youth interviewed are involved in armed conflict only in limited ways, they are powerful conflict reproducers.

In Rwanda the problems of land shortage and restricted access to education, employment, and capital, which remain unsolved in the post-genocide period, make it very difficult for young people to shake off the past and imagine a new future. Sommers's detailed discussion of the condition of youth in Rwanda today concludes that unless the "severity and expanse of youth entrapment" in Rwanda is recognized there will likely be "an explosion of widespread self-destructive acts." Like Wessells and Jonah, Sommers argues for holistic programs of aid, including "nonformal education that addresses conflict negotiation, health (HIV-AIDs education in particular), and social concerns," as well as skills training. These recommendations overlap with several offered by Cilliers in his chapter on the challenges of educational transformation in Bosnia.

As in the Israeli-Palestinian case, accords can be a trigger for a new phase of conflict, rather than a conflict resolving mechanism, with youth often at the frontlines of the backlash against the negotiation process. But after a peace process has begun and failed, there is no simple return to the conflict of the past. As part of the conflict history, the accords add nuance to the violence. According to Ghassan Andoni of the Palestinian Center for Rapprochement between People, both Intifadas emerged from youth who perceived that the preceding generation had failed to make any gains. In 1987 "generational defeat" was symbolized by the lack of attention to the Palestinian question at the Arab summit in Jordan. In 2000 it was the failure of Oslo to end occupation and the Palestinian Authority's misgovernance that in two-pronged fashion provided the spur. Andoni describes the teenage uprising as a redemptive vanguard: "Again, and as suddenly as 1987, a new generation stepped in, renewed hope, and moved the whole community toward active resistance" (2001, 214).

Redemptive violence has most appeal for youth when collective political aspirations are thwarted alongside hopes for personal future well-being. Not only was Olso increasingly seen as a "gigantic fraud" (Said 2001, 29) in terms of Palestinian sovereignty, but human rights abuses and a state of war continued. Children continued to be arrested and detained by the Israeli army for security offences. In 1998, 490 were arrested, 340 injured, and 14 killed according to Defense for Children International's Palestine Section (n.d.). Young people were also subject to rights violations at the hands of the Palestinian National Authority (Quzmar 2000). Additionally, poverty and unemployment rates increased after Olso, largely because of the Israeli policy of closure. An increase in the average unemployment rate from 3 percent to 28 percent between 1992 and 1996 was recorded by the World Bank. According to Roy, "Poverty, especially among children, is now visible in a manner not seen for at least 25 years" (2001, 92). Barber's (1999) study of 7,000 families in the West Bank and Gaza Strip suggests that intracommunal, specifically intergenerational, tensions also contribute to youth frustration.[13]

Although the Palestine-Israel situation can only be described as "post-accord" in the loosest sense—optimistically it is "between accords"—Adwan and Bar-On's chapter on the PRIME Sharing History Project is included in this volume because it reports on a peace-building initiative begun after Olso that continues today as a grassroots endeavor to prepare the ground for a new peace process. This chapter also highlights the difficulties that ongoing regional conflict— including the latest war in Iraq—places on grassroots efforts to build peace at any stage of a peace process, a point that is also highlighted in Wessells and Jonah's chapter in relation to Sierra Leone and Liberia.

POST-MILITANTS, "WORLD BUILDERS," COMMUNITY ACTIVISTS: YOUTH AS PEACE BUILDERS

The PRIME Sharing History Project involved Jewish-Israeli and Palestinian teachers writing a joint textbook containing separate but parallel historical narratives, which were then translated into Arabic and Hebrew and introduced in schools with Palestinian and Israeli ninth and tenth graders. The chapter on this project analyzes the design process and the attitudes of both teachers and pupils before and after the project. The dialogue, writing, and teaching processes that Adwan and Bar-On recount, itself a narrative of peace building, is an inspiring one, providing many lessons about the timing, format, ethos, and strategic considerations of cross-communal peace-building activities.

Like other civil society actors, such as teachers, peace-active youth are less visible in analyses of peace processes than key elites, and their effectiveness in peace building is hard to measure. But there have been a few recently celebrated examples. Otpor in Serbia has already been mentioned. Other powerful examples of youth activism for peace exist in the Children's Movement for Peace in Colombia (Cameron 2000), the various activities of Israeli and Palestinian youth involved in protesting occupation through demonstrations and street theatre (Svirsky 2001), and, perhaps, the demonstrations in the Basque country against ETA violence (Mees 2000). But much less has been written about youth peace builders than about youth soldiers. Youth violence and rebellion have important historical impact and offer high drama and compelling, vivid testimonials. But often this focus serves to obscure a fear of youth and a tendency to scapegoat them for all social ills. It may contain a skepticism about the ability of young people to analyze their life experiences and make rational calculations about appropriate ways to navigate their torn worlds. As Nordstrom's chapter intriguingly points out, when the media and scholars are offered compelling counter evidence to the narrative of youth and violence, as provided in her study of the storm drain communities in Angola, they question its authenticity.

In this volume the roles of young people in peace building are examined through numerous lenses, with a focus on projects utilizing youth leadership structures. In chapter 8 Namik Kirlic, Neil McMaster, and Nir Sonnenschein exemplify engaged youth; although it is clear that many obstacles exist to youth organizing for peace, they describe a variety of creative responses. Twenty-four-year-old Sonnenschein identifies the complexity of peace work when describing how the Jewish inhabitants of an experimental binational Jewish-Palestinian village respond to their call to military service. Some refuse on grounds that if all young Israelis did so "the occupation would have to cease," others take noncombat positions, and still others accept their legal obligation, arguing that "if all the conscientious and moral people will not serve in the occupied territories, all those left serving there will be the ones who have no moral problems oppressing the Palestinians." As Sonnenschein concludes, there are different ways to "[apply] principles of peace." In Bosnia, among a variety of activities undertaken by Kirlic's youth group was the raising of funds to take back public space and reconstruct a fountain that was a meeting place for both Muslim and Croat youth prior to the war. Educators and peace builders, these young people create a symbol for the town of their desire to be reconciled.

Cilliers's chapter makes the case for the role of local nongovernmental organizations and civil society groups, particularly youth groups, in lobbying against institutional and governmental resistance to educational change. He also discusses the importance of international agencies supporting these bodies, while being "careful not to prescribe solutions and frameworks that are not grounded in local

realities." Derived from interviews with teachers, young people, and peace practitioners, Cilliers provides a detailed analysis of the problems of transforming the
post-accord education system in Bosnia, and he offers a set of concrete recommendations targeting curricula, education structures, and political elites.

Even in contexts where civil society has been devastated by war, people manage to build peace in more informal ways, fashioning local conflict resolution
mechanisms and group survival strategies in active resistance to norms of antagonism. Nordstrom calls this "world building" (1997), and youth are some of the
most creative and committed actors in the face of destruction, often confound-
ing all the expectations of adults who view the world through hard realist lenses.
In her chapter on Angola, Nordstrom shows how orphaned and runaway youth
construct homes for themselves, even furnished with art clipped from magazines, and develop a system of supporting ideas and values that sustain a fairly
stable, cooperative, surrogate family. That these alternative communities are rel-
egated to the drains beneath the street, she argues, the only place where children
and youth are safe from adult predators, is both an indictment of adults and
an example of a hidden, alternative source of knowledge about violence and
peace. The view of young people as automatic inheritors of violence and inadequate to the task of political analysis and prescription is quite definitely
debunked by the chapters in this volume containing young people's personal testimonies, narratives, and reports of their committed advocacy, including Cairns
et al. and my studies on Northern Ireland and the chapter by Galtung. Galtung's
chapter, the last in this volume, develops a theory linking generation and gender
to violence and peace. Read at the end of this volume, as a kind of *digestive,* it
provides a valuable and sometimes provocative frame within which to evaluate
the other chapters' empirical data. One the one hand he notes the "wisdom" of
youth on the sharp end of violence and social change: "they have the advantage
of knowing where the shoe pinches." On the other, he seems to speak mostly
to youth in developed countries, particularly in the United States, in a timely
exploration of their creative and revolutionary potential as global citizen peace
builders.

SURVIVORS, BYSTANDERS, THE NEXT GENERATION: YOUTH AND HEALING/DEALING WITH THE PAST

Finally, the youth we are writing about here, whether victims, perpetrators,
bystanders, gang members, street fighters, rioters, war orphans, storm drain-
dwellers, dissidents, refugees, family heads, homeless, students, ex-combatants,
community activists, or peace builders, are all survivors. As survivors, they hold

the keys to the construction of a new, more humane era after accords. But survival also takes a toll—the least of which may be physical injury. Guilt, fear, desires for vengeance, an overwhelming sense of loss, and hopelessness are inadequate descriptions of only some of the emotional and psychological effects of involvement in armed conflict. Inevitably, a profound need for healing follows accords. Scholars have increasingly become interested in how mechanisms for healing, reconciliation, or dealing with the past may impact peace building (see, for example, Amadiume and An-Na'im 2000; Assefa 2001; Boraine 2000; Borer forthcoming; Kritz 1995; Lederach 1996; Minnow 1998; Rigby 2001; Smith and Vaux 2003, 46– 50). In this volume we focus on education, storytelling, community-based rituals of reconciliation, and youth activism as existing and potential mechanisms for addressing the past in order to promote sustainable peace.

Mechanisms for finding the truth and addressing a violent past speak to the desire of young people to do good, to make contributions, to change systems, and to redress wrongs. As Minnow writes, "Young people, understandably, want to know what has been done, and what can be done, to respond, redress, and prevent future occurrences. They ask whether it is possible to find a stance for survivors, bystanders, and the next generations" (1998, 7). In practice, usually some combination of five kinds of processes are implemented for dealing with the past and promoting healing that have specific implications for youth: individual and small group processes, community processes, education processes, national processes, and legal processes. Each promotes a conversation between past and present. Conflict memories and experiences are given center stage and valued in their own right, but usually they are also conceptualized as a bridge to new relationships between conflicting groups.

Individual and small group processes include such activities as individual trauma counseling and discussion or encounter groups. During "single identity work" in Northern Ireland, trained facilitators encourage youth to explore their political and religious identities, which to be done effectively requires an understanding of the historical origins of the conflict and the ways in which their lives are shaped by the near and distant past. This is theorized to contribute to self-awareness and identity-confidence, which form the basis for effective cross-community encounter work. In chapter 8 a young activist from Northern Ireland, Neil McMaster, addresses some of the flaws associated with the cross-community encounter approach and argues for structured and sustained "dialogue about contentious issues" as a useful methodology for constructively addressing the past. This mechanism is recommended by Cilliers in his chapter on Bosnia. Bar-On et al. have developed a method of personal storytelling in encounter groups as a way to address both past and present conflict in the Palestinian and Israeli context and with the descendants of Holocaust victims and Nazi perpetrators. Their

"To Reflect and Trust" process involves a recognition of the past in a way that transforms some of its negative potential and gives its constructive power: "the outcome of the process was not to forget or to be done with the past, once and for all, but to find new ways to live with it, perhaps in ways that are more conscious, but also less threatening and self-destructive" (Bar-On and Kassem n.d.). In their chapter Adwan and Bar-On report how the process of personal storytelling is incorporated in a peace-building project involving Palestinian and Israeli teachers and pupils. Jessica Senehi and Sean Byrne's chapter looks closely at what the process of public, local storytelling entails at cognitive, emotional, and social levels and how it can build "inclusivity in the grassroots, repair relationships, heal from trauma and reduce prejudice." They provide a rich and persuasive evaluation of storytelling as a conflict resolution and peace-building mechanism.

Clearly there is also overlap between such group processes and community processes. Community processes may involve public healing rituals or memory projects. Where youth have been active combatants, implicated in the atrocities of the past either as victims or perpetrators, mechanisms for dealing with the past are important for personal healing, healing the social wounds of war, and reintegrating combatants into communities (Honwana 1999b). Local rituals for healing child soldiers in Mozambique and Angola involve the symbolic purging of the evil of war through ceremonies constructed around bathing, setting fire to war clothing, and eating cleansing herbs while being guided by community elders. This "reconciliation from below" uses resources from everyday life, such as religion, cultural symbols, and traditions related to rites of passage, to effect a "home-made, socio-cultural healing" (Honwana 1999b, 102). The focus is on "reconciliation with oneself," as well as with one's hurt family and wronged community, to remove the common pain, shame, and responsibility; to cleanse the social pollution caused by war; and to allow the combatant to be reintegrated without bringing home "bad spirits" and antisocial behavior. In this volume Wessells and Jonah argue that addressing community and individual fears of spiritual contamination is an important element of successfully reintegrating youth combatants, but this should take place in an holistic context in which other material needs are addressed as well.

Sanford notes that the community healing model can "break the binary that counterpoises justice and healing, further challenging Western constructs of both politics and therapeutic healing" (2003a, 242). Writing about the gathering of testimonies from massacre survivors and families of those killed in Guatemala, Sanford argues that not only are catharsis and closure possible, but the process of giving testimony can also enable the survivor to play a part in producing "the written record, which can later be used in individual and community attempts to provide evidence of human rights violations and seek justice"

(Sanford 2003a, 242). Her chapter in this volume exemplifies this methodology, providing compelling and educational testimony from both youth soldiers and peace builders. Removing militaristic structures, repainting political murals, organizing demonstrations and vigils of remembrance, and erecting monuments are some other examples of local initiatives to further healing by taking back public space; the use of some these strategies is discussed by the young activists Kirlic, McMaster, and Sonnenschein in chapter 8.

Formal education venues are a third space for such activity. They may include school-based cross-community encounters or curricula aimed at building tolerance, such as Northern Ireland's mandatory Education for Mutual Understanding (EMU) requirements and its more ambitious and innovative new Citizenship Education curriculum (Gallagher 2004). Cilliers argues that educational institutions are "a powerful mechanism that can sustain an infrastructure to promote post-accord peace building" and that failure of institutions and structures (including educational institutions) to meet people's "inherent needs" is one of the major reasons for their resort to violence. The educators in Cilliers's Bosnia study reported being excluded from most of the processes associated with the implementation of the Dayton Accords. The transformation of the education system was "dominated by international actors and agencies" and hampered by the corruption of local elites. As a result, local people felt no ownership and were apathetic about involvement, making local capacity building difficult. The rewriting of history textbooks is another important component of moving divided societies toward a recognition of a shared but contested past and educating the next generations for coexistence, mutual respect, and, eventually, reconciliation. As Adwan and Bar-On argue in their chapter, the initial task is not for historically conflicting peoples to agree on one narrative (an impossible task in the short term), but to provide a common forum for the display of contested narratives on equal footing.

Finally, national processes such as truth commissions, days of atonement, memorial building, and memorial days may or may not have specific youth components (the South African Truth and Reconciliation Commission included youth depositions), but they perform important education functions for the next generation by constructing a national narrative and modeling conflict resolution. Similarly, legal processes such as war crimes tribunals and court prosecutions may not only provide a certain legal and moral satisfaction, and act as a deterrent, but their issues and procedures, and the debates in post-accord settings about whether or not to use these apparatuses, can themselves have educational value. I argue in my chapter, however, that genuine power sharing, experienced at the grassroots, must precede truth telling in Northern Ireland because youth without rights of voice will not be open to recognizing the rights of others to voice or to "truth." Sommers's study of Rwandan youth shows in a concrete and moving way how a focus on truth telling at the expense of structural change may be counter-productive. Senehi and Byrne place their analysis of the value of public, local storytelling within the context of more expensive, overly structured, slow, and top-down truth processes.

The chapters in this volume have been written by psychologists, anthropologists, educationalists, political scientists, and sociologists, some of whom are also practitioners in the field of conflict transformation and peace building and all of whom have spent extensive time working under war conditions. They utilize data from both before and after accords; their studies include cases where internal peace agreements collapsed, as well as those where they have endured under a variety of stressors, accords of long-standing and others comparatively new, in conflicts of different lengths and intensities and with different modes and levels of brokerage and external intervention.[14] The difficulties of working in the field in war zones and regions in transition from war—difficulties of access, personal safety, and work-related ethical dilemmas, stress, and trauma—are apparent in these chapters, some of which deviate at times from traditional social science methodologies to personal testimony and witnessing. They are all the more powerful as a result, and together with the different disciplinary lenses and methodologies used by the authors, and the combination of scholars and scholar/practitioners, they provide a richness of perspectives and findings. It is hoped that this interdisciplinary scholarship focused on the question of where youth, war, and peace-building intersect will illuminate that question from multiple angles and provide a body of research to serve as a resource to other scholars and writers. We intend, also, to advocate and offer conclusions relevant to policy that will not only aid peace builders concerned with preventing violence, preserving accords, and rebuilding war-torn societies, but that will as authentically as possible represent the interests, needs, experience, and perceptions of young people who have been involved in armed conflict. Although mostly invisible in international political discourse except as stereotypes, global youth have many ideas, perceptions, values, and agendas of their own. While most of the chapters reproduce youth testimony, we do not claim to "give voice" to young people, conscious that such a position implies that young people's ideas and agency are dependent for power and worth on our listening and advocacy.[15] But we attempt to amplify an already expressive but marginal voice and set of concerns and bring those to a wider audience.

In the landscape of contemporary armed conflict and peace building, young people are already economic, social, and political agents in numerous ways, expressive through violence, through labor, through peace work, and through many other creative forms. They are active subjects in their own lives and shape and create the social worlds of others: "Not only does a complex historic period impact young [people's] political images but each new generation helps to shape the historical context" (Byrne 1997b, 67). Louis Kreisberg has noted that "major conflicts have strong and enduring impacts on those reaching political maturity while they are underway" (1998, 326). Similarly, peace processes also affect and shape the next generation. The constitutive nature of the youth and peace-building challenge within an unfolding conflict life cycle is the subject of this volume.

NOTES

1. Adult in Sierra Leone, quoted in chapter 1.

2. Young people in Bosnia, quoted in chapter 7.

3. Youth in Rwanda, quoted in chapter 3.

4. Young woman from Northern Ireland, quoted in chapter 6.

5. Accords were signed in Northern Ireland in 1998; in Guatemala in 1995; in Angola in 1988 and 1994; in Sierra Leone in 1997, 1999, 2000; in Bosnia in 1995; and in Israel/Palestine in 1993, 1998, and 2003 (Geneva Accord).

6. While there are key physiological markers for when a child enters adolescence and for when puberty ends, even these stages of transition are not uniform. Most would agree that there are psychological stages to child development across a range of cognitive skills development, including the acquisition of political awareness and attitudes. But, again, these transitions occur within rough age groups and not across distinct and uniform thresholds.

7. For example, Gellner (1983) and Smith (1986) write about the role of intellectuals in the creation and reproduction of nationalist ideologies and especially in relation to oppressed groups.

8. Processes or events that effect transformation in regional and global environments, for example, such as the end of the Cold War or September 11, 2001, may change the postures and alliances of key power/peace brokers. This can result in more or less attention to specific peace processes and changes in perspective on key elements such as the definition of and policy toward "terrorism," which may significantly affect internal actors, issues, and goals.

9. This last question is dealt with comprehensively in Borer's edited volume in this series, *Telling the Truths: Truth Telling and Peace Building in Post-Conflict Societies.*

10. In this case Sharon's provocation in 2000 was only the spark to the tinder of Oslo's failure to create real change or hope of such for Palestinians.

11. For example, cross-community projects are often forced to cease operations during the summer months due to escalations in interface violence around key political/sectarian commemorations, which make it dangerous for participants to meet. They slowly build up rapport and trust again over the year only

to have the same experience the following summer in what participants have described as a defeating and depressing cycle.

12. Some time ago Frantz Fanon argued that violence provides the vehicle for an individual to regain lost self-respect and for the development of community. In embracing violence an oppressed people are bound together, argued Fanon. Violence "invests their characters with positive and creative qualities"; they are freed from despair and feelings of inferiority; they are made "fearless" and their "self-respect is restored." The war of liberation "introduces into each man's consciousness the ideas of a common cause, of a national destiny and of a collective history" (1966, 7 and 73).

13. Though the first Intifada in general was a "strong, cohering force for families and communities," and Barber (1999) found support for the hypothesis that political involvement increases resilience in children, he did find that one to two years afterwards mild antisocial behavior (in males) and depression (in females) were positively linked with involvement. His explanation of this pattern is persuasive. The Intifada gave youth increased personal autonomy, which adults attempted to reverse once the Intifada was over.

14. For a list of Internal Peace Agreements between 1988 and 1998 broken down by agreement type, see John Darby (2001, 10). The full text of peace accords is available through the United States Institute of Peace Digital Peace Agreements Collection at http://usip.org.

15. Purporting to "give voice" to or "speak for" others is often "postcolonial discourse refashioned for a post-modern world" (Nordstrom 1997, 30 n. 3).

MICHAEL WESSELLS AND DAVIDSON JONAH

Recruitment and Reintegration of Former Youth Soldiers in Sierra Leone

Challenges of Reconciliation and Post-Accord Peace Building

Following the signing of a ceasefire or a peace accord, the task of reintegrating former child soldiers into civil society is a crucial part of the ongoing process of peace building. Around the world the presence of large numbers of idling youth amidst poverty and high levels of unemployment is a prescription for crime and violence. Lacking in education, job skills, and positive options in civilian life, child soldiers often maintain their military identity and resort to violence as a means of meeting their basic needs and asserting their desire for power, wealth, and identity. In cases such as South Africa and Mozambique, former youth soldiers often engage in criminal violence that destabilizes communities, weakens peace building, and undermines development. In other cases, such as Sierra Leone, young former soldiers have contributed directly to ongoing cycles of political violence by remaining with military forces and fighting even following the signing of a ceasefire. To build peace in a post-accord environment, it is vital to engage youth in positive ways, enable them to assume a positive role in civilian society, and integrate them into communities.

The linkages between youth and post-accord peace building are nowhere more apparent than in Sierra Leone, a small West African country bordering Liberia and Guinea. The war in Sierra Leone, begun March 23, 1991, as a spillover from the civil war in Liberia, involves two main players, the Republic of Sierra Leone Military Force (RSLMF) and the opposition forces of the Revolutionary United Front (RUF) and its ally, the Armed Forces Revolutionary Council (AFRC). Promulgating a pan-Africanist ideology and claiming inspiration from the Green Book of Colonel Gaddafi, the Libyan leader, the RUF has presented itself alternately as an environmental cult (Richards 1996) and a social movement for the poor. In contrast to the presentational images, the RUF employed increasingly brutal tactics, making Sierra Leone's one of the world's most horrifying wars. The war became infamous for terrorism of villages, mass rapes, and mutilations wherein a person's arm was cut off, yielding a "long sleeve" if it was cut at the elbow and a "short sleeve" if cut at the shoulder. The war acquired an ethnic component since the RUF was concentrated for years in the border region. Richards (1996, 274) estimates that three-quarters of the RUF are Mende-speaking, although Foday Sankoh, the RUF leader, had been a Temne speaker from the north.

Repeatedly, peace accords failed because the RUF, which consisted in no small part of youth soldiers, continued fighting as a means of increasing its power and control, and it maintained control of "conflict diamonds" to finance the war (Smillie and Gberie 2000, 1–6). For example, the Lome peace agreement, signed between the government and the RUF in July 1999, lifted hopes for peace. But the RUF maintained control of large parts of the east and north, and many RUF soldiers who had been fighters since childhood and who had grown up as warriors maintained a strong will to fight. Hostilities resumed when the RUF captured approximately five hundred peacekeepers of the UN Mission in Sierra Leone (UNAMSIL). To increase its numbers of soldiers, the RUF re-abducted some of the young soldiers who had been demobilized under the Lome accord, and fighting resumed. As this grim episode illustrates, the abduction and re-abduction of children, who are then made into warriors, is an essential part of the ongoing cycles of violence. The construction of peace in Sierra Leone, then, requires concerted attention to the problem of reintegrating former child soldiers into civilian life.

The fighting that occurred in May through November 2000 was some of the bloodiest on record and included attacks on villages, beheadings of people who resisted the RUF, and torture and killing of suspected RUF members by armed, progovernment militias, the Civilian Defense Forces (CDF). Local villagers have reported that some of the worst atrocities were committed by children who were high on drugs. Subsequently, in November 2000 the Sierra Leone government and the RUF signed a ceasefire in Abuja. With support from a large UNAMSIL contingent, the ceasefire held and disarmament and demobilization occurred, allowing free elections to take place successfully in May 2002.

This chapter analyzes the tasks of reintegrating young soldiers in the post-accord environment of Sierra Leone as a means of building peace at the grass-roots level. It departs from the more standard practice of focusing exclusively on child soldiers since a wider emphasis on youth is necessary for post-conflict peace building. First, it examines the main pathways through which youth become soldiers. Next, it discusses young people's roles and experiences with an eye toward analyzing the challenges of reintegrating former youth soldiers into civil society. Then it describes a program for reintegration of former youth soldiers that interconnects economic, psychosocial, and spiritual elements and that has implications for post-accord peace building in other contexts.

Youth Soldiering in Sierra Leone

No accurate statistics exist regarding the number of child soldiers in Sierra Leone, though most estimates fall between five and ten thousand. Beneath the difficulties of secrecy and obtaining accurate figures in a dangerous, chaotic situation are deeper issues of definition. Indeed, the definition of "child" and "youth" soldiers is culture bound and needs to be problematized. Despite the wide acceptance of the Convention on the Rights of the Child (CRC) and the Optional Protocol (signed by Sierra Leone), universalized notions of "childhood" and "youth" are contested on the grounds that they are products of mostly Western and Northern cultural systems and that they clash with culturally constructed views and practices. In rural Sierra Leone, as in rural areas throughout much of sub-Saharan Africa, people regard childhood as having ended when a young person has completed the culturally scripted rite of passage into manhood or womanhood. Most often, this occurs by age fourteen or fifteen, although the number of people who complete the rites is decreasing. It is a misnomer in many parts of Africa to call a fourteen year old carrying an AK-47 a child soldier since local people may regard that young person as an adult.

An even greater gulf in definition arises in regard to "youth." Most Western societies use this term to refer to people in transition between childhood and maturity. Most often, the term is synonymous with "adolescents" or "teenagers." In contrast, many African societies have more expansive definitions of "youth," which in South Africa includes people up to thirty-five years of age. In Sierra Leone the term "youth" is more expansive still and can include people in their forties.

Although issues of definition contain thorny layers of complexity and hidden questions about power, it is worth noting that cultures are not static and unchanging. Local concepts often reflect the intermixing of ideas from different cultural systems. From this standpoint, it makes little sense to enshrine one definition of child or youth. To strike a balance between highly expansive and excessively restrictive definitions of the term "youth," this chapter defines "youth" as people between the ages of thirteen and twenty-nine. This includes the Western category of teenagers and also recognizes that in rural Sierra Leone, people in their twenties are regarded as still in transition to full maturity and are making key life choices. Although significant numbers of people under thirteen years of age have been soldiers in Sierra Leone (Wessells 1997, 32–39), the largest numbers of young soldiers have been thirteen years old or over and hence are an appropriate focus for purposes of both analysis and intervention. In the following discussion, reference will also be made to "under-18s" since in terms of international law and child protection, the age of eighteen remains an important benchmark.

PATHWAYS INTO SOLDIERING

The literature on child soldiering has veered between extreme images of brutal, forced recruitment on the one hand and voluntary entry into military activity on the other. In many respects Sierra Leone shatters extreme, simplistic images and invites analysis of diverse, changing pathways into soldiering (Richards 2002, 255–76; Wessells 2002, 237–54). Further, difficult living conditions in Sierra Leone often blur the boundaries between voluntary and forced recruitment.

The following discussion, which examines entry of child soldiers by militarized group, invites reflection on the multiple causation and the linkage of macrosocial and microsocial processes that influence entry into soldiering. It draws on previously unpublished interviews conducted in the northern province (Bombali, Koinadugu, and Tonkalili districts) by the first author with former youth soldiers in August 2002. The sample consisted of forty-eight youth, including nine women and eighteen under-18s, who were interviewed either alone or in groups of ten to fifteen people. The data offer a more complex picture than has been available previously of the variations that existed within the RUF and the CDF, of the variations in choices made by youth under difficult circumstances, and of the issues that could potentially thwart the integration of returning soldiers into their communities.

Sierra Leone Army (SLA)

Age documentation is difficult in rural Sierra Leone, where no written birth records were kept until recently. When the war started in 1991, the RSLMF attracted significant numbers of young volunteers, including under-18s, who joined for various purposes, such as to receive training or to be with older family members who had joined (Richards 2002, 265). Others joined out of desperation for food or because the RUF had attacked their villages and killed their parents. Still others reported viewing military activity as an adventure (Peters and Richards 1998, 183–89). Although it is uncertain whether the army deliberately targeted under-18s, the army apparently welcomed them and did not conduct extensive work on age documentation initially.

Following the Lome peace accord, the restructured army—now called the Sierra Leone Army (SLA)—included over 6,000 people (Coalition to Stop the Use of Child Soldiers 2001), all of whom were over eighteen and had completed training with the assistance of foreign forces. This is consistent with the government's statements that it will abide by the Optional Protocol on Children and Armed Conflict, setting eighteen years as the minimum age for combat participation. As is true of armies worldwide, the SLA also includes large numbers of voluntary recruits in their twenties. Among their reasons for joining are desire to defend their country, training, prestige, and money.

Revolutionary United Front (RUF)

As mentioned previously, the RUF often portrayed itself as a social justice organization, and it often used a mixture of propaganda and force to recruit youth. A twenty-five-year-old man in Fadugu reported "they [the RUF] attacked the mines and captured us. They said they wanted to liberate the country from poor education and poverty. I got convinced because I knew these things were lacking. . . . I played by their rules." Although it is difficult to separate the role of threat and indoctrination in this young man's decision to stay with the RUF until the cease-fire had been achieved, his perceptions of why he stayed suggest that the RUF was skillful in using ideology as a recruitment tool.

Being a relatively small force that relied increasingly on terror attacks on villages to gain control over particular territory, abduction was the dominant means of recruitment into the RUF. Particularly vulnerable to recruitment were separated children, many of whose parents had been killed and who had no source of protection or means of meeting basic needs. Former RUF members reported that youth and even young children were preferred recruits since they were easily intimidated, followed orders, were fearless, were better fighters, and had few moral qualms about what they were told to do.

It was common practice for the RUF soldiers to abduct children and youth at gunpoint and to kill anyone who tried to escape. One twenty-year-old man recounted how he had been abducted at age sixteen: "My Dad and I were planting rice and the RUF came and captured us. Dad begged the soldiers to release me, but they insisted . . . Dad trailed them since he couldn't let me go. . . . So they killed my Dad." Similarly, a nineteen-year-old girl described her abduction by the RUF at age sixteen as follows: "I was captured in Kono where I was with my aunt. Initially I escaped to the bush, but the RUF captured me and offered two options—kill or be taken." Many abductees reported that the RUF had killed relatives at the time of the abduction, leaving them little doubt that they, too, would be killed if they resisted. For some young abductees, entry into the RUF was associated with acts of forced killing or mutilation. To make sure that abducted children could not return home, the RUF often forced children to commit atrocities such as killing a neighbor or even a family member as other village members watched. A key point is that abductions often targeted demobilized soldiers. In January 2000 the RUF abducted approximately two hundred demobilized former child soldiers on their way from Kabala to Freetown (Amnesty International 2002). To some extent, this tactic of re-abduction may be a means of recouping on the investment in military training. More likely, though, it stems from the fact that formerly abducted children are vulnerable and many lack protection or a home to return to.

Gender had a powerful influence on entry into the RUF. Although boys were sexually abused in the RUF, the RUF was notorious for its abuses of girls and women (Human Rights Watch 1998, 11–23). It was common practice for the RUF to abduct girls and women as a village was attacked. Some were raped in open view of family and village members, apparently with the intent of defiling the girls and the community and making the girls unacceptable to the community (Human Rights Watch 1998, 11–23). In many cases, a particular captor took the woman he had abducted as his "wife," using her for sex whenever he wanted. Overall, this pattern of abduction, rape, fear, and killing of relatives was for many youth the beginning of a journey into a system of violence and human rights abuses that prepared the youth themselves to become accustomed to violence and to become perpetrators.

CIVILIAN DEFENSE FORCES (CDF)

As the RUF/AFRC attacked, burned, and looted villages, local people realized that the government army could not protect them. To protect their own villages, local groups of traditional hunter societies, notably the Kamajors in southern

Sierra Leone, organized themselves into Civilian Defense Forces. Acting as a civilian militia in support of government forces, CDF members typically fought with shotguns and knives, which were highly effective in close-range jungle fights, rather than the automatic weapons of the RUF. Nevertheless, the twin advantages of local support and intimate knowledge of local terrain often enabled them to repel or defeat RUF forces. CDF forces were able to protect against enemy infiltration by using secret passwords and initiation secrets that had attended their induction into the hunter societies. Although the CDF may have been necessary for local security, its rapid spread to the north from its roots in the southeast effectively militarized rural Sierra Leone in an unprecedented manner (Richards 2002, 269).

Many youth, including under-18s, joined the CDF voluntarily, that is, without immediate coercion, although their desperate circumstances afforded few other options. One former CDF major who had joined in his twenties said he joined the CDF because "the RUF were killing people, looting everywhere. . . . What they were doing was theft of a nation. They raped our wives and my sister was having her arms chopped off. . . . We ran but it wasn't safe so we fought. We had to fight for the liberation of our people." In many cases, joining the CDF was the only means of meeting basic needs. One twenty-five-year-old man, who had joined the CDF at age fifteen, said "The RUF killed my father and also my mother. I had no way of getting anything—I joined the CDF to get food and water." Many youth reported that they joined the CDF either to avenge family losses or because they had family members who had joined and whom they wanted to support. A twenty-one-year-old man who had joined the CDF at age eighteen said, "I joined the CDF since the RUF burned our house and killed my younger brother. I had to run. My only brother was gone, so I had to go with the CDF. I wanted to defend our land and village." Others said they joined because their peers had. Youth typically said they had a responsibility to protect their families and their villages, and they felt pride at what they had accomplished.

Roles, Experiences, and Implications

The roles and experiences of youth soldiers vary considerably according to the situation, gender, the armed group one is with, one's mode of entry, and individual skills and competencies in negotiating one's role within the situation and group. Because roles and experiences are highly variegated, it is inadvisable to think of all young soldiers as having similar duties or as having been affected in similar ways. The variegation of young soldiers defies simplistic images and cautions against monolithic concepts of "youth soldiers."

Typical roles included combatants, porters, cooks, spies, and bodyguards, and these roles were often performed in the same time period. Some individuals, however, had specialized roles such as torturers or sex slaves. In many respects, the common denominators were that daily activities and roles were thoroughly militarized, and experiences of death, either through witnessing or perpetration, were widespread. Although this applies to the SLA as well as to nongovernmental forces, the emphasis here is on the RUF and CDF since these groups were relatively unregulated by comparison to the SLA. Because RUF and CDF members had frequent exposure to deaths and atrocities, and many participated in killing, their members face the greatest challenges to integration.

RUF

Life within the RUF was typically hard and entailed long marches with little food, carrying heavy loads of looted goods, and forced participation in violence. Those who lagged behind or complained were usually killed. Compulsory drug use was frequently used to prepare youth soldiers for combat and terror raids. Former RUF members in the sample for the present study reported that they frequently smoked marijuana and consumed burnt gunpowder and alcohol. Entering combat, they felt no fear and experienced no pain. Some reported that they had received ritual treatments by traditional healers, making them believe their bodies were bullet proof. Brutal, ritualized treatment was often used by the RUF to prepare young soldiers for killing. Young boys were given drugs and forced to commit atrocities against family and community members, presumably to insure they would not be able to leave the RUF and return home (Richards 2002, 258). Others were forced to beat other young people. This regimen of forced participation in violence has psychological effects of normalizing violence and reducing one's inhibitions against harming others (Staub 1989, 80–85).

Not all atrocities committed by youth were in response to direct orders. A difficult reality of the war is that some youth, having grown up in a system of violence, saw violence as normal, and some even relished it. In Fadugu in the northern province, for example, former RUF soldiers told of a young comrade whose specialty had been carving the letters "RUF" into people's chests using a razor blade. Similarly, it was not uncommon for people who lived in villages that the RUF attacked to report that young people, including small children, were among the most ruthless warriors and were often the ones who committed horrible mutilations. In addition, RUF soldiers developed a norm of machismo that encouraged young soldiers to brag about their exploits, to show bravado in very frightening circumstances, and to call themselves by "bad" names such as

"Rambo" and "Cock and Fire." The prevalence of names such as "Rambo" indicates the extent to which young African men have been influenced by popular Western culture, including popular films and rap music.

The RUF employed a system of incentives calculated to exploit young people's desire for power, advancement, and recognition. Within the RUF young soldiers who demonstrated bravery under fire or who were willing to carry out the most gruesome assignments rose rapidly through the ranks, becoming commanders before having reached the age of eighteen. As commanders, they enjoyed status and privileges denied to ordinary soldiers. Youth who were former RUF commanders reported that they had enjoyed their status, felt responsible for the soldiers in their unit, and found meaning in the spirit of camaraderie they had developed with their subordinates.

It is important to note, however, that many RUF youth soldiers did not support the norm of machismo and ruthlessness and sought to negotiate a path that enabled survival while avoiding killing and atrocities. One young man, who had been sixteen at the time he was abducted by the RUF, said:

> They [the RUF] captured me on my father's farm and took me away. I was forced to leave this area. They gave me a gun and forced me to go and loot. Also I was forced to carry all the loot, and if I refused [I] would be flogged or shot. We had food only sometimes. . . . The leader told us to beat women and saw it [watched us] with his eyes. Also the leader told us to have sex with women older than your mother. I told him "no" and was flogged and made to do hard work.

Although most interviews with former young soldiers have stressed the bad things done or experienced, an untold story is of how young soldiers understand their situation and make choices that do not compromise their values excessively. Young women, too, often found ways of constructing roles that went beyond the more typical roles of sex slave and combatant. One woman in Makeni reported that the RUF had abducted twenty-eight women and killed twenty-four of them outright. They had also shot her, but the bullet had not entered her body, possibly glancing off a bone. About to be bayoneted, she was saved by a soldier nicknamed "Rambo." The women in the company elected her the "mommy queen," the leader of the women and the caretaker who looked after abducted women and girls. She reported that 130 children were in her care when the ceasefire was implemented, and she had helped to reunite them with their families. Thus, depending on circumstances, some people were able to carve out relatively positive roles within otherwise deplorable conditions. The variation in soldiers' roles and experiences cautions against treating the category of "youth soldiers" as monolithic.

Within the RUF, girls comprised a significant portion of the fighting forces (Coalition to Stop the Use of Child Soldiers 2001), exemplifying the wider, global pattern of girls' participation in armed combat (Mazurana, McKay, Carlson, and Kasper 2002, 105). In some regions it was not uncommon for girls to serve as commanders since, as mentioned above, promotion depended on demonstrated valor. Young women also served as spies, in some cases dressing themselves in fine West African clothing and living for months in villages the RUF planned to attack. An important psychological wound of the war was the powerful sense of betrayal women and men reported as the result of having accepted new people into the village and allowing them to sell items at the marketplace only to learn subsequently that they had been spies. This practice contributed to the shattering of social trust and generated much suspicion, creating obstacles to reintegration and peace building following the war.

By far the dominant role of women within the RUF was as sex slaves. Once captured by a particular soldier or assigned to a particular commander, a young woman's survival depended on her willingness to provide sexual service on demand. Resistance to providing sex on demand was a serious offense within the RUF. An eighteen-year-old girl who had been abducted by the RUF at age fourteen told her captors, "I am too young for sex, and we are not married. In Sierra Leone, people don't take such young girls." Having continued her defiance, she was taken to Freetown as part of the January 6 attack there and told to have sex with a particular soldier. When she refused, saying she was too young, they cut off her left arm above the elbow. In most cases, young women had sex because they had no other recourse. Many became pregnant and gave birth while still in the RUF. Whether through identification with the captor, gratitude for protections offered by the captor, or adherence to cultural scripts, young girls who became mothers in this manner often stayed with or near their former captors and spoke of "relationships" with them even following the disarmament and demobilization process.

The RUF practiced more brutal forms of sex slavery as well. Some abducted women were mass raped immediately and were raped repeatedly by many men over long periods of time (Human Rights Watch 1998, 11–23). Many rape victims suffered from sexually transmitted diseases (STDs), including HIV/AIDS, and reproductive health problems associated with mass rape. In addition, pregnant women were often cut open and the fetuses killed. In this manner the RUF used sexual violence as a tool for simultaneously violating women, demeaning the enemy, and asserting dominance through terror.

CDF

Not unlike their RUF counterparts, youth members of the CDF performed a variety of roles. These included serving as checkpoint guards, cooks, porters, and combatants, among others. Although in the eyes of the world the CDF occupied the high moral ground of fighting out of survival and self-defense and deplored rape and sex slavery, it is vital to look realistically at what their youth did. For example, many youth reported that with the CDF they had been required to loot villages in order to obtain food and other basic materials. The irony of these attacks was not lost on villagers in the northern province, as they saw the group of people who was supposedly protecting them stealing their food, animals, and livelihoods.

Further, some CDF members, including youths, committed atrocities against presumed or known members of the RUF/AFRC. Human Rights Watch (1998, 24–26) presented a variety of eyewitness reports of beheadings and murders of RUF members and also of disembowelments followed by CDF members eating vital organs of those they had killed. The extent of youth participation in such activities has not been documented, but it is unlikely that they remained isolated from them. As discussed below, communities often said they regarded CDF members with considerable fear and distrust. The same applies to SLA members, who were known to have committed summary executions and to have used torture to extract information from RUF/AFRC members or sympathizers.

IMPLICATIONS FOR REINTEGRATION

As a result of these experiences, youth soldiers face significant challenges to reintegration into their communities and civilian life. Some analysts have doubted that former soldiers will be able to return home in light of what happened during the fighting. Others characterize former youth soldiers as hardened killers who have been traumatized, numbed to violence, and become "damaged goods," and therefore they have little prospect of returning home or recovering. These negative images, which can become self-fulfilling prophecies, do not fit well with the resilience and flexibility of Sierra Leonean youth and communities. At the least, they need to be tempered by analysis of the challenges, which can then serve as a guide for programmatic efforts to support reintegration. Five key challenges are noteworthy in this regard.

RECONCILIATION. In order to achieve reintegration, returning youth soldiers need to reconcile with the communities to which they are returning. Reconciliation also needs to occur between former RUF and CDF soldiers who are returning to the same community. As suggested by Lederach's (1997, 23–35) framework regarding reconciliation, significant progress needs to be made with respect to four elements: truth, mercy, justice, and peace. At present, many communities fear returning soldiers, who are often stigmatized as "rebels" and "troublemakers." Because of this fear, communities are often unwilling to extend mercy, to recognize the common suffering on all sides, and to restore a sense of unity. Returning soldiers, too, fear that they will be recognized and attacked in revenge for what they had done. Initially, some returnees sought anonymity since they feared that telling the truth about what they had done might get them killed. In a climate of desperation, fear, and suspicion, conflicts will continue to erupt, making it important to create a sense of unity and security and to establish norms of tolerance and nonviolent conflict resolution. Apology, forgiveness, restitution, truth telling, and healing are needed to move beyond the pain of the past and to transform society at all levels—including the village level—away from a culture of violence.

POVERTY. Former youth combatants typically have no money, clothing, food, or way of meeting their basic needs. Deprived of education and lacking job skills, they are not in a good position to earn a living as civilians. Most report that unless they receive training or support in meeting basic needs, they will probably return to the bush and use violence to meet their needs. In rural Sierra Leone, reconciliation and economic development must go hand in hand.

IDENTITY. The humanitarian community is increasingly cognizant of the mental health needs of war-affected children and youth, particularly regarding issues such as trauma, depression, guilt, and anxiety (Apfel and Simon 1996; Danieli, Rodley, and Weisaeth 1996; Machel 2001, 80–86; Marsella, Bornemann, Ekblad, and Orley, 1994). Although the conceptual and cultural limits of this focus have been noted (see, for example, Ahearn 2000; Bracken and Petty 1998; Summerfield 1999, 28–56; Wessells 1999, 276–82), the identity issues of former youth soldiers typically receive little attention. In the authors' field experience, one of the primary reintegration challenges stems from former soldiers' difficulty transitioning out of their military identity and constructing a civilian identity. Particularly following extended stay in the military or having spent formative years in an army, they literally define themselves in terms of their military roles, values, and behavior patterns.

LACK OF A POSITIVE CIVILIAN ROLE. Complementing identity issues is the reality that many youth lack a positive social role in civilian life. Even those who have not been soldiers may be regarded as troublemakers and have few positive life options. For former soldiers who had risked their lives to protect communities, this disrespect by the community is stinging and frustrating. Since most returning youth lack the job skills and education needed to contribute as citizens, they have difficulty constructing a meaningful role and engaging in meaningful activities in communities. A key task of reintegration is to help youth achieve a positive, respected role in their communities.

Spiritual contamination. In rural areas of Sierra Leone, as in much of sub-Saharan Africa, spirituality is at the center of people's lives (Honwana 1999a, 103–19; Wessells 1999, 276–82). In addition to the dominant Islamic faith, most people believe that events in the visible world are caused by good and bad spirits. Respecting traditions of animism involving ancestor worship, they practice rituals to restore harmony between the living community and the community of the ancestors. For returning youth soldiers, conducting particular rituals is a crucial part of community reconciliation. For example, a young woman who has been abducted and raped is regarded as spiritually contaminated, and local beliefs hold that if she returns home, she will bring spiritual pollution into the community. Since this spiritual pollution is believed to cause misfortune, bad harvests, health problems, and a host of other issues, it needs to be addressed. In most communities a local healer conducts a purification ritual that is believed to rid the young girl of contamination and enable her to reenter the community. As this example illustrates, indigenous practices often play a key role in reconciliation and reintegration.

Although indigenous practices can be valuable, outsiders, too, have an important role to play in reintegration. Humanitarian agencies can bring resources that are enormously helpful in impoverished, war-torn contexts. Sometimes outsiders can help establish linkages between groups and villages that have been divided and isolated by war and suspicion. Outsiders play an important role in facilitating community development, unity, and peace building. In northern Sierra Leone, where the fighting ended very recently, the presence of outsiders who previously had no access to the area symbolizes peace and gives local people hope that war is over. Of course, outside assistance, even if well intentioned, can create dependency, support neocolonialism, and undermine peace (M. Anderson 1999; Wessells 1999, 276–82). Conducted well and with an eye toward capacity building, long-term development, and partnership with local communities, outside assistance can support peace building and reintegration in the post-accord environment (McCallin 1998, 60–75; Wessells and Monteiro 2001, 262–75). The following section provides an example of a community-based program for the reintegration of former youth combatants.

Creating Life Options Through Skills Training and Employment Generation

To address these reintegration issues, Christian Children's Fund (CCF), a non-governmental organization that is both international and nonsectarian, constructed a community-based reintegration program called Support for Skills Training and Employment Generation (STEG). Begun in September 2001, its objectives were (1) to strengthen life skills of and create positive roles for youth ex-combatants, and (2) to encourage reconciliation through economic and psychosocial support and cooperation between ex-combatants and civilians. The need for work on reintegration was severe in the northern province, where the RUF had had a stronghold in Makeni (Bombali District) and where bitter fighting and mass displacement had occurred recently. In addition, the northern province had been isolated from outside support for years due to insecurity and geographic remoteness. For these reasons, the project focused on three northern districts: Bombali, Koinadugu, and Tonkolili.

Using the psychological method of cooperation on superordinate goals (Sherif et al. 1961), the project strategy was to encourage reconciliation through cooperation between ex-combatant and civilian youth on community-selected civic projects that provided immediate employment and a small stipend. To enable ex-combatants to earn a living, the project also sought to provide skills training in locally sustainable skills followed by participation in a microcredit scheme that provided small loans and enabled income-generating activities. The strategy also included ongoing psychosocial training and dialogues about reconciliation that aimed to increase tolerance and unity, decrease stigmatization of ex-combatants, and support local mechanisms of remorse, healing, forgiveness, and conflict resolution. To increase the geographic coverage and build linkages between villages isolated by war, the project defined a community as a cluster of nearby villages, typically four or five, in the same chiefdom.

Project Activities

STEG was implemented in fifteen communities and followed eight main steps. *First,* the CCF team met traditional chiefs and elders, following cultural scripts for entering the community, and explained the purpose of the project and the partnership it entailed. Community entry was facilitated by Catholic Relief Services, which had long served the northern province, thereby helping to establish trust. The initial meetings with chiefs and elders provided important information about community structures and local community development committees, which would become important venues for community planning and mobilization. *Second,* the communities prioritized their needs, defining which kind of civic works project was most valuable. The construction of a health post, school, or latrine or the repair of a bridge were popular options. This prioritization, which often entailed animated dialogues, helped to restart processes of collective planning and action that had been disrupted by war and displacement.

Third, CCF staff conducted a four-hour psychosocial workshop for groups of thirty local chiefs, elders, senior women, youth, and other opinion leaders. Conducted in a participatory manner, this initial workshop explored topics such as human rights, conflict and its impact, nonviolent conflict management and resolution, peace, and peace education and reconciliation. The workshop provided a forum in which local people discussed the meaning and challenges of building peace and promoting reconciliation at the community level. It also provided a space in which local people recalled and discussed the relevance of traditional mechanisms for healing, conflict resolution, remorse, forgiveness, and reconciliation. In a safe context, people told stories of suffering on all sides, humanizing the Other and strengthening norms of truth telling. Using stories, proverbs, and songs, the workshop emphasized the importance of uniting, moving beyond the pain and suffering of the war, not stigmatizing former soldiers, listening to ex-combatants, and reconciling ex-combatants with civilians. The dialogues of unity were expressed well by one elder who said, "We are Sierra Leoneons—one people—and we cannot let politics or the past divide us." To continue the reconciliation process, participants in the workshop agreed to construct Community Reconciliation Committees that would carry forward the work of increasing tolerance, nonviolent handling of conflicts, and justice and inclusivity at the grassroots level.

Fourth, the communities selected the workers who would conduct the planned civic works project. Communities selected the youth workers, 60 percent of whom were ex-combatants and 40 percent of whom were civilians, according to criteria such as high level of motivation, ability to do heavy manual labor, and willingness to stay in the community. In some communities the ex-combatants included former RUF and former CDF members. In others, this mixture was not possible since all the former soldiers from the community had belonged to one group.

Fifth, to prepare the workers not only to conduct the civic works project but also to use it as a space for reconciliation, CCF staff conducted a two-day psychosocial workshop on reconciliation for the workers. Cultural activities, idioms, and images were used in a highly participatory format. Themes included healing and

stress reduction, spirituality and peace, linkages between local processes of reconciliation and the wider peace process in Sierra Leone, tolerance and forgiveness,
and local modes of conflict resolution and cleansing. Regarding the latter, a case-
based approach was used to elicit discussion of local methods. For example, in the
case of a girl soldier who had been raped or sexually abused, local people explained
that the girl would be viewed as spiritually contaminated and that she needed to
participate in a traditional cleansing ritual in order to reenter the community. Discussion also elicited descriptions of traditional processes of establishing justice and
resolving conflict nonviolently. These were valorized not only because they were
useful peace-building tools but also because the strengthening of local cultural
beliefs and practices can itself provide psychosocial support by creating a sense of
continuity and meaning in difficult situations.

Sixth, the communities conducted the civic works projects. Although CCF
helped provide the materials, community-selected foremen guided the construction planning and implementation. Overall, communities implemented 53 civic
works projects, employing 2,040 ex-combatants and 1,380 civilians, of whom
63 percent were men. The workers worked for a minimum of 20 days and 160
hours, for which each received a stipend of 53,000 leones (US$27). Although
small by international standards, the stipend enabled the purchase of basic items
such as clothing and food.

Seventh, following completion of the civic works projects, ex-combatants
could elect to participate in training for skills such as carpentry, tailoring, gara
tie-dyeing, and soap making, which could support future employment. Small
groups of ex-combatants worked with master artisans from the community
for a period of approximately eight months and received a monthly stipend
of 60,000 leones (US$18). Overall, 650 former combatants have participated
in the skills training. Since most trainees were illiterate but wanted to set up
their own businesses, the training included basic business literacy skills.

Eighth, a microcredit loan and payback initiative was made available to the
ex-combatants who had completed the skills training and also to other ex-
combatants and civilian youth. Small solidarity groups of three to ten people
who each agreed to be accountable for the others received an initial loan of
120,000 leones (US$60), which is to be repaid together with a small service fee
over a six-month period. Groups that repay successfully are eligible for a larger
loan. Loans may be used to purchase capital items such as farming tools, sewing
materials, fabric for dyeing, or other items for small business.

Complementing these activities were ongoing community dialogues about
reconciliation. The dialogue topics varied according to the context, but they
examined issues such as stigmatization of ex-combatants, recent disputes in the
community and their management, and how to enable healing and unity.

Outcomes, Challenges, and Lessons Learned

Since this project is still under way and much of the evidence available is anecdotal or based on self-reports, making it subject to numerous biases, it is premature to assess its impact in detail. Nevertheless, numerous patterns have appeared through direct observation, data collected as part of the ongoing monitoring and evaluation system, and data from focus group discussions conducted with various groups in August 2002. The main outcomes may be grouped according to the categories discussed previously.

Reconciliation

Many community members reported that the civic works project, together with the psychosocial workshop and dialogues on reconciliation, had increased unity, reduced community divisions, and improved relations between ex-combatants and civilians. Ex-combatant and civilian youth said that their cooperation on the civic works project had enabled them to talk, to make jokes, and to experience their commonalities and commitment to rebuilding the community. The ex-combatants reported that they were less likely to be called names such as "rebel" and that they felt they were treated with greater respect than they had received before the project. Significantly, in communities where former RUF and CDF forces collaborated on the civic works project and in skills training, ex-combatants from both sides said the activities had helped humanize the others, reduce fears, and develop a base of good relations.

Civilians, too, commented on the humanizing effect of the project, saying that they had learned through the collaboration to view the former soldiers not as threats or dangerous people but as human beings who themselves had suffered during the war and are now struggling to earn a living and to transition into an era of peace. One adult member of a Community Reconciliation Committee said: "We used to fear them [youth soldiers] and thought they would start fighting in our communities. When they came from the bush, we looked at them as animals. At first, it was difficult to bring them together since ex-combatants themselves were hot-headed. But then they learned to get along. The works brought them together, they learned to get along, and we say they are not animals." Elders and youth alike reported that the project had made peace a priority in their community. Many said that before the project had begun, the peace process had seemed remote and unconnected to their lives; through the project they gained new understanding of how tolerance and reconciliation at the community level contributed to the wider peace-building process.

Community members reported that the project had also increased awareness of the importance of nonviolent conflict resolution and increased the tendency of people to use traditional processes of remorse, forgiveness, and reconciliation. For example, some people recalled a local practice wherein a young soldier, on returning home, told his parents what had happened during the war. Recognizing the boy's situation and the necessity for apologizing for what he had done, the parents approached a village elder and asked him to meet with and hear the boy. To demonstrate his remorse and submission to village authority, the boy prostrated himself before the elder or made some other gesture such as touching the elder's ankle. Hearing the boy's story and apology while seeing his submission, the elder typically forgave the boy and touched him on the shoulder to put him at ease. If the boy had done horrendous things, the elder might take the boy to the bush with traditional healers, who by conducting rituals and animal sacrifices would cleanse the boy of spiritual contamination that, left untreated, would cause misfortune for the boy and the community. Local people reported that these and similar kinds of mechanisms were being used more frequently.

POVERTY REDUCTION AND MATERIAL IMPROVEMENTS

Ex-combatants agreed unanimously that the stipends they had earned had been crucial for their return and had played an integral role in reconciliation. An eighteen-year-old who had formerly fought for the RUF said "the stipends really helped . . . We were so aggressive during the war. But CCF brought us together and we joked and learned about each other during the works [civic works project]. We have new friends, and now we live in harmony." Those who participated in training expressed strong pride in their newly acquired skills and felt proud that they would be able to earn their own living without depending excessively on others. Many said that without the stipends, they would have felt marginalized and uncared for and that they probably would have returned to the bush, continuing the fighting. Some reported that having clothes and less hunger had helped to rehabilitate them as members of the community since they did not seem to be a drain on community resources. They spoke repeatedly of how having a bit of money and the ability to meet basic needs was necessary for putting the war behind them. In many respects, some of the greatest wounds of the war had been not physical but mental—the isolation, marginalization, and shame they felt on arrival in the community without shoes, clothing, or the ability to feed themselves. An ex-combatant who had joined the CDF at age fifteen echoed the views of CDF soldiers when he said: "I fought with the CDF for eight years and believed all they told me. After the ceasefire, I had no gun and got no package [that is, he did not qualify for the government benefits for former soldiers]. Now we are presentable and can survive . . . Before we had only cassava but now we have rice—this makes us believe in peace."

Although civilians showed strong appreciation of the civic works projects, which helped to meet basic needs in the community, they, too, noted the connection between material improvements and putting the war behind them. They reported that the new structures had given them hope, as if the structures symbolized their own healing and resilience. As one chief put it, "War brought everything down to ground level—everything was destroyed . . . We had no hope and the people did not attend to their children. Now we have a new school and people feel hopeful. And the young people go to school instead of fighting." Most community members reported that they had become more effective in their collective planning and action and now felt better prepared to move forward.

Positive social role

Participation in the civic works projects had a powerful effect on changing community perceptions of ex-combatants. Many community members said that before the project had begun, they tended to view ex-combatants as people who had little concern for the community and indeed posed threats to the community's well-being. Ex-combatants' participation in the civic works projects changed this perception, as the youths' work contributed to community development. Since the ex-combatants could have earned significantly more money through crime and violence, most community members attributed their participation in the civic works projects not to monetary incentive alone but also to an authentic desire to contribute to the community. The skills training also had a highly positive impact on enabling youth to assume a positive role. Community members said they recognized the value of the skills the youth were learning, how hard they were working, and their desire to be good citizens. Gradually, the dominant perceptions regarding ex-combatants changed from fear and mistrust to increasing acceptance, respect, and recognition that they add value to the community.

Identity

Former youth soldiers reported that over the course of the project, they had come to see themselves increasingly as civilians and found meaning in civilian life. In part, this may have been a matter of self-selection in that those who had chosen to return to the community may have already begun the process of identity shift and knew at some level that they were capable of making the change. Most ex-combatants said that while they missed the camaraderie and even the excitement of military life, they had grown weary of the violence and wanted to live in a secure place with family and lasting friendships. Some youth reported that the change in identity was connected with how well they were treated by their families and communities. In essence, the more they were treated with respect and as civilians, the stronger their civilian identities became.

SPIRITUAL HARMONY

By reminding people of and valorizing selected traditions, the practice of which is understood locally as increasing spiritual well-being, STEG contributed to the communal sense of spiritual harmony. The project also encouraged synergies with related projects that aimed specifically to improve spiritual harmony. In Tonkalili district, STEG was implemented alongside a project to assist sexually abused women, many of whom were former youth soldiers. This project included four elements: (1) psychosocial assistance through peer support; (2) health assistance, particularly in regard to sexually transmitted diseases; (3) economic assistance through income-generating projects; and (4) spiritual assistance through enabling girls' participation in traditional cleansing rituals, which were regarded by the community as crucial for reintegration. The girls reported that the latter element helped to put their minds at ease and to enable their reentry and reintegration into their communities. In planned extensions of STEG, efforts will be made to integrate this assistance to sexually abused girls into communities served by STEG.

CHALLENGES

These positive outcomes notwithstanding, the project faces numerous challenges. Ongoing poverty and the inability of communities to meet their basic needs fuel concerns that CCF will abandon communities at the end of the project year. The monetary stipends, although valuable initially, created excessive emphasis on money and dependence on external sources of income. The largest challenge has been the privileging of ex-combatants. In particular, the exclusive focus on ex-combatants for skills training created jealousy from other young people, who also need skills training. Further, the project benefited greater numbers of men than women. In the successor projects, greater emphasis was placed on nonmonetary payment for civic works projects in forms such as animals or seeds and tools that assist restocking or agriculture, respectively. Also, training programs provided opportunities for community youth—women as well as men and civilians as well as ex-combatants. In addition, ongoing support for community development in currently participating communities was provided.

The greatest challenges to peace building will come from the wider political and economic arena in Sierra Leone and the West Africa region. Within Sierra Leone, the occurrence of free elections is encouraging, but the situation could deteriorate rapidly if large numbers of youth remain unemployed or if leaders manipulate public fears for their own political gain, fomenting divisions that could again lead to war. Unfortunately, the 2003 war in Iraq has pulled much attention and funding away from West Africa, and the funding needed to continue the reintegration work in Sierra Leone on a large scale has not materialized.

Regional issues of peace building are also crucial. If the war began as a spillover from conflict in Liberia, the threat of another spillover increased sharply in 2003 as violence again racked Liberia. There have been continuing military incursions with the associated flight of refugees back and forth across the border between Sierra Leone and Liberia, and fighting has also occurred across the border with Guinea. This serves as a poignant reminder that post-conflict peace building cannot be a country-by-country affair but requires regional approaches. On a hopeful note, international efforts helped to oust Charles Taylor from the presidency in Liberia, thereby removing one of the main threats to regional stability. As shown by the case of Sierra Leone, a key part of the peace-building agenda, regionally as well as nationally, is the creation of positive life options and meaningful participation in civilian life by former youth combatants as well as by civilian youth.

Victoria Sanford

The Moral Imagination of Survival

Displacement and Child Soldiers in Guatemala and Colombia

> I stood in the courtyard with the other young recruits of my
> unit, strangers all; in the gloom of initial anonymity, what
> comes to the fore is coarseness, otherness; that is how it was
> for us; the only human bond we had was our uncertain future.
>
> *Milan Kundera (1982, 59)*

DISPLACEMENT AND CHILD SOLDIERS

Though the exact number of Maya youth in the army and guerrilla forces has been difficult to determine, the Guatemalan Commission for Historical Clarification found that 20,000 children under the age of fifteen were forcibly recruited into the army-controlled civil patrols (CEH 1999, 3:80). In Colombia there are an estimated 16,000 child soldiers today (Paez 2003). One in ten Guatemalans was displaced by the internal armed conflict in the 1980s, leaving 1.5 million displaced (CEH 1999). Each day violence in Colombia forces some 300 civilians to flee their homes (ICG 2003). Some 2,900,000 Colombians have been internally displaced since 1985 (CODHES 2003), and Bogotá alone is home to more than 400,000 displaced people (WCRWC 2002). Women and children represent fully 80 percent of the total displaced population, and children alone comprise more than 54 percent (Profamilia 2001, 123). If these percentages have remained roughly constant since 1985, that means that more than half of displaced Colombians, or nearly 1.5 million people, were displaced as children. In other words, the majority of displaced people are/were children at risk for forced recruitment.

The ever-increasing numbers of internally displaced Colombians presents a humanitarian crisis of epic proportions. While much has been written about displacement, in-depth comparative studies of child soldiers remain scarce. In the literature on displacement in Guatemala and Colombia, there are numerous studies about the basic needs of the displaced (Fajardo-Montaña 2001), their uncertain legal status (CCJ 1999a, 1999b; Tassara et al. 1999), and the disproportionate effect of displacement on women and children (Young 2002). Often times, the conditions of displacement are explained in tandem with the lives of refugees (Malkki 1995; Manz 1988). While the lives of displaced Maya in flight (Falla 1992; Sanford 2003a, 2003b) and the experiences of Guatemalan refugees in Mexico (Manz 1988) have been documented, there is no published study on the Communities of Population in Resistance (CPRs) or their role in postwar reconstruction. Literature on displacement in Colombia focuses on the aforementioned topics (Osorio and Lozano 1995; Hernandez-Hoyos 1999; HRW 1994a; ICG 2003; Peacaut 2001) or provides a history of displacement within particular regional studies of La Violencia (Roldan 2002; Ramirez 2001). My articles on peace communities (2003c, 2004) and this chapter on child soldiers in Guatemala and Colombia are the first scholarly studies on the topic. This chapter builds on existing literature on displacement and contributes to emerging literature on child soldiers by seeking to understand the role of internally displaced people and forcibly recruited youth and children within the complex web of internal armed conflict.

Most literature on child soldiers emerged in the fields of law, medicine, and psychology based on the reflections and efforts of human rights advocates and service providers working in zones of conflict and postwar reconstruction in Africa.[1] In her work in Mozambique, Thompson (1999) suggests that the conditions of child soldiers "erase" analytical categories of military, civilian, and child. Transformation in kinship and family situations in Sierra Leone (Zack-Williams 2001) and the cultural meaning of the category of youth in Mozambique (West 2000) have been explored in relation to the phenomena of child soldiers. Millard (2001) challenges the primarily legal approach to child soldiers, suggesting it limits our understanding and policy options. De Berry (2001) identifies state crisis and local influences as the two contexts for the emergence of child soldiers in Uganda. De Waal (1996) notes that child soldiers are part of the war aims of armed actors in Africa, who tend to be local and specific bands integrating commerce and violence to sustain and enrich themselves. This research in Africa resonates with the findings of Lovell and Cummings (2001) on children in Northern Ireland. They argue that children do not merely react to conflict, but they interpret the meaning of conflict for themselves, their families, and their communities. They suggest the need for research on families and communities to achieve successful interventions for children. Likewise, De Berry (2001) suggests the need to develop a community-based approach to the problem of child soldiers, and Wessells calls for "research on the anthropological factors that affect child recruitment and prevention strategies" (2002, 254).

This chapter seeks to take the lessons learned through the sequelae of violence as well as humanitarian and peace-building outcomes in ongoing violence and place them in a framework for peace building and the prevention of violence. This chapter recognizes the increased importance of preventive action and humanitarian intervention around the world and bears witness to the insistence that international aid be used to strengthen peaceful alternatives, not escalate wars that disproportionately take the lives of civilians. The lived experiences of children and youth who have been displaced and forcibly recruited into state, insurgent, and paramilitary armies are among the most extreme consequences common to internally displaced people (IDPs) in the new millennium. Through my comparative exploration of the forced recruitment of displaced youth in Guatemala and Colombia as well as peace-building initiatives among IDPs, this chapter challenges the nonsubject stasis often attributed to displaced people (especially youth and children) who daily remake their lives in the midst of violence.

Conflict prevention should begin before conflict starts or at least as it emerges. Successful conflict prevention involves early prevention. Bad governance and exclusionary governance lead to conflict. In post-conflict situations, governance issues are key to ensuring that countries do not slip back into conflict. Throughout the world, United Nations agencies and nongovernmental organizations have increasingly recognized women and youth as key constituencies for peace building. Peace agreements alone between male leaders of warring groups are not sufficient to bring lasting peace or to deal with structural causes of conflict.

If we can learn how the lives and survival of the displaced become part of the violence, then perhaps we will be better able to understand how and why displaced communities can also organize to generate spaces for peace and democratic participation in the midst of war. How have seemingly utopian Colombian peace communities and Guatemalan Communities of Populations in Resistance survived in war zones, and what are their prospects for the future? How do children and youth become a part of these peacemaking projects, and how does this participation transform their visions of their own future?

In this chapter I explore these questions by comparing the experiences of displaced and forcibly recruited youth in Guatemala and Colombia. I begin by offering the experiences of those surviving displacement in CPRs and peace communities. I then move on to the experience of forced recruitment as told by former soldiers and combatants in Guatemala. These testimonies of forced recruitment are then complemented by the experience of a Colombian paramilitary. I then offer an analysis of their memories of trauma. I close this chapter with the efforts of Colombian youth who today seek to avoid forced recruitment and work for peace in the ongoing conflict in their country.

The basic findings of my research are threefold: (1) displaced children and youth are more likely to be recruited by armed actors; (2) displaced children and youth participating in community peacemaking projects are less likely to seek out and more likely to successfully resist recruitment by armed actors; and (3) the moral imagination of local peacemaking projects in ongoing conflict creates new possibilities for peaceful resolution of internal armed conflict. Further, by juxtaposing testimonies of forcibly recruited youth with the experiences of Colombian peace communities, Guatemalan Communities of Populations in Resistance, and Colombian youth peacemakers, I identify some of the ways in which creative peacemaking and reconstitution of citizenship are central elements of the survival strategies of IDPs during conflict and in post-conflict situations. Creative peacemaking and the reconstitution of citizenship define new community projects of recovery that represent a new kind of political power grounded in community integrity, moral courage, and the hope, energy, and optimism of youth. Moreover, this chapter situates children not merely as victims and dangers to internal security and occupying armies but as active subjects in their own lives and crucial actors in any national and local peace settlements or refugee/IDP repatriation programs.

THE MORAL IMAGINATION OF SURVIVAL

In the early 1980s, as 200,000 Guatemalans were killed or disappeared and 626 Maya villages were massacred and razed, tens of thousands of survivors fled and sought refuge from the Guatemalan army in the highlands (CEH 1999). With no stable food source and no safe exit, survivors organized themselves into Communities of Populations in Resistance (CPRs) seeking to survive and build a just and peaceful community while under continued attack from the army (Falla 1992; Manz 1998; Sanford 2003a, 2003b). In Colombia, following several years of marginal life on the urban peripheries after being displaced from their villages by paramilitary violence, some 12,000 Colombian peasants negotiated the return to their land (in the middle of the war zone) as Peace Communities in 1999 (Sanford 2003c). Though separated by time and geographically divided by the Central American isthmus, both CPRs and Peace Communities have sought to rebuild community life as neutral, unarmed civilians. Moreover, they have sought to build interdependent utopian communities based on citizen participation, mutual respect, and collective survival. After years of struggle, both the CPRs and the Peace Communities were recognized by their respective governments and by the United Nations as civilians with the right to rebuild their lives. Since the signing of the peace accords in 1996, the CPRs have played an integral role in postwar reconstruction in Guatemala. The Peace Communities continue to struggle for their survival in Colombia's ongoing war.

Given the large numbers of displaced people living in desperate circumstances of misery, how and why have these communities sought not only reconstruction but also a better, more peaceable way of life in the midst of war? While living in war is not unique, efforts to build utopian communities in war zones represent a highly creative response by seemingly powerless peasants to the violence that crashes unbidden upon them. In an era of lawlessness, they reassert their rights as citizens. In this chapter I explore how the practices of creative peacemaking and reconstitution of citizenship represent a new kind of political power grounded in community integrity and moral courage. This power is not of a violent nature but rather derived from the moral imagination—power that creates new realities and new possibilities by pushing the frontiers of the possible in the midst of the war zone. It is power that supports Hannah Arendt's (1973) belief that violence can destroy power but not create it.

Communities of Populations in Resistance

Despite ongoing army attacks and captures as well as surrender resulting from the dire conditions of survival in the mountains, thousands of internally displaced Maya remained in the mountains struggling to establish some semblance of daily life.[2] Fleeing army attacks, massacre survivors sought refuge in the mountains. They lived in near-constant movement, sometimes able to stay in a temporary village for a few months, sometimes just a few days. In groups of twenty to thirty families they traveled through the mountains, always in search of safer ground. In northwest Quiche, northern Ixcán, and the Petén, the Maya survivors organized themselves into what became known as Communities of Populations in Resistance (CPRs). Following more than six hundred massacres during the army's "scorched earth" campaign between 1980 and 1982, the

Guatemalan army labeled any village outside the army's model village structure and control as an "illegal village."

The army relentlessly attacked the CPRs as "illegal villages" using the same counterinsurgency techniques of the scorched earth campaign: occupying villages, killing any civilians in the community, burning huts, destroying crops. And, like earlier massacres, they continued to hunt for survivors in the mountains by firing machine guns, throwing grenades, and dropping bombs. These army attacks against civilians continued into the 1990s.

Don Samuel is a small, soft-spoken, and unassuming man of forty-two. In late 1997 he was helping his neighbors make lists of their financial losses during the violence—cattle, horses, chickens, turkeys, tools, houses—and the number of dead and disappeared in each family. His house in Salquil was burned in 1981. His first site of refuge was in Bachaalte with his family. "We were hidden there for almost a year," he explains, "but after the civil patrols were formed, we had to escape. We fled when they came to destroy the village." Each CPR testimony involves numerous moments of flight, survival, and reconstruction followed by an army attack setting off another round of flight, survival, and reconstruction. Don Samuel's experience is representative of the many testimonies survivors shared with me. After fleeing Bachaalte, he recounts:

> We were about sixty families. So there were many of us. We had to find a way to protect ourselves. We organized a community structure with *responsables* and different people responsible for being lookouts and we would dig hiding places in the earth. This was how we were able to reach Santa Clara. Still, with so many people, the army was able to find some of us even though we were all hiding. They would kill anyone they found: elderly, youth, children. They would kill whoever was there simply because they were there. Each time the army would catch up with us, some of us were unable to escape. The army would catch them and kill them.
>
> We were always moving from one place to the other, looking for a place without the army. The army continued to persecute us until 1990 when we became known to the public. The army lessened their offensives against us, but they still didn't stop. Beginning in 1980 until 1990, we suffered so much in the midst of all of this.[3]

At the end of 1990, the CPR issued a public declaration announcing the existence of communities that had been resisting army capture and control for more than eight years (CPR Support Group 1993, 2). One year later, just moments after arriving at the CPR in the Ixil region in October of 1991, Christian Tomuschat witnessed an army air attack on the civilian community. Sent to Guatemala as a United Nations expert to investigate human rights violations, Tomuschat was the first official observer to reach the CPRs. When he presented his findings to the UN Human Rights Commission in Geneva in February of 1992, he condemned the Guatemalan army, government, and other security forces for their deliberate and continuous violation of the political, civil, cultural, social, economic, and human rights of Guatemalans (Guatemala Health Rights Support Project). In 1992 some 30,000 Maya massacre survivors were still living in the CPRs under army attacks. Though the army continued to harass and attack CPRs, Tomuschat was witness to the last army bombing in the Ixil area (Sanford 2003a, 2003b).

Colombian Peace Communities

In her work on displacement, Hannah Arendt wrote: "The first loss which the rightless suffered was the loss of their homes, and this meant the loss of the entire social texture into which they were born and in which they established for themselves a distinct place in the world" (1973, 293). And as recounted by Don Samuel, displacement is driven by violence. In the Uraba-Choco region of Colombia, Joselito was one of 45,000 people displaced by paramilitaries in the late 1990s. Recalling when he fled his community in 1997, he said: "Helicopters were bombing and paramilitaries were firing machine guns. To go to the river to cut bananas was to risk one's life. They burned our village and we lost all our rice. When the army would come, they would say, 'Don't be afraid of us, have fear of those who come after' meaning the paramilitaries. They had no respect for our lives. We had to leave."

According to those who have been displaced, these displacement operations are joint maneuvers between the paramilitaries and the army. The army frequently uses planes and helicopters to bomb civilian areas, forcing the inhabitants to flee while paramilitaries carry out ground maneuvers, destruction of the physical community, threats and assassination of those deemed by paramilitary lists as "subversive" or potentially so, and sometimes full-scale massacres (author interviews, 2000 and 2001). Yulian, a paramilitary soldier who had recently returned from combat, confirmed these survivor testimonies. Specifically about massacres, he told me, "Human rights are a problem. Now we can't massacre everyone, we have to kill them one by one, one by one" (author interview, August 7, 2001).[4]

Hannah Arendt suggested that the term "displaced persons" was expressly invented for the liquidation of the category of statelessness (1973, 279), which paved the way for the loss of the rights of citizenship and created a category of the persecuted as rightless people. Significantly, she stated, "The more the number of rightless people increased, the greater became the temptation to pay less attention to the deeds of the persecuting governments than to the status of the persecuted" (294). Moreover, she pointed out that this shift from the deeds of the government to the needs of the displaced constituted an innocence, "in the sense of complete lack of responsibility," that "was the mark of their rightlessness as [much as] it was the seal of their political status" (295) because as rightless people, she wrote, "their freedom of opinion is a fool's freedom, for nothing they think matters" (296).

Joselito became a peace community leader because, as he explained to me:

> When one is displaced, one loses the feeling of being Colombian, a citizen with rights and responsibilities. After many community meetings of the displaced, we decided to return together in 1999. We decided to live in the middle of the conflict because if we waited for it to end, we would never return to our lands. We opted for pure non-violence. They should respect the decision of the people. If they want to fight with each other, they can—but not on our land and we won't fight with them. As the peace communities, we have a life of peace, not violence. Our goal is to support peace, not war.

In this way peace communities reassert their rights, rebuild community structures, and transform the isolation of displacement. Colombian Peace Communities, like Guatemalan CPRs, constitute new domains of social justice, citizenship, and conflict resolution. This is not to suggest, however, that these constitutive processes of the peace communities, like the CPRs, are not affected by the violence of the armed actors who surround them.

THE FORCED RECRUITMENT OF MAYA YOUTH

It is perhaps among the youth within the communities of displaced people and their efforts to avoid or seek out recruitment by armed actors that one encounters both the moral imagination and the iniquitous monotony of survival. It is most often through displacement that violence and criminality appear to these children and youth to be their only opportunities. Displaced children and youth live without power in a world of armed power. In this section I offer abbreviated testimonies of former child soldiers and combatants in Guatemala to provide an opportunity to understand child and youth experiences in armed conflict. Rather than narrow the focus from the complications and tragedies of individual suffering of child fighters, these testimonies move through the layers of violence and organization that structure displaced lives to provide a nuanced, holistic, and complexly rendered understanding of the lived experience of these youth. These testimonies allow us a privileged lens through which we can (1) distinguish and analyze new types of public spaces and new forms of community produced by displacement and forced recruitment; (2) identify critical moments in displacement when survival strategies can feed the violence the displaced seek to escape; (3) outline recruitment mechanisms of armed actors; and (4) identify effects of forced recruitment on children and youth relationships with their families and communities.

The testimonies presented here challenge us to overcome the tendency to simply categorize these children and youth as victims on the one hand and as a danger to citizen security on the other. In both international humanitarian aid as well as popular images found in the media, these children and youth are displayed as victims of war structures that have destroyed their lives. Yet, if in order to survive the child or youth becomes a soldier, combatant, or urban gang youth member, this same child is no longer viewed as a victim but rather as a dangerous delinquent because s/he no longer fits within the framework of the innocent child, which society continues to maintain despite all realities to the contrary.

THE TESTIMONIES

GASPAR

Gaspar is a Tz'utijil-Maya who grew up on *fincas* (large farms) and in the streets of Guatemala City. He became a Kaibil after being recruited into the Guatemalan army.[5]

> *My mother gave me to a* finca *owner when I was six. I cut coffee for several months until I could escape. I went back to my mother because when one is little, you always look for the warmth of a mother's love. I never had that. My stepfather would get home drunk and beat my mother, my little sister, and me. He was very strong. He would knock me across the room and tell us that we were garbage because we were Indians, but my mother never wanted to leave him. Instead, she would give us away to another* finca.*
>
> *Once I asked a* finca *owner for shoes. She told me that my mother told her I didn't like shoes. She threatened me a lot and beat me. They put my food on the floor inside the house where the dogs ate. I wasn't allowed to sit at the table.*
>
> *I tried to kill myself because I felt that life wasn't good enough, it just wasn't worth it for me. There was a place, a lagoon of water contaminated by*

the plane that fumigated the cotton. I decided to bathe myself in the lagoon to see if I could die. But I wasn't lucky. Ever since then, I have thought it was bad luck and bad luck follows me. All I got was a rash.

Then, my sister and I went to live with my half-sister in Guatemala City. She told us we were Indians. She was very prejudiced because her last name was Juarez Santos. I have scars on my head from her beating me with burning sticks. She was trying to rid herself of rage. She beat us a lot. Sometimes, she would leave us tied up all day. Sometimes, she wouldn't let us in the house to sleep at night. She left us on the streets. I lived with her for three years and I tried to kill myself. I drank a toxic liquid but didn't get any results. I ran away from her.

I lived in the streets of Guatemala City and ate what I could find. I survived digging through garbage, begging, and stealing. I tried glue and paint thinner, but I didn't like it because it made me vomit. It is because of the way people look at you when you live on the streets. They never know the real feelings we have. Even living on the streets, I still felt I could be someone someday. But the people look at you and say you're lost, worthless, the scum of society. It was out of desperation that my friend Carlos put a rope around his neck. Afterwards, I tried the same thing, but had no luck.

Then, I went back to Mazatenango and got a job collecting garbage. I gave the money I earned to my mother to help her, but she gave it to my stepfather and he beat us. I collected garbage in the day and went to school at night. I wanted to learn and improve myself. But in the class, they laughed at me. They said I came from garbage, that garbage made me. People stopped calling me Gaspar. At school and in my neighborhood, they called me garbage man. Even the teacher called me garbage man.

When I would say my name, they would laugh at me because my surname is indigenous. I even changed my name for a while. But it made no difference, I was Indian because of my features and because that is who I am, whether or not I want to be. This created great conflict in me and I began to see a division between what is ladino and what is indigenous. I was humiliated so much that I began to hate ladinos. The hatred was so strong that I wanted a weapon. I wanted to kill my half-sister.

The army was always recruiting in the park, at the cinema, and anywhere else where young men congregated. I always got away. I was good at slipping away because I had lived on the streets. I saw that the world was made up of abusers and abused and I didn't want to be abused anymore. So, one day when I was sixteen, I let the army catch me. But they didn't really catch me, because I decided I wanted to be a soldier. I didn't want to be abused anymore.

I wanted a chance to get ahead. I saw what the soldiers did. I knew they killed people. But I wanted to see if in reality it could really be an option for me. If there would be an opportunity to get ahead, to learn to read and write. I always thought that it would be very beautiful to learn to read and write. I was always looking for a way to get ahead, to improve myself, but sometimes the doors just close and there is nowhere else to go. The army says we will learn to read and write, but when you go into the army, they teach you very little. They give you a weapon and they teach you to kill. They give you shoes because you don't have any. Many times, you join the army for a pair of shoes. When they grab you to recruit you, they say, "You don't have any shoes."

In the army, I was full of hate. I used the weapons with the hatred I had carried inside of me for a long time. Even though the hatred can be strong, you are still a human being with the spirit of your ancestors, with the spirit of peace and respect. So, inside you have great conflict. It was very difficult for me to find an internal emotional stability.

When I was recruited, there were a lot of indigenas recruited. They were beaten hard and called "stupid Indians" for not knowing how to speak Spanish. The soldiers who beat them were indigenous. The problem in the army is that no one trusts anyone else, even though most of the soldiers are indigenous.

After I was recruited, they told me that I could be a Kaibil because I was tall, fast, and smart. But I wasn't so smart. They took us to the mountains. Each of us had to carry a live dog that was tied up over our shoulders. I was thirsty. There was no water. Well, we had no water and we were given no water. But our trainer had water. He walked ahead of us on the path spilling water to remind us of our thirst. I was innocent. When we were ordered to pick up the stray dogs on the street, I thought we were going to learn how to train them, that we would have guard dogs. But when we arrived at the camp, we were ordered to kill them with our bare hands. We had to kill some chickens, too. We were ordered to butcher the chickens and dogs and put their meat and blood in a big bowl. Then, we had to eat and drink this dog and chicken meat that was in a bath of blood. Whoever vomited had to vomit into the shared bowl and get back in line to eat and drink more. We had to eat it all, including the vomit, until no one vomited.

The army kills part of your identity. They want to break you and make you a new man. A savage man. They inspired me to kill. There was a ladino recruit who said that Indians were worthless and that we didn't go to school because we didn't want to. I pushed him off a cliff. I would have enjoyed it if he had died. This is how the army creates monsters.

You become very hard in the mountains and sometimes the only thing you feel is fear. You are afraid of any man, or every man. After my first battle with the guerrilla, I decided to escape, because I wanted to improve myself and found no way to do it in the army.

MATEO

Mateo is from Pueblo Nuevo, Ixcán, and a survivor of the Mam-Maya Massacre. He joined the EGP[6] at age eleven and was forcibly recruited into the Guatemalan army at age fifteen.

Most of the [army] recruits were indigenous, but there were also some ladino students. There were five instructors and they were in charge. They would hit us. Everyday they punished us. The punishment is very harsh. Sometimes they would hang us tied up very tightly to the bed. They would leave us like that for fifteen minutes. Then we would do fifty push-ups. Then, we would have to go outside and lay on the ground. We had to roll to the other side and back until we vomited. Then they would line us up and go down punching us in the stomach and knocking the air out of us. But by then it didn't hurt so much because we didn't have any food left in our stomachs.

I never said that it hurt because if you said it hurt they would hit you more. Our training was called the Tiger Course. They explained to us, "You have to complete this course to become a real man." They would say, "You have to know a lot. You can become an important officer. You can order other people. But now you have to suffer three months. If you don't obey the rules here, you can die."

There were indigenous recruits who didn't know anything. They didn't know any Spanish; they only spoke their language. The majority of recruits were indigenous. Those who didn't know Spanish had to learn. There were some who only liked to speak their language. They were separated from each other. You could be beaten for not speaking Spanish. Sometimes you got beaten just for looking at someone or something.

There were three recruits who deserted. They were caught on the border because all their hair was shaved off. They were put into an underground jail [a pit]. Each day, water and garbage was thrown on them. They weren't given anything to eat. They were in there for almost a month. They were brought into our classroom all tied up as an example of what happened when you desert. They were kept in that cell for three more months. Then they had to start training all over again.

We were taught to use weapons and practiced with live munitions. Some of the recruits died in training from bullets and others died from bombs. In the third month, they taught us how to beat campesinos and how to capture them. We practiced on each other. They gave us our machine guns. They said, "It is better than a girlfriend." The machine gun is a jewel. The truth is that it is a pure jewel.

One day, they asked us if we liked our meal. They told us we had eaten dog. I never thought that it was dog. Some people had stomachaches and oth-

ers vomited. They fed us dog so that we wouldn't be afraid because it would have been impossible for us to withstand everything. I changed a lot after eating the dog. I wasn't afraid anymore. I just hated. I hated my compañeros. After three months, I was a very different person. I felt like a soldier.

After a year in the army, I went to my grandfather's village to visit. They looked at me differently. My form of speaking was different and my mannerisms had changed. The next day, I decided to go work with my grandfather. He said, "No, you have to stay here. How are you going to work? You are not one of us anymore."

In the afternoon, I met some friends. There are a lot of bars in the village. I had to go to a bar. I was overwhelmed with sadness. It is the only way the people in Guatemala can rid themselves of sadness. There you don't talk or discuss your problems. The only way is to go to the cantina and drink. I got really drunk and had to be carried to the house.

My grandfather said, "He had reason to drink, but he can't drink well." They all looked at me, but they couldn't hit me because I am a soldier. My grandfather said, "He has his reasons. Let him drink." So, they let me do whatever I wanted. And if I had hit them, they would have had to put up with it. I went to the cantina and drank with the soldiers.

When I was little, I remember the soldiers having good food. They had everything. They arrived in helicopters and airplanes and they had everything. I thought the army was good, that it was there to protect the people. My grandparents thought the same thing. But, a child is afraid of the soldiers because they have a weapon and a uniform and a very hard face. They don't look respectable. They can kick you whenever they want to. The army was very dangerous. You couldn't look a soldier in the eye. If you were watching a soldier, he would come over and say, "What are you looking at?" They would kick the children. A soldier could kill you. He could do it. They did it to some children.

Sometimes in Pueblo Nuevo on a Saturday or Sunday, the people were very frightened. They were very humble and didn't do anything. They never looked at the soldiers because if they did, the soldiers would grab them and take them to the base. I would go and hide behind an adult.

After the massacre in Pueblo Nuevo, we lived in the mountains. The army began to burn our homes and our people. They began to burn our animals. I cried because I saw our house burning. They destroyed all our crops. The corn, the beans, everything. They fired bullets. They threw grenades at my father's house. We were left with nothing. We returned to the jungle walking in a stream so we would leave no tracks for them to follow. The army killed my father in an ambush. He had gone to look for medicine because there were many sick people in our community. After the ambush, we all fled in different directions. It was two weeks before we could go back to look for my father.

I was very scared. I was nervous because I didn't know what it would be like to see my father dead. I was afraid from the moment we left. I felt like something bad was going to happen. The people were behind me, but I felt like I was being stalked. But I didn't say anything. I didn't say anything to my stepmother because she was nervous, too. When we arrived, I said, "This is my father's body."

He was in pieces and it made me very scared because I could see bits of his clothing and the things he had with him. Everything was in a path of blood. We didn't see his whole body. He was a puddle of blood. If his body had been more whole, I would have embraced my father. But all I could do was pick up the bones.

We had never seen anything like this. The people were watching to see if the army would come. So, we had to do everything in a hurry. There were frightening spirits there. There were haunted spirits there. Who knows if the spirit was devilish? I don't know. There was such fear there. There were flies and crows. There were hawks. They had been eating him. They had eaten a lot. The flies everywhere. The fear everywhere.

Many people died there. I lost my father. But really it was the children. I believe more little children died than adults. They died because of the cold and they died because they weren't well fed. The mothers didn't have any milk. So, they would give the baby water. Many died. Babies were born dead. Some were born alive, but in two weeks they would be dead. They did not have a great life. Every family lost some children. After my father was killed, I joined the guerrilla. I was a courier. I was eleven years old.

Later, when I was a soldier, I went to villages. Once I had to interrogate a woman. The woman didn't tell me anything, but she had to respect me because I was a soldier of the government and I had a gun. There was an officer behind me, watching me. I had to do it right because if you don't they beat you and sometimes they kill you. I interrogated the woman. So did some other soldiers. They beat her and I did, too. Sometimes they tell us, "Go get this person and beat him." A man was denounced by his neighbor. We beat him. He said, "I am just a campesino. I dedicate myself to working in the fields and nothing more." The man began to cry in front of us. I had to have such a face. I had to keep a tough face in front of the others because I had my orders and I was obligated to complete them. The man never said anything. The officer sent him to the base and I didn't see what happened to him after that.

The sub-lieutenant would ask the campesinos, "What have you been doing? What have you seen?" The campesinos would respond with their civil patrol titles. The sub-lieutenant would then ask them what they had seen. When they would respond that they had not seen anything, he would contradict them. He would lie and say that he had been told that subversives had been in the village. Then, the poor people would regret their answer and tell the sub-lieutenant, "Yes, we did see that." The army wants the people to give them information that is untrue. The only thing that matters is that the people will say whatever the army wants them to say.[7]

ESPERANZA

Esperanza is a survivor of the Q'anjob'al-Maya massacre and a former guerrilla combatant. She joined the EGP when she was fifteen years old.[8]

I found them in the mountain. I found the commander and I told him that if they would accept me I wanted to join their forces. I told him I wanted to fight the army. I told him I had seen the horrible things they did to people in my village, to unarmed people. I told him I wanted to go into combat. I told him it wasn't fair to die defenseless. That it was better to be armed and prepared and die in combat. They accepted me. That same afternoon, I joined the forces of the Guerrilla Army of the Poor (EGP) and they gave me a weapon. I began my training.

Everything went along fine. But the truth is that, after about eight days, I was finding it pretty difficult. In my house, I had hardly ever worked. My sisters and I were the smallest, so we had always been pampered. We were peasants, but we always had enough to eat because my father had a lot of land. In my house, there was always a lot of food at mealtimes and we had enough water to bathe everyday. But in the EGP, a lot of times there wasn't any water for bathing. The truth is this was my biggest desperation, that I couldn't bathe. Sometimes we didn't even have water to drink. I even told them that I felt desperate for water—for water to drink and water to bathe in.

Two or three days had passed and there was no water for bathing, there wasn't even water to drink. I felt truly desperate. I wanted to bathe. At first it seems extremely difficult—you're very hungry, you haven't gotten any sleep, you walk all night long in darkness, you trip, you fall, you get wet, and you just keep going, going, going. You see, we had to walk at night so the army could not easily locate us. In the beginning, I really regretted my decision. But, I just kept thinking, "I'll see if I can make it through today and maybe I will leave tomorrow."

And, so this is how it was and the days began to pass. I started to get used to not bathing everyday. Every two or three days, we would organize into squads of ten combatants to bathe. We would go to the water in squads of two. One squad would bathe while the other stood guard. If the army arrived, the squad standing guard would engage in combat while those bathing got dressed and withdrew. Some days we had no food, other days we had no water, some days we had neither. But some days, we had both.

I had been in the EGP for about one month when I realized we were walking through mountains very close to my village. I thought it would be very easy to walk back there alone. As I walked I thought how one month earlier, I would have run back to my house. But the day I walked near my village in the EGP platoon, I felt proud of what I had endured and the strength I had found in myself. I thought to myself, "Tomorrow there might not be food, there might not be water," and I laughed because I realized I hadn't bathed for two days. I chose not to go home. After a month, I liked being a combatant.

It was after this first month that I began to receive military training. The training was very difficult. We had to crawl through the ground on our stomachs. In the mountains, there were lots of stickers and rocks and mud. We had to crawl through like any other soldier in military training. We had to crawl across the ground, walk across ropes and jump very high.

For me this was all a great challenge. Because of my inheritance of being so chaparrita,[9] *there were times when things were simply out of my reach. This always put me behind the men because they are always taller than I, so it was easy for them. But the best thing is that it was in training that I discovered that I really loved being a combatant. I loved having a weapon at my disposal and I learned how to use it well. I couldn't jump as high as the men, but I could shoot as well or better than most of them.*

So it was in this month of training that the commanders asked me what I wanted to do when I was finished, if I wanted to be a combatant or an organizer. There was also a collective where uniforms were made for combatants. They asked me if I would like to work there in the sewing workshop. They told me there was also a workshop where explosives were assembled. They asked me what I preferred to do. I told them straight out, "I would like to be a combatant."

Our first action was to ambush a jeep of judiciales—*these are different from the army and the police. They are the squadrons, the ones that disappear and kill people. Anyway, these* judiciales *always had very good weapons. We had been informed that they were transporting weapons. So, we ambushed them with a Claymer bomb that we had actually made ourselves. This was my first experience. So, when the car passed by, I didn't know what would really happen. I had never been so close to the military. The* judiciales *passed by and the bomb exploded. Actually, right after the explosion, I stood there frozen, half-stupid. With a big explosion like that, one feels somewhat absurd immediately afterwards.*

We took their arms away and quickly withdrew from the area because almost immediately after the explosion, a helicopter arrived. It was a very bare area. There was almost no vegetation. This was my first close call. We had been running as fast as we could for about ten minutes when I felt I couldn't go on any longer. I felt dizzy. I felt like I was about to suffocate. I just couldn't breathe anymore. But then, I just calmed myself. I took some deep breaths. I told myself that my body was functioning normally and I continued to run.

We ran and ran. We all escaped the army. I learned a lot, especially about weapons. I learned how to handle them all. This was my job in the guerrilla for one year.

My next job was with the National Direction,[10] which is always located in very secure areas, in places that it would be difficult for the army to find. It was not the grand physical sacrifice I was used to, but there were many new rules to learn. The security was very tight. The arms were very good, very lightweight. But, we were very heavily armed. Sometimes, I almost couldn't tolerate it because I am so small and I was carrying a mountain of weaponry. I carried an M-16 with 300 rounds of fire, a 380 with 50 rounds of fire, 2 grenades and a dagger. And all this was around my waist. I was really full of weapons. But, I loved it. I was enchanted.

Still, I started to think that what I really wanted to do was to directly engage in combat with the army. I wanted to see if I was afraid of the army. I wanted to see how brave I was. I asked for authorization. In 1986, I joined the military unit. I was very happy because I was going to go into combat with the army.

We attacked the army base in San Lucas on December 31. We were 80 combatants. They were 800 to 1,000 soldiers. So, we were few in comparison to them. We had been spying on them for days. Every afternoon at one, they went down to the river to bathe. So, we went down to the river and we set up an ambush on the shore of the river. Because it was the 31st of December, the soldiers started to play soccer at 10 in the morning and they played until one in the afternoon. So, we knew that when they finished playing, they would come down to the river to bathe. But, at two in the afternoon, they finished playing and then returned to the barracks. We had been there since six in the morning. We hadn't eaten and we were thirsty. We couldn't move from our positions because they might see us. We had used all kinds of plants and weeds for camouflage and they tickled and itched. We were all feeling sad because they weren't coming out. Then, at four in the afternoon, we can hear everyone shouting inside the base and the first platoon comes out and heads straight down to the river.

The compañeros *positioned closest to me were four women and some other* compañeros *from the capital—these are people who suffer a lot and take a long time learning to survive in the mountains. I still didn't have much experience in this type of situation either. I saw that really we were not ready to directly combat the army when the soldiers were right in front of us. I had never before seen a Kaibil. He was four meters in front of me. He was armed and I was armed. I thought, "I am going to die here." And, I began to tremble with fear. There was another* compañero *who was supposed to fire first. And, I thought, "This Kaibil is going to be on top of me before he fires." And the Kaibil was actively looking all around himself, checking everything out. He didn't see anything. We were all around and he was looking, but saw nothing. When he was only three meters in front of me, the* compañero *began to fire and I also began to fire. The attack had begun. He was the first soldier we wasted.*

Then, the entire army force came out. While the army was positioning itself, we were gathering the weapons from all the soldiers we had killed. Then, the soldiers began to fire heavy weapons. So, we withdrew to protect ourselves. We were three, one man and two women. We were ordered to advance, fire, and take the weapons away from the fallen soldiers. At first, I didn't want to do this. There were bullets flying everywhere and I knew that if I stood up or moved forward on the ground, any hidden soldier would fire on me. Then, I thought, "Well, if I am going to die anyway," and I said to the other woman, "Let's go. Advance with me so I'm not alone." Then the man said, "Let's go. The three of us go together. If we die, we die together." So, we moved forward and we took the machine gun away from the dead soldier. But it was very difficult to get his munitions because he had his belt very tightly fastened. We kept ours tightly fastened, too. You have to keep it tight to hold all the weight. But, he even had little lassos on his belt. To make it worse, he was full of machine gun fire and it was all very hard to remove. Everything was full of bullet fragments. There were three dead soldiers there, but we were only able to remove weapons from one because another army platoon came upon us and our unit was almost wiped out. We had four injured and one dead. On top of that, a lot of our weapons weren't working.

By this time, I had fired 250 rounds of munitions from my M-16. I had 400 rounds altogether. I was afraid and I was trembling, but when I started to fire, I forgot that I could die. I forgot about everything. I just kept fighting. All I thought about was how to continue firing until I heard the order to withdraw. We continued to fire. Some of us carried the injured, while others protected us.

There were dead guerrilla combatants, too. We were able to remove them from the site. We buried them. We never left injured and dead combatants behind. The army did this. They would just leave their dead soldiers wherever they fell. The only thing the army did was remove their weapons. We had more respect for our compañeros. *We removed them from the battle site. If the dead combatant had a better uniform than one of us, then we switched uniforms. We took the best for the living because all combatants always needed uniforms. It was really a desperate situation. Can you imagine removing your dead friend's clothes before the burial? In the beginning, one really doesn't know how to adjust to this kind of life, plus it was very sad; it gave me great sadness to see the dead* compañeros, *friends I had been living with for quite some time. It was very sad.*

But, one gets stronger. You get used to seeing dead and injured all the time. It begins to feel normal. It is normal. You see a dead compañera and you say, "Well, she was lucky. She is no longer suffering. Now, she is resting." And each one of us knew that the next day it could be any one of us. We were all conscious that death could strike us at any moment.

So, these were my experiences in combat. This is how it was for me. As a woman combatant, in the beginning I really felt that I was out of place. But, I began to believe that women have every capacity that men have. Even more, I put forth a great deal of effort to be a good combatant and I succeeded in this. The only thing I really wanted was to not fall behind the men. I wanted to always be at their side, at the same level as them, to demonstrate that a woman could be just as good a combatant as a man.

In my village, men would always say, "I am the man and I can do every-thing. You can't do anything. The only thing you can do is have children." So, in the mountains, everything is different because everyone knows that every-one is capable of doing whatever a man does. I think that this is really psy-chological work for the men—that they have to look at the compañeras as their equals, that they can't discriminate against them. This is one of the things we learn—that everyone has equal value, men and women, indigenous and ladino, that no one is behind anyone else. I want my daughter to understand this, that she is on an equal plane with men.

Of course, all of this was difficult when I came to Mexico to live with my parents. My opinions are now different from theirs. I would say, "Women's freedom is the same as men's." And my mother would say, "No, my daughter. You have to let the man run the home. He is the one to give orders. He is the boss of the family." There was an entire year of these conversations. It was very hard, especially with my brother. He would say, "I am the boss of my house and my woman will do whatever I tell her. I'll make her do it." And I would tell them that he had to respect her as his partner, that he couldn't hit her. This was all very trying, but we are a very united family and we stick together. So, in the end, this is all part of our own personal liberation. I think we continue to liberate ourselves with these discussions even when they are very difficult. We learn from one another.[11]

PABLO

Pablo is Achi-Maya; he was recruited into the civil patrols and forcibly con-scripted into the army at age fourteen.

First they organized the Military Commissioners, one or two in every commu-nity. Then they organized us—the poor peasants—as patrollers. They told us that every eight days, we had to patrol. So, as more days passed, everything got even more complicated. Some of us weren't patrolling because we are very poor and needed to work because we had so much poverty. Then they accused us of being guerrillas. The army really believed these accusations against us were true. So it became even more complicated, more and more. The judiciales became even more organized, the death squads is what we call them. They started killing people. If you went to the market to buy or sell, they killed you. People carrying their load of wood on their back to sell—they killed them right on the path. The squads traveled in groups and they kept vigilance on every path. They would just grab and kill anyone. They didn't even ask questions anymore. They grabbed people as if they were no more than dogs. That's where all this began.

It was on the 15th of September when I was working in the bean field with my aunt in San Miguel Chicaj when we heard that everything was very difficult in Rabinal, that it was no longer possible to travel through Rabinal to Plan de Sánchez. So what we did is that we just stayed in San Miguel working with my aunt. She fed us and took care of us. So, it was on this day of the fiesta of September 15th that everything fell apart. The judiciales were already well-organized and prepared. At five in the afternoon, they began to kill people.[12] First, they invited everyone to attend the fiesta. They charged people for entering. The people didn't know what was going to happen to them. My brother and I didn't go in. They told us we could go in for free, that they wouldn't charge us. But I could see inside. I saw their red bandanas, white shirts and black jackets—all army-style. They insisted that we go in, but I didn't want to. Plus, my brother had been drinking beer and he was drunk. Thanks to God, the bus arrived and my brother was drunk, so I helped him get in the bus and we went home. Look, if my brother hadn't been drunk, we would have fallen into the trap in San Miguel. My uncle was there. He survived because he threw himself in a gutter and pretended he was dead. He came into the house crying, "Oh my God. Oh my God!"

After that, my mother heard about the killing in San Miguel. My mother was still alive that year. She came to get us. But we couldn't go through Rabinal. There was no longer the possibility of traveling through the center. We couldn't take a bus, we came back by foot. When we reached the entrance to Rabinal, we turned to take a path through the mountains around Rabinal. As we turned, we saw four judiciales with guns and the same style—red bandanas and black coats. We crouched down and kept moving. If we stopped to look at them, they might see us and shoot. "Dios, Dios, Dios," we passed by them praying to God that nothing would happen to us. Somehow we were saved and we got home. When my father saw us, he began to cry, he thought we were dead. We all cried.

A few days later, we were summoned by the military commissioner. We presented ourselves to the patrol commander and he put us in charge of *patrolling at night with the patrollers. Because we were obedient, we were just kids, he gave us sticks and rope to make road blocks to catch people. Then a commissioner, who had recently left the military base, said he was going to organize a company of kids and youth to go to the villages and hide in the cliffs to see who did not patrol. I was just listening. I was just a kid of fourteen and didn't think much about it.*

So that was how it was at the end of 1981. There were two men who worked for the army base. They told us their work was to "orejón" [spy]. They would hear a bad word about someone and arrive to investigate the poor people here. They said every day new squads were being organized. Our job was to watch over the house where the orejas [spies] slept at night.[13] They would be inside sleeping and we would be outside with our sticks. If we didn't obey them, they would accuse us and we would be killed. They said, "Anyone who doesn't patrol is acting like he wants to be a guerrilla." So we followed their orders.

They were killing people, but we didn't know why. Then, one day I was summoned again. They sent me to the army base. The commissioner said, "We have to take twenty-five patrollers and whoever doesn't go, well we know why." Still, I said, "But, I am underage. I am still a minor. I'm not an adult yet."[14] He ignored all that. He said, "As soon as you are called, you have to go and complete your orders. If you don't go, they will accuse you of being a guerrilla."

At that time, my whole family was still alive and they were just sitting there listening. Then my father asked, "How is that possible? My son is just a kid. He is still little. He is not an adult. What I know is that he has to be eighteen [for army service] and he isn't." But the commissioner said, "No. If he is called, he has to go." So, I went. My mother was crying. My father asked, "So, you are really going to go?" I answered, "I have to go because if I don't, they will say I am a guerrilla."

So I found myself in the army at fourteen. The first thing the base commander said to the new recruits once we were all gathered was, "Welcome to all you guerrillas. Welcome to all of you. You are all guerrillas and your parents are all guerrillas. So welcome, fucking guerrillas." The captain of the company grabbed one of the recruits by the scruff of his neck. He pulled out his bayonet and stuck it in the recruit's mouth. And this is how it was. Each day was a new punishment. They kicked us around like balls. They tied us up and mistreated us. We were just surviving. Some were crying. Others tried to flee. But there were orders to kill anyone who tried to get away. We were full of fear. We were like startled baby chicks.

I wrote to my father that everything was really screwed up in the army. He wrote that he would come to visit me at the base on July 18. But he never came. A few days later, a friend of mine came to see me. He was going to

Rabinal and asked if I wanted to send anything to my father. So, I gave him a letter. Then, that same friend returned a few days later. He asked me, "Do you know your father is dead? Your whole family is dead," he said. "No," I said, "I don't know that." "Your father is dead. Your whole family. Your mother. Your brothers. In Plan de Sánchez, no one is alive. The army did it. For God, I come to tell you."

I went to the sergeant of the company. I told him what had happened. "Who killed them?" he asked. "The army did it," I told him. "Who told you this?" he asked. "The people of Rabinal saw it. Everyone knows. Everyone in Rabinal knows it was the army. It happened on Sunday." He argued with me. "No, you are mistaken. Why would they have killed your father?" I asked him to help me investigate what had happened. "Why should I do that?" he said, "There is no killing here."

Then, a sub-lieutenant, a woman, arrived. She asked me what had happened. I told her. She helped me because women have more conscience. Still, it was fifteen days before I had any confirmation. I went to radio communications every day. Everyday, I went and pestered them until they got mad at me. But, I still went again. Finally, the brigadier called me. He told me he was an orphan, "that's why I have never hit you or mistreated you." It was true, this brigadier never beat me, never hit me, never punished me. He defended me when others wanted to punish me. It was true, the army killed my family. "Look," the brigadier said, "do you have any money? What are you going to do now?"

"What am I going to do? I want to know about my father's case," I said. "It is not just that they killed my father. What are we doing? The army says it is here to defend our families. They say that is why we are here. But the mistake is that we are here and not defending our families. No, our own compañeros are the ones who are killing our families. Here we are taking care of the army and the army is killing our parents."

I went to the colonel. I told him I was resigning from my position and was going to search for my family. "I will never again be in this army! The army killed my father, my brothers, everyone. Never! Not one more day. I am not going to stay here. I resign. Please give me a discharge," I said. "No," said the colonel, "you're not going anywhere. They will kill you if you leave." "If they kill me, they kill me," I said. I left the next morning.

When I finally got to Plan de Sánchez, it was empty. Some of the houses were burned. When I got to my house, it was still there. I found my little brother José crying inside. He was twelve. He had some birds in a cage. He was alone and there was no food. He was hungry. I had some tortillas with me. So, I killed the birds and gave him the tortillas. I told him I would be back for him.[15]

The (Para)militarization of
Youth in Colombia

The preceding Guatemalan youth testimonies chronicle forced recruitment in the early 1980s. Though separated by geography, culture, and time, their experiences resonate with testimonies of youth in Colombia and elsewhere today. In this section I offer the narrative of Yulian, a paramilitary youth in Colombia. His testimony resonates with those of the forcibly recruited Maya youth. Thus, these testimonies transcend their experiential location in Guatemala and become a site of contestation challenging forced recruitment of youth and demanding recognition of the rights of the child and international humanitarian law. Moreover, understanding their experiences provides an opportunity for international humanitarian aid programs to develop alternatives to violence for children and youth now living in internal armed conflicts.

My field research in Colombia indicates that displaced and orphaned children and youth generally have four options: (1) join the army, (2) join the paramilitaries, (3) join the guerrilla, or (4) rural to urban flight. Moreover, those children and youth who are displaced from rural villages under siege to urban *barrios* must frequently move from one urban site to another in order to escape recruitment by urban armed actors (author interview, May 31, 2003). Many people are afraid of these (displaced rural) urban youth; authorities treat them like criminals, and they are often targets of paramilitary "social cleansing." One way to escape "social cleansing" is to join the ranks of the paramilitaries. This was the case of nineteen-year-old Yulian, who lived in the paramilitary-controlled Barrio Obrero in Apartado, a *barrio* founded by displaced people in the early 1990s. He told me:

> I lived each day in fear that the paramilitaries would grab me and accuse me of a crime I hadn't committed. I had no opportunities until one day a friend of mine said, "Come on, let's go join them." As soon as we got there, they gave us camouflage uniforms, rifles, new guns and other equipment.
>
> The campesinos help the guerrilla, so sometimes we have to grab them. Grab them means kill them. They have to respect us because we wear the symbol that says, "AUC": Autodefensas Unidas de Colombia. When we kill a campesino, it is because there are really few displaced people. What there are among the displaced are a lot of guerrilla infiltrators who are very astute and intelligent.
>
> Once, some campesinos told some others that we had arrived in their community. We didn't want the guerrilla to know we were there. So, we had to kill them with machetes and chop them up piece by piece and bury them. Human rights are a problem because we can't grab thirty people and kill them all at once because that would be a massacre.

But we don't kill anyone without authorization. Because I have a family, sometimes it was painful for me when we got to a town and the civilians would be praying. But I am just a patroller and surely when a commander tells a patroller, "Kill this civilian," I really cannot ask him why. No, I simply have to do what he tells me to do. Because one goes there to kill or one is killed, right?

I am on leave right now, but if a patron here (in Apartado) comes to me and says, "Let's go do a little work, we have to grab someone," I go do it because I am part of the organization. Sometimes in a week, we have to kill five people. Maybe on one day, we kill two. If the police and the prosecutor aren't doing much, we kill more. It all depends on what we are ordered to do. We have to follow orders. This is a war without end. If you make a mistake, you pay with your life.

MEMORIES OF TRAUMA

Yulian's testimony, like each of the four testimonies from Guatemala, chronicles a childhood and adolescence of poverty, displacement, the witnessing of atrocities, and survival. Each also communicates profound feelings of powerlessness in an unpredictable world of terror mixed with nostalgia for the elusive power that came with carrying a gun. Whether ten years have transpired between the forced recruitment and the giving of testimony (as in the Guatemalan cases), or just ten days after returning from paramilitary actions (as in the Colombian case), the sensations of fear, self-doubt, betrayal, and self-hate as well as the desires for individual and community liberation and transformation remain palpable in the memories of each of these survivors. In each testimony, it was an overwhelming sense of rightlessness associated with direct or indirect displacement that led to forced recruitment. In this chapter I want to heed Arendt's caution about the slippery slope implicit in focusing on the status of the rightless and refocus the lens of analysis on the deeds of those responsible for forced recruitment. We can learn about them through the testimonies of former child soldiers and guerrilla combatants because the deeds of those responsible for forced recruitment can also be read as the constitution of available options for youth living in armed conflict.

Further, I suggest that the constitution of available options for youth living in armed conflict can be traced to the original traumas preceding forced recruitment, which are recounted in these testimonies. From his memories of familial battles over self-hate with his sister to his attempt to kill a *ladino* recruit, Gaspar's testimony reflects deep contradictions in his personal struggle with what it means to be indigenous in Guatemala, as well as the limited options available in his life when, in his own words, he "chose to be an abuser, not abused." Despite his weapon, he recalled fear of "any man, every man." The torture of his military indoctrination is mirrored by Mateo's experience of training with live munitions and the ritual consumption of dog. Though Mateo evokes the power, luxury, and danger of the army from his own childhood, as an adult he still remembers his weapon as "a jewel." Fear of superiors and hatred of their superiors, fellow recruits, and the peasants upon whom Gaspar and Mateo were ordered to carry out their actions is compounded by Mateo's grandfather's acknowledgement that "You are no longer one of us." The powerlessness of Maya adults in the face of army interrogators serves only to heighten this loss of Maya identity in the everyday life of soldiering. Recall Mateo's conclusion: "The only thing that matters is that the people will say whatever the army wants them to say." His conclusion also resonates with the experience of recruits that "had to have such a face" to escape the wrath of their commanders. When Gaspar was recruited, he lacked the security of the family structure that Mateo lost to the violence of the war. Pablo was taken from his family, and after learning of the army massacre in his village, he stands up to his commanding officer and challenges the army for destroying both his family and community. In Colombia, driven to paramilitarism by fear and poverty, Yulian sees no exit from the violence of the paramilitaries to which he has now tied his survival—however reluctantly.

Esperanza expresses pride in her physical strength and endurance as a guerrilla combatant. Though she sought out the guerrilla, she did so after witnessing army violence in her own community. She liked being a combatant. Like Mateo's memory of his machine gun as a "jewel," she recalls, "I loved having a weapon at my disposal." While Mateo, Pablo, and Gaspar's experiences are conflictive and painful memories of assaults on their indigenous identity, Esperanza's identity struggles involve her gendered position more than her ethnicity. At first, she felt out of place, but then she "began to believe that women have the same capacity that men have." While Gaspar, Mateo, and Pablo's experiences of violence in the army, and Yulian's experience in the paramilitaries, are mediated with memories of fear and hatred, Esperanza remembers nostalgically that, "Everything is different because everyone knows that everyone else is capable of doing whatever a man does [in the guerrilla]."

Today, Gaspar and Mateo live with political asylum in the United States, Esperanza is a legal refugee in Mexico, and Pablo is a leader in his reconstructed village and has a pending claim against the state for the massacre of his family. Despite these different contemporary life situations, each continues to struggle with what it means to be a former soldier, combatant, and/or civil patroller while living a disjointed existence, disarticulated from their communities of origin and struggling to survive at the margins of the state—each a product of trauma preceding their recruitment. Though each participates in Maya rights organizing, each also lives with the suspicions that their previously militarized lives continue to cast upon their present struggles. My meeting with Yulian was clandestine and anonymous, so I do not know his fate.

The experience of forced recruitment, even when remembered as consensual, is layered upon original displacement—what Arendt referred to as the "loss of social texture" (1973, 293). Forced recruitment was not the first trauma in any of these testimonies. Rather, survival of selective and massive violence, marginalization, poverty, and displacement marked each of these young people for recruitment by armed groups. In each case, this displacement or loss of social texture represents the displacement of individual and community life boundaries. This displacement of boundaries in turn defines new fields of subjectivity and memory.

Pierre Janet wrote that memory "is an action," but that when an individual is unable to liquidate an experience through the action of recounting it, the experience is retained as a "fixed idea" lacking incorporation into "chapters of our personal history." The experience, then, "cannot be said to have a 'memory' . . . it is only for convenience that we speak of it as 'traumatic memory'" (Herman 1992, 37). Further, Janet believed that the successful assimilation or liquidation of traumatic experience produces a "feeling of triumph" (41). Judith Herman suggests that those who have not liquidated their "traumatic memory" express it through "post-traumatic play," which she describes as "uncanny" in its reenactments of original trauma. She writes, "Even when they are consciously chosen, they have a feeling of involuntariness . . . they have a driven, tenacious quality"; this resonates with Freud's naming of "this recurrent intrusion of traumatic experience" as "repetition compulsion," which is no less than "an attempt to master the traumatic event" (Herman 1992, 41). Whether recruited through coercion or consent, child soldiers and combatants attempt to master previous traumas in the violent acts of everyday armed life. At the same time, the new layer of trauma produced in the everyday life of the child soldier or combatant demands consideration.

Few would dispute Herman's assertion that traumatic experiences "destroy the victim's fundamental assumptions about the safety of the world, the positive value of self, and the meaningful order of creation" (51). What is of particular interest to us in analyzing the case of forcibly recruited youth is our own underlying assumptions about trauma events and where on the continuum of life experience we choose to locate these events. Forcibly recruited youth face double trauma—the trauma of the violence that preceded and made them vulnerable to forced recruitment, as well as the trauma of witnessing and participating in violence whether as soldiers, patrollers, or combatants. While forced recruitment may be the public trauma of structural violence, each who gave testimony first shared their private traumas leading up to their recruitment.

Whether our focus is on prevention of forced recruitment or postwar reintegration, the experience of these former soldiers and combatants behooves us to pay close attention to how the fractured subject positions of Gaspar, Mateo, Esperanza, Pablo, and Yulian reflect the formation of agency and survival in structures of terror (Das 2000, 222). Here, I am suggesting that experiences of armed action are remembered within the framework of preceding structural traumas (in Arendt's words, the "deeds of those responsible") that crashed into their lives long before they ever held a gun. Weapons and their accompanying power are remembered with nostalgia because their use was a "post-traumatic play" where unresolved traumas and powerlessness were violently reenacted as a "spontaneous, unsuccessful attempt at healing" (Herman 1992, 41) pre-recruitment trauma. Thus, whether we set our sights on preventing recruitment in situations of armed conflict or reintegration in post-conflict civil society, we must problematize the pre-recruitment traumas of displacement.

Child Peacemakers

Still, there are children and youth who seek to make peace in the very same communities in which other children have been recruited. In Colombian peace communities, youth have organized to reject recruitment by all the armed actors. Alvin is a youth leader in the Costo de Oro peace community. He decided to focus his energies on youth organizing against forced recruitment because, in his words, "A weapon resolves nothing." He explains: "Weapons destroy the soul. I have seen this happen since my childhood."

When I asked him how the youth were able to organize themselves, he said:

> One of the principle sources of support for us, for the youth, is the example of the process of the peace communities. We are non-violent. We don't support what the armed actors are doing. We have developed a way of life without weapons. We have shown the Colombian government and also the world that we are capable of building peace. For this, we have become the target of the armed actors. Our future is something that we have to build for ourselves. Many times youth take up weapons because they are unaware that it is not really in their interest, nor their family or community's interest. We have to teach one another how to live together in peace. We want the children in our communities to grow up with positive feelings about the future and a commitment to the community so that

they can be leaders in the community, not obstacles to the community peace process.

When I asked Alvin and others how the international community could
support the youth, Alvin said: "I know that when people come to visit us from
outside, they leave with a weight of pain because it is inhuman what is taking
place here. But we need very simple things to develop ourselves. The most basic
and most needed is education and recreation." Others agreed:

Yes, we always aspire to have an education.

Training to improve our skills.

Musical instruments for the youth because our communities lost our
instruments when we were displaced.

Soccer uniforms so that we can exercise and have soccer tourna-
ments amongst the communities.

From 2001 to 2002 a series of violent attacks against youth leaders culmi-
nated with the assassination of Edwin Ortega, who represented the youth of
peace communities internationally and was an outspoken advocate of the right
of youth to resist forced recruitment. Rather than abandon their organizing project, peace community youth gathered on October 22, 2002, to restructure their
organization, because "It is only through our organization that we have the possibility of a future. Alone, only weapons await us." The restructuring included
two key points: First, the leadership training would no longer identify and train
youth leaders; rather, all youth would be trained and viewed as leaders. Further,
all intercommunity meetings would involve groups of youth leaders rather than
one single representative from each community. As one youth explained to me,
"If we are all leaders, we remove the individual targets from our backs" (author
interview, October 22, 2002). The second key point was to establish an international commission to begin a new dialogue with the armed actors. The youth
presented these proposals to the general assembly of the peace communities at
their meeting on October 23, 2002.

Both of these proposals were received favorably by the General Assembly of
the peace communities. During the discussion of the youth proposal, Celsa, a
mother who lost her son to paramilitary violence, said: "We have to recognize
that we must support our youth. If we look beyond the barrel of the gun, it is
our youth pointing the guns at us. We have to stand with our youth to support
them. We must unite with them to stop the armed actors from taking them"
(author's notes, Asamblea General, October 23, 2002). The peace communities

celebrated their sixth anniversary in October 2003 with a General Assembly of peace communities followed by an international anniversary celebration. A central focus of both the assembly and celebration was the right of youth to organize for peace. "We are here because we want a positive future," explained Luis. "We refuse to be targets of the armed actors. We refuse to carry their guns. We want our right to peace respected" (author interview, October 17, 2003).

It is not only in the peace communities that youth organize to provide a respite from the violence that engulfs them. Yolanda, a youth organizer in Barrancabermeja, told me, "Our work is difficult. We open a space here so that youth have a place to distract themselves from the violence that surrounds us. We have hope that this violence will end. We struggle for life" (author interview, October 12, 2000).

Conclusion

While testimonies and interviews from child soldiers indicate the connection between displacement and forced recruitment, the experiences of the CPRs and peace communities demonstrate that apparently powerless peasants can organize to survive and assert their rights in the midst of war. These collective survival strategies generate local spaces for peace and democratic participation despite the ongoing armed conflict. The survival of these seemingly utopian, community efforts deserve both the attention and support of the international community because they represent the survival of civil society in increasingly restricted political spheres. Moreover, the resilience of these CPRs and peace communities offers an opportunity for the greater civil society of both Guatemala and Colombia to learn from these experiments about the long-term strengthening of citizen participation. The value of this participation is evident in the enthusiastic participation of youth in the peace communities. In contrast to the youth who have been forcibly recruited, the youth of the peace communities have hope for their futures and see a role for themselves in shaping the life of their community. The international community should heed the call of the youth for support for education, soccer, and music. It should honor Celsa's plea that "we must support our youth."

Testimonies of child soldiers and peace activists demonstrate that youth do not merely respond to conflict, but they also interpret the meaning of conflict for themselves, their families, and their communities. These lived experiences rupture the binary stereotype of innocent victim or dangerous delinquent and challenge us to recognize these children and youth as active subjects in their own lives who develop survival strategies for themselves, their families, and their communities.

In this way, youth peacemakers reassert their rights, rebuild community structures, and transform the isolation of displacement and everyday life in the war zone. These youth peacemakers, like the peace communities, constitute new domains of social justice, citizenship, and conflict resolution. Moreover, these constitutive processes (1) connect the individual to the nation-state and international community; (2) rebuild the social fabric damaged by displacement; and (3) construct new modes of agency and citizen participation, which are necessary for peaceful resolution to the internal armed conflict as well as for postwar reconstruction. These transformations are not grounded in determinism or utopia outside of power. Rather, as Hardt and Negri suggest, the "actual activity of the multitude—its creation, production and power" is a "radical counterpower" in the present (2000, 66). This "counterpower" is evident in the everyday life and moral imagination of the peace communities and the youth peacemakers.

ACKNOWLEDGMENTS

This article is dedicated to the survivors and their children. It would not have been possible without the kindness, generosity, and trust of Gaspar, Mateo, Esperanza, Pablo, Yulian, Joselito, and other friends I am unable to name because of ongoing conflict in Guatemala and Colombia. I thank Erika Bliss and Raul Figueroa Sarti for their unconditional support and Shannon Speed, Monique Skidmore, Carolyn Nordstrom, Roberta Culbertson, and Philippe Bourgois for their comments and insights as I collected these testimonies and sought to process their meaning. I thank Siobhán McEvoy-Levy for her patience and thoughtful comments as I developed this chapter. RIREC colleagues Dan Bar-On and Michael Wessells also provided useful comments. This research was supported by grants from Stanford University, Fulbright-Hays, the Inter-American Foundation, the Life and Peace Institute, the MacArthur Consortium, Notre Dame's Institute for Scholarship in the Liberal Arts, the Shaler Adams Foundation, and a Rockefeller grant from the Virginia Foundation for the Humanities.

NOTES

1. The trauma and medical needs of child soldiers have been empirically documented (Machel 1996, 2001; McBeth 2002; Castello-Branco 1997; Pearn 2003; Somasundaram 2002; Maier 1998; Keairns 2003). Additionally, abuse and trauma of child soldiers have been explored to establish the need for rehabilitation

and/or reintegration programs specific to the needs of child soldiers (Thompson 1999; Chaudhry 2001; Rakita 1999; Alfredson 2001; De Silva 2001; Bracken 1996; Menkhaus 1999; Skinner 1999). The Rights of the Child (Ramgoolie 2001; Heppner 2002; De Berry 2001), human rights (Maslen and Islamshah 2000; Von Arnim 2000), international humanitarian law (Cohn and Goodwin-Gill 1994; Rone 1994; Human Rights Watch 1994b, 1995), the Optional Protocol on the Involvement of Children in Armed Conflict (Khabir Ahmad, "UN Resolves to Protect Children Against Wars," *Lancet*, September 11, 1999, 929; American Academy of Pediatrics 2000; Dennis 2000), and the International Labor Organization (ILO) Convention on Child Labor (Halsan 2001; Dennis 1999; Amnesty International 1999, 2000; Fernando 2001) have provided legal frameworks for the international community to condemn the use of child soldiers and establish legal protections for children (Kalshoven 1995; Abbott 2000; Campbell 1999).

2. This section draws from my books *Buried Secrets: Truth and Human Rights in Guatemala* (2003a) and *Violencia y Genocidio en Guatemala* (2003b)

3. Nebaj Testimony 3N5, March 9, 1997, 1 of 1.

4. This interview with paramilitary youth was organized clandestinely. "Yulian" is a pseudonym. The interview was granted on condition of anonymity.

5. *Kaibiles* are the elite fighting forces of the Guatemalan army. The following testimonies draw from my book, *Buried Secrets: Truth and Human Rights in Guatemala* (2003a).

6. The EGP (Ejercito Guerrillero de los Pobres, or Guerrilla Army of the Poor) was the largest of the four guerrilla groups in Guatemala and later became a part of the URNG (Union Revolucionario Nacional de Guatemala, or Guatemalan National Revolutionary Union), which was composed of all four guerrilla groups.

7. San Francisco Testimonies, Mateo, 1991–92.

8. See chapter two of *Buried Secrets* (2003a) for more of Esperanza's experiences.

9. *Chaparrita* is a colloquial expression meaning short, petite, or tiny. Esperanza's height is four feet, eight inches.

10. National Direction (Direccion Nacional) was the high command of the EGP.

11. Mexico Testimony 7, July 1993.

12. San Miguel was not the only community attacked by the army that day. On September 15, 1981, the people of Rabinal went to the plaza to celebrate Independence Day. The army had obligated everyone to participate and attend the Independence Day parade. Accompanied by *judiciales*, military commissioners, and civil patrollers, the soldiers opened fire on the crowd and killed some two hundred people. See CEH (1999, 8:144).

13. *Oreja* (ear) is a colloquialism for army spy.

14. With these statements he was attempting to protect himself from forced recruitment because by law, recruitment age was eighteen. Here again is another example of youth consciousness of their rights.

15. Rabinal Testimony no. 6–4, June 17, 1997.

MARC SOMMERS

In the Shadow of Genocide
Rwanda's Youth Challenge

In 1994 Rwanda's notorious *Interahamwe* ("Those Who Work Together") became the face of genocide: seemingly mad, rampaging, predatory, evil youth who not only killed in staggering numbers but degraded and decapitated their victims as well. How did these young people become vicious murderers who did not seem to have a conscience? Where did their rage and their desperate acts of intimidation, looting, and slaughter come from? These questions could apply to the actions of young people in a number of different contexts. Yet Rwanda remains different because of the enormity of the crime: arguably the most efficient genocide ever devised, during which somewhere between 500,000 and a million people perished in 100 days (Mamdani 2001, 5). An average of 5,000 to 10,000 people were killed per day, a rate that, during peak killing days, averaged one murder every two seconds (Peterson 2000, 252–53).[1]

In post-genocide Rwanda, the scars of the 1994 horror are becoming harder to see. Former refugees from the 1994 genocide, many of whom were involved, in some way, in carrying it out, are back in their homes, farming and trading as before. Former refugees from ethnic violence beginning in 1959 (and continuing, intermittently, into 1964) have also flocked back to Rwandan farms, pasturelands, and towns. A new government, led by President Paul Kagame and the Rwandan Patriotic Front (RPF), is solidly entrenched. The exiled *Interahamwe* (now also called "Infiltrators") menace from the Democratic Republic of the Congo (DROC, formerly Zaire), but Rwanda's military presence in eastern DROC (and in Congo's war) has limited their threat. Although war, violence, and refugees are an integral part of central Africa's current landscape, the blight of regional instability has not prevented Rwandans from carrying out their day-to-day routines. Life continues.

Most of the problems that plagued Rwandans before the genocide continue as well, including a profound sense of despair and frustration among many youth. For them, limitations seem to be everywhere: from inadequate access to education (despite government efforts to greatly expand access to primary schools and high schools) and land to the limited availability of employment and capital. As before, the spotlight has tended to shine elsewhere. The literature on Rwanda's 1994 genocide largely focused its attention on the political extremists who both organized the near-extermination of ethnic Tutsi (as well as leading moderate Hutu deemed political opponents) and manipulated Rwandans, young men in particular, into carrying out the massacres. Much less has been written about the genocide's youthful foot soldiers or the potential for renewed youth violence in Rwanda. Drawing on field research in rural Rwanda carried out between 2000 and 2002, this chapter will explore the current lives of Rwanda's rural youth and consider the potential for youth violence to again surface in the future.

RESEARCH METHODS

Field research data for this chapter was drawn from a series of seven evaluative research visits to Rwanda over a three-year period (2000–02) for the Conflict Management Group's Central Africa Project.[2] The pilot project centered on providing carefully designed training sessions aimed at "extending the skills of conflict resolution, negotiation, and joint problem solving to traditionally marginalized populations" (Sommers and McClintock 2003, 47). The central target populations were marginalized women and youth in one village (known in Rwanda as a "Sector") in Byumba Province (formerly known as a "Prefecture"), located in northeastern Rwanda.

While quantitative data was gathered, the field evaluation research centered on qualitative interviews with marginalized Rwandan youth and women—both those who participated in the series of training sessions that formed the core of the Central Africa Project and those who did not. Interviews were also conducted with local, district, provincial, and even national leaders involved in activities for marginalized women and youth. Questions addressed a range of issues, including the personal histories of informants; the history of the area (particularly the period since the civil war that began in 1990); current challenges facing informants; whether and how they had adapted skills learned in the Conflict Management Group training sessions to address specific problems; and issues and perspectives that were of particular concern both to local Rwandan leaders and the poor, marginalized majority in the village.

Background: Rural Rwanda in Context

On a continent whose population is increasingly turning toward cities, Rwanda (together with neighboring Burundi) remains an anomaly in Africa. Although it is one of world's most densely populated countries, it has very few towns with populations of any consequence. In fact, the level of urbanization in central Africa is the lowest in the world: only 6.1 percent of Rwanda's inhabitants live in urban areas (Bhutan, at 6.9 percent, is second, while Burundi is third, at 8.7 percent), as opposed to the average of 33.5 percent for sub-Saharan Africa overall (UNDP 2001, 157). While the proportion of Africans living in cities is expected to climb to more than 50 percent by 2020 (United Nations Department of Economic and Social Information, cited in Rakodi 1997, 1), UNDP predicts that Rwanda's standing as the least urbanized country in the world will continue; by 2015, only 8.9 percent of Rwandans will live in urban areas (UNDP 2001, 157). Despite evidence of rapid growth of Rwanda's capital city, Kigali (Waller 1996, 37), one needs only to look at east Africa to recognize the exceptionally high rural orientation of Burundi and Rwanda. Compared to the east African region, which has the fastest growing urban growth rate in the world (Torrey 1998, B6), central Africa is truly "a world clinging to hillsides" (Ould-Abdallah 2000, 21).

From the view of many observers, central Africa's strong rural accent should be considered an asset. The most notable example of this contention is found in the work of Robert D. Kaplan, who has described young urban men as "hordes," as "loose molecules in a very unstable social fluid, a fluid that was clearly on the verge of igniting" (1994, 46), and as prime examples of what he perceived as "nature unchecked" (1994, 54). But in central Africa the inability to congregate in cities plays into the rural isolation and fear that has fueled genocidal killing in Rwanda and Burundi. Consider the following comment on Burundi, which contains a constellation of ethnic identities, terror, and violence similar to Rwanda:

> [The] absence of big cities has had a significant effect on divisions within the country. Without the opportunity to mingle together in large numbers in cosmopolitan settings, most Burundians remain largely within their ethnic group, their clan, and their region. By contrast, many of those Burundians who live in the capital are conscious of their ethnicity only in times of conflict. . . . I saw many cases in April 1995 of young people of the capital unable to identify with an ethnic group and often attacked by both groups before they migrated abroad or chose, against their will, to be Hutu or Tutsi. Extremists on both sides despise them because they constitute living proof of the possibility of peaceful coexistence. (Ould-Abdallah 2000, 21)

The striking contrast between urban growth in east and central Africa can be illuminated by a brief comparison between the capital of Rwanda and the dominant city of its east African neighbor, Dar es Salaam in Tanzania. Dar es Salaam was a small, sleepy town when it was the capital of colonial Tanganyika. Ten years after independence in 1961, it was well on its way to becoming one of the fastest-growing cities in the world. Ankerl (1986), for example, surmised that Dar es Salaam would grow by 1,239 percent between 1970 and 2000. All of the government's subsequent efforts to "repatriate" young urban migrants, who were driving the city's astonishing expansion, back to their rural homes were fiascos. Tanzanian youth continued to flock to the capital, and the government repeatedly failed to halt their drive to the destination they call *Bongoland* (meaning "Brainland").[3]

In Rwanda the government succeeded. Rwanda became a rural-based exception by intention. Near the end of the colonial era, in 1953–54, Rwanda's urbanization rate was less than 1 percent, and the capital, Kigali, had no more than 3,000 inhabitants (Uvin 1998, 116). Belgian colonial policy restricted movement by Rwandans, and the subsequent post-independence administrations, if anything, restricted movement even more. As Uvin noted, "Internal migration was made all but impossible through deliberate government policy," a state of affairs he termed "forced immobility" (1998, 115–16). Rwanda in the mid-1990s was both the least urbanized and the poorest country in the world, with 86 percent of the population living below the poverty line and the impoverished masses stuck in the countryside. "Peasant life was perceived as a prison without escape," Uvin observed, "in which poverty, infantilization, social inferiority and powerlessness combined to create a sense of personal failure" (1998, 117).

Extreme ethnic violence has almost always overshadowed and often enveloped the day-to-day struggles of ordinary Rwandans. Indeed, the roots of ethnic difference, terror, and manipulation that have fueled a succession of brutal conflicts since the dawn of the post-independence period in Rwanda and Burundi, and that eventually led both to extensive genocide in Rwanda in 1994 and a vicious civil war in Burundi since 1993 (until the present), have been examined elsewhere at length. They will not be detailed here, except to note that the combination of civil war, genocide, flight, displacement, and an edgy return to stability has left many Rwandans with profound losses and an enduring undercurrent of ethnic suspicion and fear, trauma, and lacerating memories of the past that continue to haunt Rwandan communities. The recent past has made living with grinding poverty unusually challenging.

The post-genocide period has allowed Rwanda's landscape of difference to more easily extend beyond the Hutu-Tutsi divide. While the ethnic division between the majority Hutu and the minority Tutsi still dominates Rwandan and Burundian lives, there is also a third ethnic group, the Twa, that is by far the smallest group in both countries. Additionally, there are distinctions by class. Upper-class elites are known as "High People," while rural masses are commonly referred to as "Very Low People" and "Ignorant People." Regional identities remain influential as well. The *Urukiga* stereotype identifies northern Rwandans as crude and unsophisticated. Southern Rwandans, in turn, are still called *Abanduga* and are considered, according to the stereotype, as refined and cultured. These two identities hail back to the early colonial days, when Christian churches and Western-style schools arrived in southern Rwanda first, while Rwandans living in the north remained largely out of the emerging colonial loop of entitlement and status.[4]

Although Prunier described the two dominant ethnic groups in Rwanda (and Burundi) as a "time-bomb" (1995, 39) waiting to explode in the years before the 1994 genocide, other manifestations of the deadly cocktail of terror, social control, infantilization, poverty, impunity, illiteracy, and manipulation that grew in Rwanda were also evident. The most virulent, probably, was the plight of Rwanda's entrapped youth. "Imagine the frustration of tens of thousands of semi-educated youth spawned by the education system each year," Uvin posits, "when they were forbidden to leave the countryside, forced to stay on their meager plots, without hope for the future" (1998, 116). Many of the "zealous killers" involved in genocidal acts in 1994 were "young men who had hung out on the streets of Kigali or smaller commercial centers, with little prospect of obtaining either land or the jobs needed to marry and raise families" (Des Forges 1999, 261). Also included among the eventual *genocidaires* were thousands of youth who were part of the masses of Hutu farmers from northern Rwanda who had been forcibly displaced during the civil war that preceded the genocide (African Rights 1995, 57).

The situation confronting youth in postwar Rwanda is colored by continuing difficulties and limitations. The Rwanda AIDS Control Programme estimates that "at least 13 percent of Rwanda's 8.2 million people are infected with HIV/AIDS" (IRIN 2003, 1). Many of those infected are children and youth. The political atmosphere remains tense and sometimes intimidating. Ofcansky lists a number of particular concerns, including "increasingly harsh and dictatorial policies" of the Rwandan government; "one of the worst human rights' records in Africa" by 2001; "numerous government attempts to suppress press activity"; a sequence of accusations from Human Rights Watch, Amnesty International, and other human rights groups concerning the detention of more than 125,000 Rwandans (including as many as 4,000 between the ages of fourteen and eighteen [Human Rights Watch 2003, 2]) suspected of participation in genocidal crimes; and the Rwandan government's conduct in the civil war in the Democratic Republic of the Congo (2003, 826–28). Rwanda's first-ever multiparty elections in August and September 2003 were plagued by accusations that the Rwandan government "allegedly resorted to flagrant intimidation, harassment and even vote-rigging on the day of voting itself" (Economist Intelligence Unit 2003, 12). Intimidation of emerging political opposition parties was also reported, in addition to the outwardly passive response to such tensions by "ordinary Rwandans, who tend to be self-censoring about their actual views and are increasingly unprepared to associate with opposition parties for fear of the consequences" (Economist Intelligence Unit 2003, 13).

The atmosphere of uncertainty is greatly exacerbated by the presence of perhaps 400,000 children (a tenth of all children in Rwanda) living with one or no parents (Human Rights Watch 2003, 2), in addition to the presence of thousands of street children in Rwanda's towns and cities. Their existence is particularly problematic; Human Rights Watch reports that "many have been exploited for their labor or their property and denied the right to education at home," and they "face a near constant risk of harassment by law enforcement officials and arbitrary arrest." There have been sweeps by municipal authorities to "clean the streets" of children. "Girls living on the streets are frequently raped," Human Rights Watch added (2003, 2, 3).

At the same time, a swirl of reforms in Rwanda has inspired a sense of hope for the future. While strong social controls persist and the ruling Rwandan Patriotic Front party unfailingly dominates political life, decentralization and a still-emerging civil society suggest that at least a partial opening of Rwandan society may be at hand. "Everyone we spoke to identified decentralisation as an opportunity," Unsworth and Uvin report (2002, 10). The introduction of *Ubudehe* promises to provide each cellule—the smallest political segment of Rwandan society—with about US$1,000 per year to invest in development projects (National

Poverty Reduction Programme and Ministry of Local Government and Social Affairs, Republic of Rwanda n.d.). The remarkable experiment to address those accused of "low to moderate" crimes during the genocide, known as *Gacaca,* involves tens of thousands of newly appointed and trained judges hearing cases in communities across the country.[5] There is also a movement underway to involve more youth (and women) in local governance. In 1998 youth representatives were elected to community-level positions. In 2001 youth representatives joined the National Assembly, and in 2002 municipal elections charged one vice-mayor per district with youth affairs (another was charged with women's affairs) (UNDP and International Council on National Youth Policy 2003, 2).

Despite such encouraging reforms, the situation of Rwandan youth remains undeniably dire. Most are poorly educated, unemployed, and devoid of promising opportunities. While nearly 1.3 million Rwandan children attend primary school, less than a tenth of that figure—77,435—attend secondary school. Perhaps 7 percent of secondary students will receive tertiary education (Murison 2003, 844). Nearly half of all Rwandan females and a third of Rwandan males over fifteen are illiterate (Youth at the United Nations 2002, 1). Despite the presence of hundreds of thousands of out-of-school youth, an international agency official working in Rwanda reported that less than 2 percent of the national budget is reserved for nonformal education and out-of-school children and youth. One survey of Rwandan youth revealed that "every second adolescent had no money at all at his personal disposal" and only 30 percent had a regular paid income (UNDP and International Council on National Youth Policy 2003, 1).

OBSERVATIONS ON RURAL YOUTH LIVES

BYUMBA

Kuperman notes statistics suggesting that only 1.39 percent of the 779,665 people living in Byumba in 1991 were Tutsi. His data suggests that not one Tutsi was killed in Byumba during the 1994 genocide (Kuperman 2001, 121–22). This was not the picture of Byumba that was recorded over the course of seven visits to the province in 2000–02. Some sectors in southern Byumba, for example, had their Tutsi populations virtually wiped out. The sector where the field research took place (here called "A Sector")[6] experienced a comparatively low level of population loss during the genocide. Some claimed that their sector was special because Hutu residents had refused to kill Tutsi neighbors in 1994. "It's a real lie that people wanted to kill each other here," one A Sector leader insisted. Religious leaders explained this by claiming that "God sleeps here" at night. The people in A Sector are exceptionally religious and peaceful, they asserted. That their sector did not receive commendation for its restraint, as the Bourgmestre and people of Giti Commune (also in Byumba Province) had, one religious leader claimed, was merely a matter of "propaganda from people in Giti." Leaders from other parts of Byumba, on the other hand, stated that the genocide did not take place in A Sector because it was part of the neutral zone that divided civil war adversaries, which will be described below.

A Sector's relative peace did not prevent displacement. During the genocide some residents fled to Kigali to the south, toward Uganda to the north, or to the refugee camps near Goma, Congo (formerly Zaire). Others fled to nearby areas in Byumba, returning to A Sector when it seemed safe. One female youth described her experience as follows: "War came and we left to another commune. When we returned, the door of our house was broken and the house was looted." Those who fled to places in the general vicinity tended to return to A Sector much sooner than those who fled to more distant destinations. Many fled more than once. "We went to [the northeastern end of A Sector]," one woman recalled. "Then we came back home and farmed. But then the war returned and we went to [a commune to the northwest]." One local leader explained that the level of wealth of fleeing families determined whether and how far they fled. "Those who were rich left the area. But the poor remained behind."

The Conflict Management Group (CMG) carried out a pilot project aimed at providing conflict negotiation training to marginalized youth and women. A Sector eventually became the site for the pilot work. I worked as a consultant for the project, providing technical advice, carrying out a baseline study before the two sets of training sessions took place, and then carrying out a series of short field evaluation visits to A Sector after each of the trainings occurred. The approach is unusual if not groundbreaking in the context of post-genocide Rwanda, as it has made marginalized Rwandan youth and women, rather than civil society or government leaders, its central target groups for conflict negotiation trainings.

A Sector has an unusual history. It is an important site of what the Catholic "White Father"[7] living there calls "radical terracing," a labor- and capital-intensive method of minimizing erosion while trying to maximize crop yields for the tiny family farm plots running along the area's high, steep hills. A Sector thus has a reputation for being either innovative (in the view of its residents) or fortunate to have a White Father living among them (in the view of some living in neighboring sectors).

More than most other areas of Rwanda during the 1990–94 civil war, A Sector was a pressure cooker to live in. The civil war largely took place, albeit in fairly sporadic form, in northern Rwanda. Byumba Province was the site of the initial RPF invasion into Rwanda from Uganda, and it eventually became the RPF's base of military operations. Thus, the people of Byumba experienced war and displacement for a longer period than any other part of Rwanda. Local leaders in A Sector estimated that as many as 150,000 displaced Rwandans from northern Byumba swelled the hillsides during the civil war period. A Sector "was a refugee camp for the entire war," one woman from A Sector recalled. "All these hills in [A Sector] were full of [displaced] people." They also stated that minimal humanitarian support was forthcoming from national or international agencies to support the displaced.

In addition, A Sector also rested within the neutral zone set up in 1992 to separate the fighting forces during the civil war that immediately preceded the genocide. Stationed at the southern end of A Sector were the government forces of the former Rwandan government. At the northern end were patrols for the Rwandan Patriotic Front, the force that eventually routed the government forces while the genocide was also taking place in April–June 1994. In between the two hostile forces were patrolling United Nations peacekeeper units and residents of A Sector. A local leader described this period as extremely tense and dangerous. "Because we were in the neutral zone," the leader explained, "Men were often seen as spies or enemies" of one side or the other. "Some were also obliged to assist one of the military groups, fetching guns for one side or the other." Once the genocide began in 1994, men were vulnerable to accusations of complicity with either the government or RPF forces. But such situations attracted little outside attention or support. Surrounded by military forces, hosting displaced populations and survivors of attacks from war and genocide, A Sector became an overlooked crossroads for violence and displacement.

Most of those interviewed in A Sector did not necessarily call the violence that forced their displacement and sent others searching for safety in A Sector a genocide. Many recalled horrific stories that villagers arriving from nearby sectors told them, of invading *Interahamwe* militiamen and government soldiers, and some Hutu villagers, turning on Tutsi neighbors. The homes that A Sector residents saw burning on nearby hills and valleys, the survivors had told them, were those of Tutsi families. "We saw people arrive with amputated arms and gashes on their faces," one man from A Sector recalled. At the same time, the experience of violence and displacement in A Sector was longstanding. As a result, what was deemed a genocide in 1994 may have appeared to be the latest episode of the civil war that had begun with the RPF invasion of Byumba in 1990. This perception was supported by the specific experience of A Sector residents and those in the general vicinity, which was a tense standoff site between the Rwandan government forces on the southern edge of A Sector and the RPF to the northeast, up the road in the town of Byumba, during the 1992–94 period.

A number of people interviewed in Rwanda referred to Byumba Province as "the silent place." It is an area whose history of war and genocide is still not well known, particularly since government and international attentions following the 1994 genocide have focused on the genocide, not the civil war that preceded it. Byumba, therefore, was overlooked when foreign funds arrived to reconstruct Rwanda following the genocide. Aid agencies flocked to most other areas of Rwanda. Few came to Byumba. The fact that international attentions were focused elsewhere in Rwanda was a sensitive issue in Byumba. A Rwandan government official in Byumba argued that "Byumba needs more trauma counseling because it has suffered since 1991. We had all three areas during the civil war: an RPF zone, a demobilized zone, and a Rwandan government zone. You can't find this anywhere else in Rwanda." An A Sector youth added the following: "I don't understand what's happening in this world. The people who killed each other get assistance while we who lived peacefully do not. We are not begging for money. But we want assistance to develop our area."

The feeling that Byumba was a darkened corner of Rwanda was not, in fact, a particularly new development. Regional inequalities have a long history in Rwanda. Uvin notes that, for example, from 1982 to 1984, 90 percent of all public investment (most of it financed by development aid) went to only four provinces in Rwanda: Kigali, Ruhengeri, Gisenyi, and Cyangugu (1998, 124). Byumba remained known as the land of backward *Bakiga* peasants, and Byumba residents were well aware of how others viewed them.

YOUTH FRUSTRATIONS

The youth of A Sector face a multitude of problems ("youth" being locally defined as those between the ages of sixteen and thirty-five). The land shortage, which a former préfet of Byumba Province called "our time bomb," hits youth particularly hard. The population in Rwanda continues to surge while the amount of land remains the same. Land conflicts are commonplace in A Sector. New ones sprout almost daily, while others remain unresolved. One leader in Byumba noted how a typical family "must depend on half a hectare of land to survive." He stated that the government is planning to rely heavily on community groups (such as youth) forming cooperatives to maximize land use. But the problem, the leader reflected, is that while "we feel cooperatives are a solution to land shortages, we haven't organized them to address this solution." The situation is made even more difficult, the leader continued, by the strong tradition of polygamy (or *Urukiga*) in Byumba. Rwandan sons are supposed to inherit land from their fathers, but having more wives tends to dramatically expand the number of children belonging to the same extended family, even while the size of the land remains finite. The amount of land that is available for inheritance, then, is declining.

Such ever-increasing pressures on minimal amounts of land have yet to inspire viable solutions in Byumba. A leader from Byumba recalled a meeting of government officials from the province. When they were asked how they planned to address land scarcity in their respective districts, the collective response was, "There's no way out." Feeling trapped proved to be a common theme for those interviewed in Byumba. Another leader described the perspective of youth in the following way: "Poverty and land shortages make the youth feel hopeless. They have no vision of the future and no hope for the future."

Land shortages and social constraints form a powerful combination that confronts youth in A Sector with a diversity of difficulties. One youth put it bluntly: "Land always causes problems." A female youth, a widowed mother who had fled to the refugee camps in the former Zaire during the genocide, remarked that "Nothing goes on well here because of soil erosion. We are just patient." Increasing crop yields with radical terracing is not an option because "Only men have radical terracing. They're the only ones who can [physically] do it." She has also been unable to join a cooperative because participation is restricted: "Since I returned from Zaire, no new cooperatives have been created." The young widowed mother remarked that "I can't quarrel over land because I have none." Instead, "I live with my parents, and I work on their small land or the land they rent from neighbors." The connection between land and conflict in A Sector is frequently acute.

As in other parts of Byumba (and nearly all of rural Rwanda), land is so scarce that conflicts over it are a near-constant occurrence. The entrance of two sisters-in-law who were arguing passionately over the share of sweet potatoes that each felt they deserved, for example, disturbed a interview session with leaders in A Sector. Although the sisters-in-law had raised the sweet potato crop together, the plot where it grew belonged to one of the sisters-in-law. While the amount of potatoes involved in the dispute may have seemed small, it illuminated the level of desperation that so many Rwandans endure. Another conflict involved a teenaged male household head, who explained that neither he nor his sister were able to go to school. Instead, they worked the land he had inherited from his father. "I have a good amount of land," the youth explained. "It's not very fertile, but we find something to eat" from the crops. In his immediate neighborhood, land conflicts were common. "Bad persons exist in life," he explained, adding that conflicts arise when neighbors "change the fence." Small pieces of land are frequently claimed by secretly shifting the fences that divide one person's plot from another. What is known as "land grabbing," the youth continued, "happens to all of us" living in the neighborhood. Conflicts, feuds, and resentments between impoverished neighbors are common and frequently persist for years, sometimes generations. At the time of my last interview in his neighborhood, the youth explained that he was unable to bring his case involving an alleged land grab by one of his neighbors to a local government official because the official required a fee to consider the issue. He did not have the money. "My uncle is handicapped and doesn't have the money either," he added. The case cannot be addressed until he can save enough money from making and selling roof tiles.

Land scarcity frequently entraps youth because it serves to curtail marriage. Indeed, the prominent frustration that young men face is largely due to the fact that they cannot get married until they have built their own house and have farmland upon which to work and support a family. They worry about their ability to construct a viable economic life in the face of serious land shortages. They are also aware of the fact that their limited education has left them with few or no alternatives to farming and, whenever they can find it, low-wage, unskilled, temporary employment. Young men in A Sector are thus an agitated group. It is common to find young men drinking in one of the numerous bars in A Sector or in their homes. One male youth explained that "Most [male] youth are waiting for their parents to give them land." Another summed up his frustrations in the following way: "Struggling for life and being patient is very, very difficult."

The number of youth who have migrated to Kigali is exceedingly small. Interviews with young men revealed their fear of Kigali and inspired the thought that migrating to the capital was impossible. The mere prospect struck some of those interviewed as absurd. Migration just was not done. In A Sector, a male youth leader explained, "youth don't have the heart to go to Kigali because they don't know Kigali." Even though movement appears to be less restricted in Rwanda now than prior to the genocide, it proved difficult to gauge the degree to which restrictions had been reduced. A Sector residents, like all Rwandans, still carried around a series of cards listing their residence and identity (though ethnicity is no longer listed). Yet it appeared that even if migration were allowed, the fear of moving to a new place without assistance or a base of support made urban migration unlikely. Migration lacked precedence, and potential migrants lacked networks. As one youth from A Sector explained, any relatives that may already reside in the capital "are educated, so they have a job." And since "they are educated and I am not," the youth asked, "how can I help them? Youth can't go to Kigali because they don't know anything and they can't go just to wait around" for a job.

Some young women in A Sector, often lacking prospects for marriage, got entangled in relationships with older men, becoming "co-wives" but never being formally recognized as a legal spouse. Their "husbands" may award them land and provide a site for a house (he may or may not help her build it), but others, particularly the husband's first wife, will inevitably dispute whatever they receive. Co-wives may be castigated as "prostitutes" who prey on reputable men and wither the family's resources. A husband may be pressured to "divorce" himself from his dalliance with a young "co-wife" for either social or economic reasons. Or he may simply no longer be interested in her and begin to look elsewhere. One woman described her plight in the following way: "I am very poor, but I can't find anyone to support me. I had a husband, but he chased me away, telling me to return to my parents. He didn't want me." It was common to hear about young women who have been forced out of their homes by men who wanted to give the land parcel and house to another, usually a new co-wife. A woman who has been turned out in this way returns to her father's home disgraced. She may have difficulty finding another husband. She usually returns with children in tow. The additional mouths to feed add further stress to impoverished households.

Young women are also severely underrepresented in both youth and women's organizations. A meeting with a local youth group, for example, had a ratio of eight male youth to every female youth. Women's organizations may not fare much better. Younger women already represent a threat to married older women, given the possibility that they could become co-wives of their husbands. Young women also lack the seniority necessary to become well represented in women's groups. They constitute, by far, the most underrepresented adult population segment in A Sector, a tendency that is common in other parts of Rwanda (and beyond) as well.

As in other parts of Rwanda, nothing significant seems to take place in A Sector without the government's involvement. The development of *Imidugudu*—government-planned housing complexes that are being built on the tops of hills across Rwanda—constitute the government's vision of the community's future. The two *Imidugudu* in A Sector were financed by the United Nations High Commissioner for Refugees (UNHCR) and the European Community Humanitarian Office (ECHO). Local government officials insisted that no one would be forced to live in the new housing complexes. However, no new housing could be built in the area. Since young men are required by custom to build their own houses before marrying, the restriction essentially meant that, over time, all young men in A Sector would be living in the *Imidugudu*. This would enhance the government's ability to monitor male youth: once in the *Imidugudu,* the authorities would know where young men were living and be able to more effectively track their movements and activities should security concerns make it necessary.

At the same time, the *Imidugudu* is perceived as having a number of social benefits. In principle, those living there will reside near roads, making it easier to go to hospitals and have access to services such as running water and electricity. Yet improved services remain a distant hope for most Rwandans since they do not exist in most *Imidugudu*. The purpose of situating youth there, however, was clear to most youth in A Sector. One male youth summed up the government's intentions in the following way: "Youth are supposed to be near the favorable factors of development."

An emerging development in Rwanda is the move to increase women's and youth's participation in politics. There are new youth representatives at many levels of local government, and increasing numbers of youth are being included in local government councils, meetings, and other gatherings. Almost all of the youth involved in these new activities are male. The government is also trying to expand youth participation in cooperative economic work, but thus far in A Sector and the surrounding area government efforts have yet to get off the ground. There is little available capital for recruiting and organizing youth. Many local youth who have attempted to organize themselves have fallen into disputes with other members. A local official charged with youth development highlighted the challenges of organizing youth into cooperatives. "One government strategy is to create a youth fund. But funding is not strong," the leader explained. The leader contended that while youth required access to capital, very little government money existed to support youth development. There was not even money for sports equipment, the leader explained. Lacking skills, direction, and funding, most youth cooperatives in A Sector appeared to exist in name only.

A prominent exception to this tendency was found in youth cooperatives affiliated with Protestant churches. Field interviews with youth cooperative members associated with one Pentecostal church suggested that they had gained some stability, although the level of involvement and control of Pentecostal church leaders over youth activities appeared to be high. Despite their apparent success, the degree of profit from youth cooperative work that actually returned to youth themselves appeared to be small.

CONCLUSION: "NO WAY OUT"?

Before Rwanda's period of civil war and genocide (1990–94), Uvin detailed the situation of rural farmers. Citing a number of surveys of the views of Rwandan farmers in the 1980s, he noted that they "equated their own occupation [farming] and lifestyle with failure and humiliation" (1998, 118). The majority of farmers in one survey concluded that "only those who could not escape would remain on the farm" (Uvin 1998, 118). Policies that served to forbid migration and make self-employment costly "pleased many experts who appreciated the lack of shantytowns in Rwanda." But for the rural majority, the policies "signified one more damper on hope for escape. . . . Young men were hit especially hard: they had far less land than their fathers and were incapable of supporting families or even marrying . . . They were blocked in their educational advancement, were limited in their employment and migration options, and lacked the resources to make a decent life in agriculture" (Uvin 1998, 118). Uvin notes that this state of affairs was already in place before Rwanda's economic crisis leading up to the genocide accelerated the problems of Rwandan farmers.

Does the dire state of limited opportunities, government restrictions and control, and impoverishment without much hope of improvement still exist for Rwandan youth after the genocide? Can the future for Rwanda's youth be characterized by the reported view of officials in Byumba that "There's no way out"? Is the land shortage issue truly the "time bomb" that Byumba's former préfet considers it? Changes are in the air in Rwanda in a lot of ways, and some were prominent in A Sector, particularly the *Imidugudu* and the expansion of political participation to include more women and youth. Kigali has grown to a size that is, for Rwanda, unprecedented. Urban migration is rising, albeit slowly, but it must be said that a sizable degree of Kigali's growth is due to the presence of refugees from the 1959–64 violence settling there. Most of these urban migrants have recently returned to Rwanda; for many it is their first time on Rwandan soil, having grown up in exile.

Without question, peace building and development that directly involve the marginalized youth majority in Rwanda remains a daunting and seriously underemphasized challenge. In general, the shift from youth feeling entrapped to feeling empowered has yet to take place—indeed, it could be argued that youth have never had much of an opportunity to explore political, social, and economic options in modern Rwanda. While much more needs to be learned and appreciated about the specific difficulties confronting marginalized male and female youth, particular attention still needs to be paid to the unusually limited political, social, and economic options available to poor female youth.

Some of these concerns are addressed in the Rwandan government's National Youth Policy. It suggests a variety of ways in which youth can be better incorporated into development planning. Among the options suggested is to hire jobless youth to work in planned "labor intensive activities" such as constructing local infrastructure and schools (UNDP and International Council on National Youth Policy 2003, 2). Yet the policy statement suggests just how difficult even this effort will be: "If jobless youth would be included in such works a high amount of vocational training would be needed. Trainers of existing vocational training centers would have to be motivated to undertake on-the-job training in this field, together with the teaching of entrepreneurial skills" (2). In addition, the tone of this statement is merely suggestive: vocational education trainers require "motivation" to train youth. Another option raised in the policy statement—"allowing productive youth associations to benefit from the money spent for micro-projects" (2)—may be hampered if youth associations are largely weak or nonexistent, as they were in A Sector.

While these and other ideas suggested by the government constitute promising steps forward, they will most likely prove insufficient because the underlying problem facing Rwanda's youth is both structural and extensive. Dependence on land and rural living simply cannot meet the pressing needs of many if not most Rwandan youth. Youth need access to capital and holistic nonformal education that addresses conflict negotiation, health (HIV/AIDS education in particular), and social concerns, in addition to economic skills–based training. Alternatives to farming need to be energetically explored and promoted. Youth should also be encouraged to be mobile, to explore viable economic options in towns and cities.

Rwanda's land shortage "time bomb" is still ticking. Population pressure remains alarmingly high. Viable alternatives to farming continue to be slow to arrive. Educational achievement levels are low. While all of these pressures confront Rwanda's youth, perhaps the most worrying sign of potential trouble lies in signs of their frustration about the present and fear about the future. Plans to include more youth in the political process and economic programs are truly promising developments. Nonetheless, when life for so many continues to be grim and looks to be grimmer down the road, an explosion of widespread self-destructive acts carried out by Rwanda's youth, surfacing in violent as well as nonviolent ways, remains a real possibility. To prevent this from occurring, a swift and truly dramatic increase in investments for youth development, in urban as well as rural areas, and broad recognition of the severity and expanse of youth entrapment are required.

ACKNOWLEDGMENTS

An earlier version of this paper was presented at Youth Policy and the Policies of Youth in Africa Conference at the Program of African Studies, Northwestern University, Evanston, Illinois, on May 10–11, 2002.

NOTES

1. More recently, a Rwanda expert noted that "The generally accepted figure for the number of people killed during the 1994 genocide is 1 million, or

perhaps a few thousand more than that. Even the most conservative estimates don't go below 800,000 anymore" (interview by the author).

2. Conflict Management Group (CMG) is a 501(c)(3) nonprofit organization based in Cambridge, Massachusetts. Founded in 1984 by Harvard Law School professor Roger Fisher, CMG offers a range of negotiation and leadership skills training and consulting services. The author gratefully acknowledges the support of the Conflict Management Group over the course of his contribution to the Central Africa Project. The project is described in detail in Sommers and McClintock (2003).

3. Youth life in Dar es Salaam has been detailed in Sommers 2001a and 2001b.

4. These and other Rwandan identities, including the popular nicknames for different groups of Rwandan refugee returnees (such as Waragi, Dubai, and Guarde Présidentielle) and genocide survivors (Sopekiya) following the 1994 genocide, are reviewed in Sommers and McClintock 2003.

5. See Gasibirege and Babalola (2001) and Sommers and McClintock (2003) for more information.

6. Out of respect for the privacy of its residents, the actual name of the sector will not be used here.

7. While "White Fathers" (Pères Blancs) remains "the most used name of the Catholic Church missionary group, their formal title is the Roman Catholic Order of the Missionaries of Africa" (Eggers 1997, 142). The White Fathers have been present in Rwanda since the dawn of the twentieth century (Hoben 1989, 10).

CAROLYN NORDSTROM

The Jagged Edge of Peace

The Creation of Culture and War Orphans in Angola

I wish I could write something about the way the full moon rises, yellow, over the high buildings; how it glides up silently from behind the forlorn office blocks, but I can't.

Instead I feel the hot breath of war puff into my face and make my eyes sting with the ash of burning villages; ash from the burning of thatched roofs; ash from the torched corn stores. War has crept in on its belly through the long grasses of the dry season and crossed the dry riverbeds to come close, close to me here in the city where bush war should not reach. War wants me to see that it is more powerful than anything good, that it cannot be held at bay by non-war. Non-war is just a butterfly or soft petals. Strong wind or beating sun shrivels it.

But war, war howls with the taka-taka-taka of machine-gun fire tearing up the edges where sunset meets night; tearing up the curtain behind which life is supposed to be safe. It is the numberless refugees marching down like a column of ants to reach Skyline and safety. It is Bernard's untold nightmare. It is the terrible stories unfolding next to a steaming enamel teapot and baked maize bread in Princess's flat. (Pinnock 2000, 34)

Societies are fragile processes. They are not the product of an innate imperative, nor an inescapable human teleology. They are creative processes. And, like the humans that compose them, they can thrive or wither. But these processes are not easily visible to the research eye: communities are little given to explain themselves, and researchers have few tools to plumb the depths of what creates, and devastates, humanity in the plural. There has been a habit in academic history of looking to the sites of mass culture (media, education, religion) and elite culture (the architects of justice, political systems, and the arts) to explore the dynamics that sustain societies. These studies tend to take place in stable societies, where social cohesion already exists— where societies are maintained and nuanced, not created anew. This is a sufficiently dangerous practice in peaceful times: how can we understand the creation of society, indeed ourselves, when we begin with the already created? But in times of upheaval, war, and despair—in times when societies are torn asunder rather than thriving—the danger is multiplied; in these conditions the very creation of self and social universes is not a heuristic epistemological process but a matter of survival. Untested assumptions about the sources of violence and peace and the foundations of morality most affect societies' powerless: children, war orphans, homeless youth, and the most disenfranchised—those who find themselves unarmed on the frontlines of wars they neither support nor control. To understand society and survival in war—to delve into the true toll of violence and the innovations of resistance—it is crucial to go beyond raw physical descriptions to explore the ontologies, the deep experience, of war lived, as the opening quotation captures. Political violence is not a simple story of broken bodies and shattered regimes. War howls, as this quote says, alongside the everyday of baked bread, down the streets in the steps of refugees, and into our very dreams of tonight and the hope for tomorrow. Taking analyses of childhood, war, power, and the creation of social worlds to the front lines, and out of clean peacetime offices and theories thought rather than lived, can play hell with cherished academic notions. For example, from a frontlines perspective, what is the outcome of suggesting that war orphans and homeless children living on the streets of Angola may be a valuable site for understanding the generative processes of community and the values that sustain it?

THE INJURY

> More children are killed in wars today than soldiers. These are statistics of shame.[1]

The boy was part of the group of children that lived in the storm drains under the busy city streets of Luanda, the capital of Angola. He was in his early teens. One day, walking down the street, he was hit by a speeding car, and his leg was badly broken. The car, seeing it was a street child, did not stop. The call went out immediately among the other street children to help. They knew the "free medical care" at the hospital was not free: doctors had received little in pay or supplies for a considerable time due to the war budget, and they charged for treatment. The children fanned across the neighborhoods and began to make money as quickly as possible. They hauled and carried for pennies; they shined shoes and washed cars; some stole simple items, and others called in favors and begged from adults. If they had anything worth selling—a toy, a shirt, a pair of shoes—they sold it. Within a short period of time, about as long as the wounded boy could tolerate the pain, they gathered together and carried him to the hospital. They found they had enough money to have a doctor set the leg and stabilize it with a proto-cast, but they did not have enough to have a cast put on. The doctor would not proceed without pay. The street children then made arrangements to visit Padre Horacio's center for homeless children several kilometers from the city center. Padre Horacio is one of the few adults the children trust: word on the street is that he grew up on the streets himself in his native home in Latin America. He understands not only the violence but the dignity of the streets, they say. The trip is not easy: penniless children of ten and fourteen made their way around congested streets, through the roiling industrial outskirts of Luanda, and across conjoining towns to the Padre's center to ask for help. The center gave the help and worked hard to have the boy return to his extended family in Luanda to recuperate. The debate went on for three days as they treated the child: he wanted to return to the storm drains, but the people at the center did everything they could to convince him otherwise: "He has some family," they said to the wounded boy and his friends, "this is the place to be when one is so seriously wounded. How can he recuperate well from such a serious injury in a storm drain with other children?" He refused to go to his family and returned to the storm drain to be cared for by his street orphan friends. When the boy returned to the drains, he told me: "This is my home. Where else would people take such care of me? These are the people, this is the place, I trust."

Why would a person elect to recuperate from a dangerous, and possibly crippling, broken leg in a storm drain under urban streets instead of going to a relative's home? The answer rests in the intangibles of cultures created and resisted. Theories about the origin of good, of systems of justice and human rights, of the very creativity of culture originate with adults. Children are viewed in these theories as the recipients of these achievements of civilization. The role of children varies by approach. In Christian theology children are conceived, physically and conceptually, in original sin. For secular modernists children are vessels to be filled, and in postmodern theory they are constituted through interaction with the larger world. For many of these theoreticians—from those who believe a child's character is forged in biology to those who see humans constituted through ongoing complex interactions—children must be guided carefully by adults through the maturation process. Without this guidance they personify the "proto-human": the nature and the beast that culture must conquer. They are the children of William Golding's *Lord of the Flies*. Few adults, from theologians to postmodernists, would suggest children are capable of forging the laws and justice systems that (fail to) govern their lives. But for the children living in the drains under city streets, adults are the cause of violence and fellow children are the solution.

STORM DRAIN CULTURE; OR "LORD OF THE FLIES" IS WRONG

There isn't anyone to help you. Only me. And I'm the Beast ... Fancy thinking the Beast was something you could hunt and kill! ... You knew, didn't you? I'm part of you? Close, close, close! I'm the reason why it's no go? Why things are the way they are? (Golding, *The Lord of the Flies*, 142)

In 1998 I discovered the world of storm drains quite by chance. I had worked in war zones in Africa for a decade and had come to realize that if children constituted half of all war casualties in the world, they should make up a significant portion of research attention. The war in Angola had taken nearly a million lives and produced several hundred thousand orphans.[2] HIV/AIDS, with infection rates running from 10 to over 30 percent of the population in southern Africa, constitutes a holocaust in its own right. However, you could count the number of orphanages on one hand. One Friday night in Luanda, I was talking with a young street boy who was cooking something that looked like glue in a scavenged tin can over a small fire in the grassy part of a roundabout on a major street intersection. I called him chef, complimenting his cooking skills; pleased, he looked me in the eyes and asked if I would go home with him. When I said yes, he grabbed my hand, pulled me down the street while dodging oncoming traffic, and then ran over to the side of the road and jumped down a storm drain. Everyone "knew" about the storm drain children, but what they knew rested in the realm of speculation, myth, and fear. Children were seen popping into and out of the drains, and they were considered feral, violent, and unpredictable. "These kids are dangerous," people said, shaking their heads in both sympathy and fear of the children, "they're violent." Jumping into the storm drain after this child near midnight seemed stupid but, for an anthropologist, unavoidable. It was like a storm drain in any country, a small opening at a roadside. For street children, a drain is its own natural security system: a full-size man could not fit into it. In my mind's eye, when I had heard about children living in the drains under the streets, I had visualized decaying, dirt-encrusted tunnels with children huddled in dismal conditions amid stagnant water and rats. Everyone I knew held the same idea. But when I entered the drain, I felt the world stop, existentially, for a moment—and my view of the human condition, in its most profound sense, expanded.

In this drain the children had created a home and a community. It was spotlessly clean. I remember being surprised that there was no smell. Some twenty children lived in this one section of the drain. Children with no change of clothing, no running water, and no money to buy soap managed a place that smelled fresh. The children had lined the walls with pictures from magazines, no small feat for children with no money for food and clothing, much less glue. The "living room" had pictures from action movies and music groups, while the "bedroom," farther down from the drain entrance, had pictures from advertisements with images such as women in long white dresses walking on island beaches. An old inner tube from a tire served as a chair. The children had somehow acquired scraps of fabric and rug and placed them on top of cardboard, lining the floors in home-style comfort. Some meters down the drain they had fashioned a wall, and at the end they had constructed shelves that held the few possessions they had managed to acquire. On one shelf stood a battered old vase that held a bouquet of paper flowers the children had made. Little bits of art, collected here and there from what the rest of humanity throws away, decorated the shelves and tiny tables—for example, a picture frame they had filled with a collage of magazine photos and some old Christmas tree tinsel, possibly from an embassy party. Holding my hand and leading me down to the end, the children sat me down next to an old powdered milk tin can connected to a strange assembly of wires and small bits of transistor boards connected by yet more wires. Delightedly, they turned on the radio. They had even fashioned a dial so they could tune in different stations. I followed the trail of wires to what looked like a pile of white Styrofoam, on which sat a small mountain of worn-out batteries the kids had patiently collected from the trash. No single battery had enough energy to power anything, but in a mass, they produced music. I asked the children who had made this. They pointed to a boy of about eight, who grinned in recognition. When I told them that even though I was a teacher, I could not make a radio from junk-heap scraps if my life depended on it, they thanked me for being polite, assuming I was lying: making such a radio is a survival skill for an eight year old here.

As I turned to leave the drain, they pulled me over to show me a sleeping boy wrapped up in a blanket and began to gently pull the blanket from him without waking him. Wrapped up and sleeping with the boy were four plump, healthy puppies. Clearly, the children had shared what food they could manage with the puppies. They treated these puppies with a tenderness they themselves might

Home, inside the storm drain.

With pet puppy, inside the storm drain.

The fishermen—dinner for a street community of a dozen children.

Crashed car, home to four girls.

Collage: boy and the drawing he gave me of "the home I'll have someday . . ."

never have known. This was the feral violent community I had so often been warned about when I walked on Luanda's streets.

The children said I was the first adult to visit them in the drains. I asked if I could come back the next day and take pictures of their home and have them explain more about how they set up their community. They agreed, proud of the family community they had created.

(INVISIBLE) MORAL UNIVERSES

The next day the children explained to me the codes of conduct that governed their community. And this is a community in the fullest sense. They share everything they have with each other equally. If one has food, they divide it among all; it would be unthinkable for someone to have two shirts if another had none.

Stealing is not allowed within the community of street children or within the larger community of those among whom the children live. They assign chores, with some of them washing clothes and bedding, others cooking, and yet others cleaning. I asked them if at night, when they were all comfortable in their beds before they went to sleep, they told stories about their ancestors and history. "Yes, of course," they answered, "it's our job to educate the young." They instituted a security system for protection. If one is taken by the police, all the others go out to find odd jobs to scrape together the money to take to the jail and get their friend out. If someone does break the rules of the community, the children have a governing council where everyone sits down and finds a solution.

These children have come to Luanda from all over Angola, running from the war, from harsh conditions, or from impossible family situations. They are orphaned, abused, or the children of extreme poverty. They live in a world largely hostile to them. From Luanda to Manila to New York, most of the "civilized" world walks past them without seeing them. "Some people kick at us as they walk by," one child told me. Yet in extreme deprivation, they have created not only a functioning community in the most adult sense, but they have also created as peaceful a one as possible. They have fashioned family and support networks as best they can. In a world of violence, they have sought to create stability and accord. As one youth told me, "I carry a little bit of peace in my heart wherever I go, and I take it out at night and look at it."[3]

In the months that followed, I explored the numerous communities of street children in Luanda. They differed in age and size. The group that lived in front of the press center was small, about six boys, and in 1998 the oldest was eleven. The group that lived on the hill below the university was large, over forty, and hosted both boys and men in their late teens. The group that lived in the abandoned crashed car lot had both men and women, children and older teens. Men's and women's quarters were segregated by cars—younger males and females tend to live in single-sex groups with links to groups of the opposite sex. The group that lived in a collapsed house was female and ranged in age from teen mothers to their infant children. Men and women formed partnerships across the gendered living arrangements. The older males would bring their girlfriends "home" to give a sense of family to the younger children under their care. The older teen females would partner with males their age to provide a sense of stability and protection to their group. Love and romance, as well as familial duties, defined most of the relationships I saw. Some of these romances endure well into adulthood and into marriage and become the basis for new communities—for example, when a couple has a child, finds new living quarters like an abandoned or bombed-out house, takes in young desperate street children, and raises them as a family.

No matter the age, the size, the gender, or the composition of the group, all followed codes of conduct similar to the storm drain community I had visited.

The different groups were linked in a Malinowski-esque kula ring set of relations.[4] Like small countries, each group maintained good relations with the others in their area. They traded constantly. I would bring one group a toy or some
prized piece of clothing and be able to chart its progress through the street communities of the sprawling capital of three million people—traded as much to
maintain community ties as to get other important goods and services. These
ties were crucial: if one child had a fight with his group, he could join another.
If one group had special problems, say with the police, they could request assistance from another. If a new set of war orphans arrived, food, clothing, and
places to sleep were always found for them. Indeed, the very idea that orphanages had set limits to the number of people who could stay was inconceivable to
these children: "We never turn a child away, no matter what, there is always a
place for them." The fact that they can take care of twenty children in a small
storm drain while people live above them in spacious quarters occupied by a few
is an irony that is not lost on these children.

If the children institute creative communities, they also create rich philosophical systems. The jarring differences between the rich and the homeless became
the theme of a dialogue the children developed to remind everyone to share
equally what few resources they had. When one child wants to keep more than
the others, to lord over others, to control, the rest respond: "Illusion. What you
are saying is illusion. Like the big shots with their big cars and big guns. Like what
got us into this mess [the war, poverty, injustice] in the first place. You want more
than the rest of us?" they sneer. "Don't be like that. That's just illusion."

When I discussed this with Lidia Borba, who works in UNICEF/Angola's
Children in Difficult Conditions Bureau, she said: "These children understand
the politics of power thoroughly. Never would I have thought children so young
would understand these complex issues. But they do, and they critique them.
Illusions."

A BETRAYAL

There are 100 million street children in the world. Many of these
children disappear, are beaten, illegally detained and confined, sexually exploited, tortured and systematically killed by agents of the
state. (Millett 1994, 294)

If that many people were in one country they'd have a seat at the UN.[5]

I took the pictures I had taken inside the storm drains to several organizations
dealing with children in Angola such as UNICEF, UNDP (United Nations Devel-

opment Program), Christian Children's Fund, and GOAL (an Irish organization working with street children). Against their awareness of the sheer sophistication of these children's communities rested an international wall of habitual ignorance. One day a friend came up to me and sadly handed me a copy of the *New York Times.* On the front cover was an exposé on Angola's war and war orphans. The title read "Street Children Live like Rats in Filthy Sewers." Clearly the journalist had not entered the drains. Several times I was contacted by European journalists who asked me to take them to the drains and, upon arriving, refused to enter. I can only imagine the stories they submitted. But this is not an ignorance that is innocent. It is an ignorance that can cost lives, and worse, justify that cost, as the following story illustrates.

THE DEATH

"Nada é permanente neste mundo, excepto a morte!"—disse ele . . .
Se soubesse que naquele momento a sua vida fazia a mais curta contagem regressiva por ele nunca imaginada, talvez proferisse todos versos e verbos; os existentes e os inexistentes. Mas pode ser que talvez não.

"Nothing in this world is permanent, except death!"—he said . . . If I knew in that moment that his life would make the shortest telling he could ever have imagined, maybe I would have offered all the verses and verbs, all those existing and those not existing. But maybe not" (Baptista 2000, 1; translated by the author).

One day the police took a boy who lived with his group on the streets near the central market. The police do not necessarily take street children under suspicion of breaking a law; children told me that, for example, they are routinely picked up and taken to the police station and made to clean, then released. These were times of fear for the youth: they could be ridiculed and even harmed; girls faced sexual assault. As is their code, the rest of the group fanned out to make as much money as they could to take to the police headquarters to seek the release of their friend. When they arrived at the police station, the police told them their friend was not there any longer, that he must have gone elsewhere. The children knew this was a lie: the boy would have come back to his home to check in with his friends. The street children persisted in asking for their friend. Finally, a policeman gestured to the area behind the police station where trash was thrown and said, "Forget it, get out of here, he's gone. You know, garbage, going out with the rest of the garbage." The group went out back to find a dump, and there was the body of their friend.

The children retrieved the body and took it to the mortuary until they could arrange a funeral. This was a decision that was not made lightly. In war-time Angola energy was a scarce, and expensive, commodity. City power was neither constant nor widely available. The mortuary told the youth that if they wanted the body of their friend to be kept cool, they would have to pay. The children did every kind of job they could to raise the money for the mortuary, in many cases going without the food they needed to pay for their friend's refrigeration. The police began harassing the children: to hold a funeral was an indictment of the police.

The children had confidence in two Angolan woman—Casimira Benge and Lidia Borba—who worked in UNICEF's Children in Difficult Circumstances Bureau, and they went to them for help. They asked two things: that the woman help them arrange a funeral, and that they help make a public statement that the police should not develop a culture of violence against street children like that in Brazil—that Angola should set a new and more humane path. UNICEF went to the police, who denied everything. But the children had the body. The police increased their harassment and threats against the children, who refused to relent; and in the midst of this, the youth continued to work daily to pay the morgue to keep the body of their friend. The women from UNICEF told the children not to hold the funeral because it would endanger them, but the children insisted that it be done. Together, the children and UNICEF wrote a formal letter to the government asking that the murder be investigated; they also asked that Angola create a more civilized way of dealing with the tragedy of war and poverty than street children face in countries where police violence is a norm. Angola, they said, should rise above this. They took the letter to government officials and to the press. The public exposure helped protect the children against police vendetta, but UNICEF still felt the children would come to harm if they arranged and attended the funeral. As it was unconscionable for the children to let their friend die without ceremony, the people from UNICEF who had been helping the children agreed to hold the funeral while the children met in another place special to them to observe their own ceremonies.

For the children, the *New York Times* article, and all like this, is a nail in their coffin. Average society fears "Rats Living in Filth"—these are the harbingers of chaos, disease, violence, and lurking threat. To kill rats in filth is a public health issue. It is justified. You can throw them in the dump behind the police station. Killing "real" children, of course, is unthinkable.

THE IRONY

If children are loved and valued, why are they still being used as cannon-fodder? (UNICEF 1996, 10–11)

Adults are the architects of a world where they are the guardians of children. In this world, adults speak for children. It is inconceivable in the world we live in that children would be asked to help draft laws, sit on juries, hold jobs at UNICEF, sit on school boards, or develop public policy. This entire framework exists on the conviction that adults are the moral guardians of humanity. The conviction endures only as long as adults speak for children and children remain silent. Or silenced.

The children living on the streets of Angola are there for the same reasons children live on the streets in the rest of the world's countries: war; abuse in the home; the severe inequality of social hierarchies that produces lethal poverty; the violent abuses of forced child sex work and labor; a dearth of social services. When you walk the streets with homeless children, you see the world from their point of view: it is adults who cause the violence that leaves them homeless. It is children who take them in and help. Indeed, a child who finds himself suddenly on the streets discovers his first line of help is other children, not adults.

This is the *illusion* that children on the streets refer to: to maintain a community of peace, one can *not* emulate adults per se. In a curious happenstance, just as I was having these conversations about the illusions of power with the street youth, I picked up a book that began with the following words:

> The illusion is performed out of doors, often in a dusty field. The magician works inside a circle surrounded by spectators, assisted by a young girl, his obedient daughter.
>
> Near the end of the show, the magician suddenly and unexpectedly takes hold of the girl, pulls a dagger from beneath his cloak and slits her throat.
>
> Blood spurts, spattering their smocks and sometimes the clothing of the spectators nearby. The magician stuffs the body of the girl into a bulb basket he has used throughout the show. Once she is inside, he covers the basket with a cloth, and mutters incantations. Removing the cloth he shows the audience that the basket is empty, the body of the girl gone. Just then the spectators hear a shout from beyond the circle. They turn to see the girl gaily running through the crowd into the magician's waiting arms. (Frost 1997, 1)

When I read this, I realized yet a further level of critique invoked by these child philosophers. For the war orphans living in drains under the road, the illusion refers to the very real, and very dangerous, politics of power. The purveyors of war suddenly pull out daggers and slit throats, and then for the grand finale—peace—they attempt to show that no one really died, that no harm was really done, that no street children orphaned by the war exist.

I met another group of street children who lived in a part of Luanda where the drains ran open across a field. One night, the police burned them out. I arrived just after the attack and found the children devastated by their loss. Like the storm drain communities, they had worked hard to create a "home," putting up pictures, making "furniture" from scrounged makeshift items, even growing plants in battered tin cans. The police had rushed in at four in the morning—beating the children, even burning the little plants they had coaxed to life—and hauled several kids off to jail. "What do they expect you to do," I asked, "disappear?" One child looked at me sadly and said "Yes. The rich don't want to look at us. We are not supposed to exist in their world." Illusion.

THE THEORIES

Among the paradoxes of this long century of violence is the paucity of reflections within contemporary political theory, including democratic theory, on the causes, effects and ethico-political implications of violence ... While there are certainly plenty of case studies of wars, civil wars and other violent conflicts, political reflection has lagged far behind empirical events. Of course, the sheer quantity of violence heaped by the twentieth century upon itself is enough to make even the most cheerful philosopher pessimistic, and since "optimists write badly" (Valéry) and pessimists tend not to write, the silence of those parts of the political theory profession which have been shocked by this century's cruelty is understandable. Elsewhere in the profession, the silence is simply inexcusable, for it is as if professional political theory is incapable of learning to think in pain or even that it has forgotten the experience of pain, that it has succeeded in doing what people normally cannot bring themselves to do: to overcome the animal pity that grips those who witness or hear about the physical suffering of others. (Keane 1996, 6–7)

I have researched wars across the front lines of several continents for nearly two decades. While I investigate the reality of violence in people's lives, my enduring focus is always the inspiration whereby average unarmed civilians survive atrocities of the worst kind through creating self, society, and world afresh in innovative ways against the hegemony of violence. I have published and spoken in formal venues widely on this—and, when speaking of adults, have never been critiqued for my approach, never had my data called into question. No one has approached me to claim I am biased, that average people cannot be that creative, that good, that enduring; no one insists that I am ignoring the wicked in people because of some laudable but misdirected reason. But every time I have presented the data on the street children to a professional, Western, adult audience, these charges have been laid against me: "The picture is too rosy; you must be ignoring the bad."

The Lord of the Flies must be right. Without the direct supervision of adults, children *must* revert to some kind of savagery. It is only through these beliefs that adults can maintain the *illusion* that we are, unquestionably, the architects of the moral order, and we hand this order down to the raw material of upcoming generations.

Of course, the children who land on the streets have landed there because of violence: war, assault, rape, starvation, battery. Some do reproduce what has befallen them, but most do not. Indeed, the children I meet seek to escape the violence they have encountered in the world of adults. They seek to craft a world of greater care and concern. Without guidance from adults, without the benefit of the stability of societal law and community in their own lives, they create these. It is a remarkable accomplishment. But it is not one my audiences want to hear. "There must be bad there."

Perhaps such sentiments come from the view that if children mirror adult society—wreaking violence as well as peace—we adults are not implicated in the fact that it is we, not children, who seem to be the architects of aggression. This would mean violence is not a biological imperative, nor a foundational feature of the human condition, but something adults can craft out of choice in the pursuit of power and perfidy.

THE CREATION OF THE HUMAN CONDITION

So where, in the final summation, is the font of human society and the peace that undergirds it? Since it may well emerge from places mainstream theory tells us are unlikely, even impossible, let us return to the ruminations of the children who live on the streets and in the storm drains of Angola. The children take great exception to the common statements that children born and bred in war are a "lost generation." This phrase is heard from Angola through Sudan, up to the Balkans, and over to Burma. It is intended to capture a generation of children who have grown up knowing severe political violence and who have been deprived of settled communities, stable families, schooling, and the creative nurturance that peace imparts. But there is an underside to these comments. The jagged assumption is that these children are indeed "lost": that they will be prone to violence, instability, and aggressive poverty; that they will be limited in their ability to envision and create a better future; that they have looked into the eye of war and will reflect what they have seen. "Illusion," the children respond.

> We know how we came to live this way. We can see who has and who doesn't, who gives and who takes. We know we take better care of each other here than any of us would find in the places we ran from. If you can tell us of a peaceful home that will take us, we will go today.

> But the people with the nice cars and big homes are not asking us home. In the meantime, we create a life as best we can, and we do a pretty good job.

> You want to know what we need? We need to go to school. There is a school just down the street, and we watch the regular kids come and go, and when we go there and ask if we can attend we are turned away. We need a place to keep our things. If we get a book or some clothes, how can we keep them on the street? Someone just comes along and takes them. We need a chance, schooling, work, people to believe in us.

Michael Comerford, an Irish priest and scholar working in Angola, responded to this story by asking: "Who is lost? The children, or those who drive by them without seeing?"

Perhaps what is most distressing about the phrase "the lost generation of children" is the fact that in the mere saying of this, the creative communities and peaceful supportive traditions these children make are not recognized. The "lost generation" is used as a marker of deprivation and violence, not of creativity and peace building. The designation of "lost generation" invokes *The Lord of the Flies* philosophies. And it conveys the impression that there is war, *or* there is peace: if children grow up in war, all they know is violence and suffering. But as Lidia Borba of UNICEF/Angola said when I was talking with her about where these children learn such peaceful strategies:

> But it is natural they should know these things. For the war orphans, before they lost their homes, they grew up with daily kindnesses. They were loved and cared for; they saw people come to visit and treated with dignity and respect, they saw their family set up ways to support each other through good times and bad. Even for children who have fled abusive homes, they walk the streets and see the goodness their cultures have to offer: the acts of helping, the community strength, the deeply held beliefs in the dignity of people.

> Peace is everywhere in the midst of the war: in every act of daily caring. These children have seen this, they have thought on this, they have

grown in this way, they have been nurtured in a culture that values these things, and they too have grown to value them. You know, it is how the children survive the streets, how we survive the war, by keeping these traditions of humanity alive in living day to day.

What is most interesting in this context is that having been exposed to both dignity and violence, these children generally choose to enact the former and to mitigate the latter when facing even the harshest of circumstances.

Postscript: Philosophy

I asked the group of children who lived on the streets in front of my boarding room if I could *passear*–go about—with them one day. Sure, they said, and came to collect me the next morning. They ranged in age from eight to twelve. After hitting the restaurants and shops to see if any food had been thrown out, checking with the other nearby street communities, scrounging for "treasures," and looking for simple jobs like hauling or washing, they settled on the steps at the oceanfront to talk and rest. Curious what they would say, I asked them what it meant to be human. One boy touched the middle of his chest and said this is what made us human. No, said a second, it resides here, he said, touching his throat. I wondered if the boys were talking about their hearts and breathing, or something more. The third boy cleared this up: "It's both together: it's when we combine feeling, caring, with voice." All nodded. I paused to wonder if academia, by this definition, constituted part of the human condition. Then the children leaned back against the steps. "We always take rests—you can't walk too far unless you've eaten properly."

Notes

1. UNICEF (1995, 2). In the last decade, approximately 2 million children have died in wars; between 4 and 5 million have been physically disabled; more than 5 million have been forced into refugee camps; more than 12 million have been left homeless, and 10 million are psychologically traumatized. Twenty-eight million minors live in war zones (UNICEF 1996, 13).

2. Angola achieved independence from Portugal in 1975. The country went from a war for liberation to a civil war within the span of a year. In 2002, with the death of the rebel leader, Jonas Savimibi, a peace accord was implemented and continues to hold at present.

3. After leaving Angola in 1998, I traveled to Mozambique, where I spent time talking with street children there to ask them about the similarities and dif-

ferences between their lives and those of the children in Angola. One youth stood out to me in speaking of the intersections of violence and peace building. This teenage boy was one of the toughest I had met. He had a hard edge and acted the role of the street boy thug—but he had fashioned a necklace out of an empty plastic container for sugar tablets. He was willing to take me to every corner of his life but resisted showing me where he slept. After gaining what for him was probably the ultimate trust, he took me to see his sleeping quarters with a shyness I had never seen. It was an old broom closet in an abandoned, broken-down home. He had only a tattered straw mat and a very old and worn blanket, but above his head on the wall he had put pictures of the most gentle scenes common to magazines: people holding hands, holding babies, smiling in idyllic locales. Directly above his head was a ballerina literally flying through the air in an embracing leap. He went over to place his hand on this picture, looked at me sheepishly, and then, having shown his vulnerability, took my hand to pull me back down the hallway. He had no problem showing me his toughness, his pain, the violence of his life; his vulnerability lay in showing his ballerina.

4. Malinowski (1922) helped develop economic studies in the twentieth century with his work showing that people inhabiting a series of islands in the Pacific maintained a complex set of institutionalized trade relations that linked them socially, politically, and interactionally, as well as economically.

5. Bruce Harris, interviewed by Richard Swift, *New Internationalist*, July 1995, 31. Harris, who works with an NGO dedicated to children's rights in Guatemala, continues with an example: "Guatemala City is divided into 15 zones. We've only worked in four but we've initiated 195 law suits and are suing 123 policemen and 48 members of the military for the torture and murder of children." And this in only one quarter of one city in the world.

ED CAIRNS, FRANCES MCLERNON, WENDY MOORE,
AND ILSE HAKVOORT

The Impact of the Peace Process in Northern Ireland on Children's and Adolescents' Ideas about War and Peace

The ceasefires in Northern Ireland, which ended some thirty years of political violence, presented researchers with a unique opportunity to study children's ideas about peace and war in a society that had just recently made the first faltering steps toward a transition from war to peace (see Cairns and Darby 1998). The present chapter reports a series of studies in which we attempted to use different methods to capture something of the way in which the unfolding peace process impacted the ideas of children in Northern Ireland. Before reporting our work on the impact of peace, we will begin by briefly reviewing what is known about children's ideas about war and peace in general; in particular, we will examine the limited evidence there is from other societies that these ideas may be influenced by living in societies where there is war or political conflict.

Children's Ideas about War and Peace

Work in this area dates back to at least the early days of the Cold War (Cooper 1965; Tolley 1973). What this research demonstrates is that by about age seven or eight, children have developed reasonably well-defined ideas about peace and war. Ideas about peace, however, tend to involve "negative peace"—that is, a state defined simply by the absence of violence. Much less is known about children's ideas about "positive peace," defined by knowledge of such concepts as "cooperation" or "harmony."

A leap forward in both knowledge and methodology did not come about until recently, as a result of a pioneering study in this area by Hakvoort and Oppenheimer (1993). They interviewed 101 middle-class Dutch children between the ages of eight and sixteen years. The interviews focused on children's definition of peace and their ideas about how to make peace. Because the young peoples' responses were all categorized according to the same specific criteria (see Hakvoort and Oppenheimer 1993), this made it possible to make comparisons across studies carried out at different points in time where researchers have used the same scoring criteria.

All the children appeared to have acquired a comprehensive concept of war by age eight. Only at age ten, however, had the same level of knowledge been acquired regarding peace. Of interest is the fact that more girls (74 percent) than boys (43 percent) at age eight years had grasped the concept of peace. Girls also were more likely to use interindividual ideas when trying to define peace, while boys relied more on war-like terms by defining peace as the absence of war. As predicted by earlier research, all the children tended to think of peace mainly in terms of "negative peace." That is, they tended to conceive of peace as the absence of war or "with a state of stillness." Only from age ten years on did children begin to use concepts such as human rights.

When asked to give their suggestions as to how to make peace, the vast majority of the younger children made suggestions that involved solving or preventing quarrels at an individual level. Among the older children this strategy was gradually replaced with strategies involving more global events such as preventing war between nations. However, only the girls who were interviewed, in particular the oldest (sixteen-year-old) girls, "thought tolerance and respect between people" to be an important component in any strategy to attain peace (Hakvoort and Oppenheimer 1993, 71).

Not only do we need to know how the concept of peace develops in children over time, but we also need to know if this development takes a different trajectory in children who have been exposed to political violence, for example, children who have grown up with the constant background of war. This information is essential if we are to understand how to enable such children to contribute to the development of more peaceful societies.

Effects of War on Children's Ideas about War and Peace

War

Relatively little research has been carried out worldwide concerning the effects of war on children's ideas about peace, and much of the research that exists in this area has tended to be contradictory. For example, one result of experiencing war is general pessimism about the possibility of achieving peace in the future. Gillespie and Allport (1950) found that 60 percent of the college students in their sample (whose childhoods had been dominated by World War II) expected a third world war within fifteen years. More recently, Punamaki (1987) was similarly pessimistic about the effects of war on children's ideas about peace. She concluded that the Palestinian and Israeli children in her sample could not be socialized into peace-loving citizens and that children who experience violence within their society are more likely to use violence to settle their disputes.

In contrast, Bender and Frosch (1942) reported that children during the Second World War believed that peace should be sought after. Again, more recently, similar views have been expressed by South African children (Liddell, Kemp, and Moema 1993) and by Ugandan and Sudanese children during periods of political conflict (Dodge 1990). In particular, Spielmann (1986) noted that children living in violent areas of Israel are more inclined to stress the active factors of peace, such as the changes that peace will bring, including freedom to travel, better social relations, and greater prosperity. The passive aspects of peace, such as the disappearance of war, fear, and compulsory army service, were less frequently alluded to. Spielmann also observed that "children's vision of peace is always richer and more colourful when the children are in a state of hope, which stimulates imagination" (1986, 64).

Conflict in Northern Ireland

A small number of studies have provided some insight into Northern Irish children's ideas of peace. For example, McWhirter (1982) found that when asked to write about "violence," two-thirds of a sample of 637 children in Northern Ireland spontaneously expressed negative views. It was hypothesized, however, that over time children in Northern Ireland would become habituated to the violence and accept it as normal, thus distorting their ideas about peace.

Hosin, McClenahan, and Cairns (1993) found no evidence to support this hypothesis in their study that involved comparing essays entitled "My Country" written by children in Northern Ireland in 1980 and 1991. The participants in the study were 288 twelve year olds and 319 fifteen year olds, seen in either 1980 (n=455) or 1991 (n=152). All were Protestant children attending religiously segregated schools in Northern Ireland, with approximately equal numbers of boys and girls. Content analysis was carried out on the children's essays using a number of preset categories that involved counting the number of children who mentioned such things as loyalty and violence in their essays. The most striking result drawn from this study was the finding that regardless of whether the children had grown up in the 1970s or in the 1980s, or whether they were aged twelve years or fifteen years at the time of the study, the one feature of Northern Ireland that they were most likely to mention was the political violence.

Qualitative analysis carried out on the two studies suggested, however, that the contexts of the violence mentioned differed markedly between 1980 and 1991. In 1980 the children perceived the violence in a more matter-of-fact way, concentrating more on its political aspects, as shown in the following statement: "Northern Ireland is not a very peaceful country because of the Troubles" (male, twelve years, 1980). In 1991 the children were more likely to mention the violence in the context of a wish for peace: "I like my country a lot apart from the war between religions. I would like my country to be free from war. I wish there was no IRA or bombs" (male, twelve years, 1991). The authors argued that this demonstrated that the twelve and fifteen year olds who wrote their essays in 1990, despite the fact that they had lived all their lives surrounded by conflict, had not habituated to the violence. Certainly, there was no evidence that they accepted it unconditionally, nor had they lost the desire to live in a peaceful society.

A second study carried out by McClenahan and Cairns (1993) reinforced this conclusion. In this study the terminal values section of the Rokeach Values Survey was administered to 315 eleven-year-old and 398 fourteen-year-old children in Northern Ireland, equally divided between Protestant and Catholic and between male and female. It was found that all the children, except for boys in the older age group, placed "a world at peace" in the first position of importance. This result was compared with a similar study carried out ten years earlier, in which McKernan (1980) had asked 751 fourteen year olds (equal males to females) from Northern Ireland to complete the same Rokeach Value Survey. Also at that time, "a world at peace" had been the highest ranked value for both boys and girls. The conclusion was reached, therefore, that children in Northern Ireland overwhelmingly wish for an end to violence and a world at peace.

Effects of Peace on Ideas about War and Peace in Northern Ireland

This wish for peace in Northern Ireland appeared to be close to fulfilment when, on Wednesday, August 31, 1994, after twenty-five years of relentless violence, the Provisional Irish Republican Army (IRA) announced a ceasefire. This was followed by ceasefires from various Loyalist groups, culminating in the Good Friday/Belfast Agreement in 1998. This agreement has had a checkered career. It received massive support (more than 70 percent of the total population of Northern Ireland) in 1998, but since then this level of support has been falling steadily in the Protestant community. A recent survey (Mac Ginty 2003) showed that in 2003 less than 40 percent of Protestants would now vote in favor of the Good Friday/Belfast Agreement.

For the children and young people of Northern Ireland, the ceasefires have meant a lessening, if not a complete end, to bomb alerts, British army vehicles, armaments and personnel on the streets of the city, security searches, and the constant bombardment with information about killings, bombings, and violent attacks on the police and army. Instead there is now a political climate in which the validity of the ceasefires is constantly questioned in the face of the continuing sectarian violence. The studies reported in this chapter represent our attempts to monitor the impact of this fluctuating peace process on the way children and young people in Northern Ireland think about peace, war, and conflict resolution.

Peace Begins

In our first study (McLernon, Ferguson, and Cairns, 1997), we tried to capture the thoughts of young people in Northern Ireland about war, peace, and conflict resolution before and soon after the 1994 paramilitary ceasefire announcements. Concepts of war, peace, and conflict resolution were elicited by means of a self-completed questionnaire. Aside from requests for information about age and gender, the questionnaire had just four questions:

1. What do you think of when you hear the word "war"?
2. What do you think of when you hear the word "peace"?

3. What do you think could be done to bring an end to the trouble in Northern Ireland and prevent any more fighting?

4. Is your country one of the following:

At War / At Peace / Not Sure   *(Please circle)*

The first three questions were based on the semistructured interview devised by Hakvoort and Oppenheimer (1993) to elicit ideas about war and peace and about how peace might be achieved. Adolescents were asked to describe their thoughts and associations connected with the words "war" and "peace" and to suggest what could be done to bring a war to an end and to avoid starting another war. The final question was devised for this study to determine participants' ideas about the state of war/peace in Northern Ireland. The adolescents' responses to the questions on the concepts of war, peace, and strategies to attain peace were categorized using the scoring manual compiled by Hakvoort and Oppenheimer (1993).

Analysis of the responses of 117 adolescents aged fourteen to fifteen years showed differences in their attitudes toward war and peace and in their strategies to attain peace before and after the ceasefires. Concepts of war, which were portrayed before the ceasefire as static and unchanging, showed a significant difference after the ceasefire. In addition, the perception of war, seen before the ceasefire as a struggle between national leaders, shifted significantly to a more general view of war in terms of war activities and their negative consequences. Perceptions of peace as active showed a marked swing after the ceasefire to a more abstract view of peace as freedom, justice, and liberty. Before the ceasefire adolescents were reluctant to provide strategies to attain peace, but after the ceasefire such strategies were suggested with more confidence. There was also an indication in the results that adolescents prefer an alternative to violence in the resolution of conflict. Perhaps most surprisingly, the proportion of adolescents who said the country was "at peace" did not change significantly after the ceasefire, while the percentage that expressed ambivalent feelings about the status of Northern Ireland in terms of peace increased significantly. McLernon, Ferguson, and Cairns (1997) concluded that at the time of the study many young people had not fully accepted the reality of the peace process.

LEARNING TO LIVE WITH PEACE

Of course our first study (Ferguson, McLernon, and Cairns 1994) provided only a very quick snapshot of the possible impact of the ceasefires on children's thinking in Northern Ireland. Further, the children's responses were, to some extent, limited by their literary skills. To overcome these problems we undertook a more detailed investigation using a semistructured interview involving a three-part longitudinal design (McLernon 1998).

The interviews were used to elicit concepts of peace and war and strategies to attain peace from a sample of eight- to ten-year-old Protestant children from a district of Belfast that had experienced above-average levels of political violence. The interviews took place in December 1994, June 1995, and January 1996. Thus, the data were gathered during what was arguably the most dramatic event in the history of the peace process in Northern Ireland: the first IRA ceasefire, which lasted from August 1994 to February 1996.

All children were interviewed individually. The interview began by asking children about their concepts of peace, in particular their free associations with peace and definitions of peace. The children were then asked to formulate strategies to attain peace from differing social perspectives, first from an unspecified perspective and then followed by the more specific perspectives of head of their own country and head of the world. There followed a cluster of questions dealing with the children's knowledge about individuals and institutions responsible for peace in Northern Ireland and the strategies these bodies might be using in the search for peace. The data were then coded using the Hakvoort coding frame, and hiloglinear analyses were carried out using gender and time of interview as independent variables.

All children in the study expressed well-developed concepts of peace, with the majority concentrating upon an explanation of peace as the negation of war. McLernon (1998) interpreted this as reinforcing the views of Oppenheimer (1996) and R. Hall (1993) that until the age of ten years, children's concepts of peace do not differentiate into multifaceted aspects of peace such as abstract concepts about universal rights and human attitudes.

Overall, McLernon (1998) concluded that during the period 1996–98, the young Northern Irish Protestant children she interviewed revealed concepts of peace that were in general no different from those reported in studies involving children living in peaceful societies. Further, there were few statistically significant time-related changes during this period. However, marked fluctuations were observed in the children's responses at the second assessment, and at the third assessment their responses reverted to a level similar to that of the first assessment. These fluctuations were attributed to the influence of media messages at the time of the second assessment in June 1995, which tended to focus on problems surrounding the peace process.

Finally, when asked about peace in Northern Ireland, the children tended to be indecisive. Indeed, it was clear that the majority of children did not know that there had been peace in the history of Northern Ireland; rather, they appeared to believe conflict was always part of Northern Irish life.

PICTURING PEACE

The studies noted above, of course, still have limitations. To begin with, although one study used questionnaires and the other interviews, both relied on verbal skills. Further, while we were able to compare our data with those gathered by other investigators in other societies, we had gathered no comparative data ourselves.

In our next study (McLernon and Cairns 2001), therefore, we used drawings to study the impact of political violence on children's ideas about war and peace. This time the participants (100 boys and 81 girls aged six to seven years) came from three state (that is, Protestant) primary schools in Northern Ireland and three in northeastern England. All children were asked to draw two pictures entitled "peace" and "war," and the drawings were then coded using Hakvoort and Oppenheimer's (1993) system (see Figures 1 and 2).

Some differences were detected between the drawings of the Northern Irish and English children, indicating that the Northern Irish children were more likely to conceptualize peace as a negative construct—that is, as the absence of war. Although, as we noted at the time, it is difficult to draw a negative image such as the absence of war, Northern Irish children were more likely to produce drawings of war memorials, armies laying down their weapons, or downcast soldiers filing onto a ship to go home. On the other hand, we found no evidence that children from a high-violence area of Northern Ireland were any more likely than children from a low-violence area or from England to draw more detailed war pictures, for example, with more explicit portrayals of weapons and soldiers.

Finally, the data from this study confirmed previous research by showing boys in the younger age group to have a greater knowledge of war than girls

Figure 1. Peace.

of the same age. McLernon and Cairns (2001) related this finding to claims that boys are either more likely to be exposed to prevailing cultural norms or are more sensitive to such norms.

POEMS OF PEACE

It could be argued that peace and war are emotive topics and that by approaching them with semistructured interviews, a more cognitive framework may be imposed on the children's ideas. In particular, there is always the possibility that demand characteristics associated with this format will lead children to answer in the way they believe the interviewer (adult) expects them to. We hoped that poetry, because it allows more room for personal, even private, expression, would elicit more personal reflections on peace and war, relatively free from demand characteristics. To examine this proposition we (McLernon, Smith, and Cairns 2002) investigated the influence of gender, age, and culture on children's ideas about peace in children's poetry.

Figure 2. War.

A total of 809 children (482 females and 327 males) took part from four primary schools (mean age 9.08 years) and four secondary schools (mean age 11.61 years) in the Londonderry/Derry area of Northern Ireland. The children were asked to write a short poem entitled "What Peace Means to Me."

The poems were read and concepts of peace identified and assigned to the categories devised by Hakvoort and Oppenheimer (1995). As expected, the children in this study were able to express well-developed concepts of peace, which again emphasized the position of peace as secondary to war.

My Dream of Peace

Live at 6.00 it's on again,
I don't want to hear them scream,
That bomb that killed so many.
Please God let it be a dream.

PEACE

A father shot late last night,
His son was in his bed.
O daddy, daddy where are you?
It's a dream, please don't be dead.

PEACE

Three little boys burnt to death,[1]
Their parents what will they do?
A lonely home forever,
A dream this can't be true

PEACE

Peace

Peace is when people can walk
down the town without getting shot,
And also elderly don't have to be
afraid in their homes anymore.
Once more the children can play happily outside
Because there is no fighting or arguing outside.

Peace is when Catholics and Protestants
can be neighbours,
Peace is when the police don't have
to arrest people anymore
Most people are happy
Only some are sad
But I am glad.

We interpreted this as evidence that the children had been socialized to understand peace mainly as the absence of war. In addition, we noted two other dominant themes in the poems on peace. The first was an emphasis on positive emotions at an individual level, such as playing together and being friends. This is a common theme observed by other researchers investigating children's ideas about peace (Hakvoort and Oppenheimer 1995). The second was the frequent use of war-related images to describe peace. This discovery is not a common theme in previous research carried out in other countries, but it had been observed in one of our earlier studies of Northern Irish children's ideas about peace (McLernon 1998). McLernon had interpreted this emphasis on war-related images as evidence that Northern Irish children's ideas about peace are distorted by their perception of the state of peace in Northern Ireland, which is formally acknowledged by the presence of a ceasefire while acts of conflict such as beatings and paramilitary shootings continue to be carried out (Dunn 1995).

Also of interest was the fact that a considerable number of children (32 percent) used religious images to depict peace. Although church membership is important in Northern Ireland (Rose 1976; Cairns 1991), this is something we had not encountered in our earlier studies. We concluded that the emphasis on religious imagery in this study may be due in some part to the poetic medium used to elicit the children's ideas about peace and in part to the fact that the data were gathered in the run up to Christmas.

PEACE

I give my family peace.
I get peace playing my computer.
I get peace in the house.
You get peace when you are a sleep.

I get peace.
I always get peace.
Peace is quietness.
Peace is silence.

I like peace.

PEACE PROCESS POEM

When fighting has started
Look out John Hume[2] is about
When riots start
People can't go out

The bomb in Omagh[3]
was a tragic death
The fathers and mothers
Are very unhappy yet

The lads who did it
Come out wherever you are
If you don't
get very far

Peace is the answer
It's the only way
To solve this problem
Amidst our country today.

Peace, Eight Years On

In our most recent study (Cairns, McLernon, and Hakvoort 2003), we returned to the study of adolescents' views on war and peace and carried out a partial replication of our first study (McLernon, Ferguson, and Cairns 1997). The 2002 study, however, involved a much larger sample from Northern Ireland[4] than did the 1994 sample. Further, in the 2002 sample we used quota sampling techniques in order to ensure that the sample was made up of approximately equal numbers of Catholic and Protestant young people, with each denominational sample made up of approximately equal numbers of young people from working-class and middle-class backgrounds. Our aim was to examine Northern Irish children's concepts of war and peace some eight years after the initial ceasefires to see if these concepts differed in relation to the children's denominational backgrounds. In general terms we entertained two hypotheses. The first was that because the Catholic community in Northern Ireland appears to be embracing the peace process somewhat more enthusiastically than Protestant, Catholic young people would differ from Protestant young people in the way they were thinking about war, peace, and strategies to attain peace. Secondly, given that the peace process has now been going on for some time, we expected to find differences between our 1994 data and that gathered in 2002.

PARTICIPANTS: All of the participants were aged fourteen or fifteen years and were students at one of four high schools in Belfast, Northern Ireland. This age group was chosen because it matched our 1994 sample and also because this was a cohort of children who had spent their formative years (from age six onwards) in a Northern Ireland where (officially at least) peace reigned. The schools were chosen because of their location both in a middle-class or working-class area and because they were attended predominantly by either Catholic or Protestant students. A total of 346 young people provided usable data, of whom 59 percent were Catholic and 41 percent Protestant; 46 percent were working class and 54 percent were middle class, and 51 percent were girls and 49 percent were boys.

QUESTIONNAIRE: All participants completed the four-item questionnaire described above, as well as indicating their age and gender. School attended determined denomination, and social class was based on area of residence. The remaining questions elicited concepts of war, peace, and conflict resolution by means of open-ended questions. Questions 1–2 were identical to those used in the semistructured interview designed by Hakvoort and Oppenheimer (1993) to elicit ideas about war and peace. Question 3 was also similar to Hakvoort and Oppenheimer's (1993) original question about how peace might be achieved, but in the present study this question was set in the context of the Northern Irish troubles. Question 4 dealt with the adolescents' perceptions of whether or not their country or community was at war.

SCORING: We scored all responses to questions 1–3 using the scoring strategy devised by Hakvoort (1995), which is outlined below. In addition, responses to question 3 were subjected to a limited content analysis (see the appendix).

RESULTS: It is clear from table 1 that the majority of our participants did not think there is peace in Northern Ireland; in fact, only 4 percent held this opinion. This is a somewhat surprising result given that the peace process has now been ongoing for the last eight years. At the same time, only half of the sample were clear that the absence of peace indicated there is war, while the remainder were ambivalent. As we noted earlier, the perception is that Protestants are somewhat cooler toward the peace process than Catholics. A further surprise in our results, therefore, is that significantly more of the Catholic young people believed that there is war and significantly more of the Protestants fell into the "unsure" category.

Despite this we found no statistically significant differences between the Catholic and Protestant young people when we examined the concepts they held of either "war" or "peace." For both groups it was clear the majority thought of war primarily as involving activities such as killing and shooting (70 percent), and it is something that has negative consequences (people die, are unhappy, etc., 60 percent). Of particular interest was the fact that, for both groups of young people, peace was thought of primarily as the absence of hostilities between *groups,* not between individuals (60 percent).

In turn, we noted this definition of peace was probably related to how they tended to view strategies to attain peace. We made this observation because

TABLE 1

CATHOLIC AND PROTESTANT PERCEPTIONS OF WHETHER NORTHERN IRELAND IS AT PEACE OR WAR

	Catholic		Protestant		Total	
	N	%	N	%	N	%
War	120	58.3	61	43.6	181	**52.3**
Peace	9	4.4	4	2.9	13	3.8
Ambivalence	76	36.9	71	50.7	147	42.5
Total	206	100	140	100	346	100

NOTE: Column totals may exceed N because respondents could answer in more than one category. For the shaded categories, p < .05. Percentage in bold is modal response.

responses to the question "What do you think could be done to bring an end to the troubles in Northern Ireland and prevent any more fighting?" most often elicited responses that were categorized as "ending conflict at a global[5] or inter-group level" (59 percent). Further, while this was the modal response for all par-ticipants, significantly (p < .05) more Catholic young people (66 percent) than Protestant young people (49 percent) used this category.

What is interesting about the responses to this question on peace strategies is that the second most frequently used response is not, as it was with the con-cepts of peace responses, positive emotions at an individual level (52 percent). Rather, this time the second most common response was coded as positive emo-tions at a *global* (that is, intergroup) level (33 percent). Responses coded in this category emphasize the need, for example, for "different peoples to talk and to be involved in cultural exchanges." Finally, while only a minority (14 percent) of all responses could be categorized as "negative evaluations of peace in North-ern Ireland," this response was used by significantly (p < .05) more Protestant young people (19 percent) than Catholics (10 percent).

An innovation in our 2002 study was that we introduced content analysis for the peace strategies question. That is, as well as using Hakvoort's coding sys-tem, which is designed so as to be content free, we analyzed the actual responses given to the peace strategies question in terms of their specific Northern Ireland content. We were able to identify fourteen different types of response (see appen-dix), which included such things from "no solution is possible" or called for the elimination (or displacement) of the out-group, to more conservative strategies such as "get everyone to like each other" or "create a climate of equality."

It is encouraging to note that potentially divisive solutions such as "eliminating the out-group" were only employed by small numbers of respondents. In fact, just four categories accounted for most of the responses. These were, in rank order, integration/equality, political concrete, accept/like each other, and legal/military (see table 5 below). We also found statistically significant Catholic/Protestant differences on only two of these Northern Ireland–specific strategies. These were "United Ireland," which no Protestants mentioned and just 12 percent of Catholics mentioned, and "displacing the out-group,"[6] mentioned by 10 percent of Catholics and 17 percent of Protestants.

In addition to comparing the responses given by the Catholic and Protestant young people, we also compared the two data points in 1994 (before and after the ceasefire) with the data gathered in early 2002. Admittedly, this is a somewhat speculative exercise as the 1994 sample was much smaller[7] and less carefully drawn. Another problem was that we had no data to fill in the gaps between 1994 and 2002. Nevertheless, given the scarcity of data in this area, we felt justified in carrying out this exercise.

There were differences (between 1994 and 2002) in five of the twelve categories we used to code the young people's concepts of war (see table 2). Three of these categories appear to indicate an increase when comparing 1994 and 2002 data (weapons/soldiers, war activities, and negative consequences); only one indicates a decrease—conflict (one-sided). What is interesting about these results is that they have taken place against a background of a marked decrease in military activities (both state and extrastate) in Northern Ireland over the same time period.

Our interpretation was that with the beginning of the ceasefire people in Northern Ireland moved away from using denial/distancing as a coping mechanism and were able to acknowledge for the first time that they had been living through a war. This resulted not just in more conversations about the Troubles but also more retrospective media coverage, particularly television programs. While the participants in our study were unlikely to have employed denial/distancing before the ceasefires (they would have been only about seven years of age in 1994), they have been exposed to this additional discourse about the Troubles and the increased in-depth media coverage, hence the increased references to weapons, war activities, and the negative consequences of war in particular.

It is also interesting that our 2002 participants were less likely to define war as a one-sided conflict. It could be argued that a major obstacle to peace in Northern Ireland has been a lack of insight into the "mutual character" of the conflict. We take the fact that young people's tendency to view war in this one-sided way is apparently decreasing to be an encouraging trend in our results.

TABLE 2 _____

CONCEPTS OF WAR, 1994–2002

	1994, Before Ceasefires (%)	1994, After Ceasefires (%)	2002 (%)
(N)	**(56)**	**(61)**	**(346)**
Missing or don't know	0	2	0
Peace-related	0	0	0
Weapons/soldiers	9	31	36
Quarrel (individual)	2	3	2
War activities	27	43	**70**
Human aspects of war	0	5	1
Negative consequences	25	**46**	60
Positive consequences	0	2	3
Negative emotions	7	26	26
Conflict (one-sided)	**61**	25	15
Qualitative evaluation	34	26	29

NOTE: Column totals may exceed N because respondents could answer in more than one category. For the shaded categories, $p < .05$. Percentages in bold are modal responses.

Given the differences noted above involving concepts of war, it was puzzling that, despite eight years of the peace process, there were very few differences evident when we examined concepts of peace (see table 3) and strategies to attain peace in Northern Ireland (see table 4) in the 1994 and 2002 samples. A much larger proportion in 2002 (52 percent) mentioned positive emotions at an individual level when thinking about peace (the 1994 figures were 12 and 21 percent pre- and post-ceasefires, respectively). Also, when talking about strategies to attain peace, more 2002 participants (59 percent) mentioned negation of war at a global level than had done so in 1994 (30 percent before and 28 percent after the ceasefires).

Finally, and perhaps not unrelated to the results noted above, fewer of our 2002 participants than from any other time reported that Northern Ireland was a society enjoying peace (see table 5). In fact, the 2002 sample was evenly split between war and ambivalence. Apparently, any belief that there was peace in Northern Ireland—a sentiment that appeared to be growing among young people in 1994—may now have evaporated.

TABLE 3
Concepts of Peace, 1994–2002

	1994, Before Ceasefires (%)	1994, After Ceasefires (%)	2002 (%)
(N)	**(56)**	**(61)**	**(346)**
Missing or don't know	7	3	1
War-related	0	0	1
Religion/church	2	2	10
Material-related	0	0	0
Nature/pollution	0	0	3
Positive emotions (individual)	12	21	52
Positive emotions (global)	32	10	20
Negation of war (individual)	5	7	1
Negation of war (global)	**66**	**64**	**60**
Disarmament	4	8	3
Human attitudes	16	8	12
Universal rights	2	15	1

Note: Column totals may exceed N because respondents could answer in more than one category. For the shaded categories, $p < .05$. Percentages in bold are modal responses.

Conclusions

The studies we have reported here have adopted slightly different methodologies and have used a wide range of age groups drawn from different parts of Northern Ireland. Despite this it could be argued that a coherent pattern can be discerned in the various results. This is because, overall, one gets the impression that if anything the peace process has had an impact only on the concepts of war and peace of older children and adolescents. However, this has not been a consistent impact but rather one that has been as varied as the peace process itself. As in the Northern Irish population at large (and particularly the Protestant portion of that population), it would appear that the peace process had its biggest impact at its very beginning, in 1994–95. This is when the most dramatic changes were noted among adolescents. Since then an optimistic reading of our data indicates that there may have been some permanent gains, but these have not been as marked as the changes that took place in 1994.

TABLE 4 —————————————————————————————————

STRATEGIES TO ATTAIN PEACE, 1994—2002

	1994, Before Ceasefires (%)	1994, After Ceasefires (%)	2002 (%)
(N)	(56)	(61)	(346)
War-related	3	0	0
Religion/church	0	0	2
Material-related	0	0	0
Nature/pollution	0	2	0
Positive emotions (individual)	2	2	11
Positive emotions (global)	**43**	**41**	33
Negation of war (individual)	5	8	4
Negation of war (global)	30	28	59
Disarmament	5	23	13
Human attitudes	39	7	23
Universal rights	7	7	1

NOTE: Column totals may exceed N because respondents could answer in more than one category. For the shaded categories, p < 05. Percentages in bold are modal responses.

TABLE 5 —————————————————————————————————

ANSWERS TO SURVEY QUESTIONS, "IS THERE WAR/PEACE IN YOUR COUNTRY?" 1994–2002

	1994, Before Ceasefires (%)	1994, After Ceasefires (%)	2002 (%)
(N)	(56)	(61)	(346)
War	**62**	30	**52**
Peace	29	**44**	4
Ambivalence	7	30	43

Note: For shaded categories, p < .05. Percentages in bold are modal responses.

Where younger children are concerned, it is probably correct to say that the peace process has only had a minimal impact on their conceptions of war and peace. Further, this has been true regardless of the methodology we have used in our attempts to overcome young children's lack of verbal ability. With hindsight all of this is not surprising given the, at times, subtle or even confusing messages emanating from the ongoing peace process. In an earlier report on this program of research (McLernon and Cairns 1999), we were perhaps rather more optimistic. Then we were impressed by small changes that we noted had taken place over a short period of time. What we are now suggesting is that these changes have not been consolidated, at least in the minds of younger children in Northern Ireland.

On the positive side it is of course encouraging that we have found relatively few Catholic/Protestant differences. One worrying note, however, is that there is a hint in our results that Catholic and Protestant young people may have slightly different views of what constitutes peace. In particular, young Catholics are more likely to see peace as involving an equality agenda than are Protestants. This observation reinforces that made by McEvoy (2000), who in 1998 conducted focus groups with Catholic young people in Northern Ireland. What she noted was that among some of these young people, "peace was envisioned as practical parity of esteem for all citizens" (97).

Perhaps the most surprising of our conclusions is that Northern Irish children's basic understanding of peace as the absence of war is little different from those of children living in societies free from political conflict. Furthermore, age-related changes amongst Northern Irish children reflect developmental changes observed in previous studies in other countries. The main differences in the peace images of Northern Irish children are in the children's emphasis on war-related images, thereby underlining the confusing effect of societal events on the children's understanding of the concept of peace. This in turn may be related to Jagodic's (2000) comment that younger children possess more affirmative attitudes toward war perhaps because their "developmental level does not allow them to understand the ideological dilemma of war" (253). All of this could of course be interpreted as suggesting that the conflict in Northern Ireland has had only a minimal impact (if any) on Northern Irish children's concepts of war and peace. Indeed, this is the interpretation we favor. On the other hand, it is worth raising another possible interpretation.[8] This is the possibility that children in all Western societies are being influenced by a global culture of violence. If this is the case, it may be that peace education faces an even bigger challenge, and not just in societies such as Northern Ireland.

Overall, however, we would contend that at the very least our work has again underlined the need for further research in this area where "Knowledge about the developmental course of children's and adolescents' understanding of peace and war is scarce" (Raviv, Oppenheimer, and Bar-Tal 1999). Further, as these authors point out, while we know something about children's ideas about war, what we do not know enough about is how children acquire knowledge about peace defined in terms of harmony, cooperation, and coexistence—in other words, positive peace (see Galtung 1985).

Only when we acquire this knowledge can we institute what Cairns (1996) has argued is necessary—peace as an integral subject in the curriculum. Certainly this is what McEvoy (2000) suggests is required in Northern Ireland when she notes among young people a "pessimistic inability to imagine peace" (2000, 101) because "the depth of their vision and their expectations have been shaped by their experiences" (2000, 102). This, above all, is what we would conclude from our research: that the political and historical context in which children and young people find themselves, however confusing this may be, does impact their ideas about war and perhaps particularly their ideas about peace. What we now need is more research investigating which factors mediate between the sociocultural context in which children find themselves and their ideas about peace so that, in turn, we can help to create a true culture of peace, particularly in post-conflict societies.

NOTES

1. The author of the poem refers to the deaths of Richard (eleven), Mark (ten), and Jason (nine) Quinn in Bailymoney, County Antrim, in July 1998. The three brothers were killed by a petrol bomb thrown into their house in a sectarian attack by Loyalists.

2. John Home was the leader of the Catholic/Nationalist Social Democratic and Labor Party (SDLP) between 1979 and 2001.

3. An IRA dissident splinter group called the Real IRA (rIRA) exploded a bomb in Omagh, County Tyrone, in 1998, killing twenty-nine people and injuring more than two hundred.

4. The 2002 study did not take place in the exact same locations as the 1994 study.

5. Here and elsewhere we have chosen to interpret Hakvoort's use of the term "global" to include any response that did not indicate that the respondent had in mind an action involving individuals acting as individuals.

6. Examples of such strategies included "send them back to where they came from," or "let them live in the South if they like it so much."

7. Further, given the small numbers in 1994, we had to treat the sample as one rather than making separate Catholic and Protestant comparisons.

8. We are grateful to Siobhán McEvoy-Levy for drawing this alternative interpretation to our attention.

Appendix

Categories for Content Analysis of Specific Northern Irish Peace Solutions

Category	Label	Example
0	No Answer	
1a	Accept/Like Each Other	Wise up (vague); understand each other; just get on; stop fighting; forget the past
1b	Integration/ Equality	Live together; go to school together, mix more; treat all equally; eliminate religions; no flags
1c	Separation	Keep sides apart; divide Northern Ireland into Catholic and Protestant areas
1d	Religion	Follow Jesus, love thy neighbour
2a	Political Vague	Bring leaders together; think about lives lost
2b	Political Concrete	Get a compromise; start talks; get a peace agreement; two sides talk to each other
2c	United Ireland	United Ireland; all one country; Ireland to be free
2d	Decommissioning	Get rid of guns; give up guns; disarming
3a	Legal/Military	Eliminate paramilitaries/gangs; stop punishment beatings; longer sentences, more police; more soldiers
3b	Legal/Military	Send army away; new police force
4a	Out-group Eliminated	Kill all . . . .
4b	Out-group Displaced	Send out-group back to . . . ; Brits out; send out-group home
5a	No Solution Can Be Found	Nothing can be done; it's hopeless; it will go on for ever
5b	No Solution I Can Think Of	I can't think of anything

Siobhán McEvoy-Levy

Politics, Protest, and Local "Power Sharing" in North Belfast

A young girl sporting a Celtic top came rushing up the street to her mother, gasping: "They're not letting any of our ones through but they're letting the Orangees through." Her mother told her to calm down but she ran off in excitement to where crowds of nationalists had gathered.... The police aim was to keep protestors off the Crumlin Road in order to allow the Orange parade[1] a safe passage. But the main rioting erupted in a side street off Ardoyne Road around 7PM as police pushed nationalists right back into their neighbourhood. At first minor skirmishes broke out between individuals and police, which led to sporadic surges of people towards police shields. Riot police then ringed off the garden of an end-terrace at the corner of Estoril Park and faced men, women and children who stood shouting abuse from the garden. I don't know what triggered it and certainly nothing was thrown, but suddenly police had scaled the fence and, using their shields, were pushing people into the open doorway of the house. One woman was severely battered with a police shield and another was rammed against the wall of the house. Similar scenes happened minutes later at houses on the front of the Crumlin Road. Cries of "you're trespassing" and worse expletives fell on deaf ears as police seemed determined not just to move people off the streets but to pen them into their houses. There were shrieks and scuffles and at this point everything degenerated. A mob of mainly young men advanced towards Ardoyne Road from Estoril Park which was sealed off with a line of police. The heavens then opened and police were pounded with showers of bricks and bottles. Angry youths grabbed anything they could get their hands on as the rioting turned vicious. One man standing on a wall dropped a car wheel on the head of a police officer, smashed a mop handle off his shield and, when he had exhausted all possibilities, spat on him. A wheelbarrow, screwdriver and saucepan were among the collection of items hurled at police and overly-keen journalists. As the missiles continued, water cannon were deployed. It was a security operation in itself to manoeuvre the huge black tank past the fleet of Land Rovers and into Estoril Park. Rioters were blasted with jets of water but the cannon quickly emptied and by the time the alternative tank came in, police had taken another battering. A constant stream of injured officers were dragged to safety and first aid was administered on the rubble-strewn pavement as onlookers cheered. And all this before an Orangeman was even in sight. A police message repeatedly warned rioters that baton rounds would be fired if calm was not restored—but the battle was just starting. (Anne Madden, "Chaos as Night Is Lost to Angry Mob," *Irish News*, July 14, 2001)

This news report is just one of scores of accounts illustrating that post-accord does not mean post-conflict in Northern Ireland. Four years after the Good Friday/Belfast Agreement (1998), one manifestation of the continuation of war by other means in Northern Ireland is the increase in public disorder at marches and interface fighting or "recreational rioting," as it is sometimes called when youth are involved (Jarman and O'Halloran 2001). Although all sectors of community take part, a recent official report, *Managing Disorder,* notes: "Over the past few years, the role played by young people in recreational rioting and sustaining tension in interface areas has been widely noted by local residents, community workers, by political representatives and by the police" (Jarman 2002, 33). This chapter reports on part of a study began shortly after the Good Friday Agreement in 1998, the last focus group interviews of which were conducted in late 2001. The aim of this study was to generate themes useful for designing peace-building[2] practice from the deliberations of young people about their lived experience of the conflict and peace process. This chapter reports on focus groups conducted in North Belfast in June of 2001. North Belfast has been the location of some of the worst violence during the conflict; despite the peace process, localized interface violence continues there, as well as intracommunal feuding over extortion rackets and drug dealing territories.

The thesis of this chapter is that young people create politics, whether they or adults are aware of it or not. They do so through their actions, through the meaning they give to those actions, and through their narration of their actions and experience among themselves, with their families, and in formal settings for dialogue such as these focus groups. Although the politics (political meaning) they create often aids conflict reproduction, paradoxically, it is also in these politics that young people's peace-building potential can be found. This peace-building potential emerges in their critical questioning of the status quo, but it is a potential inhibited by structural and cognitive factors. The structural factors are their insecurity and political exclusion, and the cognitive factors are their inability to imagine peace and experience empathy in relation to the "other." The crucial task for peace builders is to address those cognitive barriers by changing the structural barriers.

Looking at youth involvement in post-accord violence as primarily a problem of "recreational rioting" leads to solutions based around diverting young people's attention to leisure and training. This is a good in itself but would not be enough to end the phenomenon. Similarly, to focus on the role of parents or community authority figures including paramilitaries, while important, is only a partial solution because the power these groups have over young people is ambiguous and contested. National or economic structural change is a long-term endeavor; thus, it is important to provide meaningful ways for young people to address both their insecurity and their political exclusion in the present. The conclusion offers some recommendations for how this can be done by developing a model of local power sharing through which young people can have political voices and work actively to address violence in its many forms. Changing local structures of political exclusion and realistically addressing the problem of youth, particularly young male, insecurity is the first step toward changing mindsets; toward instituting grassroots democracy, dialogue, and a futurist orientation; and a means to meet the "other" in collaborative peace building. Lederach (2003, 1) has identified "the lack of authentic engagement of the public sphere" as one of the most "significant weakness[es]" of post-agreement peace building to date. Through the following excerpts from the focus groups, I hope to show that young people have the ability and the will to be active political participants in the peace process and that the conditions of their existence as subjects of that peace process make it imperative to include them or risk conflict escalation.

METHODOLOGY

The young people were consulted through focus groups conducted in community centers, youth centers, and schools. Focus group interviewing, as defined by Morgan, is a research technique that collects data through group interaction

(1996, 129–52). The strengths of focus groups, according to Morgan and Krueger, are their capacity for providing observed data on "the extent and nature" of agreement and disagreement in groups; their ability to offer "insights into the sources of complex behaviors and motivations"; and their "unique" provision of a respectful, "humane" environment for "emotionally charged" discussions (1993, 16–18). Johnson argues that critical social scientists might use focus groups for "raising consciousness and empowering participants, rupturing rather than reproducing underlying relations of exploitation and domination" (1996, 519–39). Feminist researchers have emphasized how focus groups enable the participants to direct, shape, or curtail, if not gain interpretative control, of the discussions (Nichols-Casebolt and Spakes 1995; Montell 1995). The focus group method has been found to be useful in identifying "cultural knowledge," providing the researcher with the appropriate language, concerns, and conceptual frameworks to enhance the effectiveness of expanded studies (Hughes and Dumont 1993) and, it is hoped, to derive appropriate peace-building techniques.

In the focus groups, Freire's "generative themes" approach was adopted (Freire 2001, 96–97). The participants were invited into a dialogue about their experiences by first defining three abstract concepts—peace, violence, and community. Beyond this initial structure, the conversations were allowed to take their own form through unstructured interviews, with each group of young people setting their own agenda and the researcher following up with related questions. The purpose of this approach was to probe young people's experience and ideas without activating conventional wisdoms about the nature of the conflict or peace building or conformity with the perceived expectations of the researcher.[3] If the aim is to produce effective mechanisms for violence prevention and peace building with youth, it is important to reproduce for reflection and analysis the ways in which young people themselves perceive and interpret their experience, reflecting on the conditions of their own existence, their own analyses of the reasons for conflict, and their own ideas for effecting change. The data is analyzed following Scott's (1990) identification of "public" and "hidden" transcripts in popular discourses. In my analysis the "public transcript" is the reflexive, close-to-consciousness, everyday reality that the participants reproduce. It is somewhat performative, rising to expectations, but also strategic and certainly political. The "hidden transcript" is also political and consists of items unsaid, obliquely referred to, glossed over, or denied. It is important to look for both forms of discourse in a long-divided, conflicted society where a great deal of political and sectarian speech occurs and where there are perils of internal and external censure or even physical harm attached to political speech.

Additionally, the young people's dialogues are examined as strategic thinking relevant to the conflict trajectory. "Once a conflict has acquired a certain dynamic (for example, escalatory, de-escalatory, violent or peaceful), the dynamic tends to feed on itself and become prolonged" (Reychler 2001, 7). Strategic thinking conducive to conflict escalation, according to Reychler, involves zero-sum perceptions; negative stereotyping; a preference for tactics involving threats, violence, and exclusion; goals of hurting the other and winning; fear of losing face; and a perception of violence as the "most cost-effective option." De-escalatory strategic thinking as identified by Reychler involves win-win perceptions; deconstruction of stereotypes; preference for tactics of persuasion; problem-solving and integration; goals of "doing well"; war weariness and perception of stalemate; and no fear of losing face (8). Finally, the dialogues are also examined for the extent to which they involved creative and constructive "imagining" of the future and of peace. Boulding (1990) argues that peace must be imagined before it can be built. Cairns (1996) states that understanding how young people perceive "war" and "peace" is essential before evaluating their potential for conflict reproduction and transformation (see also Hall 1993). Haavelsrud and Hakvoort and Oppenheimer identify "dialogue about what peace is and how it can be achieved" as central to peace education (Haavelsrud 1987, 363; Hakvoort and Oppenheimer 1993, 65).

"To tell you the truth, I love riotin'"

This excerpt is from a focus group conducted in the summer of 2001 with a group of young women, aged between thirteen and eighteen, in Mount Vernon estate, North Belfast.[4] McKay describes this particular public housing estate as follows:

> Mount Vernon is one of the estates in which the paramilitary presence is most obvious. It is like a broken-down fortress. Built on a steep hill, the estate of redbrick houses, maisonettes and blocks of bricked-up flats looms over the Shore Road, its entrance marked by a huge, crudely painted mural of armed and masked men. "Prepared for peace, ready for war" its equivocal message. Almost every lamp-post had a purple UVF flag. The area was the centre of several ongoing feuds in 1999 . . . The UVF in Mount Vernon was said to be well armed but paralysed by fears that some of its members were informers. (2000, 60)

Despite the Good Friday/Belfast Agreement and official ceasefires, the participants in the Mount Vernon focus groups describe continuing conflict conducted at the micro level, neighborhood by neighborhood, through street violence and intimidation. Although the initial agenda entailed the abstract questions on peace and community, the participants chose to refocus the discussion on an issue that most energized them that summer: local riots and antagonism between Protestants and Catholics. The young women describe riots as fun—"it's brilliant," "I love it"—supporting the "recreational rioting" thesis; but they also view rioting as "protest." What are they protesting? Initially, they cite the rerouting of the Drumcree[5] parade and perceived local Catholic encroachment on their "territory." They list places by name that they fear they will lose (mostly other public housing estates all within a few square miles of each other, each in a state of considerable economic deprivation). But later they protest a different reality—a political exclusion specific to their youth status (rather than an ethnic/national group exclusion). These different forms of protest coexist with the actions of building and policing barricades. In the dialogue the "public transcript" is of being under siege from neighboring working-class Catholics who are "taking over everywhere." But these youth are also subject to internal policing and to the wider vilification of other Protestants and society at large, and this marginality is contained in a "hidden transcript" of how even their own group fuels their sense of vulnerability.

LINDSAY: If it wasn't for them there would be peace.

Q. Why do you say that?

ELIZABETH: Because they won't let the Orangemen walk up the Garvaghy road.[6]

LINDSAY: And this is our country. This WAS our country and we gave them one county and they're takin' it all over now.

Q. You gave them one county? Which county?

LINDSAY: My mother was telling me the other day. I don't know but it was one of them.

ELIZABETH: Well the way I put it is it's our fault for letting them take over. They should a done something about it. They should've fought.

SARAH: Yeah, fight. We should fight.

LINDSAY: They'll never take over Mount Vernon though.

MICHELLE: They're takin' over everywhere. Sure they're taking over the [Tiger's] Bay next.

ELIZABETH [UNDER HER BREATH]: They'll never get it.

Q. What exactly would happen? Do you mean Catholics would move in?

ELIZABETH: Yeah. They'd move in and then it would be all Fenian, [apologetically] all Catholic. But they're not going to take over Mount Vernon. They'll never take over the Shankill either.

LINDSAY: All up Fortwilliam and all used to be all Prod. That's all Taigs [Catholics] now.

Q. Does it make you angry? Does it make you frightened to think about it?

ELIZABETH [QUICKLY]: Doesn't make me frightened.

SARAH: No.

ELIZABETH: To tell you the truth, I love riotin'.

LINDSAY: It's brilliant. We'll all get to walk again—the Orangemen.

Q. How do the riots start?

SARAH: We go out at about half four or five [for] everybody coming from work.

ELIZABETH: There's [little] kids but they don't stand in the road, they wait at the bonfire [*sic*] field, you know what I mean. Then there's the likes of us, 13 to about 18, 19. We're the ones that blocks the road and then when all the riotin' starts, the older ones arrive. We all look out for each other.

SARAH: Don't get me wrong like, see when we do have a peaceful protest and wee old men and women come along in cars like, I probably let them through.

ELIZABETH: But you can't.

LINDSAY: You can't or there's no chance.

[. . .]

ELIZABETH: It's not that we riot, we protest [emphasized] and then the peelers [police] aggravate it

MICHELLE: Yeah.

ELIZABETH: And then we end up riotin'. But it's the peelers that start it, get people out.

MICHELLE: We're just protestin'. It's peaceful. It's our community. All we're doin' is just blockading the road.

SARAH: They come with their landrovers. Sure, they near knocked me down one year.

ELIZABETH: They were goin' to mohawk me last year.

[. . .]

Q. Why do you think the police do that?

SARAH: It keeps them uns busy.

ELIZABETH: You know what it is. It's the money. If there's any riotin' they get paid more. See if they're on 7 pound an hour, they get triple that. In case any of them get hurt. That's why they love it, they get more money.

[. . .]

Q. So have the community leaders ever had discussions with the police about it?

ELIZABETH: We have community police. They take the young ones out but nothin's happened.

LINDSAY: Until they kill a child.

Q. What would happen in that case?

ELIZABETH: There'd be murder.

LINDSAY: There would.

ELIZABETH: And it doesn't matter a policeman still has to go to jail because it's still murder.

LINDSAY: But the police ARE goin' to kill a child one of these years.

MICHELLE: It isn't just the police, all the cars that try to get past the protest too.

[AGREEMENT]

ELIZABETH: It's innocent people gettin' hurt too. Why a child of five that doesn't know what protestin' or riotin' means.

SARAH: Then there'll be the Catholics to blame too for not letting the Orangemen walk.

LINDSAY: It's excitin'. It's fun. It's amazin'.

ELIZABETH: Then there'll be the Catholics to blame too.

LINDSAY: I can see the world comin' to war. I can see Britain comin' to war again.

Q. What do you mean? War with who?

Lindsay: The Catholics. Like years ago, before I was born, before my mummy was born. There'll be war and there's all innocent people hurt. Like up the Shankill that was all innocent people hurt.

[. . .]

Q. So how has the peace process/agreement changed your lives?

Elizabeth: Hasn't.

[Long silence]

Michelle: Become more angrier at the Fenians [Catholics].

Sarah: You can see people angry around the barricades.

Elizabeth: The peelers are never out of here. Like up in Ardoyne there was a whole lot of innocent people hurt.

Sarah: There was all riotin', putting the Catholics out and them uns putting the Protestants out [of their houses].

Q. What's the explanation for it? Why is it happening now?

[In unison]: Because they're not letting the Orangemen walk down.

Q. And if they did would the riots stop?

[In unison]: No.

Elizabeth: Well. Huh [laughs] then the Catholics would start it. You see you can't please no one.

Q. There wouldn't be peace?

Elizabeth: Nobody knows what peace is. You could ask that question to anybody and nobody will know what peace is.

Sarah: Or what it's ever goin' to be like.

Michelle: People lie in bed at night and maybe think about peace. But there'll never be peace and Protestants and Catholics will never come together.

The impossibility of peace frames this discussion of the young people's involvement in street violence. First, it is the intransigence of the other that is reflexively noted as the barrier to peace. But by the end of the discussion they seem to reach an agreement that a lack of peace is due to a universal inadequacy. In making the assertion that "nobody knows," Elizabeth points us to the wider failure of society, adults, and politicians to make peace meaningful. Michelle portrays it as a something people dream about in private. The youngest of the group, Lindsay, eventually tries to put peace in a biblical context, describing it as if trying to recall Sunday school teachings from a long distance:

LINDSAY: God put us in this world to have no violence, peace. That's why the two doves, peace.

Q. What doves?

LINDSAY: Was there not a dove? They came out of Noah's ark to see if it was still rainin'. That means peace—two doves means peace.

This inability to imagine peace except as something distant, fabulous, or achieved through divine intervention contrasts with the personal efficacy these young women express in their authoritative descriptions of riots. Three years on from the Good Friday accord, the only meaningful reality is one of war, and their chosen identities are those of combatants and community defenders. In their own analysis the peace process has changed their lives little in practical ways and only made them angrier and more hard-line. As zero-sum thinkers—if we get what we want, they, the Catholics, will riot and vice versa—their concern is with remaining alert and maintaining a line. Images of the besieged collectivity are reflected not only in what they say about being under threat but also in how they say it: they speak in collaborative sentences—one backing the other up—in short, defiant statements of solidarity. In other language they also reference themselves as beleaguered. They talk about nearly being "mohawked" (killed) by Catholics and the police, and here the unconscious reference to themselves as settlers fighting against attacking Indians is broken down since the police too are the threatening "other," co-opted in defense of the unruly natives. Using Reychler's rubric, conflict escalation would be predicted by their zero-sum thinking; negative stereotyping; a preference for tactics involving threats, violence, and exclusion; goals of hurting the other and winning; and their fear of losing face.

A sense of vulnerability and the reactionary response is not only produced from a perception of being under threat from Catholics, however. In fact, a triple set of opponents is described: Catholics, Protestants who try to get through the barricades, and the police. The police are viewed within an individualist frame, operating out of economic self-interest; this reflects the changing relationships over the last decade between members of the security forces and working-class Protestants. There is residual resentment toward the police, who were once integral parts of Protestant working-class communities but were seen to have turned against these communities during civil disturbances related to the Anglo-Irish Agreement (AIA) of 1985. Members of the police force were threatened and attacked by Protestant/Loyalist protesters and many moved out of working-class neighborhoods to mixed or middle-class areas as a result. Although there has probably always been tension between working-class Protestants and the police,[7] since the peace process the rift has deepened, with the Drumcree parade controversy only the most visible example of how the conflict architecture has gradually shifted to pit Protestants not only against Catholics but against the security forces as well. Invariably in the focus groups, young Protestants perceived that the police unfairly targeted them. As Elizabeth expresses it, "the peelers are never out of here." Further extending the gap is the view that the educational qualifications needed for entry into the police force are now higher than those of most working-class Protestants.[8] While, in the short term, reforms under the Good Friday Agreement to make the police service more representative and inclusive of Nationalists crystallize a nostalgic loyalty (although it is not evident in the Mount Vernon discussion), in the long term they threaten further Protestant/Loyalist alienation.

Contrasted with the police, the young women's own self-images are of a morally virtuous collective who "all look out for each other," who are also kind to "wee old men and women" (though there is disagreement about the strategic consequences of this), and who are concerned for the safety of children. An important dramatization takes place when these young people state that eventually a child will be killed at the barricades. The prospect hangs there as an inevitability in the exclamation that there will be no change in their relationship with the police "until they [the police] kill a child." This parent-like statement reflects the disengagement of adults who are at best ambiguous about the involvement of their children in these protests (Jarman 2002). The young women pose themselves as substitutes for adult protectors, and, like the adults they replace, their concern seems more rhetorical than practical. Yet their limited power to effect change makes this rhetorical intervention significant because it contains within it a critique of the status quo—in posing the killing of a child as an inevitability, the speakers shock us to attention. The imagined consequences that escalate from the killing of a child to the "murder" of a policeman to "war with the Catholics" are a dramatization, a crescendo in the conversation, that make a case for change. As Shor argues, "Routine habits need dramatizing because they tend to fade into the background and become experienced as unchangeable nature rather than as transformable culture" (1996, 28). In this sequence, the young women resist the naturalization of their involvement in the riots, proposing the violence as transformable. Of course, this fantasy of an escalation in violence stands in stark contrast to the young women's inability to imagine peace and underscores the psychological barriers that violent ecologies place against peace building.

Jackson and Scott point out that "Children's participation in constructing their own everyday world takes place within the constraints set by their subordinate location in relation to adults" (2000, 153–54). These young people did explain their actions in direct relationship to the presence and attitudes of significant adults. One says, "I stay out [at the barricades] until I see my uncle coming and [then I] bolt"; another, "If I'm not in by 11 my mother knows there's riots on . . . she supports us, so she does." The first reflects a negotiated submission to adult control and the second autonomy granted by parental permissiveness. Both of the relationships described and the power distribution are ambiguous. Young people are uncertain of their power, as are their parents and communities. This ambiguity helps explain why youth workers, local politicians, and even paramilitaries claim that young people are not under their control. At the same time that they have uncertain roles in their communities, they are loyal and socially oriented and see their own actions at the barricades to a certain degree as altruistic community defense. The relationship between adults and youth is criticized in general, but loyalty to *the* community is unquestioned in public (and certainly not to a stranger). For example, they stated that they attended a young women's group but the activities of this group were "all confidential": "we're not allowed to tell you about that." These phenomena provide an entry point in terms of peace building with youth, suggesting that it is important to engage both their "mediating" presence and their developmental need for meaningful social action (see Berman 1997) while working within the realities of a communal deterrence system (a system that involves strict internal control as well as external opposition).

There is striking dissonance between the activism of the young women, who by their own admission helped build and defend barricades, and the discourse they adopt of how the police unfairly target "even women and children." They are dislodged in the patriarchal scheme—reinforcing it and challenging it at the same time. This is another example of how youth can occupy middle space between conformity and resistance. As adolescents/young adults, they occupy a liminal space, and it is unclear whether their actions at the barricades show youth leadership or followership. Nationalist struggles militate against rebellion in the classic sense of breaking with a community or familial norm. But the view that these actions are only due to conditioned sectarianism, manipulated by adults, is too simple. Even given the permissiveness of adults and the pressures to conform, these young women do assert a limited rebellion. One, who had attended an integrated school, later takes on the others in asserting that "not all" Catholics are untrustworthy. Although this claim ends in a shouting match, it is nevertheless debated by the group. More significantly, while the group did not really question the sectarian status quo, they did describe their own struggle to be heard and, in a way, to be politically counted.

In the analysis offered, the riots are posed at one level as a form of recreation but not as a habit that could never be reformed. The young women describe the riots as a response to external and internal stimuli including events (Drumcree), other actors (Catholics, adults in their own community, the police), rhetoric (war and peace talk from all sides), and rumor and misinformation (a perennial trigger of conflict).[9] The young women also perceive the riots within a wider context of their own political exclusion and moral marginality. The political exclusion experienced is both internal (local to their community) and external (at the state level).

Q. What would you tell the government or politicians needs to be done to make peace?

MICHELLE: We don't know. We can't go to the government and say what's got to be done. We'll never come together and there'll never be peace.

ELIZABETH: Our opinion? The government would rip that up and throw it in the bin. THEY don't care. They only listen to Gerry Adams.[10]

Q. Why's that?

SARAH: Maybe he paid them to listen to him.

Similar to their analysis of police action, the young women's tentative analysis here is that their economic marginality contributes to their political invisibility. The gap in political understanding (and lack of voice) is filled by a sense of economic victimhood. This suggests that political education/ignorance and economic vulnerability mesh, a second factor that ought to be operationalized in peace building.

In the discussion, however, only one of the voices on display is the pro-Orange voice. The other, quieter voice, is that of class and generation. As established above, the young women are angry at the economically more advantaged police, but they also express discontent with adults in their own community.

ELIZABETH: People don't listen to us.

MICHELLE: People say kids should be seen and not heard.

ELIZABETH: But where do parents get all their information from? Kids! If there is anything happening on the Shore Road, where do they get it from? The kids! If there's any fightin' about.

SARAH: If my mother doesn't see me until about 11 o'clock, she knows there's riotin'.

ELIZABETH: What can you do?

The conclusion drawn here is that young people are denied recognition although they are vital sources of information and a barometer (and fuel) of conflict. But remedying this lack of recognition is beyond their control: "what can you [one] do?" Their invisibility leads to a certain irresponsibility in regard to conflict reproduction. But, again, as in the imagined scenario of a "war" brought about by the killing of a child at the barricades, this complaint contains within it a description of "transformable culture." The transformable culture is that of their own silence about their lived experience and their marginality from political decision making. It is evident from their narrative that pent up frustration and energy needs some outlet. "I actually was dying to get it all out," said one of the Mount Vernon participants when asked for their reactions to the session. "Nobody ever asks us our opinion about this," said another, "Everything else but this. Drugs and all that. Sex education." They explained this lack of political recognition as follows:

MICHELLE: Because people don't believe in what young people have to say. I don't think that's right.

ELIZABETH: Nor do I because, you see now, we're all goin' to have to grow up. It's our future. And they're sayin' vote for the future. So we're the one's that should be having the opinion because its goin' to be our future that they're fightin' for. So we have to have an opinion.

SARAH: And we have to tell our kids and keep it going through.

Noticeable is the future orientation of these claims to political voice; they are not a claim to political voice in the present. One implication of this is that if the aim is to counter the reality of war, young people such as these need access to forms of constructive, activist telling (to replace violence) and need to be given real roles in the present peace process, a theme that will be revisited in the conclusions below. But would this kind of opening of the political system to youth voices promote conflict reproduction or transformation? Sarah says that her political action in the future will entail passing down to her children the need to "keep it going through"—in other words, to hold the line against Catholic/Nationalist encroachment. On the face of it, this does not engender optimism. But this is Sarah's future projection based on present realities. It may be possible to change the future through the act of consultation because in actual democratic participation would be concrete lessons about, and practice in, power sharing.

Finally, there is the problem of a wider, social exclusion. Compared with the community defenders theme, the theme of economic marginality is not well developed beyond the argument that the police are motivated by danger money and another exchange on the relative worth of local politicians based on whether they were successful in getting people showers or gas lines in their homes. But these two economic rationales—for involvement in riots and for supporting certain politicians—identify the young women's limited economic opportunity structure. Some more attention was given in the discussions to the young women's sense of their moral marginality. Mount Vernon estate is known not only as a source of sectarian violence; it is also known because of violence associated with paramilitary drug dealing and internal Loyalist feuding. In some newspapers it has been called "Mount Vermin," a term coined by the father of a British soldier killed by the Mount Vernon Ulster Volunteer Force (UVF)—an illegal paramilitary organization—over drug dealing (McKay 2000, 60). Later in the interview I asked the young women, "What do you think that people from outside think of you?" They were in agreement: "They hate Mount Vernon."

SARAH: They do, they hate Mount Vernon. It's always in the paper in all. About drugs and all in Mount Vernon. But there's no drugs. Just evil people, that's all that is. Because our community's coming together people have to try and ruin it.

MICHELLE: It says that in the papers that it is a drug estate and all and there's none of that in Mount Vernon.

ELIZABETH: They've had their mistakes like. Like in every estate.

Q. What kind of mistakes?

[THERE ARE A FEW LAUGHS, THEN SILENCE]

Q. Don't want to go into too much detail?

ELIZABETH: No.

In the euphemism "mistakes," and the refusal to articulate or admit to them, we can read a "hidden transcript" involving habituation to violence and fear of becoming targets within their own community by speaking against the paramilitaries involved in drug dealing, as well as an unwillingness to collaborate in defining their own marginality.

Overall, the focus group discussion and the actions it described are an expression of, and a demand for, agency. In their narrative of involvement in Drumcree-related protests, setting up barricades, and rioting, these young women assert their control over their environment while recognizing its instability. One says she would let some people through the barricades but another replies, "you can't, or there's no chance." The assertion of their (limited) control over territory and local people's comings and goings substitutes for other forms of political agency; they have no role in ceasefires and settlements, no sense of ownership of the peace process, ambiguous, confusing roles in their own community, and little control over how they are portrayed and viewed from outside.

This lack of roles is filled by a number of self-constructed social identities: Orange defenders, community defenders, members of a morally virtuous youth gang, economically marginal, morally marginal, undervalued in their own community, silent witnesses, voiceless, and "kids."

When Elizabeth says, "To tell you the truth, I love riotin'," this is not so much a confidence as a commentary about "truth" and a defiant response to the question, "Are you frightened?" The "truth" serves a purpose, in this case to express autonomy and choice but also to perform as expected. In this contradiction lies the problem of youth. They resist but also seek to serve and be included. In the Mount Vernon discussion the sectarian and ethno-political discourse is the "public transcript"—exclamations that the Orangemen will march again and that they (Catholics) are taking over everywhere. The "public transcript" is performative, a fulfillment of an expectation but also strategic in that it creates boundaries and threatens. Its performative qualities do not make it fake or apolitical but only part of the political story. There also exists a "hidden transcript." In it, claims such as "But where do parents get all their information from—kids" and that the police are against them involve speaking truth to adults and to the Protestant establishment. Yet there also exists an even further buried transcript of glossed over "mistakes" and "confidential" meetings that remind us not only of adult influence behind the scenes and of the limitations placed on young people's own identity development and behavior by the dynamics of communal deterrence (see also Darby 1986, 1990) but also the social and political context at the micro level that must be engaged. Each of these layers must be addressed when considering the meaning young people attach to their actions.

As shown in the Mount Vernon discussion, interviewing young people in a community setting in a community or youth center makes possible spontaneous group dialogues that closely mirror real life conversations but also reproduce the community tensions and censorship that mark everyday life. In the next example, the young people are interviewed in a school setting, and this forum seems to have enabled a more analytical approach. The participants stay closer to the script of abstract questions and sometimes adopt a problem-solving stance (part of Reychler's predictor of conflict de-escalation). But like the Mount Vernon participants, they also display escalatory strategic thinking. The discussion is also frank, but it contains less personal admissions of involvement in interface violence, perhaps illustrating a self-censorship given the school environment. Clearly, both methods have advantages and disadvantages. This focus group discussion is between young Catholic men from St. Patrick's College in North Belfast and was also conducted in the same week of the summer of 2001.[11] The members of this group were older, all aged between seventeen and eighteen. The participants were local people from the Nationalist sides of some of the interface areas in North Belfast, including Ardoyne and New Lodge.

"You'd rather get a beatin' than get shot dead, you know. [As] long as you wake up"

While the Mount Vernon participants perceived that peace was so unlikely as to be beyond discussion, the focus group of Catholic boys from North Belfast defined it in ways that echoed the Protestant girl's concern with control over space and person. Their answers to the question "What is peace" were immediate and succinct and dwelled on a theme of personal security and freedom of movement:

Q. What is peace?

KIERAN: Freedom to walk wherever you want.

MICHAEL: Not havin' to watch your back.

KIERAN: Goin' to or from other areas.

JOHN: Freedom to be everything you want to be.

MICHAEL: Havin' places where you can learn Irish culture and language—for everyone.

[GENERAL AGREEMENT]

SEAN: I would say no violence.

MICHAEL: And no worry.

Their narrow definitions of peace as the absence of violence are expanded by the two respondents who cite freedom to develop one's full potential (John) and freedom to learn about and practice Irish culture (Michael). This last definition received general approval. However, as the discussion progressed and the participants were asked what they thought their lives would be like in ten years, none developed an expansive definition of peace or social justice. None held the apocalyptic vision of the "world coming to war" that the Mount Vernon group expressed. But only one, John, envisioned a major transformation from the status quo into the form of a united Ireland. The rest agreed with this analysis:

MICHAEL: What will the future be like? Exact same thing we're doin' now. There'll still be people talkin' 'bout violence on the streets. There'll still be Catholics moanin' that there's no opportunities and there'll still be Protestants moanin' that there's no opportunities for Protestants. . . . Oh, it'll be what *you'll* call peace. But at the same time the drug trade will go up, there'll be more cocaine, heroin and harder drugs on the street. Northern Ireland already has a lot of ecstasy. There'll be more cases of AIDS.

This pessimistic view of the future, although it seems resigned to conflict, contains a social and political critique. Michael places himself in opposition to a perceived societal agreement on "what you'll call peace." In the dramatization he creates he questions whether peace is the right word for a world of localized sectarian violence and increased drug use and crime.

When discussing the question "What is a community?" Michael defined it as people who were "all in the same ghetto." Asked to elaborate, one in the group defined a ghetto as a place where Catholics and Protestants are separate, "like blacks and whites." Another defined it as a "working class area." A third countered tendentiously, "Have you ever been to the New Lodge?" The New Lodge is a working-class housing estate, and this young person's sarcastic response is a challenge to the interviewer's seeming ignorance and distance from reality. Two define a ghetto as a place to which Catholics are restricted, kept in their community by Loyalist violence, as in this excerpt:

JOHN: They're [ghettos are] still developing areas. They still bein' developed. People haven't developed to their potential in the likes of New Lodge. Sometimes they're not being allowed out by what's on the streets and so you'll get them coming home from school, just knocking about on the street, getting blocked [drunk] and all that.

Although John begins by describing a state of unfulfilled potential, presumably economic and social, his definition turns into a description of social problems (youth alcohol abuse), which he attributes to the sectarian/security situation. The group only obliquely touched on economic issues.

Similarly, in describing what would make their lives better, these young people do not think in terms of social and economic justice, their own job futures, or even leisure or recreation.

Q. What would make your lives better?

JOHN: A united Ireland.

MICHAEL: North Belfast would be better if people weren't so bigoted that they couldn't understand other people. The DUP[12] still won't sit in the room with Sinn Fein even though in the last election they had the biggest majority. Sinn Fein are the biggest Nationalist party.

KIERAN: To be able to walk places—we're not safe.

SEAN: To be able to practice our faith.

MICHAEL: Not being afraid of stray cars driving down with no lights on. Not jumping into the bushes every time you see one.

[General agreement and laughs]

John: A bit of relief.

Nationalist identity and representation and a lone religious priority, but mostly physical security, dominate their concerns.

The same focus emerges in the response to the question "Do you think that politicians have young people's interests at heart?"

John: Not all the politicians. You look at the DUP's Nigel Dodds, he's on and on about IRA decommissioning, but he's not answering the question why should the IRA decommission when Loyalists are not decommissioning? The IRA may be in fear of another spree of tit-for-tat killings. It's only four years ago that they stopped killin' Catholics on the streets. So, what if that happens again and IRA weapons are decommissioned? There's no threat on the Loyalists to decommission their weapons. Just the other day there was a thousand pounds worth of semtex found in a block of flats where kids and all were livin'.

John expresses a politics developed in a lived environment where violence is a pragmatic response to a threat. Youth interests are reduced to self- and community preservation. As in the Mount Vernon discussion, the insistence that "kids" are imperiled makes the case urgent. In both of these cases, it could be argued that the use of the image of the child serves to demonize the opponent and justify violence and that the young people making these statements are exploiting children much in the same way adults do for political gain. However, as in the Mount Vernon discussion of the killing of a child at the barricades, this young Catholic evokes an image of endangered children, thereby underscoring his own vulnerability. This vulnerability is evident in the group's narratives of their everyday lives, having to "watch your back," "jumping into the bushes" to avoid suspicious cars, getting a "beatin'" or a "kickin'." John also has direct knowledge of a Loyalist attempt on a family member's life:

John: My stepdad dandered out sure and there was a bomb underneath his car, pipebomb underneath his car. He got up and was going out in the car but just looked underneath it and there was a bomb underneath it. Terrorists, Loyalists, had put it underneath his car.

The boys' preoccupation with their own physical security shapes their evaluation of the peace process, as in this excerpt echoing the zero-sum thinking of the Mount Vernon girls:

KIERAN: No. There'll never be peace. If a decision is made its goin' to affect
the Catholics or its goin' to affect the Protestants and they're not goin' to
stand for it because they haven't stood for it all these years and they're
not goin' to stand for it now. I don't think there's ever goin' to be peace.

The rest of the group used this statement as a launching pad for discussion of
the politics of the peace process, about which they expressed tangible resentment and disillusionment.

MICHAEL: 62% said yes in a Northern Ireland referendum[13] and you can't
turn back now and say we don't want that now. 62% said yes and that's
it and that's why it should go forward. That includes decommissioning,
demilitarization, and a new police force. Not reform of the police force, a
new police force for Northern Ireland. But the DUP and the UUP want
to wreck that. But you can't just because it isn't goin' your way and say
you want a new referendum.

KIERAN: It was agreed.

JOHN: It was agreed. They all signed it.

KIERAN: I don't think it will be implemented. There's still goin' to be people
complaining. Just like he says, the DUP are just hard-line Loyalists that
won't accept it and will keep their own guns. And then they say the IRA
should decommission. But what happens if they do decommission and the
referendum's implemented? There's no British troops on the streets.
There's this new IRA. There's this new police force. Do they all carry
guns or batons or what? Do they walk around in short-sleeved shirts?
Do they wear bulletproof vests? Then, the next thing the Loyalists carry
out a big killin' spree. That's what would happen then.

Kieran expresses incredulity that a "normal" state of law and order would be possible or even desirable. He grapples with, but cannot quite imagine, such conditions. The uncertainty of the peace process fuels this anxiety. His resistance is
rationalized by a vision of being defenseless.

Even under conditions of all-round decommissioning and demilitarization,
the gain, the group argues, would be "more security" rather than peace (previously defined as free movement and no worry). They would still be on the alert.

Q. What would have to happen for you to feel secure?

MICHAEL:The Loyalists would have to give up their guns.

Q. Would you feel secure then?

Michael: We'd feel securer.

Kieran: Securer.

John: You'd rather get a beatin' than get shot dead, you know. Long as you wake up.

Q. What would have to happen for you to feel secure?

John: Never happen.

Michael: You'll never . . . See in America, would a black man feel secure in a white man's neighborhood? No. Look at England now, would an Asian feel safe in parts that are all white? No. There's never goin' to be that in Northern Ireland. There's never goin' to be a utopia where everyone's holding hands saying Auld Lang Syne. It's never goin' to happen. Your goin' to need to stop looking for that there. Your goin' to need to look for somethin' that's goin' to end killin'. That's it, end killin'. It's never goin' to be what everybody perceives it to be.

Kieran: Its never goin' to be the way people think it will be, Protestants and Catholics all joining hands across New Lodge and all. It's never goin' to be like that.

John: Up in Ardoyne? [All laugh]

To general agreement, Michael again positions himself as speaking truth to liberal, middle-class notions of peace. The only relevant search he maintains is for a means to prevent deaths. All other aspirations for reconciliation are hopelessly utopian. As Michael illustrates, the ability to imagine peace is constrained by the demands of surviving in a still dangerous environment. In his experience, post-accord Northern Ireland remains a war zone. Michael rejects what he perceives to be a "touchy feely," liberal, "do-gooder" kind of peace of "why can't we all get along," but he does not have any other language or theory of conflict transformation through which to construct a more nuanced, socially situated, progressive peace. This is the entry point for peace builders/peace educators.

Michael also thinks beyond that narrow sphere to make comparisons with other situations of racial and ethnic conflict. His insight is that when there is a history of violence or injustice between people, the effects of that interaction leak into subsequent generations despite structural or institutional attempts to legislate or politically engineer solutions. Viewing racial and ethnic relations in the United States and Britain in this way promotes an understandably cynical or distanced view of a similar peace in Northern Ireland. Such cynicism is reinforced by the vagaries of the peace process itself. Michael's and the others' complaints about the decommissioning question illustrate how peace process crises and the sectarian nature of the political discussion and assembly dynamic erode popular support for peace. This is a different reason for disillusionment than that of the Mount Vernon girls, for whom the peace process had no original attraction or even solidity of form. The Catholic group's willingness to engage in defining peace illustrates their relatively more invested positions. But as the dialogue suggests, even Catholic investment is eroding.

Another takes it further to say: "I've lost interest because I think that if there was decommissioning and no war between Protestants and Catholics, and the Irish and the British, I think it would just go the way London is. There would be drugs and racism. A lot of places in America are like that too." The participant intuits that the kind of peace that may be created in Northern Ireland will not change their essential marginality. As (mostly working-class) young people they will bear the brunt of future social problems. He also challenges external judgment, pointing out that the Northern Ireland conflict is not an aberration, some stereotype of Irish irrationality; rather it is the rule, and many people who judge and comment upon it—such as academics and journalists—come from places with their own, similar, problems. "A lot of things have been said about this place. The first thing I'd say to people outside of here," says Michael early in the interview, "is it's not as bad as you think."

The discussion reveals a tension between a sense of self as victim and oppressed minority and a resistance to that as stereotyping. There were other examples of resisting or deconstructing stereotypes. One of the participants said that a student from a state/Protestant school would be more likely to get a job than someone from their school: "You'd just get a feeling that the interviewer would pick them because they would have a better upbringing or something." As he suggests, it is the "feeling" that there is discrimination that is so destructive to a sense of efficacy and opportunity. But another admonished him, saying, "See, she'll say after this that there's no opportunities for Catholics but there is. They're all out there for Catholics if you want them." In this intervention the participant acknowledges his own agency in collaboration with a researcher constructing a perspective—creating knowledge about life in Northern Ireland—and a sense of responsibility for the uses to which that knowledge is put. He asserts his own dignity but also demonstrates a recognition that he does not have ultimate control over the interpretation.

Although Catholics are still more likely to be unemployed than Protestants, this young Catholic rejects the status of victim. Likewise, one of the most radical participants, John, repeatedly used the language of "developing potential" to describe his own community, Ardoyne, and others experiencing social disadvantage. In this way the group rhetorically attempted to achieve a balance between pessimism and optimism, between insisting on their grievances and asserting their dignity and power, in their narrative. Most shared the belief that the root of the conflict was "the work of British injustice in Ireland," but they did not comfortably occupy the position of "second-class citizen." To admit second-class citizenry is to collude in defining their own marginality, something they refuse throughout the discussion. As John says, "I think everyone has their potential no matter what." When discussing "negative" phenomena such as Catholic "ghettos," youth drinking and violence, and prejudice, they emphasized these as rational and normal actions in the circumstances by turning questions back on the interviewer: "Were you ever 18?"; "Would you not expect somebody livin' in this area to crack up?"; "Have you ever been to the New Lodge?"; "Would a black man feel safe in a white man's neighborhood?" This struggle to define self in opposition to expectations and to opportunity structures, and to challenge negative judgments, is important for peace builders to engage.

Moreover, young people's will to be active in support of change must also be addressed.

JOHN: If you're brought up in this way. If you're brought up in this community, it's in your head, like, that that's the way life is. You either learn to accept it or you try to make a change.

KIERAN: I'd say more Catholic people should stand up for themselves but in a different way. They should not be bigoted but stand up and let their voice be heard and not just stand back and say that's wrong, that's wrong, but actually do somethin' about it.

Although they expressed this desire to be engaged, they only partially associated this with the political process. They disagreed on whether changes in perception should precede or follow structural change such as "a new police force, demilitarization, decommissioning of all weapons, stronger connections with the North-South body AND with Britain." One who favored change of perceptions first said: "I would be more interested in not as big stuff as that. Normal people have to change perceptions. It can't all be down to politicians and prime ministers. Because no matter what they say there will still be riots and stuff." This statement again underlines the young people's belief in the limitations of politics. The expression "you've got to change mindsets" or perceptions was used over and over again but unconnected in a positive way to the peace process.

Q. How often do you talk about politics and the peace process amongst yourselves? How often do you think about it?

MICHAEL: Every time someone gets killed.

JOHN: Whenever there's a riot. And in the next few months that'll be a hel-luva lot. [Laughs]

KIERAN: I think we talk about it just like we talk about here. It's just that if there's riots or something during the 12th we're talking about just how much you hate them. It's not really how can we fix this. It's just how much you hate them and how much you want to get into them with a petrol bomb.

[. . .]

Q. Do you feel that your voices are heard?

SEAN: No.

MICHAEL: I would say 88% (of young people) wouldn't care.

JOHN: I think that's wrong but I think they just don't know how it would be heard.

KIERAN: What do you do, like? Do you just go down to the Sinn Fein center and say well I want this?

SEAN: People don't know where to go or what to do.

JOHN: There's places where you can go to get your voices heard.

SEAN: Where do you go? Where do you go to start off with?

JOHN: Up in Ardoyne there's places where you can get your voices heard. Not political like. But see with [the case of] the Provies and the hoods, joyriders and all. There was a case up in Ardoyne—a lot of joyridin' up there. So they called a meetin' to see what the children wanted to stop them doin' it. And that was good because they got their voices heard then and they're getting a new house built down in Alliance road for them, for a community center to keep them off the street.

The majority think that young people want their voices to be heard but per-ceive that there are no practical mechanisms for that to occur. John takes the opportunity to educate the group on some of his local experience. However, John does not see this negotiation between the local IRA and joyriding children as po-litical. Is this because the political is associated with opposition to "the other" and with failure? He has experience of what can be achieved through young people expressing their needs and interests to community authority figures. That he does not see this as a political process suggests that the peace process and politics are associated with failure to agree and with exclusion, rather than with voices being heard, and that politics fail to exist outside of the frame of sectarian violence.

The North Belfast Catholic's sense of being without voice is not as pronounced as that of the young Protestants in Mount Vernon, but it is significant. "An individual's orientation to the social future is a function of the manner in which he/she experiences the relationship between rulers and ruled" (Danziger 1963, qtd. in Cairns 1996, 142). As these narratives suggest, each group's experience of the relationship between rulers and ruled follows historically entrenched patterns, but this is slowly shifting. The tensions within each group emerge clearly in the language used. The young Catholics strive for "freedom" of various kinds—the main part of their definition of peace—and experience the world as a minority struggling to be recognized and heard. But they also imagine and place themselves within a future in which they are rulers rather than ruled. The young Protestants assert their control and fear of being "mohawked" and "taken over," but they also find themselves marginal and voiceless and imagine a catastrophic future in which they are no longer rulers but ruled. Although there is much common ground between young Catholics and Protestants, these differences and their dynamics must be mapped, recognized, and accommodated by peace builders.

Apart from social, economic, and political exclusion, the clearest shared theme across both groups is their lack of empathy for each other and tendency to devalue and depoliticize the other's story and experience. The Mount Vernon group said "only for them there would be peace" and that the reason there is conflict is because "Catholics never grew up"; "They believe in Holy Mary and we believe in God"; "They believe God hasn't rose and we do." They ventured that the leading Nationalist political representative Gerry Adams "maybe paid" the government to listen to him. The St. Patrick's students said that "Protestants are more bitter," and that "I don't see what they've got to be so bigoted about." One notorious Loyalist "was abused as a child, that's what made him turn against Catholics." However, in each group one member challenged these interpretations from within even while perpetuating them in other parts of the discussion. At Mount Vernon, Elizabeth, who had attended an integrated school, said that "there's some of them you can trust." She recalled being with "a group of about 30 Catholics and not one of them hit me." Michael went even further in identifying with Protestants his own age: "Everybody thinks a Protestant fella and I are completely different. But we're not. Lots of Protestants our age are probably doin' the exact same thing we are, sittin' with our mates in a bar or goin' out to play football at the weekend. They're just the same." And, in fact, the devaluing, demonizing statements were much less dwelt upon than the act of explaining themselves. Both of these are examples of deconstructing stereotypes, which is important for conflict de-escalation (Reychler 2001). Moreover, while holding fast to a particular view of what has to happen in the peace process (the agreement's full implementation), the Catholic group did engage in more malleable problem solving when discussing youth political engagement (also a sign of conflict de-escalation, according to Reychler).

The "public transcript" in the St. Patrick's focus group is their cynicism about peace and their pragmatic refusal to be enthusiastic about its prospects. The "hidden transcript" emerges in the critique built into their cynical evaluations; they do pose the situation in North Belfast as "transformable culture," and they do express their own responsibility for social change. The struggle they experience between cynicism/pragmatism and idealism is important for peace builders to recognize and address. Another part of their "hidden transcript," one they share with the young women from Mount Vernon, is economic and social exclusion, which they refer to only obliquely in their references to the "ghetto" and fair employment. They resist it as both not an immediate priority but also as stereotyping. They are more self-conscious in this activity than the Mount Vernon girls, but both groups share, for obvious self-preservation reasons, this tendency to rank violence over social disadvantage. While the "hidden transcript" in the Mount Vernon dialogue involved veiled references to intracommunal paramilitary policing, the Catholic group did not avoid this topic in their discussion but made it part of a definition of violence with many layers:

Q. What is violence?

SEAN: Well, here it's paramilitary violence.

JOHN: That's too hard a question, you could go on for years on what that is. There's abuse, physical and mental, verbal.

MICHAEL: Domestic violence.

JOHN: You could go on for ages on violence.

MICHAEL: Here in North Belfast its beatins with metal bars.

JOHN: Beatins within your own community. Beatins because you're in the wrong community. State violence. But there's also domestic violence where someone gets stabbed because they were fightin' with their wife or there's fights in bars, spillin' over into local communities.

KIERAN: There's bullying is violence, like slagging [teasing] people and all.

MICHAEL: Mental abuse—would you not expect somebody livin' this area to crack up?

As this illustrates, another part of the St. Patrick's group's "hidden transcript" is all of the violence to which they are vulnerable as young men: even domestic violence is defined as a husband being attacked by his wife. To build peace, people must first be able to imagine it (Boulding 1990). If we listen to these young people we hear that imagining peace involves feeling safe, feeling able to both control change and stimulate change. Indirectly, we hear that imagining peace begins with telling one's own war story—with being heard.

Finally, the gender dimensions of these narratives are important to explore, and briefly, the following aspects should be outlined. While the young women adopted militant roles, they often focused on the dangers to children and to elderly people in the vicinity of the riots. They addressed these issues as a collective—arguing, finishing each other's sentences, and constructing a narrative based more on an accumulation of fragments of thought than on exchange of individualized opinions. While the focus group format undoubtedly fosters this result, the tendency to *build* a collective narrative was more pronounced for the female than the male group. While the young men also offered a collectively endorsed narrative, it was not presented as "in creation" in the way the women's discussion emerged, but was less tentative and more authoritative. One of the young men did make reference to the danger to children, but for the most part the male participants were most concerned about their own vulnerability and security issues. They are, in fact, more likely to be victims and perpetrators of violence than women. The young men also more comfortably inserted themselves into the elite political process and spent considerable time debating about the politics and politicians of the day, which the young women's group seemed unable or unwilling to do.

The young women talked about cross-communal relationships while the young men did not, indicating perhaps a greater intersection between the personal and the political in the young women's experience and interpretation of the conflict. In references to family members in each group, the girls talked about their distant, supportive mothers or stern, disapproving uncles—adults understood in terms of how much they attempted to circumscribe their autonomy—while the boys talked about male relatives experiencing various forms of violence—uncles subject to attack, male paramilitaries, and a man being stabbed by his wife as a form of domestic violence. Their world of violence seemed to be a completely masculine world, which sits oddly with the girl's presence as conflict participants—strangely invisible to their opponents as women and, when seen at all, seen only as a male or genderless "other." This is one further level of marginality experienced by the young women from Mount Vernon. All of this does suggest that even though on the surface both groups were involved in similar street violence, the context within which each group understands that violence may be quite different and partly mediated by gender. The single-sex focus groups reproduced the segregated schooling system in Northern Ireland (a system still mostly segregated by gender as well as by religion), and if the focus groups lent themselves to a gender exclusive (and therefore partial) analysis, this challenges the potential for that system of schooling to foster peace.

CONCLUSION:
YOUTH AS POLITICAL PEACE AGENTS

This chapter problematizes participation in peace processes and expands its meaning. The focus groups tell us a lot about what young people think, the ways in which they make connections, and the extent to which they are political beings. In neither case did the participants treat themselves as subjects to be researched. Instead, they developed and insisted upon their own narratives, created their own frames for understanding the problems discussed, and insisted upon their own knowledge and authority. They analyzed, explored, hypothesized, compared, pronounced, offered evidence and polemic, reasoned argument and invective, diagnosed and debated. Politicians, they emphasized some points, underplayed others, and invoked silence where it was prudent to do so. These young people are participants in politics and conflict reproduction whether or not they or adults realize it. First, they create and reproduce politics as they construct, expand, and disperse these narratives of who gets what, when, and how (Lasswell's [(1972) 1990] classic definition of politics). They do so in their everyday lives, and their knowledge and political reproduction is developed through their interaction with violent events. In telling these stories, they reinforce their own socialization and influence others. They are both mediators and educators. Second, in their actions on the barricades and on the streets they also play important roles. They influence how communities relate to each other and among themselves. They are sometimes the triggers of interface fighting, which begins around specific incidents of interpersonal violence or the spread of rumors. They participate in marches and riots, and, symbolically, their presence, their vulnerability, and their activism help crystallize adult perceptions of community solidarity and righteous self-defense. They stimulate intracommunal debates about punishment beatings/internal policing and restorative justice and wider debates about the police and law and order, social disadvantage, schooling, employment, and leisure. All of these kinds of political participation are underrecognized and need to be addressed in policy.

The peace-building potential of youth needs to be activated through the means of political peace education. Such political peace education needs to be socially situated and progressive, emphasizing collective struggle. Making peace a reality involves imagining peace as complex, rewarding, and relevant. In the working-class Northern Ireland context, that means expressing it as a collective endeavor for dignity, well-being, and participation. As Freire argues, "human beings in communion liberate each other" (Freire 2001, 133). Writing about the use of Freirean ideas with youth in an American urban setting, De Oliveira and Montecinos (1998) argue: "It is insignificant to educate for . . . the child to stay in the same situation, [or to educate young people] for the purpose of obediently inserting themselves into a society marred with injustices. The political challenge resides in educating those who are disenfranchised by guaranteeing spaces for their critical participation in a collective struggle to create a society based on social justice." Toward that end it is necessary to disengage from demonization of certain communities and political parties. Young people are anchored within their communities and are loyal to them. Their will to be involved in positive social change is intimately connected with that ethic of community loyalty (see Cairns 1996). Socially situated peace building begins with awareness raising and practical work to achieve social justice within communities. It is illogical to talk about reconciliation, empathy, and cross-communal peace building within a wider rhetoric of demonization—blaming certain parties or sectors of the community.

A MODEL OF RITUALIZED/INSTITUTIONALIZED POWER SHARING

This study finds that there are two key structural barriers to young people imagining and then being active in support of peace.[14] They are their continued insecurity (vulnerability to violence) and their political exclusion (lack of voice in decision making). Implementing a model of ritualized power sharing may be one way to constructively address these two problems. The term "power sharing" has a long history in the Northern Ireland context, usually taken to mean joint authority of Nationalist/Catholics and Unionist/Protestant representatives in some form of devolved government (such as the Good Friday Agreement). Here, however, is a recommendation for local power sharing through committees established in individual communities, with periodic local cross-community meetings in (paramilitary) protected spheres, as a grassroots peace-building mechanism supporting the operation of power sharing at the elite level. Where these youth committees differ from all of the important work already taking place in the community development sector is in their overtly political nature, their role in informal peace education, their institutionalized ties with the political process, and their combination of education, dialogue, reflection, training, and service activities for youth. Such an approach will complement initiatives to introduce civic and citizenship education into Northern Ireland schools (see Education for Pluralism 2002; Arlow 2003). International funding will be well spent if it is used to support such activities, including conferences for youth to present their work to media, scholars, and policy makers, which will allow them to begin to take control of outside interpretations of them and their communities.[15]

RECOMMENDATIONS

The following are recommendations for bringing youth into the peace-building process:

1. Establish local power-sharing committees as active experiments in democracy that institute the political peace education and training of young people and their involvement in a variety of community-based activities, such as community-needs surveying and youth-designed social service projects. These youth committees would provide feedback to community leaders and politicians and also meet with the committees from the other community for joint reflection and problem solving.

2. Utilize local power-sharing committees as stepping stones for young people's participation in the peace process. Periodic youth policy camps targeting working-class and interface communities would prepare recommendations for their assembly representatives. Do not presume a lack of competencies, but where needed provide training in the necessary competencies as a long-term investment. In the absence of a functioning assembly, it is even more important to continue to actively involve young people in this way.

3. Invest in teams of detached (street-based) youth workers to advise the power-sharing committees, and also consult on the streets because youth often ridicule and avoid youth centers. This would involve training local young adults who have credibility in their communities. They could be teamed with "outsider" participants—youth workers and gang workers from the United States, for example—who are well-educated in the history and issues of the conflict and established residents in local communities. As the study showed, many young people are interested in the comparison between Northern Ireland and other areas of conflict.

One clear outcome of the discussion was the young people's disinterest in an integrative politics: power sharing seems impossible or is caricatured as "holding hands" across the barricades. Only zero-sum, antagonistic politics are real to them. The full implementation of the agreement, political elites changing their discourses, and an end to violence on the street at marches and interfaces would help counter these rational perceptions. At the same time, the challenge is to organize young people to be agents of their own transformation (De Oliveiria and Montecinos 1998) and in so doing effect social change from below. This begins with work to understand the young person in context and recognizing their human dignity and their right to a role in the political decision making affecting their lives. This challenge is one of activating an imagined peace through young people's active participation in diagnosing their own and their community's problems, learning skills to address those problems and make them politically visible, and finding ways to imagine "the other" as eventual collaborators in development for the mutual benefit. Young people are disenfranchised even within their own communities, and this local power-sharing formula would challenge the socialization of young people in an unequal, undemocratic status quo (where they are excluded). That lesson of inclusion will help shape a future orientation toward "the other." "Shared authority helps create the conditions for critical study of knowledge, power and society" (Shor 1996, 155). Those who are themselves without voice are unlikely to see "the other" as deserving of rights of voice. For this reason any move to introduce large-scale truth-telling processes in Northern Ireland should be preceded by initiatives to include youth. Local power sharing indirectly addresses the problem of violence because it undercuts the need for violence from youth by providing other avenues for expression. And as John's Ardoyne anecdote suggested, an inclusion principle regarding young people allows paramilitary, internal policing to assume a political form. Ritualizing power sharing at a local level and from an early age is conducive to conflict transformation because, as Mach argues, "identity is not a static phenomenon. On the contrary, it is par excellence dynamic and it is formed and developed through a continuous process of identification" (1993, 15). "Rituals or ceremonies," states Mach, "make social change happen" (1993, 75). We are familiar with rituals aiding conflict reproduction—marches, annual commemorations, or seasonal street violence (not to mention decommissioning crises), for example—but the activities of these committees would be rituals for conflict transformation. They would not change or be designed to change ethnic or national allegiances; rather, they would be designed to develop transgenerationally an understanding of the other in deep context (social, economic, historical, political, and cultural) and institutionalize political problem solving. As research in other contexts suggests, there is a relationship between the developing child's defining political (and conflict) experiences and the content of later political attitudes (Byrne 1997a; Cairns 1987, 1996; Coles 1986; Kriesburg 1998; MacManus 1996). There is a need for much more research in this area and further methodological experimentation in designing appropriate, democratic research within the studied populations.

ACKNOWLEDGMENTS

The author would like to thank the following for their comments on an earlier draft of this paper: Sami Adwan, Craig Auchter, Dan Bar-On, Ed Cairns, John Darby, Andrew Levy, Carolyn Nordstrom, Victoria Sanford, and the participants at the RIREC conference at Notre Dame. Special appreciation to the young people who participated in the focus groups and to the following teachers and youth leaders who arranged the meetings: Michelle, Frank, Liam, and Ciaran.

NOTES

1. "Orange parade" refers to a march by members of the Loyal Orange Institution or Orange Order, a Protestant fraternal organization that promotes the Union of Northern Ireland with Great Britain. The name comes from William of Orange ("King Billy"), the Protestant king who defeated the Catholic James II at the Battle of the Boyne (1690) and at the Battle of Aughrim (1691). Orange order members (called Orangemen) march annually to commemorate these battles and other events in the Protestant religious, cultural, and political calendar. Members of the Orange Order consider it a religious organization for the expression of Protestant culture and identity. Catholics/Nationalists in Northern Ireland view the Order as sectarian, triumphalist, and anti-Catholic.

2. For a working definition of "peace building," see the introduction to this volume.

3. For the researcher to front-load particular ideas into the discussion runs the risk of making it authoritative and limits the possibility of generating authentic creativity. See Shor (1996) on this process as it applies to the classroom.

4. The focus group was conducted by the author at Mount Vernon Community Center, North Belfast, in June 2001.

5. The Drumcree parade is a disputed Orange Order parade that takes place annually on the outskirts of Portadown, County Armagh, and that includes a religious service at Drumcree church.

6. The Garvaghy Road is a Nationalist/Catholic area on the traditional route of the annual Orange Order Drumcree parade in Portadown. Since 1998 the Northern Ireland Parades Commission has rerouted the parade away from this area to prevent sectarian violence. The participants in the focus groups are not from this location, but Protestant protests about the rerouting of this parade have occurred throughout Northern Ireland.

7. I am grateful to Ed Cairns for pointing this out.

8. From a focus group conducted by the author with Progressive Youth at

the Ulster People's College, Belfast, in February 2000.

9. Innovative strategies for violence prevention by intercepting rumors have been tried with some success using community workers organized into mobile phone networks.

10. Gerry Adams is the leader of Sinn Féin, the largest of the two Nationalist/Catholic parties in Northern Ireland, which is supportive of the Irish Republican Army (IRA).

11. The focus group was conducted by the author at St. Patrick's College, Bearnageeha, North Belfast, in June 2001.

12. The DUP is the Democratic Unionist Party. It is the largest of the two main Unionist/Protestant political parties in Northern Ireland and opposed to the Belfast/Good Friday Peace Agreement.

13. The Belfast/Good Friday Peace Agreement was put to the people of Ireland for approval in two popular referenda. In Northern Ireland 71.12 percent of the population voted "yes" (in favor of the agreement) and 28.88 percent voted "no" (against the agreement). 94.4 percent of voters in the Republic of Ireland voted "yes" (see the CAIN Web site at http://cain.ulst.ac.uk/issues/politics/election/ref1998.htm).

14. By "young people" is meant the young people studied, not all young people.

15. This could involve training in conference organizing and public relations skills as another long-term investment in peace building through economic development.

JACO CILLIERS

Transforming Post-Accord Education Systems
Local Reflections from Bosnia-Herzegovina

The chapter will examine the challenges societies face when transforming education systems after peace accords have been signed. The violence that precedes the signing of peace accords impacts young people enormously. Leaders often use education systems to ensure that divisions and negative stereotypes are reinforced. Therefore, it is very important to transform education systems after peace agreements have been signed to ensure long-term peace-building efforts among youth can be successful. The chapter will specifically analyze the difficulties involved in transforming the education system in Bosnia-Herzegovina. It will outline some of the lessons that can be learned from peace practitioners, educators, and young people in their efforts to promote post-accord peace building.

A lot of progress has been made to better understand what needs to be done to overcome the challenges of building long-term peace in societies after peace accords have been signed. However, Elise Boulding

(1997) argues that the challenges for scholars working in the field of conflict studies is to develop not only theories but concrete arguments for practitioners and activists that can help them transform the barriers that hinder long-term peace-building efforts. Education institutions are powerful mechanisms that, on the one hand, can often hinder long-term peace-building efforts or, on the other hand, can constructively influence young people to work toward a peaceful future and coexistence. Understanding the challenges involved in transforming educational institutions after peace accords have been signed, then, is important for post-accord peace-building efforts.

This chapter is based on information gathered from educators, young people, and peace-building practitioners in Bosnia-Herzegovina. Reychler and Paffenholz argue that "the learning curve could be shortened if debriefings of people who have acquired peacebuilding experience would be taken more seriously" (2001, xiv). This study is also based on data gathered from a previous research project conducted in Bosnia-Herzegovina from 1996 to 2000 (Cilliers 2001). It is more focused in scope, however, and also includes data gathered from subsequent research conducted between 2001 and 2002. The principal research method for gathering the information was a series of interviews and focus groups, with participant observations and document reviews also being used. A total of forty people were interviewed in Bosnia-Herzegovina during the research.

This chapter will address two general research questions:

1. From the perspectives of individuals directly involved in the conflict in Bosnia-Herzegovina, what are the challenges and obstacles to transforming education systems after peace accords have been signed?
2. What roles and influences can young people and educators have on efforts to transform educations systems and promote peace-building efforts during the post-accord period?

A "purposive sampling" method, which focused on educators, young people, and peace-building practitioners, was applied to the research. Berg (1998) indicates that purposive sampling is used when researchers use their background knowledge about and experience with groups to select subjects who represent a certain part of a population. It was determined that these three groups would provide insights regarding the research questions. First, the large amount of data that was gathered, primarily through the interviews but also during the field visits through observations, field notes, and the gathering of documents, was coded. An open coding or grounded theory process was used, whereby themes emerged inductively from the data. Nine identifiable themes emerged from those people who were dealing with the day-to-day challenges of promoting peace-building efforts. The themes were then grouped and sorted. Since one purpose of the research was to present reactions from key individuals involved in educational efforts, there were occasions where unique factors were listed by certain individuals even if they were not necessarily repeated by others. There were, therefore, certain themes that were listed by only one or two interviewees. These reflections were still included in the presentation and description of the cases in order to ensure that as many as possible of the relevant "local reactions" were analyzed and recorded.

During the interviews, participants were given an overview of the research problem and how the interview would be conducted. Interviewees were informed that their answers would be anonymous. These field visits provided opportunities to observe and hear from people directly involved in post-settlement peace-building efforts about the ongoing challenges they confront and to gather the information needed to address the research problems. These field visits provided an opportunity to "get underneath the labels and concepts used in either documents or discussions and observe a phenomenon directly" (Yin 1982, 49). I was also fortunate to live and work in Bosnia-Herzegovina for nearly two years between 1996 and 1997.[1] These experiences provided unique perspectives of the challenges of building long-term peace after the signing of the Dayton Peace Agreement.

The next section will briefly introduce relevant literature in the field of conflict studies dealing specifically with the challenges of transforming structures and institutions and what can be done to enhance peace-building efforts during the post-accord period. This will be followed by a brief contextual history of the conflict in Bosnia-Herzegovina. The main findings from the research will then be presented before I make some brief conclusions.

Theoretical Insights

Throughout this chapter the terms "peace building"[2] and "conflict transformation"[3] will be used interchangeably. When looking at some of the theorists that contribute to our understanding of these terms, there are a number of insights on why it is often so difficult to transform education institutions after peace accords. Conflict theorists such as Galtung (1965, 1975–88) and Curle (1971) have emphasized the importance of taking structural factors and power relations within institutions into consideration when attempts are made to *transform* violence and conflict and enhance peace-building efforts within societies. Crocker and Hampson (1996) point out that after agreements have been signed, there is nearly always a breakdown of the political authority and the radical altering of social and educational structures. The post-settlement phase is often characterized by ongoing violence because parties try to control the situation and establish their dominance within these systems. Darby and Mac Ginty (2000) argue that there are numerous factors that can result in violence re-erupting after peace accords have been signed. The strength of peace processes will be tested by these ongoing conflicts, which may become violent. How well educators and young people deal with these ongoing challenges will be important for long-term peace-building efforts.

Lederach (1995) points out that a transformation approach to solving conflicts within societies that have been plagued by long periods of violence must take into consideration what can be done to establish an "infrastructure for peace." This implies the creation of various peace-building efforts within multiple leadership levels within a given society as well as within institutions that can promote sustainable peace processes. Educational institutions, therefore, can be seen as a powerful mechanism that can sustain an infrastructure to promote post-accord peace-building efforts. Boulding (1988) argues that it is important for individuals to have a clear vision of how their future will look, especially if they have been involved in wars for extended periods. Individuals can benefit from educational institutions that can provide insights into what can be done to repair damaged relationships and build trust among former enemies. She asserts that social institutions must provide educational guidance for people to help them visualize alternatives and to create opportunities where people can work together in a peaceful civil society.

Within a post-accord society such as Bosnia-Herzegovina, where leaders played a significant role in contributing to the ongoing violence, it is important to also reflect on the positive or negative role they can play in promoting peace-building efforts after the signing of peace accords. Numerous conflict theorists make reference to the important role that leaders play in transforming structures that prevent peace-building efforts (Gurr 1993; Hampson 1996a; Kriesberg 1998; Rothstein 1999). Many of them argue that it is important to understand the reasons why leaders make certain policy decisions, why they tend to be resistant to efforts that can promote peace, and how they can manipulate certain institutions to promote political ambitions and ethnic hatred. Ferguson (1980) argues that in order to transform conflict situations it is crucial that leaders show their followers that new political and educational institutions will not promote further confrontation and violence but rather reconciliation efforts. Ronen (1995) indicates that it is important for leaders to be conscious of the need for "messengers of new ideas," which will eventually lead to constructive peace-building efforts. Reasons why some leaders are more successful than others include the education they received, their culture, their life experiences, and their personal motivations. Rothstein claims that "chances for stable peace are greater if strongly supported leaders who favor compromise are in power on both sides and if external patrons also support compromise, are willing to commit resources to the settlement, and are not intent on using the game itself for their positioning purposes, domestically or internationally" (1999, 9).

The signing of the Dayton Peace Accord and the subsequent post-accord period in Bosnia-Herzegovina has been characterized by the heavy involvement of outside international organizations as well as numerous nongovernmental organizations (NGOs). Weis and Nazarenko (1998) and Spencer and Spencer (1995) argue that state structures and people working within large government systems, such as educational institutions, are often resistant to efforts that can bring about change and transformation. They argue that NGOs as well as strong civil society groups, including youth groups, can put significant pressure on these institutions to ensure they change for the better. NGOs and civil society groups can create opportunities where former enemies can create spaces to deal peacefully with their problems. Although this can enhance peace-building efforts, certain theorists like Wallensteen (1991) contend that the involvement of international NGOs during the signing of peace settlements, together with the involvement of parties from inside and outside the conflict, can often contribute to more complexities and challenges during the post-accord period. Lederach (1995) argues that external actors often lack a true understanding of the cultural and contextual dynamics of a conflict; therefore they impose models that are based on "outsider-partial" perceptions and norms. He claims that peace-building efforts should be based on elicitive methods that develop models grounded in the local context. Therefore, outsiders to a conflict, such as those involved in reconstructing and developing post-conflict education models and institutions, should be careful not to prescribe solutions and frameworks that are not grounded in local realities.

Mitchell (1981) contends that a comprehensive approach is needed when efforts are made to understand how structures and institutions contribute to conflict situations. He argues that conflicts within education institutions, for instance, are comprised of three interrelated components, namely *conflict situations, conflict behaviors,* and *conflict attitudes and perceptions.* The *conflict situation* arises out of the perception of mutually incompatible goals. This happens as a result of the interaction between social values, structures, and perceptions of resources within institutions. The *conflict dynamic* arises out of a three-level structure of interaction, which includes the intragroup, intergroup, and group environment dimensions. *Conflict attitudes* refer to the psychological consequences of human interaction, which serve to complement the conflict situation.

All these elements are central to dealing with conflicts at the structural level; approaches to transform conflict into situations where sustainable peace can be ensured will have to address all of these interlocking factors.

It is important, furthermore, to be aware of the relationship between the needs of the individual and the various structural factors that prevent individuals from meeting those needs and living together peacefully. Individuals will often resort to violence if they feel structures and institutions are not meeting their inherent needs. Institutional, systemic, or structural changes that can address the frustrations of people are of the utmost importance, especially when dealing with protracted and multiethnic conflicts.

Van der Merwe (1989) stresses that reconciliation can only be truly accomplished in protracted conflict situations if institutions and structures are put in place to support peace building. Reconciliation efforts are especially crucial where governments or regimes have used oppressive measures to sustain power or where atrocities were rampant within society. Processes should be created to address grievances and rebuild damaged relationships comprehensively (Van der Merwe 1989). Authors such as Montville (1993) and Volkan (1988, Volkan and Julius et al. 1990) argue that there are clear indications that the persistence of violent conflicts can be attributed to people not dealing with the history of trauma, aggression, and retribution that plagues conflict societies. It is only when the victims of conflicts can heal from their experiences that societies can move toward true reconciliation. At the same time, there should be opportunities where former adversaries can perform acts of acceptance and recognition in order to strengthen relationships and build trust. The education system that emerged out of the post-accord period in Bosnia-Herzegovina was uniquely placed to address many of these concerns raised by the theorists. During the interviews with young people and educators, however, it was clearly pointed out that in many ways the exact opposite occurred.

In the conflict literature there is an acknowledgment that systemic and structural causes of conflict are major reasons why conflicts tend to become violent. In the research and through the perspectives of those directly involved in peace-building efforts, it also emerged that structural causes continue to be major obstacles to peace-building efforts in the post-accord period.

HISTORY AND CONTEXTUAL BACKGROUND

The division of the education system in Bosnia-Herzegovina into three separate institutions that primarily promote the various cultural and religious values of the Bosniac, Croat, and Serb populations has a long history.[4] The war that lasted from 1992 to 1995 fueled these separations, but historically there were many incidents that contributed to these conditions. As mentioned by Kolouh-Westin, "the future will tell if the tripartite presidency and state of Bosnia-Herzegovina will support educational conditions which can lead to the flourishing of reconciliation, human rights and democracy, or if the political development will end up in three ethnically cleansed mini-states with three different education systems, three histories and three different languages" (2002, 42). This section provides a brief overview of some key historical events to provide a context for some of the findings that resulted from the research.

The oldest inhabitants of the area now known as Bosnia-Herzegovina were the Illyrians. They lived in large communities and were involved in fierce battles against the Romans. After the Romans conquered the Illyrians at the beginning of the Common Era, the area was annexed to the province of Dalmatia, which was part of the Roman Empire. Many of the Illyrians became Romanized and were recruited into the Roman legions. However, when the Byzantines annexed Bulgaria in 1018, Bosnia came under the control of the Byzantines. The area then changed hands again when it was annexed by Hungary in 1137, but soon afterwards it reverted to Byzantine rule. After 1180 Bosnia mostly became free of outside influence and was governed by rulers referred to as "Bans." Ottoman Turks occupied areas around and within Bosnia during the fourteenth century. The battle of Kosovo Polje (Blackbird's Field) in 1389, where the Ottomans' victory over the Serbs became the center of Serbian political history, occurred during this time.

An unstable Ottoman rule continued in Bosnia during the eighteenth and nineteenth centuries. There were continual conflicts, wars, and rebellions that resulted in a complicated social, political, and economic configuration. People from the same ethnic background and language became divided by the three main religions in the area, namely, Islam, Orthodox Christianity, and Catholicism. During the nineteenth century these three religions became the religious identities for the Bosniacs, Serbs, and Croats, respectively, which resulted in three different cultural legacies being created. There was also a growing Jewish population, which emigrated during the fifteenth century from Spain and Portugal, and a smaller group of Roma or Gypsies, who lived all over Bosnia. In general, the Muslims adopted the Turkish-Islamic culture but with creative and significant differences. The Serbs inherited the Byzantine and Slavic traditions, while the Croats were heavily influenced by the Western Christian and Catholic traditions. At the Congress of Berlin in 1878, the Austro-Hungarian Empire received a thirty-year mandate to occupy Bosnia-Herzegovina. Although Bosnia-Herzegovina remained under the sultan's sovereignty, the Congress of Berlin signaled the end of Ottoman rule. Austria subsequently annexed Bosnia-

Herzegovina after the mandate expired in 1908, but Muslims and Orthodox Christians were awarded political and cultural autonomy. On June 28, 1914, in Sarajevo, a Serbian nationalist, Gavrilo Princip, assassinated Archduke Franz Ferdinand, who was the heir to the Austrian throne. One month later, Austro-Hungaria declared war on Serbia, signaling the start of World War I.

The end of World War I brought about the end of the once powerful Austro-Hungarian Empire. Between 1918 and 1941 Bosnia-Herzegovina became part of a new south Slavic configuration known as the Kingdom of Serbs, Croats, and Slovenes, or later referred to as the "first Yugoslavia" (*Yugo* meaning south and *Slavia* meaning Slavs). The "second Yugoslavia" was declared in the Bosnian town of Jajce on November 29, 1941, by Tito, who led the "Partisans" and who eventually took control of Yugoslavia at the end of World War II. During his rule of Yugoslavia, Tito introduced innovative domestic policies that relied heavily on socialist self-rule. These policies would eventually have profound consequences for the various educational institutions. During the first part of his rule, Tito introduced a process whereby schools became the property of the state. From the early 1950s, however, educational institutions were encouraged through decentralization to become more independent in the various republics. General recommendations, such as guidelines on textbooks, were made by the Federal Council of Education, which was controlled by the central government. A high level of educational development was reached, and a nationwide network for levels of education was achieved. Qualified teachers were trained and school education was compulsory and free.

Problems started to emerge during the 1980s, however, as a lack of diversity in the education system and serious economic constraints surfaced. During the final years of his reign, Tito introduced various forms of liberalization, and the lack of repression and control resulted in open hostilities and competition between the various ethnic groups throughout Yugoslavia. With the breakup of the Soviet Union and the constant pressure throughout southeastern Europe for national and democratic rule, Yugoslavia decided to call for multiparty elections in each of the six Yugoslav republics. Nationalist movements dominated the elections, and these influences were also carried over to schools, universities, and other educational institutions. The elections held in Bosnia-Herzegovina in November 1990 ended in the three nationalist-based parties—the Serbian Democratic Party (SDA), the Croatian Democratic Union (HDZ), and the Muslim-favored Democratic Action Party (SDA)—winning nearly 86 percent of the 240 seats in the Bosnian Assembly. The authority of the Yugoslav federal government was steadily eroding, and minorities within the boundaries of the republics were starting to express nationalist feelings, which were exploited by the leaders. There was also a considerable quantity of arms being distributed to the Serb communities living in Croatia and Bosnia-Herzegovina. These weapons came from stockpiles of the Yugoslav People's Army (JNA). During 1991 there were also large numbers of "illegal paramilitary units" being established throughout Croatia, Serbia, and Bosnia-Herzegovina.

When Slovenia and Croatia proclaimed their independence in June 1991, a full-blown war resulted. The JNA, under the control of Serb leadership in Belgrade, intervened to protect "Yugoslav territorial integrity" and in the process started to support Serbian separatists' movements in Croatia and Bosnia-Herzegovina. A referendum was held on March 1, 1992, in which people overwhelmingly (more than 99 percent) voted for independence. The Serbs living within Bosnia-Herzegovina did not participate in the vote and insisted that Bosnia-Herzegovina remain within what was left of Yugoslavia. They also proclaimed their own constitution, and shortly after the referendum vote, forces of the JNA launched attacks against the newly declared "Republic of Bosnia-Herzegovina."

On the day the European Union recognized the independence of Bosnia-Herzegovina (April 6, 1992), Serbian snipers in the top floors of the Holiday Inn hotel in Sarajevo opened fire on peace demonstrators. This signaled the beginning of the devastating war that would last until the end of 1995. The Bosnian Serb forces, led by Radovan Karadzic and the leader of his military force, Ratko Mladic, launched a campaign to take control of large parts of Bosnia-Herzegovina. In comparison, the Bosnian Territorial Forces (initially comprised of Bosniacs and Bosnian Croats) had mainly small arms when the war started. Tensions over resources, sovereignty, and symbols eventually led to the so-called second Bosnian war between Bosnian Croats and Bosniac forces in Herzegovina and central Bosnia. An agreement was signed in March 1994 that called for a "Bosnian Federation" between Bosniacs and Bosnian Croats. The Bosnian Federation created an uneasy peace between the former allies, but it would eventually be central to the creation of two future "entities" encompassed by the Dayton Peace Agreement. The Dayton Peace Agreement, signed on December 14, 1995, in Paris, called for the establishment of a new state structure with two separate entities (the "Bosnian Federation" and "Republica Srpska"). The Dayton Peace Agreement brought an end to the fighting that left nearly 300,000 people dead, hundreds of thousands more displaced, and the country largely separated along ethnic lines.

The impact of the war on educational institutions was dramatic. Cousens and Cater state that "for years Bosniacs, Croats and Serbs have maintained three different curricula, strongly discouraged minority enrollment, and continued to resist efforts to develop a more inclusive and integrated system" (2001, 81). School buildings were often transformed during the war into fortresses where soldiers and peacekeepers had their offices. Children had to be protected from snipers as they walked to school, and informal classrooms had to be established since it became dangerous for children to sit in school buildings, which became targets during the war. As the war continued over nearly four years, the teachers, administrators, and various educational institutions changed to adapt to the reality of trying to educate young people during wartime. Berman quotes Mujo Musagic, the editor of the *Education Gazette* in Bosnia-Herzegovina, who indicated that "war schools" started to emerge in Bosnia-Herzegovina. Musagic stated that "Children did learn, teachers did hold classes, the educational process did take place on the basis of a reduced program written by the Ministry of Education. However, my impression is, the most important value of schools during the war can't be measured by numbers and the statistics but, as I would put it in words, it can be measured by the value of the significance of life" (Berman 2001, 5–6). Transforming an education system that had been physically destroyed and, more importantly, after a war that left mental and psychological scars on nearly all the students and educators would prove to be very challenging.

The history and background of the region were important to the way the peace agreement was developed. It also had a considerable effect on the eventual role that the international community played in not only helping broker an agreement but also in assisting with the post-accord peace-building efforts. One interviewee stated, for instance, that Bosnia-Herzegovina "has a history of being taken over by foreign armies and groups" and that "the international community did not understand the dynamic and history when they started getting involved in helping us transform our education systems." The lack of trust that remained from previous conflicts also resurfaced during the war and was exploited by those leaders who wanted to promote their own nationalist agendas. The historical situation in Bosnia-Herzegovina, therefore, is crucial to understanding many of the tactics, problems, and challenges that appeared after the signing of the Dayton Peace Agreement. A historical description of the conflict also puts in context many of the local reactions and responses that were gathered during the research. As one interviewee reflected, "Bosnia-Herzegovina is not a society in transition since the latest war broke out; we have always been a society in transition and were constantly transforming ourselves." Kolouh-Westin argues that

> at present there is a tension between tradition (e.g., emphasis on national subjects, and rediscovery of religious belonging and values) and modernity (e.g., shift from collectivism to individualism, emphasis on liberal democratic ideas, and human rights). These contradictory trends that can be traced within education policies are the result of pressures from a tripartite national level and from the international arena. The question is how Bosnia-Herzegovina will develop

its education system and if the educational conditions will be developed which all ethnic groups will accept. (2002, 42)

The following section summarizes the main themes and perspectives gathered from local people about why a shared education system has not emerged, and what the prospects are for a successful transformation of the education system.

Local Reflections on the Post-Accord Transformation Efforts in the Education System

Through the research nine distinct themes emerged. These were

1. Lack of leadership and corruption
2. Lack of ownership and dominance by "outsiders"
3. Relationships needed to rebuild the education system were torn apart by ethnic divisions
4. Severe brain drain and lack of hope among young people
5. Transforming education systems requires financial support
6. Lack of educators and young people involved in peace accords and peace processes
7. Teaching methods to promote critical thinking are absent
8. Need to integrate peace education
9. Comprehensive and holistic approaches are required for transformation

These nine themes will now be explained in detail before general conclusions about the findings are made.

Lack of Leadership and Corruption

There was a high level of frustration among educators and young people I talked to in Bosnia-Herzegovina concerning the lack of commitment and involvement of local leaders in constructively transforming the education system in their country. They felt that the leaders were continuing to divide the ethnic groups within the country through their actions and that schools and other education institutions were polarized and manipulated in order to emphasize ethnic, religious, and cultural differences. Local leaders designated by the parties to work on transforming educational institutions during the post-accord period were seen as unwilling to confront extremists within their parties who wanted to introduce curriculum that taught ethnic hatred and separation.

Interviewees who were directly involved in conflict resolution and peace-building efforts also stated that they found it difficult to encourage people from the various ethnic groups to reconcile with one another when they saw the "leaders at the top" still unwilling to work together or rebuild the relationships. Efforts undertaken by local NGOs or community leaders at the "middle-range," therefore, were undermined by leaders at the "top" who wanted to promote their own nationalist agendas through schools and universities. For instance, a high level of frustration was expressed by a student working on a youth project who said: "how can we build an integrated and multi-ethnic education system in Bosnia-Herzegovina if the same leaders who brought us war now have to bring us peace?"

Unfortunately, there was apathy among citizens during the post-accord period, creating an environment that was not conducive to changing the current leadership or contributing to post-accord peace-building efforts. People were either too scared to voice their disagreement with the leaders in charge of the education system or they lacked confidence in the ability of civil society or ordinary people to bring about constructive change. It was stated during interviews that "change will occur when the people are tired of the politicians and say that they have had enough of their manipulation"; "we must improve the commitment of the people at the grassroots level to take initiative and create a strong civil society"; and "normal people from all ethnic groups must show that they are not satisfied with what is happening in our schools." The distrust that fueled the war was also blamed for creating environments after the peace accord where people were too scared to support anyone opposing the nationalistic political leaders. The political leaders continued to exploit the fear and mistrust for their own gain.

Corruption among government officials, especially after the influx of large post-accord aid, loans, and financial resources that were supposed to help with the transformation of the education system, was also highlighted. The fact that individuals in top leadership positions were enriching themselves and possibly engaging in illegal activities at the expense of the young people who would be the future of the country was negatively influencing peace-building efforts. Increased transparency, public and civilian scrutiny and monitoring, as well as "watchdog mechanisms" were seen as examples that should be considered to minimize corruption after the signing of peace accords. Corruption among those in charge of building educational institutions was perceived as a major reason for the difficulty of implementing policies that would benefit the next generation.

Lack of Ownership and Dominance by "Outsiders"

There was a great appreciation for the role that the international community played in finally ending the violence and helping to establish a military presence that "prevented" the war from breaking out again in Bosnia-Herzegovina. However, interviewees were rather critical of the role the international community played in the signing of the Dayton Peace Agreement and in subsequent efforts to transform some of the larger government institutions, such as the education system.

The peace process that resulted in the signing of the Dayton Peace Agreement in Bosnia-Herzegovina was primarily done through international "shuttle diplomacy." The intervention that brought the major parties together at Dayton can be seen as a "mediation with muscle" approach, where the international mediators used strong-arm tactics to bring the parties together to sign an agreement. It was pointed out that those involved in drawing up the accord were mostly focused on traditional Western problem-solving methods that emphasized "outcome-based agreements." Very little time was spent on the process or on creating opportunities where people could interact face-to-face with one another and build relationships. When processes were established to bring opposing parties together to implement the agreements reached during the peace talks, the people from opposing sides were extremely distrustful of one another. This was also the case for those individuals at all levels who were tasked with helping to transform the education system.

The fact that local educators and teachers were not included in many of the post-accord processes was seen as problematic. In addition, it was felt that the majority of the efforts designed to transform the education system in the country were being dominated and initiated by international actors and agencies. This resulted in apathy and lack of participation by local educators and young people. It also prevented local capacity in peace-building skills from developing within the country. There was criticism of processes initiated by "outsiders" or "international people" to "transform the education system that is supposed to help us and not them." Another respondent stated that peace-building efforts within schools and education institutions must be "by the people" and not "for the people."

The director of a large youth project stated that because the international community was making all the decisions, Bosnians were not taking responsibility for peace-building efforts and were always pointing a finger at the other side. She indicated that young people in the country needed to learn how to make their own decisions and see examples of how to do this from their teachers and professors. The fact that they did not feel ownership of the problem, as well as the fact that local groups and people were never involved during the settlement process, was seen as a contributing factor to the apathy in the country. There was also a perception that "the international community tended to disregard and not value the solutions and ideas of local people."

The lack of ownership of the processes put in place to create a more multi-ethnic education system in the country was a disturbing reality. A local teacher mentioned that "the willingness to make a success of what we will teach in our school will only come once there is an internal commitment from local teachers to work towards peace."

RELATIONSHIPS TORN APART BY ETHNIC DIVISIONS

Policies put in place during the war to promote "nationalist tendencies" and propagate specific ethnic symbols, languages, and beliefs among ethnic groups were still being used four years after the peace accord was signed. It was indicated by a teacher that history classes entailed general history and then, if you were in a Bosniac class, for instance, also readings about Islam and by Muslim authors. Serbian and Croatian schools were also intolerant of other ethnic groups and followed similar practices. People thought of themselves as Serb, Croat, or Bosniac and not as a citizen of a country. By recalling the atrocities that various ethnic groups committed against one another in the past, and emphasizing those issues in schools, young people were still being "mobilized to hate others."

The tension, confusion, and frustration involved in creating three education systems, or "government structures," to appease the needs of all three major ethnic groups in the country were seen as major obstacles to long-term peace. The constant emphasis on creating three institutions "was draining the resources of the country and taking away funds that should be applied to other educational programs." In addition, it was mentioned that the way "territorial integrity" was outlined in the Dayton Peace Agreement created a situation where educators from the various ethnic groups could continue to promote intolerance without ever being required to work together. The creation of educational institutions that saw themselves as "mini-states with their own authority" was the result. It was also mentioned that it had become very difficult to rebuild relationships between young people as a result of the physical and geographical boundaries established by the Dayton Peace Agreement. The agreement created "too many government and decision-making levels within Bosnia-Herzegovina, which complicated any efforts to transform the education systems." It was mentioned that the country had a federal government, followed by the various entities (Federation and Republica Srpska), then canton governments, local governments, and municipalities. As a result, "there are just too many laws, regulations, and various legal processes within the education systems that are confusing to everyone involved."

Respondents indicated that opportunities and initiatives should be created where people can start rebuilding relationships destroyed by the war. The need to rebuild interpersonal relationships through reconciliation initiatives was seen as very important if there was to be real success in transforming the education system. In Bosnia-Herzegovina this was a painstaking process because ethnic groups were not encouraged to reach out and rebuild relationships.

Very little was done after the signing of the Dayton Peace Agreement to create opportunities where antagonists could rebuild relationships or to establish processes where the level of trust between groups and individuals could be strengthened. Young people from the various ethnic groups had very few opportunities to participate in activities, games, and sporting events since hardly any multiethnic schools existed. Atrocities by other ethnic groups and negative stereotypes were continuously highlighted in schools during the war. The need to reverse those perceptions was subsequently seen as very important. Unfortunately, it was pointed out that those individuals and groups who were essentially teaching hatred and who were against peace efforts continued to employ tactics to prevent people from coming together to build peace. Including reconciliation efforts within the education system was seen as very important, but unfortunately it was given a low priority. It was mentioned by one educator that "young people don't hate one another; it is only if they have been provided with negative stereotypes that they start seeing themselves as different."

Severe Brain Drain and Lack of Hope among Young

The lack of opportunities being provided to young people, as well as the fact that some of the brightest teachers and educators in the country were leaving, were seen as major reasons why post-accord peace-building efforts were so difficult. There was an alarming "brain drain" in the country, and young people of various ages were leaving to explore opportunities in other countries. It was felt that the future of the country was being lost, which was not encouraging for post-accord peace-building efforts. A prominent academic from Sarajevo pointed out that "as a result of the war many well-educated people and some of our best professors at universities have accepted positions outside the country." A number of respondents also made reference to the fact that "the quality of professors and teachers at universities and various educational facilities has deteriorated significantly." There were also few incentives for skilled people to return to the country since unemployment was high and people had little hope that things would improve.

When young people were asked what could reverse this "brain drain," the responses varied from "we need to create universal values and a multiethnic society that all of us in Bosnia-Herzegovina can be proud of," to "we need to know that we will find a job one day" and "young people have to start believing in the future." When talking to educators and people involved in peace-building efforts, they also stressed that it was crucial to reverse the negative perceptions that young people have of the situation in the country and that more should be done in schools to provide them with hope and optimism that they can have a peaceful and prosperous future in Bosnia-Herzegovina. As one young person noted, "we have a lot of new buildings and reconstruction projects, but we are not seeing a bright future for ourselves."

TRANSFORMING EDUCATION SYSTEMS REQUIRES FINANCIAL SUPPORT

The devastation and destruction caused by the war to schools, universities, and other educational buildings meant that a considerable amount of resources and international aid had to be provided to help the country with reconstruction efforts. Huge sums were subsequently spent on renovating many of these buildings. Unfortunately, very little funding was made available for components to help support the "human and logistical development" that was also required to ensure quality education could be provided to young people.

Teachers were often not paid their already small salaries, and teaching materials were limited. This resulted in low morale among those who were supposed to train and educate the future leaders of the country. The international community and the local politicians made unfounded promises during the signing of the Dayton Peace Agreement that "those working in the education system would receive adequate compensation and salaries." When this did not materialize, well-qualified teachers left the education system and pursued other opportunities. It was felt that both the local and international parties involved in the peace agreement should have prepared educators for the difficulties that would follow during the post-accord period.

There was also frustration expressed about the fact that hardly any funding was available to coordinate peace-building efforts among the various ethnic groups. It was pointed out that it was difficult to get funding for projects aimed at encouraging young people, educators, and teachers from various ethnic groups to work together on joint projects or initiatives. Funding sources often had a very "narrow vision of what should be funded and there were always strings attached." Reconstruction efforts were easily funded, while efforts to build peace through the various education systems were often overlooked. In addition, it was mentioned that "the majority of funding sources during the post-accord period continued to focus on only providing funding for specific projects in one or the other entities in Bosnia-Herzegovina." Education systems in the various entities and areas controlled by certain ethnic groups were not required to integrate or promote multicultural approaches. The lack of investment in "human development," "multicultural," "relationship-building," or comprehensive "trust-building" initiatives was seen as a major reason why the education system in Bosnia-Herzegovina was struggling to promote post-accord peace-building efforts.

Lack of Educators and Young People Involved in Peace Processes

The lack of involvement by young people and educators was seen as a major obstacle to post-accord peace-building efforts. It was stated by one respondent that "local teachers and even young people on the ground were never involved, consulted, or even informed about the implications of the peace agreement for their lives before it was signed." This lack of participation has contributed to ignorance about the peace accord and what can be done to maximize efforts to transform schools and universities. The fact that a "nucleus of reform-minded people working in the education field" was not involved, or even consulted, during the signing of the peace accord was seen as problematic. By excluding these actors, as well as people from other civil society sectors, from the peace process in Bosnia-Herzegovina, the international community was seen as "losing the opportunity to have people and groups that would have been interested in rebuilding relationships and trust."

The lack of involvement of young people in any decision-making structure has resulted in apathy and a perception that "decisions are made for us by people who do not have an idea of what we are faced with on a daily basis." The perception of "those mediators working in Dayton that peace accords can be signed without the active involvement and consultation of civil society groups" was seen as very problematic.

Teaching Methods to Promote Critical Thinking

Difficulties within the education system as a result of the way education was developed and had operated in Yugoslavia during the pre-settlement phase were mentioned by a number of interviewees involved in educational institutions in Bosnia-Herzegovina. Respondents indicated that "the education system during socialism made people believe everything they were told." It was structured in such a way that it "did not make us think and challenge what we were being told." Therefore, the need to develop a critical way of thinking was stressed as an important requirement that was never fully developed in the education system in the pre-settlement phase. It is only when "people are taught how to think for themselves that they will start to challenge the current lies that are being told by one group or another and children will start to challenge stereotypes." A university professor indicated that a study conducted by researchers from Sarajevo University concluded that as long as children continued to be educated by means of the current books developed during the war, which were still being used in the school system, the prospects for a multicultural society in Bosnia-Herzegovina were slim.

INTEGRATING PEACE EDUCATION

Respondents stressed that during the post-accord phase, education systems must focus on peace education to build trust among children. This entails designing new teaching styles such as workshops and encouraging students and young people to express their ideas on civil society. It was felt that students should have forums to express how they saw the future of all nations within Bosnia-Herzegovina. A teacher interviewed mentioned that "there needs to be a concerted effort to train teachers in new teaching methods. There is, for instance, a lack of trained teachers to deal with children traumatized by the violence." Another teacher expressed that "one would assume that after what we went through during the war that the introduction of peace education should have been central during the settlement phase and included in the Dayton Peace Accord." The reality, however, is that in Bosnia-Herzegovina the introduction of peace education is an ongoing challenge. A peace activist indicated that "it has become very difficult to promote peace education in the post-accord period because school leaders are scared that they will be perceived as opposing the official party policies that still promote separate education for every ethnic group."

Apart from emphasizing the need to develop new textbooks, respondents also strongly felt that there was a great need for conflict resolution and peace-building training in school and university curricula. Young people should have the skills and methods to deal with the continuing conflicts and challenges they are faced with on a daily basis. The value of improving interpersonal skills, therefore, was seen as being very important to peace-building efforts. One interviewee, who conducted conflict resolution training in schools after the signing of the peace accord, commented on the important practical value of improving the communication skills of those who attended the trainings. She felt that the introduction of conflict resolution methods within the school system had contributed to changing negative perceptions and stereotypes among young people. Additional conflict resolution skills and techniques currently not available to teachers and educators are needed to overcome obstacles. One of the interviewees provided the example of teachers who participated in a conflict resolution training session and then became catalysts for change and reform in their schools and divided communities. They started to use methods to encourage children to use nonviolent techniques to deal with their problems. They also began sending girls to empowerment workshops that were offered in youth centers in the area.

At the same time it was indicated that conducting trainings that only provided people with skills and techniques to manage and resolve their interpersonal conflicts was not enough. The need to have a strategy to encompass all development programs in a "holistic peace-building framework" was seen as very important.

Comprehensive and Holistic Approaches Are Required for Transformation

It is clear from the research that more attention should be paid to establishing holistic approaches to the implementation of peace agreements. In Bosnia-Herzegovina interviewees indicated that humanitarian efforts and the delivery of aid were hardly ever integrated with comprehensive peace-building efforts. Interviewees felt that projects aimed at physically rebuilding the infrastructure of the country during the post-settlement phase, such as basic housing and water supply and sanitation systems, were mostly done in isolation. These initiatives were never integrated within peace-building efforts or, for instance, with strategies to transform the educational institutions in the country. The international community was also working mostly with high-level national leaders and not empowering local actors to participate in decision making, which compounded the problem.

When participants in a focus group were asked what could be done to ensure that better coordination and planning took place to help transform educational institutions, they provided a number of suggestions. The group indicated that there should always be an analysis of the needs in the communities, schools, or other educational institutions. This analysis should include the voices of young people and those directly and indirectly involved in the education process. The needs assessment would provide an outline of the various capacities that would be required to transform education systems and schools. This should be followed by the establishment of an inclusive decision-making structure that could settle problems and challenges that might arise. Everything possible should be done to make the process transparent to those involved, and they should feel that they are always a part of what is being decided in the process. The various activities and programs should then be coordinated at all levels. It was stressed that local leaders and resources should be given preference. Lastly, it was stressed that effective monitoring and evaluation criteria should be developed to ensure suggestions and recommendations were successfully implemented.

CONCLUSION

In Bosnia-Herzegovina the education system was used to introduce ideologies that prevented opportunities for ethnic cooperation or the possibility of a "multicultural" society. It was especially interesting to note that the educators I talked to in Bosnia-Herzegovina observed that an education system controlled by the national parties was ruining any chance of transforming the hearts and minds of young people and that it was reinforcing stereotypes that made peace building very difficult. The introduction of programs and trainings focusing on prejudice reduction, multi- and intercultural understanding, conflict resolution, and peace education within the school and education system generally during the post-accord period were seen by respondents as very important in order to build sustainable peace. It was stressed that education programs should be aimed at improving dialogue and relationship-building initiatives where possible to strengthen peace-building efforts.

On the basis of this case study, some concrete recommendations for how to enhance peace-building efforts within education systems might include the following:

- Develop "white papers" or "discussion documents" that encourage dialogue around contentious issues
- Provide training in conflict resolution, nonviolence, and transparency during the post-accord period to help educational institutions become institutions that promote peace
- Establish partnerships and cooperation between government, civil society, and education institutions

- Ensure young people and educators are adequately represented when peace accords are developed
- Introduce peace education programs that can break down stereotypes and negative images of other groups
- Minimize the "brain drain" to keep skilled and qualified people involved in peace-building efforts during the post-accord period
- Develop holistic peace-building efforts and coordinate education initiatives with other civil society efforts
- Minimize corruption among government officials and promote efforts that reward leaders who encourage peace-building efforts

These are just some examples that can be highlighted from the research. They illustrate the value of generating constructive ideas from people directly involved in conflict areas and are very encouraging. Research initiatives that look at efforts to resolve ethnic conflict situations might want to explore how such efforts can be done more comprehensively in the future.

On October 28, 2002, the head of the Organization for Security and Co-operation in Europe (OSCE) in Bosnia-Herzegovina, Ambassador Robert Beecroft, announced: "I propose a vision for education reform that includes modern schools, where all parents and students have a voice, where teaching is as interactive as possible, and where students' creativity, individuality and diversity and special talents are encouraged and used to drive the learning process." This vision can in many ways be built on the hard lessons that have been learned from local people involved in efforts to transform the education system in Bosnia-Herzegovina.

Notes

1. I worked as the Conflict Resolution Program Manager for the United Methodist Committee on Relief (UMCOR) and was based in Zenica and Sarajevo.

2. The term "peace building" is used by theorists in various ways. With the publication of *An Agenda for Peace* in 1992, the then–secretary general of the United Nations, Boutros Boutros-Ghali, defined post-conflict peace building as the "action to identify and support structures which will tend to avoid a relapse before violence breaks out." Peace building in his framework is associated with the post-accord phase that follows "peacekeeping" and "peacemaking" activities (Boutros-Ghali and United Nations Department of Public Information 1992, 11). Lederach, on the other hand, argues that "peace building" is "a comprehensive concept that encompasses, generates, and sustains the full array of

processes, approaches, and stages needed to transform conflict toward more sustainable, peaceful relationships" (Lederach 1995, 20). The term "peace building" is used in this chapter as an all-encompassing term that transcends various phases and stages.

3. The term "conflict transformation" developed out of a recognition that conflicts can not necessarily be "resolved' or "ended," but more accurately they should be viewed as being "transformed" into new dynamics. Similar to the term "peace building," "conflict transformation" is mostly used to reflect the fact that comprehensive and holistic approaches need to be considered when attempts are made to constructively deal with conflicts (see Rupesinghe 1995; Clements 1997; Notter 1995; Lederach 1997; Vayrynen 1991).

4. The history and contextual background for this section are drawn from the following authors: Pinson 1994; Donia and Fine 1994; Davis 1996; Malcolm 1996; Samary 1995; Lampe 1996; Udovicki and Ridgeway 1995; Andripc and Juricipc et al. 1990; Kolouh-Westin 2002; Ivic and Perzic 2002.

Jeff Helsing, with Namik Kirlic,
Neil McMaster, and Nir Sonnenschein

Young People's Activism and the Transition to Peace

Bosnia, Northern Ireland, and Israel

This chapter reports on three short addresses given by young people who have been active in peace building and youth empowerment in their communities, where violent conflict has been endemic.[1] In particular, they have been very active in youth organizations and thus provide us with a young person's perspective on their respective conflicts and the role youth have played in Bosnia, Northern Ireland, and Israel. One of the most important messages that these young people have to offer—and one that they have lived—is that there can be no peace where there is exclusion. They have, each in their own way, worked across barriers, divides, and cultural or ethnic lines. For them, inclusion and equity are essential to peace. What is also remarkable is that they are optimistic overall, even though they and their communities have witnessed so much pain and suffering. At the core is a belief that people are fundamentally good.

Young people rarely have a sense of ownership or any place in a peace process, yet we see countless examples of young people making a difference in their own communities. Since we see that they can be very effective agents of social change and peace, it might be useful to consider how to empower young people and the positive effect they might have in their nations or regions. In many conflicts there is too often a lack of hope among young people. Despair and impoverishment help sow the seeds of conflict as well as of terrorism. So it is important to spotlight those young people who are working for peace and what they have been able to accomplish in providing alternative outlets for their peers. It is equally necessary to promote the efforts of young men and women who have found ways for young people to make a difference in their own communities as well as give their peers a sense of hope and accomplishment. They and countless others have helped to break down stereotypes among young people and helped create positive rather than negative images of the other. They have also helped break down stereotypes of young people as disengaged, lazy, and self-centered.

As Siobhán McEvoy-Levy notes in the introduction to this volume, young people are rarely included in a peace process. Yet, while they may be marginalized in a political sense, they often are at the center of the debates within a society or community in conflict. In Israel, for example, five young men spent almost two years under detention and in jail as conscientious objectors, arguing that they could not serve in an occupation army. At the same time, some young people serving in the Israeli Defence Forces have joined ranks with settler groups in proclaiming that they will never act as accomplices to the use of military force to compel settlers to withdraw from the occupied territories. The voices and actions of these young people mirror the critical issues and debates within Israeli society, and how such young people act is closely watched by the larger populace.

One of the conscientious objectors, Haggai Matar, first joined a youth program dedicated to peace and mutual understanding in the ninth grade when he participated in a two-week Israeli-Palestinian program, the "NIR School." He subsequently participated in other peace-related activities as a teenager. Before his release from jail, he wrote, "One of the most amazing letters I got came from a Palestinian youth who lives in the occupied territories. He told me that he grew up believing in Hammas, wanting to be a suicide-bomber. Then he writes: 'But when I heard of your decision, I realized that there are actions which trigger greater echoes than any bomb ever could—and I have forsaken the road of violence'" (Matar 2004). Here, the voice of the youth as peace builder had an impact on the youth who was on a path toward violence.

In many post-conflict or post-accord situations, there is a growing recognition that youth must be addressed. This is now the case in Bosnia and Northern Ireland, even among political and governmental authorities. Young people can be agents of change and, obviously, have been affected greatly by the conflict and violence. Thus, much of the work with young people is designed to give them hope—both to move them beyond the past and work toward the future with a positive, hopeful outlook. At the same time, to have a meaningful impact on the future, they need skills—skills that can enhance their contributions to sustaining or creating peace in the areas of organizational management, conflict resolution, nonviolence, or citizenship.

One of the keys to each of the three programs that are discussed below is that they help make young people more secure in themselves and more sensitive to others. Ultimately, such programs may not bring peace to their countries or change their communities, but they clearly help transform individuals. And, epitomizing grassroots change, the more individuals who can be transformed, the greater the possibility of peace being built and sustained when peace agreements emerge. This is particularly the case with young people who will later be in positions of leadership in their communities if not their countries. As each of these young men implies, young people have less of an interest vested in the status quo than adults and thus have the greatest incentive to push for change.

Bosnia-Herzegovina

Since the end of the war in Bosnia, many programs have emerged as ways to engage young people. Such initiatives tend to focus on job training and economic development or conflict resolution, human rights, and nonviolence, or some combination of the above. Essentially, these are efforts to develop more responsible citizens while at the same time providing hope and the necessary skills for them to become productive members of society. There is a desire to open new horizons and orient the young people toward the future in a post-conflict environment. But much depends on getting politicians and administrators in Bosnia to view youth development as an integral element of reconstruction, rehabilitation, and reconciliation. This has begun to occur in the past couple of years. The government helped sponsor two major youth forums in the spring of 2004—one was global in its scope and participation, the other European. Education for Peace programs have been introduced into many schools throughout the country in the past few years. Many outside organizations, including the United Nations Development Program (UNDP) and the World Bank, have put a great deal of effort into peace and conflict resolution programs, including summer camps that promote interethnic education and understanding. While the environment for such programs is better today than it was immediately after the end of the war, young people often remain disaffected and see little hope for the future, much less a shared future in a multiethnic society.

The following is an account of one young person from Bosnia.

Namik Kirlic (age 20)
Gornji Vakuf/Uskoplje, Bosnia-Herzegovina

The devastation of the war in Bosnia in my town of Gornji Vakuf/Uskoplje was quite significant. Not only were many killed and many parts of the town destroyed, but the town became ethnically divided. One street in the center of the town completely separated the two communities of Bosniac Muslims and Bosnian Croats. The result was that both communities developed into communities that functioned independently from each other. In addition, the war led to significant unemployment, dissatisfaction, and disillusion.

As a way to break out of the cycle of disillusionment, segregation, and violence, the Omladinski Centar of Gornji Vakuf/Uskoplje (OCGVU) was established. The center was located on the division street and aimed at bringing children from both communities to learn and develop together. OCGVU is an organization in which children and youth develop educational programs, learn and grow, and connect two communities separated by war. The ultimate vision of the OCGVU is to take care of children and young people and those who have influence on forming their personalities, such as teachers and parents. OCGVU has adopted a holistic approach to addressing the psychosocial needs of children and young people by using education, recreation, and creative activities in programs that are aimed at promoting civil society, multiethnic dialogue, tolerance, and leadership.

OCGVU has grown from a small organization that only taught English and informational technology/computer studies to an organization that has become an important educational factor in the community. It has grown from a singular focus on educating children and young people to educating teachers, parents, and authorities. Its activities today include information technology, English, German, music, art, dance, drama, and video/photo studies. OCGVU has established or promoted a library, club, Internet café, cultural events, art colonies, and exhibitions, theater performances, summer and peace camps, peace workshops, civic education, youth initiatives, teacher trainings, youth partnership projects, and a teen group.

The center's leadership structure allows young people themselves to participate in the decision-making processes, organization, and leadership. The Teen Group consists of the young people who have expressed a wish to work on various projects and take over part of the responsibilities the adults had in the OCGVU. In order for these young people to be able to do so, they regularly attend workshops and seminars on conflict resolution, nonviolent communication, civil society building, leadership, media, gender issues, project proposal writing, evaluation, and others.

The Teen Group consists of both Croats and Bosniacs, and many of the activities of the group helped eliminate differences between them. The center itself was the only safe environment where young people from both groups could work or come together. Various speakers were heard on topics such as nonviolence, drug abuse, sexual violence, and violence in the family. Posters were designed and posted that called for cooperation and togetherness. But many of the activities also had a functional purpose and were not geared primarily to bridge a divide between Bosniacs and Croats. These included classes at the community center as well as specific projects such as ecology activities to clean up the town's parks and other areas and also to raise the awareness of the issue of ecology in Gornji Vakuf. Art and music festivals were also created.

As the coordinator of the Teen Group, I was always proudest of our "Fountain" project, which we realized in the summer of 2001. A few of us in the Teen Group felt as though the workshops, seminars, and public campaigns for peace were not enough. We wanted to feel peace. We wanted it to be visible to everyone. In 1980 the town's own architect had designed and built a fountain in the center of town. Throughout the years it had served as a hangout for young people. It was in the center of the town on what after the war served as the division street. As with most of the town of Gornji Vakuf/Uskoplje, it was completely destroyed. The fountain's architect had been killed in the war and his family had left the city. Moreover, they were Croats who had lived in the Bosniac part. Six years after the war, the downtown was rebuilt and the reunification process had started. But no one had mentioned the fountain. It didn't belong to anyone.

Our Teen Group, therefore, wanted to give this symbol of youth back to our town. We wrote a project proposal and were able to secure financing for the idea from UMCOR (United Methodist Committee on Relief) through a fund designed to be used by young people in various youth centers in Bosnia. We were given the necessary approval from the municipal authorities as well. For the opening day we organized a big festival/concert on the division street and invited the family of the architect from 1980 to perform the opening ceremony. We wanted our past, our present, and our future to come together. The rebuilt fountain was to become a symbol of a united youth who know their roots and their past and who are willing to make progress and a better life for all. We wanted a symbol that gave hope but that also served as a lesson.

The work of the Teen Group and the community center work often had to overcome significant problems and obstacles. These included a lack of understanding from the community, teachers, peers, and parents. Nationalism was still very strong and on both sides we were called pro-Muslim or pro-Croat. Few politicians ever wanted to understand our work, nor did they try to help us. We were the only youth program in the country that had to pay rent. When we advertised our activities, prominent politicians in the town would walk behind us and take our posters down. We always had to go the extra mile in order to obtain permission for our activities in the town and we were always hassled in the process.

In addition, teachers did not appreciate the knowledge we gained outside their classrooms; they often opposed our time spent away at seminars and workshops and would always try to punish us through unexpected and unnecessary oral examinations. Our parents often supported us, but most of the time they did not understand what exactly we were doing. They were glad we were off the streets, but the whole idea of peace building was not something that they would tell their friends that their kids were doing. Often parents would not allow their kids to spend too much time at the OCGVU as they feared the reactions of others.

Peers most of the time had no interest in what we were doing and often tried to belittle our work with jokes. There was always an attrition of young people. Sometimes they would simply go off to college, but often they would give in to the pressure the community would put on them and stop participating in the OCGVU activities. The conflict itself and the very difficult economic and social situation had a dramatic impact on the activities of the OCGVU, especially those of young people. Many youth become disillusioned and give up. They are not interested in improving the situation. They are waiting for someone else to do it for them. They also feel like they can not do anything. Many constraints are put on them by politicians, parents, and education. Many are, however, attending colleges, but most are not looking forward to graduating, as they will not be able to find jobs. As a result, more and more young people want to leave Bosnia and search for a better life elsewhere.

Education in Bosnia-Herzegovina is also not conducive to peace building and giving young people hope that their lives will get better. The country has three different education systems, which together only have one aim—to create further divisions and create an obedient population. The learning conditions are terrible and technology not well developed. Much of the learning is still done the way it has been for decades and generations. Professors are not paid enough and are thus inflexible and unmotivated. University dormitories are awful, and often students from certain areas cannot stay there because their local governments have not provided sufficient funds. Finally, upon graduation there are no jobs. Some estimate the unemployment rate to be as high as 60 percent. The World Bank and other NGOs, as well as the CIA, claim the figure in 2002 to be around 40 percent, although taking into account the "shadow" economy in which employers often keep employees off the books to avoid taxes, the figure could be as low as 25 percent (Oslobodjenje, May 13, 2002, 1). For young people, unemployment is higher than the average.

But young people also face considerable pressures at home. Many parents are abusive and domestic violence is a growing problem. There are no facilities for young people to seek psychological help, nor are there good systems of support. Alcohol, cigarettes, and drugs are extremely accessible to the youngest populations and they often abuse them. A pack of cigarettes costs the same as a liter of milk. There is absolutely no education in schools concerning drugs, alcohol, and safe sex. Very few young people vote or are remotely interested in politics; politicians are not trusted. And many young people question whether the international community has the power or desire to bring about positive changes. Too often, it seems, the rhetoric and the monetary pledges do not make a difference on the ground.

The political situation can be blamed for much of the attitudes of young people. The Dayton Peace Agreement stopped the war but seemed to fail at most everything else. It divided the country into two and in practice created three parts. So many levels of government result in little ever being implemented. Ethnic issues remain the most salient for most politicians. Moreover, we cannot speak about peace building in Bosnia unless we speak of one united country, where all are working toward the same thing.

But the international community stands behind the Dayton Peace Accords and hence behind the continued division. In addition, international support has lately been for the nationalistic parties, the same parties that led the country to war. This compounds the fact that most people in Bosnia-Herzegovina have no sense of belonging to anything anymore.

In addition to an improved economy and education system, peace building needs to be sustained and rewarded. If lives do not improve, there will be little faith in peace. In a situation where people are living poorly and are unsatisfied, it is easier to blame the other side, which will always be the other ethnic group. Democratic parties, which want to work for a united Bosnia, need to be given attention, rather than the nationalistic parties whose presidents not so long ago were Milosevic, Tudjman, and Izebegovic. Too often, it seems that most people in Bosnia-Herzegovina do not share a sense of belonging to the country or feel any responsibility to their fellow citizens. Rather, they feel tied to the community in which they live and often only to their own ethnic group. For many, that would mean they have a greater sense of belonging to Serbia or Croatia than to Bosnia. For Bosnia to succeed and its people prosper, such divisions need to be bridged, and certainly the law and constitution should not make such divisions legal and embedded in the society. The international community has too often not provided enough support for democratic political parties while working too closely with the nationalist parties, which, after all, were the ones involved in the design and execution of the Dayton Peace Accords. The international community invests too much in nationalist parties who have little or no interest in a united Bosnia-Herzegovina. Thus, the international community should focus less on working with these nationalistic parties and more on creating prosperity for young people by investing in their education, and thus creating more opportunities for economic development. But most of the responsibility for Bosnia's future lies with the citizens of Bosnia themselves.

And yet, there remains room for optimism. In Gornji Vakuf/Uskoplje today, through the community center, Bosniacs and Croats are partners and not enemies. The municipality is providing the center with a larger space for its activities for a much-reduced fee. The political situation in the town is changing. The town has increasingly become united about the community center, and the authorities have realized that they benefit politically by supporting the center. The community center has become involved in all important decisions and processes that involve youth in the town. Its cooperation with schools and sports clubs on both sides has greatly increased.

Children now use the things they learned at the OCGVU in classrooms and at homes and thus attract parents and teacher, for whom the center provides education programs as well. They have become more active in other things in the town. Children who regularly attend activities at the center have done better at school. These students are reportedly more outspoken and more interested in the material. We are making them modern citizens of our country who are willing to speak out for themselves. They are willing to speak with politicians and work on a better future for all of us. They are not passive or lazy but willing to seek higher education and give back. They have learned that voluntarism pays off as well as the power of giving to others. They have also developed evolutionary and revolutionary minds. This seems the essence of youth empowerment.

Our greatest success has been that we have shown ourselves, our teachers, and our parents that Croats and Bosniacs can live, work, and be productive together. Furthermore, we all became friends for life and, more importantly, created models of positive and constructive friendships and relationships not based on our territorial, religious, and ethnic boundaries. We have also traveled all over the world and begun to realize what it means to be citizens of the world, not just one of the ethnic sides of the divided Gornji Vakuf/Uskoplje. But young people need to be provided with an even greater sense of hope that their lives can and will improve. Otherwise, they will develop into adults who will not be able to take this country anywhere. Then, they will not be peacemakers or troublemakers; they will be passive, not-opinionated adults, who will be easily swayed by any political faction.

The mission of the Omladinski Centar of Gornji Vakuf/Uskoplje is the recovery and reconciliation of a community divided by war through working with children and young people. The Omladinski Centar began in 1997 and has adopted a holistic approach to addressing the psychosocial needs of children and young people by using education, recreation, and social activities in programs that are aimed at promoting civil society, multiethnic dialogue, tolerance, leadership, and, ultimately, the reconciliation of its communities. The target groups are mainly children and young people between five and eighteen years old and include refugees, returnees, and children with social or learning difficulties. The program emphasizes that the recovery of children and young people in such a post-conflict environment should be based within their communities and in structures that are most familiar to them and to which they can relate. If young people of Gornji Vakuf/Uskoplje are to be able to overcome the nightmares of the past and play a role in rebuilding their country for the future, social, recreational, and educational activities must take place in an atmosphere that is safe, nonthreatening, and positive. Funding sources include the United Methodist Committee on Relief (UMCOR); European Commission; United Nations Development Program (UNDP); International Rescue Committee; Catholic Relief Services; Stichting Kinderpostzegels Nederland (SKN); Balkan Children and Youth Foundation (BCYF); German Committee for Human Rights and Democratization; Organization for Security and Cooperation in Europe (OSCE).

ADDRESS: Omladinski Centar, Bratstva i Jedinstva 10, 70240 Gornji Vakuf-
Uskoplje
Bosnia i Herzegovina
PHONE: 00 387 30 26 05 20
E-MAIL: ocgv@gmx.net
WEB SITE: http://omladinski-centar.port5.com or http://notrix.net/centar

Northern Ireland

For many years there have been a variety of people-to-people exchanges between young people in Northern Ireland. Such programs usually incorporate an equal mix of Catholic and Protestant youth, often a mix of males and females, and target different age groups (up to age twenty-five). The aim of such programs is to attract young people from all over Northern Ireland and bring in youth from different social and economic backgrounds. They are usually structured around different themes and might include socializing, outdoor activities, arts and crafts, sports, and stays with host families. There are a number of programs that take young people from Northern Ireland abroad, in the belief that they will more easily mix outside of their own society as well as learn about another culture.

There is also a presumption that young people will more easily form relationships as they explore together something quite different from their own experiences. This helps them find points of commonality between them.

However, too often such programs have a short-term impact on young people and seem too far removed from the Northern Ireland experience. Thus, many programs for young people, and by young people, have moved beyond promoting mutual understanding and toward a more active, collaborative orientation toward peace and, increasingly, responsible and active citizenship. A number of programs try to develop a sense of participatory and responsive democracy in young people. There is also an attempt by the government and education authorities to reinforce the notion of citizenship. In the Northern Ireland context, this can become a very powerful tool of engagement for young people because citizenship education quickly becomes a means by which young people engage in the planning, or development, of a new society. This can happen because there is no preexisting consensus about such a society in a polarized polity such as Northern Ireland (author's discussion with Anthony Gallagher, Professor of Education at Queens University, Belfast, May 3, 2004). The following is an account from a young person in Northern Ireland.

NEIL McMASTER (age 20)
Ballycastle, Northern Ireland

I am not a professional or an academic in this field, so I will attempt to offer insights based on my personal experiences of volunteering, working part-time, and participating in youth schemes. While providing a somewhat simplistic view of the situation in Northern Ireland, I want to give a brief look at youth work schemes that have not worked in my experience, a little bit about the background to the organization I work with and why I think it works, and conclude with perhaps naïve hopes for the future. Northern Ireland has two main communities, Protestant and Catholic, both of which feel they are victims and are insecure in their position and the intentions of the other community. Both are looking to win, or at least win the peace, and prevail over the other. The main differences and fault lines between the communities are religion, nationality, and identity. Northern Ireland has approximately 1.7 million people, about 43 percent of whom are Catholic, leaving 57 percent Protestant, agnostic, or other (CAIN n.d. a). In the most recent cycle of violence over the past thirty years, there have been around 3,600 killed and many more injured (CAIN n.d. b).

I found it very interesting to hear quite often in workshops and conferences on peace and conflict that Northern Ireland is an area where peace is working. While one truly hopes this to be the case, recent research and expe-

riences provide hints of a long way to go. In many ways, the two communities continue to draw further apart, despite the best intentions of the peace process. Before the "Troubles" of the past thirty years, 40 percent of the Northern Irish community lived in mixed areas of Catholics and Protestants; now that figure is down to 7 or 8 percent. Workforces have also become increasingly segregated, with only 5 percent of Catholics employed by companies in areas dominated by the Protestant community and 8 percent of Protestants holding down jobs in Catholic areas. About 63 percent of the population in Belfast lives in enclaves that are more than 90 percent Protestant or Catholic (Shirlow 2002). This seems to demonstrate an increased polarity between the two communities and a lack of understanding about each other.

Other research shows that 68 percent of young people in interface areas of Belfast have never had a significant conversation with someone of the other faith (Shirlow 2002). This highlights problems that exist even with peace in place, particularly what seems a situation in which peace has not brought the two communities closer together but seems to have kept them frozen apart.

Attempts at bridging the gaps between Catholic and Protestant youth have often reinforced the status quo of separation or ultimately fail to make any difference. In my own experience there are certain types of approaches to working with youth that do not work and can have damaging effects on any further community relations work.

Under the country-wide program to develop curricula and programs for young people that will teach tolerance, called Education for Mutual Understanding, the results are mixed. While young people have been brought together to learn more about each other, too often their separateness ends up being reinforced. Schools are brought together but the busses remain segregated, just as most of the students' neighborhoods and towns are.

Even more intensive youth schemes such as children's holiday programs have not been very successful. Such programs, which take Protestant and Catholic youth on joint holiday excursions and travel abroad programs, have had limited success. Too often the primary goal of such programs is contact with others from another faith. But contact is not sufficient to always make a difference and does not promote long-term learning. And, too often such contact programs revolve around social and sporting activities, which are not the difficult issues.

However, this isn't a story of doom and gloom. There have been a vast number of initiatives that have made a huge difference and without which the situation would be much worse. The organization I became part of as a young person and where I currently work is an excellent example. It is called the Spirit of Enniskillen Trust. The background of the organization is itself quite remarkable and inspiring and gives me hope that similar schemes can work as a bridge between Catholic and Protestant young people.

The trust emerged in the aftermath of the Remembrance Sunday 1987 bombing in Enniskillen, Northern Ireland. The Provisional IRA bomb killed eleven people and sixty-three more were injured. Gordon Wilson's daughter Marie was one of those killed. It could have provoked a response of anger and revenge; instead what emerged was a dignity that reflected tolerance, understanding, and reconciliation—the true Spirit of Enniskillen. Some would later note that Loyalist (Protestant) paramilitaries were intent on retaliation but may have been stopped by the words of Gordon Wilson when he was interviewed on television about the death of his daughter. His emotional words seemed to touch the hearts of many when he said: "I have lost my daughter and we shall miss her, but I bear no ill will. I bear no grudge. Dirty sort of talk is not going to bring her back to life. She was a great wee lassie." He forgave her killers, saying, "I shall pray for those people tonight and every night." It was from this message of reconciliation that the Spirit of Enniskillen Trust was set up in 1989.

The Spirit of Enniskillen Trust pays tribute to this spirit and to the efforts of those who brought good out of evil. The trust celebrates the ability of the community to work together to overcome division. Since 1989 over five hundred young people and adults have participated. One of the big assumptions that we have at the Spirit of Enniskillen is that for a fair, peaceful, and pluralist society to emerge, change has to happen at all levels. It cannot just be a top-down change at the government level. And, whether people like it or not, young people are essential to any change. The slogan of the Spirit of Enniskillen is "Where young people make a difference."

We follow a program called "Citizenship for a Shared Future," which we hope can help young people to communicate across barriers of mistrust and suspicion to build relationships and tackle difficult issues. We want to encourage them to believe that you can make a positive change. One of the main problems we have to tackle is the "avoidance culture" in Northern Ireland. It has been commented that in Northern Ireland to talk about the "difficult" issues such as politics and religion is not polite, and while people would meet at all levels of society they would avoid these issues. What we try to do is give the young people "ownership" of the program. We want to empower them to establish their own agenda, which is great and necessary, because as we all know, teenagers will not listen to adults anyway. As it happens, the young people pick the "difficult" issues that we want them to talk about anyway; but now they feel added passion because they set the agenda and picked the issues themselves.

All too often decreased communication and lack of political accord has led to increased polarization and mistrust between the two cultures. Underlying the practice of the Spirit of Enniskillen is an acceptance that young people are naturally curious about themselves and others and have a real need to learn about and to widen their experience of the world. They often also want to be personally involved in current issues of the day and, contrary to much popular opinion, have a strong desire to make a positive contribution for the good of society.

The essence of the Spirit of Enniskillen program is to encourage young people to broaden their horizons by traveling to other countries—also experiencing community divisions—where they gain firsthand experience of how people from different backgrounds are learning to live together. On return, participants are expected to reflect on their experiences and invited to become part of a "critical yeast" promoting the principles of equity and interdependence between all communities. When they do choose to work back in their communities, their efforts can have a constructive impact well beyond their immediate circles.

Another thing that I have noticed while working and participating in youth schemes is that theory and practice have to come together. I have read thick textbooks of ideas which seem great—until you try them with young people because we can be quite a strange and hard to please age. The theory has to be relevant for young people, and therefore theory and practice must go together. It is also important to be well prepared and to be flexible. One must practice the activities and approaches, consistently evaluate the programs, and change things when necessary.

There is also an international element to the scheme, where groups go overseas to learn about other cultures and religions in contested areas. This is intended to open the eyes of the young participants and take them away from the insular reality that Northern Ireland has. But this also gives the young people an opportunity to step outside their emotional ties in Northern Ireland. In so doing, they usually become less guarded and more willing to discuss issues.

The annual program brings together fifty young people who are then selected for five groups of ten. The selection process begins with the participants submitting an application to the scheme, and after careful review of the application forms around eighty are selected to come for an interview. The interviews are all done by past participants of the scheme, therefore they have a good insight into the type and diversity of people needed to get the greatest amount of learning. The fifty participants prepare together but travel as separate groups.

These groups have at least one past participant, which is essential because they have experienced the Spirit of Enniskillen and are well equipped to deal with the emotions of the group, which can be difficult as it can be quite a daunting challenge for many young people. The groups are equally balanced between Protestant and Catholic, male and female, and, most importantly, represent a cross-section of Northern Ireland from all social, *educational, geographical, and economic backgrounds, not just working-class or middle-class or paramilitaries. This mix is crucial in order for young people to learn about each other. The learning processes we emphasize are ones that confront the difficult issues but at the same time develop the interpersonal ability to have dialogue on difficult issues. The key skills that we try to teach are active listening, assertiveness, empathy, affirming, challenging, planning, reviewing, analyzing, and facilitation. However, we do realize that there has to be a balance between work and fun.*

One of the criticisms this type of work often leads to in Northern Ireland is that it dilutes one's culture, makes us all the same. But we find that participants actually return from the programs more secure in themselves but also more sensitive to the hopes and fears of others. They do develop leadership and communication skills that help them to work together. A real hope of the Spirit of Enniskillen is to show that you can be an active citizen in Northern Ireland.

There is also an underlying premise that "while we are not responsible for Northern Ireland, we are responsible for our own contribution." And, with this in mind, many of the young people make a positive contribution. In addition, participants get something concrete from the scheme. It is accredited and they receive qualification in youth work that they can show employers. One of the biggest criticisms of the trust is that it only works with fifty young people a year. But the program is trying to widen its sphere of influence—we have formed a follow-up group called "Future Voices," which is a group run by young people for young people. Currently, the Future Voices program is working to go into schools to do skills development, as well as training for political influence.

Through my own work I have witnessed the success and value of the Spirit of Enniskillen programs both as a coordinator and as a participant. But it is important to stress that this approach may not be suitable everywhere; we just find it works for us. A lesson that has emerged from the work and programs of the trust is that by empowering young people and giving them hope, they will make a positive change. Young people are very curious about each other and want to learn; few of them desire conflict and segregation. So the real challenge is how to nurture the hope of young people before they become jaded with failures and disappointments.

The Spirit of Enniskillen program encourages young people to broaden their horizons by traveling to other countries—also experiencing community divisions—where they gain firsthand experience of how people from different backgrounds are learning to live together. On return, participants are expected to reflect on their experiences and invited to become part of a "critical yeast" promoting the principles of equity *and* interdependence between all communities. If they so wish they may also join and get further support from the Future Voices project formed and run by past participants of the scheme. Funding sources include Belfast City Council and private donations.

Address: The Gordon Wilson Centre, 97 Malone Street, Belfast BT8 6EQ
Phone: 028 9038 1500
E-mail: info@soetrust.co.uk
Web site: www.soetrust.co.uk

Israel

Since the beginning of the second ("Al Aqsa") Intifada, most youth organizations or programs have disbanded or are unable to continue. Young people remain active members of groups protesting the occupation (on both sides of the line) but do not work together or meet as they had previously. A major reason for this is it has been very difficult for Palestinians to move about the occupied territories, much less come into Israel itself. In addition, security remains a major concern for both Israeli and Palestinian youth (and their parents), so interaction becomes very problematic. One exception to this has been the Seeds of Peace program, in which Palestinian and Israeli young people meet during the summer in the United States at the Seeds of Peace camp in Maine. The Seeds of Peace organization has an office in Jerusalem as well. The young people often stay in contact after their return to their communities, but it is very difficult to meet. And, as some Seeds of Peace graduates have noted, until and unless there is a Seeds of Peace office or presence in the occupied territories, many in the Palestinian community will view the program as an American institution that has little relevance to the Palestinian struggle and that does not provide any sense of Palestinian ownership.

The Palestinian-Israeli experience in organizations such as Seeds of Peace reflects the difficulties that young people face when engaged in peace-related activities when the conflict revolves around a vicious cycle of violence. They meet their "enemies," which can be a stressful situation, and when they return home they often are viewed as traitors for having met with the enemy. As a young Israeli peace activist noted recently in a conversation with this author, "We have to put more energy into gaining acceptance in our own communities than we do in our work with Palestinians." And, when violence breaks out—when suicide bombers strike or when young people are gunned down by occupying forces or helicopter gunships—many young people who participate in such programs struggle with whether they have let their own community down or whether they have been dupes. They question whether the new friend they met at a peace camp is actually the enemy, might actually be happy at the suffering of one's own people or community. How does one defend an Israeli or Palestinian friend when members of his or her community have killed people—including many young people—in one's own community?

In addition, as a result of the ongoing conflict with Palestinians in the occupied territories, Israeli Jews have grown further apart from Israeli Arabs. The following is an account from a young person in Israel.

Nir Sonnenschein (age 24)
Neve Shalom/Wahat al Salam, Israel

I live in a small village in Israel called Neve Shalom/Wahat al Salam (which translates into "Oasis of Peace" in English). The village is a binational Jewish-Palestinian village where the Jewish and Palestinian inhabitants try to lead their lives together and hold educational activities to further peace in the region. There are currently two separate but linked problems facing Israel. The first is the occupation of the West Bank and Gaza and the military rule and oppression of the Palestinians there. The Israeli military and governmental policies regarding the Palestinians have long been making their lives miserable with prolonged curfews, barricades on roads, military excursions into heavily populated areas, the "separation fence" currently being built, and recently assassination of "key figures" in terrorist organizations, incursions that often harm innocent civilians as well. The Palestinians in turn have been carrying out attacks against both the military and civilians with many suicide bombings of public places. The second, less discussed problem is the discrimination against Palestinian citizens of Israel and the relationship between the Jewish majority and the Palestinian Arab minority. The Palestinian citizens of Israel have suffered from discrimination from both the Jewish citizens and the government—in funding, in development, in their relationships with the police, and in many other areas. Funding for Arab municipalities and schools has historically been, and probably to some extent still is, lower than their Jewish counterparts. Obtaining building permits is a problem in Arab communities, for example. To give just another recent example, in the protests/riots of October 2000, eight Arab citizens of Israel were killed by the police, and the police used weapons against the civilian population. This never would have happened in my opinion if the riots/protests were composed of Jews. The society inside Israel is very segregated, and even the few joint Jewish-Palestinian cities are divided into Jewish and Palestinian areas. Many of the Jewish citizens will go through their entire lives without really meeting or having a seri-

ous conversation with a Palestinian, nor do they have much exposure to Palestinian views through the media. This is why the existence of an unsegregated community like Neve Shalom/Wahat al-Salam, as well as educational work to further the understanding of both sides, is so important.

The two main educational facilities in the village are the elementary school and the School for Peace. The elementary school is a binational, bilingual school that developed naturally from the village's need for a school in which to educate its children. Initially, it was created for the children of the community, but over time it has expanded and welcomed children who are bussed in from the surrounding Jewish and Palestinian villages. There are currently three hundred children in the school, 90 percent of whom come from outside the Neve Shalom/Wahat al-Salam community. The school is unique in that it teaches both languages to all children from a young age. The Israeli school system teaches Arabic but at a very basic level and only in higher grades. Thus, most Jewish children usually graduate from Israeli high school without even speaking basic Arabic. The elementary school is roughly evenly divided into Jewish and Palestinian teachers, and each teacher instructs in his or her native tongue. The children also learn not only about their own culture but also about the culture, holidays, and customs of the others. The school celebrates a single holiday from the Muslim, Christian, and Jewish religions each year with an open event. The elementary school serves as an important meeting ground for Jewish and Palestinian children who otherwise would not ever meet or associate with each other socially.

The second educational facility is the School for Peace (SFP). It has greater outreach into the larger Israeli-Arab and Jewish communities and focuses on youth. The School for Peace began by running encounter workshops for Jewish and Palestinian eleventh-grade high school students and later expanded to other areas of conflict resolution and peace building, including encounter workshops for students from Israel and the occupied territories, university courses in conflict resolution, encounter workshops for professionals from Israel and the occupied territories (such as journalists, lawyers, and educators), binational and uninational women's workshops, and workshops and professional cooperation with similar organizations in other conflict areas such as Cyprus, Northern Ireland, and Kosovo. A great deal of the School for Peace's work is still with youths (high school and college students). Over 30,000 youths (and over 35,000 people over all) have participated in the workshops in the School for Peace since its founding in the early 1970s. The workshops for high school students (in which I have participated) are not limited to a "we are all human so let's get along" school of thought. In the School for Peace approach, there is an initial phase of meeting the "other side" and seeing that they are much like us. But the participants also confront the cultural and even more importantly political differences with the other group. This is very important, especially for Israeli Jews because they are very rarely exposed to the opinions of Palestinians. At the end of the workshop there is a simulation "game" between the two sides where they negotiate about the future nature of the state of Israel and its relationship to and impact on its Palestinian citizens. This really makes the participants on both sides think about where they stand on many of the key issues and to understand what the opinions of the other side are. Many of the graduates of the School for Peace's programs have gone on to become peace activists.

Over the years, there have been considerable successes, some failures, and many challenges for the village and its youth. The greatest success is the very existence of the village as a symbol for the possibility of Jewish-Palestinian coexistence, even if it is only on a very small scale. This success is supported by the friendships and open discussions that exist in the village. The pursuit of a more equitable society continues to be an ongoing process we in the community strive to achieve. One of the most problematic issues remains that of language. The Jewish residents of the village are a lot less fluent in Arabic than the Palestinians are in Hebrew, and a majority of the conversations that involve Jews tend to be held in Hebrew. This is one of the inequalities and asymmetries in Israel that is reflected to a smaller degree in the village.

One of the difficulties facing young people in the village, especially the Jews, is military service. There is mandatory military service in Israel, and service in the army is part of the consensus of mainstream Israeli society. However, the inhabitants of the village are very opposed to the military occupation of Palestinian lands and the continued oppression and humiliation of the Palestinians there. This is a very complex issue because it is not easy to get out of army service and not a trivial decision to attempt to do this. Each Jewish youth in the village handles this slightly differently: some have chosen to get out of military service altogether; others have gone to serve in noncombat positions, while some have served in combat units, each with his own reasons. To understand the complexity of this choice, I will quote a friend of my brother's who is not from the village but believes in its ideals. This young man serves as a combat soldier in the occupied territories. He remarked that "if all of the conscientious and moral people will not serve in the occupied territories, all those left serving there will be the ones who have no moral problems oppressing the Palestinians. I try in my service to make their lives a little easier and show them that not all Israelis are that bad." This young man's opinion is quite different in applying principles of peace. Others hope to promote another view or implementation: "if every young Israeli man and woman were to refuse to carry out his or her military service in the occupied territories, then the occupation would have to cease." Thus, the conflict remains incredibly complex for most of the youth in the village.

Neve Shalom/Wahat al-Salam, Hebrew and Arabic for "Oasis of Peace" (Isaiah 32:18), was established jointly by Jews and Palestinian Arabs of Israeli citizenship to engage in educational work for peace, equality, and understanding between the two peoples. The members of Neve Shalom/Wahat al-Salam have demonstrated the possibility of coexistence between Jews and Palestinians by developing a community based on mutual acceptance, respect, and cooperation. Democratically governed and owned by its members, the community is not affiliated with any political party or movement. Its School for Peace assimilates the principles upon which Neve Shalom/Wahat al-Salam was founded in courses and seminars conducted for Arab and Jewish youth and adults in Israel and the Palestinian Authority. Funding sources include American Friends of Neve Shalom/Wahat al-Salam, the Goodwin Foundation, the Abraham Fund, the Canadian Embassy, the New Israel Fund, the Cohen Foundation, the Blaustein Foundation, Foundation for Middle East Peace, Public Welfare Foundation, United Colors of Benetton, Inc., and Northern Trust Bank of California.

ADDRESS: Neve Shalom/Wahat al-Salam, Doar Na Shimshon 99761, Israel
PHONE: 02 9915621
E-MAIL: pr@nswas.com
WEB SITE: www.nswas.com

CONCLUSION

Young people who live in war zones or in areas of violent conflict often live with constant upheaval, destruction, and violence. Some respond in kind. Others, like Namik, Neil, and Nir, have become leaders among their peers and devote themselves to working for peace in their communities. They want to help ensure that violence and intolerance do not become routine. In large measure, young people have a great stake in securing peace. In the past decade and a half, millions of children and youth have been killed in wars, many more millions have been disabled or disfigured, and an even greater number have been uprooted, made homeless, and lost their families. To ignore these victims in peace processes is terrible; to ignore them as the future of any sustained peace is self-defeating. Too often the international community views young people and children primarily, if not exclusively, as victims of violence. In most policy recommendations by international governmental organizations and nongovernmental organizations these groups see their role as advocates for these young victims. While that is very important, too little attention is given to the role of young people as leaders, as advocates and activists, and as agents of social change and peace building.

One of the great challenges for senior leaders who are attempting to make peace in their respective countries or societies is to negotiate an agreement or secure commitments that will create a sustainable peace. And, ultimately, sustainable peace is about the future. True peace is not just the absence of violence or the reduction of tensions; true peace is building a future together. It requires energy, dedication, initiative, and creativity. Many young people have been able to engage with the world around them with these same attributes. They may not have developed grand political solutions or critical negotiating positions, but they have dealt with conflict in a very meaningful way on the ground in their communities. John Paul Lederach has noted that to achieve sustainable peace, people "must imagine and articulate the kind of community they desire. They must not envision the future as a final destination that is mechanistically planned, but must instead engage one another, as communities, in the process of looking toward the horizon of reconciliation, toward that place where they can envision living in an interdependent and commonly defined future" (Lederach 1997, 116–17). As Namik, Neil, and Nir have demonstrated, many young people are doing just that.

In this way these young people are working to build conditions for peace that would make the conditions for war less likely. Young people today are ultimately our chance to move beyond continuing cycles of violence. In order to avoid societies backsliding into more violence, young people will need a sense of hope and opportunity. They can be an effective insurance if we invest much more in them and their future. But too often today young people are simply marginalized by their political leaders, by their societies, and by peace processes. Even in the fall 2003 Track Two Geneva Accords between unofficial Israeli and Palestinian delegations, there were only two mentions of youth in a twenty-plus page document, and only then as simply one of a number of potential exchange programs between the two communities. There were also only a couple of minor references to education and no specific language or clauses in the agreement that dealt with the critical area of education and youth empowerment. As with so many peace accords, few acknowledge the central and long-term role that education and young people will need to play in sustaining peace.

Thus, it would seem advisable for the diplomats and the peacemakers to create a role for young people in efforts to implement a peace agreement or peace process. They need to have a stake in any negotiated peace, but they also have something positive and necessary to contribute to the process of peace building. Youth groups should be empowered. Education should be strengthened. This should be done not just by focusing on content or bricks and mortar but by developing education curriculum that encourages experiential learning as well as places a greater focus on the student as individual. UNESCO

(1995) argues that education must create a climate that models peaceful and respectful behavior and demonstrates the principles of equality and tolerance. What is remarkable about young people such as Namik, Neil, and Nir is that they do not just make a case for peace but they attempt to achieve peace by living peace.

At the same time, it is important to note that the impact of young people on peace, or on politics, may come over time and as a result of, or having moved beyond, failures. In Serbia in the early 1990s, there were a number of antigovernment student movements, but many of these movements were nationalistic, intolerant, and narrowly focused and found little country-wide or grassroots support. Yet, a few years later, a new youth- and student-dominated movement, Otpor, is credited with a significant role in bringing down the dictatorial regime of Slobodan Milosevic. Many Otpor activists came from the initial failed movements but coalesced around a less ideological, more pro-European movement that was very well organized and extended its reach throughout Serbia. A local study of Otpor concluded that "The political culture of Otpor activists is in sharp contrast with the traditionally intolerant Balkan political culture and is distinguished by an incomparably more modern and quite unusual style as far as these regions are concerned. . . . Otpor's success is due not only to the enormous enthusiasm of its activists, but also to an enviable proficiency in political marketing" (Ilic 2001, 71).

One of the most interesting conclusions drawn from this study was that many of the students were very pessimistic about education culminating in personal or professional achievement. Because the prospects of a job seemed very low, fewer students were devoted to their studies and attending classes. Thus, they had more time on their hands to engage in political activities, and they channeled their frustrations and energies into "changing the system," thus improving the prospects that their education might some day pay off (Ilic 2001, 15). What seems remarkable is how young people—like those in Otpor, or like Namik, Neil, and Nir—see the status quo as something to transform, to be overcome. Through their energy and a desire for change, and despite a bleak landscape, they turn pessimism into optimism, despair into hope.

Finally, it is also critical to understand the link between opportunity (with jobs, education, protection of minority rights) and young people believing in a better future and their willingness to invest in that future. Of course, in tandem with this must be energy and resources directed to post-conflict reconstruction that helps provide young people with jobs and educational opportunities. Otherwise, they will become disillusioned and provide little or no support for peace, or they will find alternative means, often violent, to try to challenge the status quo or change the world around them. Involving young people in building peace can give them hope. If the enemy of peace is despair, hope is an important pillar upon which to build a sustainable peace.

NOTE

1. The addresses, sponsored by the United States Institute of Peace, were given at the University of Notre Dame on September 13, 2003, during the Peacebuilding after Peace Accords Conference. The conference was part of the Joan B. Kroc Institute for International Peace Studies' Research Initiative on the Resolution of Ethnic Conflict (RIREC).

SAMI ADWAN AND DAN BAR-ON

Sharing History

Palestinian and Israeli Teachers and Pupils Learning Each Other's Narrative

> The aim of this project is to make the Palestinian and the Israeli pupils know what the other thinks. The whole point is that your independence-day celebration is our day of Nakba (Catastrophe). — Khalil (a Palestinian teacher)
>
> It is like two blind people shouting their story without listening to the other. — Eshel (an Israeli teacher)

This chapter describes five workshops conducted by Peace Research in the Middle East (PRIME) in which Palestinian and Jewish-Israeli teachers developed a joint textbook. The textbook included two narratives (one Israeli and the other Palestinian) in regard to three important historical dates in their mutual conflict: the Balfour Declaration, the 1948 war, and the first Intifada. Throughout the project, these activities took place under extremely severe conditions of asymmetry of power relations, with the occupation of Palestinian communities and suicide bombings against Israelis. The teachers taught these two narratives in their classrooms and summarized some of their pupils' reactions, as well as their own, before developing additional narratives. The pupils' negative initial reactions helped the teachers express their own negative feelings but did not lead them to forgo their commitment to continue their joint work on writing a book that contained the two narratives. The process, described chronologically, helped the teachers realize that they must develop narratives more inclusive and sensitive to each other, more interdependent though still separate.

THE DEVELOPMENT OF TEXTBOOKS IN VIOLENT CONFLICTS

In periods of war and conflict, societies and nations tend to develop their own narratives to explain the conflict, which become the only true and morally superior narratives, in their perspective. These narratives are morally exclusive (Optow 2001), and they devaluate and sometimes dehumanize their enemy's narrative. If the enemy's narrative is described at all, it is presented as being inferior and the enemy is depicted as a faceless entity, immoral with irrational or manipulative views. In conflict situations, "the experience of identity invariably evokes codes of exclusion, difference and distinction. Belonging to a collectivity always concerns the delimitation of that collectivity and the application of a logic of conflict and contention" (Tawil, Harley, and Porteous 2003, 7). These narratives become embedded in everyday culture, in the national and religious festivals, in the media, and in children's textbooks.

Textbooks are one of the formal representations of the society's ideology and its ethos. They impart the values, goals, and myths that the society wants to instill in the younger generation (Apple 1979; Bourdieu 1973; Luke 1988). "The basic working assumption is that there is a dialectical relationship between schooling and violent conflict and that this relationship needs to be explicitly recognized and explored for the process of educational change in the wake of civil strife and to be a meaningful contribution to post-conflict reconciliation and peacebuilding." Therefore, "it is a major concern in post-conflict situations to avoid replication of educational structures that may have contributed to the conflict" (Tawil, Harley, and Porteous 2003, 7).

Palestinians and Israelis do not see themselves as currently being in a post-conflict situation, especially after the failure of the Oslo Accords and the second Camp David summit that took place in August 2000 and the outbreak of the Al-Aqsa Intifada in October 2000. Children growing up during times of war and conflict know only the narrative of their people. This narrative is supposed to convince them, overtly and covertly, of the need to dehumanize the enemy. It usually indoctrinates children to a rationale that justifies the use of power to subjugate the enemy. This not only causes the development of narrow and biased understandings among children, but it also leads to the development of negative attitudes and values toward the other (Bar-On 1999). This state of affairs is true also for the Palestinian/Israeli situation.

Since the early 1950s, Palestinians have been using Jordanian and Egyptian school books in their schools in the West Bank and Gaza Strip, respectively. The use of these school books continued after Israel occupied the West Bank and the Gaza Strip in the 1967 war, but the books underwent censorship. Palestinians started preparing their own school books immediately after the establishment of the Palestinian National Authority (PNA) in 1994. In the 2000–2001 school year the first Palestinian-produced textbooks were introduced into the schools for grades one and six. Each year the Palestinian Curriculum Center, under the supervision of the Palestinian Ministry of Education, produced textbooks for only two grades. They gradually substituted the Jordanian and Egyptian books with Palestinian ones.

The Palestinian educational system is characterized as being a centralized one. This means that the Ministry of Education is the sole producer of the textbooks and all schools use the same textbooks. Israelis have a longer history of producing their textbooks. It goes back to before the State of Israel was established. The Israeli system of education is more decentralized; schools and teachers have some freedom to choose the textbooks they want to use from the list approved by the Ministry of Education. To a limited extent, teachers also may choose the texts from the open market.

Research on textbooks has shown how each side, the Palestinian as well as the Israeli, presents its own narratives. In an analysis of the presentation of the 1948 Palestinian refugee problem (Adwan and Firer 1997, 1999) in Palestinian and Israeli textbooks that have been used since 1995, it was found that both sides failed to talk about the complexity of the refugees' problem. The Israeli texts put most of the blame on the Palestinians and the Arabs for the refugees' plight, while the Palestinian texts mainly blamed the Israelis and the British (IPCRI 2003).

Another comprehensive analysis of narratives in Palestinian and Israeli history and civic education (Adwan and Firer 1999) shows that the texts reflect a culture of enmity. The terminology that was used in the texts had different meanings. What was positive on one side was negative on the other side. For example, the 1948 war in the Israeli texts is called "The War of Independence," while in the Palestinian text it is called "Al-Nakba" (the Catastrophe). While Israeli texts refer to the first Jewish immigrants to Palestine as "the pioneers," the Palestinian texts refer to them as "gangs" and "terrorists." The heroes of one side are the monsters of the other. Furthermore, most of the maps in the texts eliminate the cities and towns of the other side. The texts show the de-legitimization of each other's rights, history, and culture. There is also no recognition of each other's sufferings. The Holocaust is barely mentioned in Palestinian texts,[1] and, similarly, the trauma of the Palestinians is ignored in the Israeli texts. Some of the texts have even failed to agree on the facts. For example, the Israelis write that there were between 600,000 and 700,000 Palestinian refugees from 1948, while the Palestinians write that there were more than one million Palestinians who became refugees as a result of the 1948 war.

Based on these studies, we concluded that the Israeli-Palestinian conflict is not yet ready, and perhaps will never be ready, for the production of one joint narrative. Therefore, we decided to develop an innovative school booklet that contains two narratives—the Israeli and the Palestinian—that center on certain dates or milestones in the history of the conflict. This would mean that each pupil would also learn about the narrative of the other, in addition to studying their own familiar narrative, as a first step toward acknowledging and respecting the other. We assumed that a joint narrative would emerge, if at all, only after many years of a clear change from a culture of war to a culture of peace. This requires time and the ability to mourn and work through the painful results of the past. We could not expect this to take place while the conflict was still going on. Still, we did expect that through the process of developing the narratives with the teachers, the narratives could become less hostile in their expressions, more sensitive to each other, and interdependent but still separate (Levinas [1961] 1990).

We had to consider the roles of teachers. Studies have shown that teachers have more power than mere written texts in forming children's understandings and value systems (Nave and Yogev 2002; Angvik and von Borries 1997). As a result, this project focuses on the central role of the teachers in the process of using shared history texts in the classroom. We believed that it should be the teachers who develop these narratives and try them out in their ninth- and tenth-grade classrooms. Through their mutual interaction, we hoped that they would become more sensitive to each other's pain, making it possible for them to be able to develop more interdependent narratives.

THE PARTICIPANTS

The co-founders of Peace Research in the Middle East (PRIME), Sami Adwan and Dan Bar-On, and two history professors, Adnan Massallam (Bethlehem University) and Eyal Nave (Tel Aviv University and the Kibbutz Teachers Seminar in Tel Aviv), chose the team to work on this project. The team includes an equal number of men and women teachers: six Palestinian history and geography teachers (ages 28–67), six Jewish Israeli history teachers (34–65), and five international delegates (four women and one man, ages 24–37), as well as one Jewish Israeli woman observer. The teaching experience of the teachers ranged between 7 and 35 years. Most of the Palestinian teachers, who are from Hebron, Bethlehem, and East Jerusalem, had never before participated in dialogue encounters with Israelis. Several of the Israeli teachers, who teach in high schools in the center and north of Israel, had participated in previous encounters with Palestinians.

THE WORKSHOPS WITH THE TEACHERS

WORKING UNDER VIOLENT CONFLICT

All the participants convened five times for three-day workshops at the New Imperial Hotel in the Old City (eastern, Palestinian part) of Jerusalem in March, June, and August 2002 and in January and April 2003. As the political and the military situations were very fragile, it was unclear until the last minute whether the Palestinian teachers would get permits to enter Jerusalem, or if they would be able to reach the places where the permits were issued. The workshops were called off several times, but each time we found ways and the energy to reschedule them again, and finally we succeeded in bringing the teachers together for all of the meetings except for the planned March 2003 seminar, which was delayed due to the war in Iraq and our inability to get permits for the Palestinian teachers. This meeting eventually took place in April 2003.

As the project was operating within the reality of the conflict, it is critical to note the contexts from which the participants came. First, while the situation on both sides was bleak, difference and asymmetry exist with respect to the intensity of the general realities on the ground (Maoz, 2000c). For Palestinians, the reality has an unrelenting effect on day-to-day life with experiences of occupation and living under the thumb of the Israeli army. This translates into restricted freedom of movement, curfews, border checkpoints, and a great fear of shootings, killings, and house demolitions. Most Palestinians have suffered serious losses and have had their own homes or those of relatives damaged. Meanwhile, for Israelis, because of Palestinian suicide attacks, the everyday reality reflects itself mostly in fear. This involves fear of riding buses and of going downtown or anywhere where there are crowds. Many on both sides even fear sending their children to school.

The Israeli participants had to become even more attentive to the fact that there were limitations on the Palestinian teachers' movements and that they were threatened for their participation in such a joint project. Israelis had more freedom to move around; they had to arrange the Palestinian permits, bring the permits to them, and help them get to the meeting. This is not a pleasant "advantage" as it gives the representatives of the powerful side more power. Therefore, it had to be done tactfully, as a matter of fact, without too much talking. In addition, many of the Palestinian public often reacted aggressively to people who were seen as "betraying the common cause" or in favor of "normalization," as it has been defined in the Palestinian public discourse. Therefore, it was important that the Palestinian teachers maintain a low profile and not draw too much attention from their own social surroundings.

A Palestinian teacher described the hardship of conducting such seminars during the continuous occupation and violence:

> I live in Adna (a village) and I teach in Ramallah. During the week I stay in an apartment together with five other teachers from different disciplines. Because of the closure I cannot return home. My friends were surprised that such meetings take place when there is an Intifada, and people are killed. The period that we are working under is very hard for all of us. The questions that are raised are: Why is this done now when many people are martyrs? It is a tormenting experience. We have here a good time together but when we go home we hear that something happened. There is a contradiction between meeting and trying to build some trust and the outside circumstances that definitely do not help. I have to go through humiliating experiences every day. I feel that I have a split personality, I live two lives.

One can feel how the Palestinian teacher was torn between his "two lives" and how difficult it was for him to participate in such a project while there were daily events of humiliation and violence toward him and his people by the Israelis. At the same time, there were also some expressions of hope and persistence. A Palestinian teacher commented that "we should look into other ways of resolving our conflict and this project is an example for such a way." One of the Israeli teachers mentioned during the fourth seminar: "This work over the last year was my only source of hope in the current desperate situation."

We have decided to avoid the media and both the Palestinian and Israeli Ministries of Education. When almost everyday people are being killed by suicide bombers on the Israeli side and the Palestinian people are under curfew, have to move through checkpoints, and are being killed by Israeli army assassinations or shootings, the public in general, and the Ministries of Education in particular, are haunted by the violent conflict and paralyzed in terms of the peace process. Therefore, we estimated that such premature publicity would hamper the possibility of continuing our process rather than accommodating it.

The Process: Getting Started

In the first (March 2002) workshop, teachers got acquainted with each other by sharing personal details ("the story behind my name") as well as stories such as that by the Palestinian teacher above. It was not easy to listen as stories that contained painful moments were related to the other's violence or oppression. But it was a necessary process because it enabled the teachers later to work together on their joint tasks more openly (Albeck, Adwan, and Bar-On 2002). The interpersonal story-sharing process was an essential aspect of peace-building work under extreme conditions. The outside asymmetry of power relations and violence had to be represented in the room through personal experiences of storytelling before a pragmatic task-oriented approach could be introduced with more symmetrical expectations (Bar-On and Kassem, n.d.). One actually has to envision a future different (post-conflict) state in order to accomplish this task. Such an act of envisioning could take place after people were able to share some of their pain, fear, and mistrust; this sharing had to be done at the beginning of each joint seminar because of the intensity of the events that occurred between the seminars, which eroded some of the closeness that had been reached during the previous meetings.

After the story sharing and a joint dinner (that we needed for relaxation and unwinding), we formed three mixed task groups. Each task group created a list of all the events that were relevant to the Palestinian-Israeli conflict and chose one event they wanted to work on. In the plenary the teachers discussed their lists and preferences and chose three events. One mixed group focused on the Balfour Declaration of 1917, another on the 1948 war, and the third on the first Intifada of 1987. A program was set up so that the groups could communicate and coordinate their relevant narratives to be reviewed at the second workshop. The history professors, Naveh and Mussalam, provided their professional views of how such narratives should be developed and what they should include. It was the role of the international participants to do some of the translations, when necessary, to summarize the task groups' work, and to write an evaluation at the end of each seminar. An additional activity in our seminars were our evening strolls in the Old City of Jerusalem, which members of both groups had not done in recent years because of the severe security conditions. In a way we felt like we were in a self-created bubble, disconnected from the hostile surroundings in which we usually lived.

In the second (June 2002) workshop, teachers developed their narratives, partially by working in the original task groups and partially by working in their own, national, groups. We also devoted time to continuing our personal acquaintance and our joint walks, as these became important ingredients of the work, especially with the current hostile atmosphere outside the group. Between the second and the third workshops, the narratives were translated into Hebrew and Arabic (the workshops were conducted in English).

During the third (August 2002) seminar, the teachers had their first opportunity to read both narratives in their own native language, the way they would have to present these narratives to their pupils in the following year. This time, most of the work was done in the plenary. We expected it to be a very difficult encounter, as there was a dilemma of how to be accountable to one's own society (which was used to hostile verbal expressions toward the other) while being sensitive to the narrative and feelings of the other. Therefore, it was interesting to follow how all the teachers accepted these narratives, not only those who created them. Surprisingly, most of the questions posed during these sessions were informative: Was the translation precise? Who was the person you mentioned in 1908? Why did you try to describe this event so briefly, while the others are described at length? At that stage, there were almost no attempts to de-legitimize the other's narrative.

According to our interpretation, the fact that each side could feel safe with their own narrative made it easier to accept the other's narrative, even though they were so different from one another. But one could perhaps foresee that the more difficult issues would come up when these narratives were presented to the pupils in the classrooms and the teachers reported their reactions.

At this workshop we learned about the sudden death from cancer of one of the participating Palestinian teachers from Hebron. There was some deliberation if we should stop the workshop, but the Palestinian teachers felt that he would have liked them to continue, and they decided to stay and continue our work. The entire group later decided that the forthcoming joint booklet would open with his picture and a dedication to him. The groups departed with the task to introduce corrections in their narratives as a result of the discussion and to develop a glossary for the teachers and the pupils concerning definitions of terms that the other side might not be familiar with.

The booklets were supposed to be ready much earlier (November 2002) than they finally were; however, the continued and renewed curfews of the Palestinian towns and the additional necessary proofreading of the texts and their translations did not enable us to follow the original timetable. In February 2003 the booklet finally came out in Hebrew and Arabic (the English version came out in June 2003). The teachers started to test it out in their classrooms, which meant that in this experimental phase already hundreds of Israeli and Palestinian pupils were exposed to the new booklet.

The January and April 2003 teachers' workshops focused on sharing the pupils' first responses, making corrections, supporting the teachers in their work, and developing three additional narratives around new dates.[2]

The Teachers Discuss their Classroom Experiences

We will describe here the chronological development that took place during the discussion among the teachers in the fifth workshop (April 2003). This discussion related to the initial impressions of the teachers after presenting the booklet in their classrooms. During the previous three months, all of the teachers had presented at least one event out of the three (usually the one they helped to develop) in at least one class for one to three sessions. It is a common practice to give a seminar to teachers to accommodate some new learning material and then let them implement it in their classrooms and leave them on their own, without following up on what actually happened in their encounters with the pupils. We knew that with our new approach of presenting students with the two narratives, especially under the harsh conditions of the conflict, we would have to follow up because the encounter with the pupils could be problematic.

We will describe the process that developed when the teachers recounted their experiences of their initial interactions with their pupils. We will first present the hardships they expressed, which also caused them to openly express their own doubts about the project and to discuss their negative emotions toward each other. Some groups get stuck at this point and cannot find a way out. Later during this workshop, however, the teachers succeeded in finding a pragmatic way of rewriting the two narratives so that they would become more interdependent and sensitive to each other but still separate.

The fifth workshop started with the teachers reporting on their pupils' responses to the two narratives. In general, the teachers reported that presenting the two narratives caused a surprise that created interest and curiosity but also some resentment among the pupils. We will focus now on the reports of the pupils' resentful reactions.

THE PALESTINIAN REPORTS

The Palestinian pupils' responses were affected by the difficult situation of their everyday lives—living under curfew and occupation—and many of them related to the two narratives through that experience. It was much harder for them than for the Israeli pupils to listen to the other side's narrative. For example, Khalil (P-M)[3] reported some of his pupils' reactions to the Israeli narrative of the Balfour Declaration:

> "They have no place in our land."

> "If they suffered from persecution, why do they do it to us?"

"I am not sorry for their persecution by gas [during the Holocaust]."

"This is our natural right; this is the land of our fathers. Who gave them the right to settle in our land?"

"Arabs are never taken seriously. The British chased us out and brought others instead."

"There was a commitment of the British to bring the Jews to the land. They should not have done it."

"They do not have a historical right in Palestine. We have a right since ancient times."

"Britain was a big country then. They committed themselves before the League of Nations, the way the UN is in the hands of the Americans now."

"They see us as aggressors but we are the original inhabitants of this land. They came from far away and they are aggressors."

Khalil tried to defend the Israeli narrative: "This is their story." But then his pupils wanted to know what he thought about the validity of the Israeli arguments. Here is what followed in the teachers' workshop:

ESHEL (I-M): Did you find yourself representing the Israeli side?

KHALIL: It was not easy, when you do not agree. For example: When I taught the history of the Maccabeans [Jewish heroes during the Roman Empire], it was easier. But when I talk about the present, it's harder. It is like you said, that your pupils saw you as a traitor. But the pupils know me, like your pupils know you.

We can sense some of Khalil's dilemma of being untrustworthy in the eyes of his pupils: Why did he teach a text he did not believe in and that represents the "other side's point of view"? Why did he not just denounce it? Sonia had a difficult time, as she also identified with some of her pupils' arguments:

SONIA (P-F): I taught the 1948 narratives. They raised many questions about the subject. Some pupils were angry and some were sad, because they live next to a refugee camp [where refugees from 1948 live]. They were angry about the Israeli narrative. Some of them were ready to listen to the Israeli narrative. The majority was resistant. They asked, "Why should we accept the Israeli narrative when in reality we lack security for our people?"

Shai (I-M): So the problem was not with the narrative, but with the reality [today].

Sonia: In the Israeli version they read about the terrible things that the Jews suffered in the Holocaust. At the same time they ask, "Why do we have to pay the price for their suffering?"

In this exchange, Shai tried to make a differentiation between the narrative and the present reality, but Sonia's answer shows that for the Palestinian teachers and pupils, this differentiation is not valid at this point in time. Khalil and Sonia present how some of their pupils' cannot accept the Israeli narrative in a positive or understanding way. By doing so, they also express some of their own similar reactions to these texts. It is the present reality that colors their reactions, and this reality is still locked up in the conflict.

THE ISRAELI REPORTS

The Israeli teachers also reported difficulties and resentment expressed by their pupils:

Eshel: I taught the three narratives in my 12th-grade class for one week, which was not enough time. My pupils are 18 years old, before their army service. There were different reactions. Some said that they do not want to get to know the other. "Look at their narrative . . . There's no basis for talking. We came here to learn about our history and we are not interested in theirs." Some expressed doubts whether teachers on the other side also teach their pupils the two narratives. Some put me in the category of being left wing. Some were curious about the other side's story. Some of the pupils took home the booklets in order to read them, although I did not ask them to do so.

Naomi (I-F): The children said something that reflected what I felt: that the Palestinian narrative is not history. It is propaganda. They said: "The narrative is always attacking the Israeli point of view. In the Palestinian narrative we see how much wrong the Israelis did, and what about them [the Palestinians]?" . . . The pupils said that after the first lesson they thought that it would be interesting, but they saw that it is only blaming us and being victims without offering any solutions.

As we see from the above, the teachers from both sides were confronted with issues of their own credibility in the eyes of their pupils. If these texts are the "enemy's propaganda," why teach them in class, especially at this time of violent

conflict? Consequently, the teachers themselves took a new look at the narratives they had created and agreed about earlier. Suddenly arguments came up that
had not been addressed before: "Why do we have to pay the price for their Holocaust?" "Our narratives are facts, theirs are propaganda." This created a crisis
among the teachers concerning the purpose of the project. If the narratives
simply replicate the conflict over legitimacy, what is the sense of teaching them
in the classroom?

MOVING OUT OF THE DEADLOCK

At this point, the group easily could have become stuck, justifying their own narrative, de-legitimizing that of the other side, and following the reactions of their
pupils. But by doing so, they would have undermined everything that they had
invested in and developed up to this point. This created a conflict situation.
Should we move forward, reclarifying what the goals of the project actually are
in order to be better prepared for future classes, or would we move backward,
back into the ethnocentric narrative that supports the conflict (Steinberg and
Bar-On 2002)? The reactions of the pupils helped bring to the surface the teachers' own negative emotional reactions, especially under the harsh conditions in
which they were working, that they tried to repress or could not express earlier. But it did not cause the group to regress to the ethnocentric discourse that
dominated the societies they lived in. This crisis actually created a new self-
examination that was essential for the process to move forward.

It was helpful in overcoming this crisis that not all the pupils' reactions were
critical or full of resentment. Some of the teachers also received supportive feedback, like the following:

RACHEL (I-F): I want to bring a different perspective, because I have more
    comments from my pupils. A few of them said that it was important for
    them to see that there is also another side. Some said that it made them
    hate more, since the Arabs hate us from many years ago. One said that
    he understands that every conflict is like that, that there are two sides to
    each story. They argue, but it opens their minds. I see that it works.

ESHEL: First, it is a good booklet. It is an achievement, but it should be
    improved. It is like two blind people shouting their story without listen-
    ing to the other. One thing that is lacking is dialogue. Most of the dia-
    logue that we had among us did not enter the booklet.

ABDEL HALIM (P-M) We should not have high expectations. . . . There are
    ups and downs. Things that we see as facts, you see as propaganda.

NAOMI: I do not say that propaganda is not facts, but it is only a partial picture.

Then the discourse among the teachers took a turn. The teachers made some new observations: that the narratives they had created represented more extreme views than those they had expressed in their earlier encounters, and that they had to create a dialogue between the narratives. Instead of mutual exclusion they had to introduce some level of mutual inclusiveness. Instead of propaganda, a new term was introduced: "partial picture." The teachers had an incentive to continue and try to work out a way to introduce changes into their original texts. Furthermore, they reacted to some specific sensitivities expressed by their pupils. For example, some of the Palestinian pupils did not want a picture of the Israeli flag on the top of each page of the Israeli narrative, and they were willing to give up showing the Palestinian flag for that purpose. Therefore, both flags were taken out of the booklet. The following extracts show how the new narratives were developed with the previous discussion in mind.

SARA (I-F): We should tell the story that we believe in, but the question is how to tell it. What is your goal when you write it in a certain way? You wrote for example: "One day before the Intifada broke out an Israeli driver deliberately ran over Palestinians . . ." *Deliberately*—what is the purpose of this phrasing?

RULA (P-F): It is true. This is how the Palestinians saw that incident. It was not seen just as an accident.

ESHEL: We saw it as an accident. They saw it as deliberate.

EYAL (I-M): This is the kind of dialogue that we should develop, and in the end we will decide if the word "deliberate" will stay.

ADNAN (P-M): People usually interpret events in the light of their own way and according to their experience and beliefs that enhance their own position in the time of conflict.

One can sense that it was still hard for some of the teachers to accept that "what is an accident for one side is a deliberate act of violence for the other" (such as the instigating event of the 1987 Intifada). But a different discussion developed, one in which teachers from both sides expressed their feelings and thoughts more openly, trying to redefine what this project was actually about. They did not want to create a bridging narrative but rather a better dialogue between the narratives, creating some interdependence between them. The teachers tried to resolve the conflict mentioned earlier by developing a pragmatic approach to the narratives themselves. The two narratives could be rewritten again and again, according to where the teachers are in their own process and in relation to what happens outside the workshop.

EYAL: We have to think about what our final goal is. If nothing changes and the feeling of victimhood remains, what is the use of presenting both narratives instead of one? Otherwise the product—the two narratives—remains the goal, and nothing else. We cannot just congratulate ourselves for presenting the two narratives; we have to continue to work on improving them.

ADNAN: Yes, but we have to be realistic about what we can expect. Still the conflict goes on and we have to go through this phase before we go to the next one.

SAMI (P-M): At a conference in Mexico we were asked how we could promise that this book will not strengthen the hatred. We have to be careful about this. We have to think how not to reinforce our self-centered attitudes. I see myself in the process in comparison with the beginning. I have the impression that something has changed in each one of us. Clearly, the current violent situation outside does not help.

DAN (I-M): I agree with Eyal that just writing the texts is not enough. The narratives are necessary but not sufficient. I would put the finger on legitimization. We have to help pupils learn to deconstruct the texts. When pupils deconstruct only the text of the other side, we have to point out that the other side can also deconstruct their text. Legitimization of the other side's narrative is very important. It is important that the pupils become more critical about the texts that they are presented with: news, newspapers.

At this point, it became obvious that there should be some interdependence between the narratives. Up to this stage, it seemed that each side wanted to tell their own story and include in it only what that side saw as important. By the end of the April 2003 workshop, there was a feeling of readiness to cooperate, to negotiate, and to reach an agreement about events or issues that each side wanted to mention, while also taking into consideration the feelings and attitudes of the other side. For example, a Palestinian teacher did not think of mentioning Black September (an event in September 1970 in which the Jordanian army crushed the Palestinian Liberation Organization [PLO] in refugee camps in Jordan and caused the leadership to move to Lebanon). The Israeli teachers saw it as important for understanding the nature of the Palestinian hardship and suffering, and they convinced him to include it in the Palestinian text when writing the next narrative. At the same time, the reverse happened around Karame (an attack by the Israeli army on a Palestinian camp in Jordan in 1968, in which the PLO was relatively successful in withstanding the Israeli military attack and caused the latter serious casualties). While the first event was omitted by the Palestinians probably because it exposed internal Arab disputes or political sensitivities, the second was avoided by the Israelis because it reflected a relative Palestinian victory over the more powerful Israeli Army.

The group had reached a new stage. In the room there was a general feeling of overcoming a crisis; the idea of the two narratives survived, even if there were initial problems with that idea. The teachers felt ownership in spite of the difficulties they faced in their classrooms and the deteriorating external situation. There was a feeling that the group had reached a higher level of communication during this workshop.

Both sides acknowledged that they had learned from the other something that they did not know before. For example, the Israelis, who knew about the massacre of Jews in Hebron in 1929, learned that Arab families also had been massacred. A Palestinian teacher, who thought that the British exiled only Arabs during their mandate, admitted that he was surprised to hear that extremists from both sides were expelled.

The organizers of the seminar gave credit to the teachers for what they had achieved, and they gave the teachers their support concerning how hard it is to teach the two narratives given that the two groups are still in the middle of a violent conflict. Both sides tried to teach their pupils to look at the other side's narrative as legitimate, while the reality outside the classroom did not match this mood of cooperation, particularly for the Palestinians, who live with daily oppression and humiliation. However, the organizers also stressed the point that the situation is not yet ripe for the creation of a bridging narrative and that the aim of this project was not to create such a narrative. They pointed out that it was normal and expected, for at least some of the pupils, to have initial negative reactions to the other side's narrative, and that just making the pupils aware of the other side's narrative is important in the current situation. One could also sense some different abilities of the teachers to withstand their pupils' pressures and to try and make them look differently at the other's narrative.

Conclusion

This chapter described five workshops in which Palestinian and Israeli teachers developed a joint school textbook of two narratives, one Israeli and one Palestinian, with regard to three dates in their mutual conflict: the Balfour Declaration, the 1948 war, and the 1987 Intifada. The teachers taught these two narratives in their classrooms and summarized some of their pupils' reactions, as well as their own, before delving into developing additional narratives. All these activities took place under extremely severe conditions of occupation (of the Palestinians) and suicide bombings (against Israelis) throughout the project. This process and report are not yet finished. Four more narratives will be created, and more pupils from both sides will be exposed to the joint book. In addition, a teacher's guide will be developed. Hopefully, the political and military situations will also improve and will enable us to develop this small-scale experiment into a widespread practice.

We suggest that this attempt to produce a joint history book makes us part of a genuine bottom-up, minimal peace-building attempt to make a difference in a situation that seems almost hopeless (Maoz, forthcoming). The high motivation of the teachers to continue this process, even in light of the difficult situation and some of their pupils' harsh reactions, is an indicator of how important this process is and what it has achieved. It is our opinion that this group of teachers is not highly selective; most of them actually represent the average Israeli or Palestinian teacher.

The idea to develop two narratives is linked to the proposed political two-states solution. In other post-conflict contexts (like South Africa), where a single-state political solution was developed, one could think in terms of developing a bridging narrative (like the one developed through the Truth and Reconciliation Commission). However, when there are two societies that wish to live separately, side by side, a two-narrative solution seems more suitable.

It was interesting to observe the initial response of the teachers from both groups. When they had their own narrative, they felt more open and secure to accept the validity of another narrative. Perhaps this could be an indication of how insecure both societies are concerning their own national identity. One should remember that the Palestinians never had a state of their own, and the Jewish Israeli state has existed for only fifty-five years. This mutual insecurity is one of the basic social-psychological characteristics of this conflict. This could partially account for the need to have two separate narratives at this stage of the conflict.

When the teachers were confronted with their pupils' reactions, they found that their separate narratives were still embedded in the conflict and created some negative reactions among the pupils of the other side. This realization, which they had not paid attention to earlier when developing the narratives, demanded that they modify some of the expressions and content to make the narrative more inclusive rather than exclusive, more interdependent, and more sensitive to each other's special needs.

In the third year we plan to run a formal evaluation by comparing, for each teacher, the two-narrative classes with single-narrative classes. In the second phase (2004–07) we plan to recruit more teachers and use the first group of teachers as assistants for accommodating the new ones. Perhaps by then the political situation will change to the extent that the Ministries of Education also will be able to adopt this concept and practice.

The violence that took place around us also often affected our interactions. Yet we were rewarded with glimmers of hope and enthusiasm about the implementation of this project in the schools. We assume that the success of this project, in comparison to earlier projects with Israeli and Palestinian teachers that were less successful, was related to three important aspects:

1. The timing of the project introduced an aspect of urgency to create a positive counterweight to the violence we experienced outside our workshops. The fact that we always made time first for the teachers to express what they were feeling about these harsh conditions, in the form of storytelling, perhaps enabled the teachers to become so involved in their mutual tasks.
2. We, the authors and the initiators of the project, tried to serve as role models for the participants so they could see that it is possible to attain academic, professional, financial, and managerial symmetry. This symmetry has rarely been experienced in similar projects (Maoz 2000a, 2000b). Cleary, the two of us were further ahead in our own dialogue, thanks to our long-term commitment to PRIME, which started several years earlier and has been maintained by us even during the new outbreak of violence.[4]
3. The creation of real texts, as something concrete that can be given to pupils and can be related to in both contexts, was very important for pupils and teachers who have difficulty with abstract forms of discussions and evaluations. As mentioned earlier, presenting the pupils' reactions helped the subsequent intergroup process of the teachers.

The teachers' presentation of their pupils' responses was a legitimate way to express the teachers' own feelings toward the other side's narrative, feelings that they did not dare to express openly earlier. Citing the most extreme reactions enabled an open discussion about the two narratives, about Palestinian-Israeli relations in the past and present, and about the goals and realistic expectations for the project under the current circumstances. After getting everything out in the open, and seeing that the other listened, the sides were ready to start a dialogue on a different level, to listen, to negotiate, and to cooperate in a less monolithic way.

We acknowledged to each other that peace could only be a result of both sides winning; a "peace" in which only one side wins has no value. Sami said: "The disarmament of history can happen only after the disarmament of weapons. But one can prepare for it now." Events of the last few years have high-lighted the fact that we are not yet getting close to a formal peace agreement. A bottom-up peace-building process, involving face-to-face encounters between Jewish-Israeli and Palestinian peoples, will be necessary in order for a sustainable peace to be achieved. Furthermore, the booklet these teachers are creating and their implementation of it will provide a concrete way to spread the effects out-ward from these face-to-face encounters among a small group of teachers.

ACKNOWLEDGMENTS

We are thankful to Dr. Dieter Hartmann and the Wye River People-to-People Exchange Program of the U.S. State Department for their three-year grants and to the Ford Foundation for their two-year grant that helped us implement this research project. We also wish to thank Dr. Shoshana Steinberg for her help in developing an earlier report and to Linda Livni and Bob Loeb for their administrative help.

NOTES

1. While this chapter was being written, a group of Israeli Palestinians, headed by Emil Shufani, a Greek Orthodox priest from Nazareth, traveled to Poland in order to visit Auschwitz as part of their wish to learn about Jewish suffering there and its impact on contemporary Jewish Israeli society (Hava Shechter, personal communication with the second author).

2. The teachers decided in favor of historical continuity of the booklet and chose the following three additional dates: the events of the 1920s, the events of 1936–48, and the 1967 war. These additional dates would fill in the gaps among the initial dates (1917, 1948, 1987–93) and create a continuity of dates. The teachers divided the dates between them and committed themselves to pre-pare a draft for the following workshop (August 2003).

3. I-M denotes Israeli Male teacher, I-F an Israeli Female, P-M a Palestin-ian Male, and P-F a Palestinian Female. This marking will appear only when each person speaks for the first time.

4. During a recent conference in Wuertzburg, Germany, on Family Con-stellations (May 2003), the authors led a workshop in which German therapists were asked to role-play the Israeli and Palestinian teachers who were writing their texts about two historical dates (1948 and the 1987 Intifada). It was a very powerful exercise, and the participants agreed at the end that they learned a great deal about the conflict and the difficulties of reconciliation. Another work-shop was organized in Rejika (Croatia) in June 2003 for a group of practition-ers from fourteen countries. They went through a similar process, and they also said it helped them reflect on their own experience.

JESSICA SENEHI AND SEAN BYRNE

From Violence Toward Peace

The Role of Storytelling for Youth Healing and Political Empowerment after Social Conflict

Maria Montessori wrote that "establishing a lasting peace is the work of education; all politics can do is keep us out of war" (1972, viii). After the high-profile and glamorous work of establishing a peace accord, the work of peace building, community building, healing, and re-envisioning society must begin in all strata and arenas of society; these are highly gradual and long-term processes, which are typically much more diffuse, less visible, and more difficult to evaluate than the actual accord that ended fighting. In the aftermath of war and protracted social conflicts, peace accords crafted by political elites create a critical, if somewhat fragile and unstable, negative peace. An enduring positive peace, characterized by shared power, mutual respect, and an "awareness of self in context," as John Paul Lederach (1996) puts it, is a profound process of social readjustment and adaptation—a process of education, broadly conceived.

It is critical to include youth in these processes for many reasons. Youth can bring great energy to peace building; youth are usually the

vanguard of social movements (Braunguart and Braunguart 1996). The young
people of today are the citizens and leaders of tomorrow. Meanwhile, political and
social conflict impacts the political socialization of youth (Cairns 1996; Byrne
2000). Repeated exposure to political violence increases the risk that young adults
will engage in future violence and antisocial behavior (Raviv, Oppenheimer, and
Bar-Tal 1999). During their formative years, young people can learn to accept
violence as the norm to solve problems, which becomes difficult to change in
adulthood (Byrne 1997a, 1997b). Meanwhile, many youth become participants
in the violence themselves. If violence re-erupts, youth may be recruited into
that violence willingly or unwillingly. Research also demonstrates, however, that
most young people have the cognitive capacity to cope with violence providing
the necessary parental and communal support is present (Garbarino and Kostelny
1997). But, it is necessary to include young people in the political process so that
they move from a position of being disenfranchised to sharing power (see chapter
6 in this volume).

Many contemporary peace and reconciliation techniques and institutions—
from trauma therapy to truth commissions—utilize narrative approaches. But these
can be expensive, very structured and controlled, slow (for example, truth commissions), and overly individualistic (for example, trauma therapy). Public but
locally based storytelling, on the contrary, offers an appealing complement to these
processes because it is easily organized, accessible, and able to take many forms,
and it provides for a collaborative process of meaning making and relationship
building that is a necessary first step for social change and that mediates between
the personal and political. This is particularly important for youth because it
engages them in an interactive and natural process that empowers their voices.
Many peace-building projects have used the cross-ethnic, cross-community dialogue
group as a means of building relationships. Two prominent examples are the Seeds
of Peace project, which involves bringing together Palestinian and Israeli youths to
a summer camp in the woods of Maine (Wallach 2000), and the "To Trust and
Reflect" dialogue groups, which bring together people from both sides of a protracted divide—for example, descendents of Holocaust survivors and descendents
of Holocaust perpetrators and Palestinians (Bar-On 2000). This chapter contributes
to knowledge about how storytelling works as a peace-building technique by reporting on research conducted with storytellers who offer special knowledge about the
role of story and storytelling in transforming conflicts. Although this research
was conducted predominantly with American storytellers working in U.S. schools
and local communities, it offers findings with implications for post-accord peace-
building practice in many contexts. Also, the work in the U.S. involves reconciliation and community-building among groups historically in conflict within
the nation. Similarly, many international contexts of post-accord peace building

involve work among groups in conflict within nations or relatively small geographic regions.

The thesis of this chapter is that storytelling is a significant and appropriate methodology for post-accord peace building that involves and empowers youth. This is due both to the substantive aspects of storytelling (what stories are about) and the process of storytelling (how storytelling operates). The role of meaning in storytelling provides for the examination and expression of identity, experience, problems, and morality in a social context. Importantly, storytelling is a highly accessible and flexible process, and therefore it promotes participation and the development of projects tailored to meet the needs of a particular context. Storytelling embodies the sharing of power. Stories create culture and society.

Like all discourse, stories can be used for a great number of reasons depending on the needs and intentions of the speaker. Stories (and other forms of discourse) draw on a shared body of cultural understanding; at the same time, they can be reformulated and used contextually to comment critically and persuasively on social life. Therefore, discourse is a site where the intersection of structure and agency can be examined. This is part of the process of the social construction and negotiation of meaning.

The thesis of this chapter is developed below. First, "empowering storytelling" is defined. Second, attention is brought to the role of storytelling in producing meaning: by defining identity, as a means of education and socialization of society's members, for expressing and engendering emotions, and for articulating and establishing understandings of morality. Third, the storytelling process as it is understood by contemporary storytellers is described, focusing on how storytelling can be inclusive and collaborative and thus build relationships and bonds of community.

EMPOWERING STORYTELLING

"Storytelling" as used here refers to the art of telling a story; it includes all forms of oral (or signed) narrative and involves a teller and at least one listener. Thus, it is a social interaction (Ryan 1995). Stories may be fictional tales or they may relate personal experience or group history, but all stories and other narratives are never pure fact or fiction. Even a fantastic tale may be used as a parable to express something that the teller sees as true. Meanwhile, narratives of personal or group experience are constructed and interpretive. Historical accounts are selected, framed, and used—often to make a point about the present in order to affect the future (Consentino 1982; Scheub 1996; Tonkin 1992).

While the relationship between narrative and truth is complex, not all narratives are equal; they may be evaluated and some deemed better than others

(Haraway 1989). Different persons may respond to a narrative differently by embracing the story, by taking an oppositional stance to it, or by reframing the story in some way (Bobo 1996). Within a particular context, meaning is negotiated through narratives, and certain versions will not have currency with the group and will not be circulated (Myerhoff 1992; Urban 1996).

Further, it is critical to recognize the interrelationship of story and social structures. Even though group history and personal narratives may be formulated in the interests of the narrator, certain events and experiences will still be acknowledged. Just because cultural knowledge is socially constructed does not mean that conflict is all in one's head—that is, that there are no structural bases of conflict (for example, structural and social inequalities) or that socially constructed ideas (for example, gender or race) do not have material consequences. Rather, the production of meaning is an important process in social life and in intractable conflicts that can have high stakes. It is the role of storytelling in the production of meaning—and access to that process—that is the focus here.

Importantly, this is not to suggest that storytelling is necessarily good or peaceful. Discursive practices—such as storytelling—may intensify social cleavages when they privilege some cultures while silencing others, generate or reproduce prejudicial and enemy images of other groups, mask inequalities and justice, inflame negative emotions, or misrepresent society. Or, discursive practices may enhance peaceful relations when they involve a dialogue characterized by shared power, engender mutual recognition, promote consciousness raising, serve to resist domination, or teach conflict resolution strategies.

Our use of the term "empowerment" draws on Schwerin's (1995) definition of empowerment as characterized by shared power ("power with") and as an alternative to coercive power ("power over"). Storytellers who were interviewed for this study described a highly inclusive and collaborative process through which persons can participate in the social construction of meaning and establish bonds of community. We call this "empowering storytelling." Storytelling is *not* empowering if it is characterized by a power imbalance and only one person or one group does most of the talking or controls the production of knowledge. (Even silence can be used as a power play by superordinate persons or groups to prevent commentary or dialogue that challenges the status quo.) Empowering storytelling grants everyone access to and inclusion in the storytelling process. This allows for a diversity of stories to be told and presents an opportunity for the de-silencing of experience. In these ways, the storytelling process is congruent with the concepts of mutual recognition (inclusion), empowerment (power sharing), and critical consciousness (honesty and awareness-of-self-in-context) that are fundamental to positive peace (Senehi 1996, 2000, 2003).

The Meaning of Stories

A premise of this chapter is that stories are a critical method (see figure 1 in the appendix). They are a means of articulating knowledge that gets at the complexity of lived experience. Belden Lane, storyteller and professor at St. Louis University, sees storytelling as a distinct way of knowing: "What story says is that truth is impossible to grasp in a purely linear way. What happens when you run up against the deep problems of life and the *mystery,* you find that there aren't any easy answers" (personal communication, 1996).

Stories articulate group identity; individuals and groups are known by the stories they tell. Stories are a means of socializing group members regarding cultural knowledge, norms, and worldview. They engender emotions as they tap into profound understandings and meaning. Stories teach and contain understandings of morality. Thus, to participate in storytelling as a teller or as an audience member who has direct access to the teller is to participate in the construction of meaning. This has the potential to be both profoundly empowering and transforming.

Of course, this process is complex and unpredictable. People respond to stories in their own ways. There are often terrains of knowledge and morality and group norms that are contested. Identities may be complex, involving multiple heritages, dissension from the group, or confusion. What is critical is the power dynamics involved in storytelling and other forms of cultural production: "Who's doing the talking?"

Children consistently report that they love storytelling, and teachers and storytellers contend that even aggressive and typically disruptive teenagers loves stories. Because storytelling appeals to youth (Senehi 2000), and because storytelling engages meaning at a level that is arguably more complex, more multimodal, and more persuasive than linear reasoning, it can be an effective means for youth to reflect on and make sense of their experiences and develop their worldviews in the context of social conflict. Story-based activities may involve both listening to stories and also taking the position of storyteller. To take the position of storyteller and begin to choose, shape, and express stories (either fictional tales or personal narratives) is to become empowered in the profound sense that the individual begins to grapple directly with important issues in a social context.

Ruthilde Kronberg taught storytelling to all students in an elementary school on a weekly basis. This class often involved students retelling stories or putting information into the form of a new story. As one fourth grader commenting on these exercises put it: "I think that when we tell it back, we really have a chance to use our imaginations. We can express ourselves. We can really do anything." Such creativity teaches young people to look for alternatives, to create their own vision, to articulate that vision in exciting ways, and to be confident public speakers. These skills are significant both for listening and for analyzing discourse as well as for participation in the construction of discourse in both the private and public spheres. These skills are critical for participation in civil society.

IDENTITY

Despite severe antagonism between identity groups, which may involve dehumanization of the other (or at least placing the other in a narrow category), the relating of personal experience is a form of storytelling that can transcend barriers. As Belden Lane theorized, story—encompassing metaphor and paradox—is able to articulate profound ideas about identity and life in a language that people can understand: "They're a different kind of tool, a different kind of method, and a lot of people sneer at them, but they're *the only way* to get at subjectivity, to get at the heart of the human person" (personal communication, 1996). Stories articulate the teller's identity because people choose stories that are congruent with their values. As storytellers put it, "you are known by the stories you tell." Storytelling performance is a process of sharing identity, which is distinct from rhetorical deliberation (Fine and Speer 1992).

Usually, intergroup conflicts are framed in terms of identity. In long-standing intractable conflicts, the conflict itself becomes a part of group identity (Northrup 1989). Identity-based violence may involve forced assimilation or punishment by murder, expulsion, marginalization, or oppression based on one's identity (Galtung 1990). For youth growing up in divided societies, understandings of the conflict and the parties to the conflict are encoded in group identity and are passed among generations through everyday storytelling and socialization processes. Youth are more likely to be shaped by the stories they hear, especially when they hear those stories from beloved family members and elders whom they respect. While individuals may interpret their social milieu in different ways, as part of the process of identity formation young people must come to terms with and make sense of their experiences and the wider political context and where they fit into it. These conclusions will shape their future political choices and actions.

Storytelling can be part of the process of peace building, specifically by addressing the misunderstanding, disrespect, and dehumanization of the other. Empowering storytelling involves persons both having access to a greater diversity of stories and having more opportunities to take the position of storytellers. This can impact understandings of identity because the process of listening to a story involves walking in the narrator's shoes and generates empathy. Stories translate well across culture, and mutual recognition is fostered when people listen to each other's stories—even across cultural divides and in the context of social conflicts.

It is important to note that "mutual recognition" does not refer to a universalizing view where one party embraces another party as essentially the same as itself, but rather it refers to a struggle to articulate and examine differences. While developing understanding across boundaries of cultural difference may never be complete or unproblematic, it seems that trusting relationships require a desire on the part of all parties to recognize the dignity and experience of the other.

The Seeds of Peace program has brought together Palestinian and Israeli youth in the United States. The program has provided a safe space for them to share their personal stories and listen to those of others and has helped to build relationships and mutual recognition across a highly charged conflict divide. The University on Youth and Development—organized by the North-South Centre of the Council of Europe, Youth for Development and Cooperation, the Spanish Youth Council, the European Youth Forum, and the Spanish Youth Institute—took place in Mollina, Spain, for the third consecutive year in 2002; it included a workshop on storytelling skills in order to provide training on how storytelling could be used as a means of cross-cultural conflict resolution and relationship building. In an urban and often violent neighborhood in Tucson, Arizona, youth gathered local stories from the past and present about their community from community members; this was a process of reexamining the meaning of their regional identity, which resulted in an increase of regard both for their locality and themselves (Eisele 2001).

SOCIALIZATION

Socialization involves the passing on of a culture's images of one or more outgroups, which may represent enemy images of, or the demonization of, the outgroup. Socialization also encompasses cultural norms for dealing with conflict—for example, the glorification of war. Robert Coles (1986) makes the point that childhood learning reproduces the fundamental mode of conflict in a particular political context. Even though socializing processes are always impacting persons, clearly children are more likely to be the objects rather than the subjects of socialization. Images of the enemy and political information, encoded in cultural parades and festivals attended by families, may be fused with childhood affections, making them hard to question or challenge (Susan Snow Wadley, personal communication, April 25, 1995).[1]

Educational institutions may deny identity needs in ways that are exclusionary. Educational curriculum may omit the achievements and perspectives of certain groups of people. Textbooks may misrepresent history or the experience of particular groups.[2] Still, M. Fine (1989) and Coles (1986) argue that young people, regardless of socioeconomic background, have a high level of political sense with regard to their perceptions of violence as well as their political views. It is critical to find ways to foster young people's own critical analysis of their political and social world so that they develop more agency in their own political socialization.

Many have called for peace education as a means of political socialization to create alternative visions of dealing with conflicts and to promote the development of a peaceful world (Brock-Utne 1985; Reardon 1993; Lantieri and Patti 1996; Harris and Morrison 2003). Storytelling can play an important role in this process.

In Mozambique the UNICEF-funded "Circle of Peace" used traditional music, art, and drama to teach peace building to children (Kolucki 1993; Lederach 1997). In response to the U.S.-Iraq war in 1991, storyteller Margaret Read MacDonald (1992) collected *Peace Tales: World Folktales to Talk About.* In response to the 9/11 terrorist attacks in the United States, New York City storyteller Laura Simms (2002) collected traditional stories in her book, *Stories to Nourish Our Children in a Time of Crisis.* Sometimes new stories are developed: in Germany's Weimar Republic (1919–33), political activists wrote alternative utopian fairy tales (Zipes 1989).

Importantly, children and youth may take part in crafting these stories themselves and articulating their experiences of conflict as part of a process of healing and envisioning a better future. Child survivors of the genocidal violence in Rwanda tell their stories through drawings in *Witness to Genocide,* which was put together by Richard Salem (2000), a mediator and former journalist, after he visited Rwanda's National Trauma Center in Kigali in 1997. Recent conflicts throughout the world have impacted child survivors. Mladi Most, which means "Youth Bridge," is a community center in Mostar, Bosnia, for Bosniac and Croat youth between the ages of sixteen and twenty-five. There, Austrian photographer Uli Loskot mentored youth in a collaborative project of photographing images of war, resulting in an international exhibit of their work, "Crucible of War 2000." These young people worked in mixed groups on a superordinate goal and shared with each other their own personal experiences of war. Their shared stories became an alternative means of education.

EMOTIONS

Emotions such as fear, anger, and frustration are often associated with persons and groups choosing more violent means of addressing conflicts. Emotions may be manipulated by political elites or those with access to mass media. Emotions may be the result of atrocities committed during conflict and part of post-traumatic stress syndrome, and they must be dealt with. After conflict, emotional healing can be constrained by biological changes to the brain (Goleman 1996) associated with post-traumatic stress syndrome.

Destructive stories may tap into intense emotions—for example, the love, grief, and anger associated with the violent death of a loved one—in order to foment hatred. Or, narratives justifying violent interventions may draw on memories of past humiliations. When collective trauma (and all the emotions subsumed therein) remain unacknowledged, fear and mistrust intensify; this can serve as an obstacle to a group's healing and reconciliation. For youth in conflict, dealing with the emotional challenges of conflict and loss may be especially challenging.

Stories simultaneously engage mind and heart. Through storytelling and other cultural rituals, information and argument is conveyed, but the participants gain added power through the emotional impact of the story that they sense and feel (Urban 1991). Storytelling in a safe place, such as in the home, among persons who share a common hardship or set of experiences can be an occasion when their perspectives, silenced elsewhere, become prominent. This storytelling can be both an emotional comfort and a form of resistance. Storytelling is part of the treatment for post-traumatic stress disorder (Goleman 1996). Such a safe place becomes a site where people are no longer objects but rather regain their "humanness" and engage in subject-subject dialogue in order to comment upon, interpret, strategize about, and heal from their difficulties (hooks 1990). The more this kind of space can be carved out in public contexts, the more these dialogues can become part of the public transcript and generate change.

De Palazzo (personal communication, September 9, 2003) argues that it is important for young people who have experienced prejudice to state in their stories how the incident made them feel because people change their perspectives based on this emotional connection rather than reason.[3] When youth hear others tell their stories, they identify with the feelings of the narrator under the circumstances described, and, as De Palazzo puts it, "recognize that people are alike in ways that are more important than their differences." This is not to ignore or diminish the real differences that separate persons and groups but rather to allow for the possibility of a transcendent identity that creates the potential to address these differences more constructively and, perhaps, bravely after bonds of community and trust are developed. Peace educators Linda Lantieri and Janet Patti have also found that for students to appreciate other cultures and overcome prejudices, "it's not enough for students to learn about those cultures; they need some emotional connection with other groups and direct positive experiences of being on equal footing with one another" (1996, 17).

MORALITY

Conflicts framed in moral terms are particularly difficult to resolve. Often, adversaries see the cause of a conflict due not so much to the situation but rather to character flaws in the other. Methods for waging conflict may also be evaluated in moral terms. The early development of children's moral reasoning is an important aspect of their overall development. Young people are involved in continuous reciprocal interaction with their environment, and thus moral development relies on interpersonal communication, relationships, and concern for others (Bronfenbrenner 1979). Young people will be challenged to deal with the moral dimensions of conflict and violence that are often overwhelming even for adults.

Stories often have a point that implies how things should be; therefore, stories are often about morality. Stories may also evoke what Robert Coles (1989) calls the "moral imagination" so that individuals are provoked to question their assumptions and are empowered to make choices that are selfless. Sometimes, because of its emotional appeal, a story can be a persuasive appeal to listeners' moral conscience; they can also be a form of moral protest. Still, the recipients of a story, even youth, do not necessarily and should not accept stories uncritically. Rather, storytelling can be a means of engaging with the issue of what is right and wrong, as well as consciously considering what one values and what the consequences of being loyal to those values might involve.

When students become creators of their own stories or discuss particular stories, they become engaged in a process of moral reasoning. They can present their own moral views when they choose a particular story to tell or construct one from their experience. Storytelling is also usually followed by discussion, either informally or formally, where ideas get critically examined and others may bring their own experience to bear on a question. The significance of this for youth in the aftermath of violent intergroup conflict is enormous because healing from violence that has involved many atrocities is ultimately, perhaps, a moral problem.

The topics of identity, socialization, emotion, and morality are intertwined and part of the human search for meaning, individually and communally. Meaning is not always the preeminent concern in storytelling. Sometimes simply the joy and fun of sharing is dominant, but the opportunity for people to express themselves in a public setting, to negotiate meaning, and to establish shared understandings can be of great significance. For Paulo Freire such a process was essential for developing a critical consciousness: "To exist, humanly, is to name the world, to change it" (2001, 69).

The Storytelling Process

In this section, the process of storytelling is examined (see figure 2 in the appendix). It is argued that storytelling as a process has special attributes that make it a significant methodology for conflict resolution approaches. This analysis is based on research with storytellers who are using creative and innovative interventions based on storytelling and expressive culture specifically as a means of developing cross-cultural understanding, peace education, conflict intervention, and post-conflict peace building.

An examination of process is relevant to conflict resolution and peace building because process and outcome are inextricable; peace must be obtained by peaceful means. John Paul Lederach describes the need to balance issues of process and outcome, discussed by Mohandas Gandhi as "Gandhi's dilemma": "transformative peacemaking is based on understanding fair, respectful, and inclusive process as a way of life and envisions outcome as a commitment to increasing justice, seeking truth, and healing relationships" (1996, 22). Peaceful process as described here is congruent with peace as defined above. Peacemaking must be an inclusive, fair, and respectful process; that is, it allows for *mutual recognition.* Peacemaking must be a collaborative problem-solving effort; that is, it allows for *empowerment.* The goals of seeking truth and increasing justice involve developing a *critical consciousness.* All of these are important for healing relationships, which are the basis of community. Peacemaking and peace building may involve *resistance* when the oppressed group confronts oppressors in order to seek justice and positive peace.

Further, process and outcome are inextricable because process, in fact, contains substantive information about values and personal relationships. For example, being excluded may teach us that we are not valued. On the other hand, collaboration teaches us that our input is worthwhile, that we share power, and how we can work together to solve problems. Collaboration builds trust and safety.

Storytelling Is Low-Tech

One of the reasons that storytelling is accessible is because it can be used anywhere at any time. No special equipment is required except the ability to talk or use sign language. Storytelling exists in all cultures regardless of technological advancement. Because storytelling involves no costly equipment or special training, it is accessible to all economic classes. Mary LaCompte, who teaches storytelling to youth, tells educators that "If you're looking for something that is free, storytelling is free" (personal communication 1996). While no expression is completely without limitation, storytelling is an expressive medium that has few obstacles relative to other media. Story-based projects for peace building can be conducted regardless of economic restraints and in the dire conditions that often exist after war and violence. Even in the most meager of circumstances, storytelling is still possible.

Everybody Gets It

Stories can be interpreted in different ways, and they can convey coded messages that outsiders do not understand. Still, in general, storytelling is a process that can be understood by everyone, including very young children and special needs children. Understanding stories takes no special training. In educational settings, anxiety about performance is reduced during storytelling sessions. Storyteller Marilyn Kinsella, a former teacher, describes the difference between a storytelling session and a typical teaching session:

> Unfortunately, in most classes you have different levels of math or whatever it is, and so you've got some kids done in ten minutes and there's kids struggling with the first problem. So you have a lot of competition. And you have a lot of feelings of frustration in the classroom that a teacher has to deal with whereas most of the time with a story, I've got everybody with me. You know, there's not one kid that's not understanding the story. They're all with me, and they're all bringing their experiences into it. (personal communication, 1995)

Storytelling's accessibility may be a clue to its significance. Information critical for society needs to be understood by and expressed by all persons. The intellectual accessibility of storytelling makes it a valuable medium for youth. While understanding stories across cultures may be problematic and incomplete, stories do translate fairly well across cultures.

In the context of conflict, the fewer the impediments to understanding the better. Further, everyone needs to be involved in peacemaking, not just those who have the advantages of education or particular training. Everyone can be involved in a story-based intervention on relatively equal footing.

Storytelling Skills Are Easy to Acquire

Storytelling is accessible because anyone can acquire the title of storyteller. No expensive training or intimidating process of certification is required. While an individual's transition to an identity of storyteller may be facilitated by the storytelling community or a supportive audience, becoming a storyteller is largely a self-driven process with few constraints. A key axiom of storytellers is "Everybody's a storyteller," and this is an ethos of inclusion. According to this ethos, storytellers do not (or should not) set themselves up as experts or prodigies. Often storytellers deemphasize their skills and even their agency by stating that they are merely conduits for the story.

It is possible for a young person to assume the role of storyteller successfully, and in the process they will develop their skills. Also, as people develop their storytelling skills, they develop their thoughts when they have a place to express them, hear them, reflect on them, and be heard. It is usually feasible to implement story-based projects because it is reasonable to expect that people will be able to tell stories even if they have not done so self-consciously in the past.

Awareness-of-Self-in-Context

Because storytellers pick stories that are important to them, storytellers must inevitably speak out of their belief systems and convictions. Sometimes this is a somewhat unconscious process and a process of self-discovery as a teller may not be exactly clear at first what attracts them to a particular story. In fact, it is common for storytellers to say, "I didn't choose the story; it chose me!" Through this process, storytellers identify and clarify not only to others but also to themselves what is important to them and what they believe.

In conflict situations, especially protracted social conflict or social division, storytelling can be a means of developing awareness of one's values and experiences. Personal storytelling done in groups can be a means of consciousness raising and community building among persons whose lives may be shaped in similar ways by social conditions. For youth from different conflict zones, getting together to share experiences may be an effective way to reflect critically on one's own experience. Also, previous research found that having a space to tell stories actually led people to develop a clearer sense of their values and to assess how they could achieve particular objectives (Senehi 2000).

Openness

While people are known by the stories they tell, this can be more or less a direct process. For example, storytelling can range from selecting a classic fable to telling an autobiographical narrative. This implies that storytelling is a means of the teller being open to listeners, but the degree of openness can be controlled.

For a conflict resolution project, this means that a story-based project can allow for a gradual—and thus safer—entry into the process of getting to know others. People can reveal as much—or as little—as they want as part of a gradual process of trust building. People can share their values indirectly by telling a story and seeing how others react. By sharing a point through a story, one may be more distanced from the message because a storyteller can be understood as simply a conduit for a traditional wisdom endorsed by generations (depending on the source of the story). Meanwhile, people can share what they want to about themselves without the constraints of other media. If someone wants to address a particular issue or share a part of themselves, it is possible.

A SAFE ENVIRONMENT

Storytellers—especially those who tell stories to children—can be intentional about creating an environment where the participants in their storytelling activities feel safe. They do this in at least two ways: by emphasizing themes of respect in their storytelling, and—perhaps more importantly—by modeling inclusion and respect through their storytelling process. Storytellers also seek to create a safe world through the lessons of inclusion, interdependence, and respect that they incorporate into their storytelling. Ultimately, inclusion and collaboration—and community building and peace—are matters of respect. Annette Harrison believes that stories can engender both self-respect and hope, which is the most important reason stories are effective in teaching.

Annette Harrison, who has developed a story-based program for teaching conflict resolution skills in schools, sees the issue of affirmation or respect as fundamental to conflict resolution:

> When I say conflict resolution story, I'm talking about the range of
> feeling like a valued person, respected, feeling that people are listening
> to you, feeling competent and that you have skills, that you can
> explain how you feel. All my stories that touch on all of these and
> being able to work it out, in some way say, "I choose peace. No matter
> what and we're gonna work this out." So that's how I see conflict
> resolution stories. A lot of the stories are about being honest and a
> good person. And we're not going to be that way unless we feel that
> we're respected. (personal communication, November 24, 1994)

Storytellers can model respect and empowerment through their collaborative, nonthreatening, interactive style—in a context of shared pleasure. This can often create a safe situation where meaning and identity can be examined, renegotiated, and potentially altered. Dan Bar-On (2000) and others have brought people from different sides of protracted political divides together in seminars called "To Trust and Reflect" (TRT), in which the participants share their personal experiences and listen to those of others. Evaluations of these seminars emphasized the value of storytelling that this space made possible: "Hearing the stories of the 'other' and learning more about their pain and suffering, was something that left an impact on me. Storytelling and the care, support, safety, and protection of the TRT group to others made it easy to open up and trust" (Maoz 2000b, 152).

THE TELLER IS ACCESSIBLE

Because storytelling is an in-person exchange, the storyteller is accessible to the receivers of the story. The storyteller's accessibility creates an opportunity for exchange and relationships among the storyteller and participants in the storytelling event. If the position of storyteller is a position of leadership and power, audience members have access to that power. If they want to share further with the storyteller or oppose the storyteller, it is possible to do so. Storytellers define good storytelling in large part by the relationship created between the teller and the audience.

SHARED EXPERIENCE

Storytelling builds community because it is a shared experience. Storytelling—even when stories are scary—can be a pleasurable activity in which everyone can participate. Storytellers talk about storytelling being profoundly joyful. Storyteller Ed Stivender is known for his belief that "storytelling is breathing together" (personal communication). Storyteller Angela Lloyd builds on this by suggesting that laughter is literally breathing together because we have to breathe to laugh (personal communication, 1996). Storyteller January Kiefer urges, "Don't forget to laugh!" She explains that laughter "is another one of those moments when you realized you're engaged . . . when you're not separated" (personal communication, 1996). Storytelling is often a shared and pleasurable experience. This builds bonds of togetherness and community.

The fact that storytelling can be pleasurable adds to its power as a potential peacemaking and peace-building methodology. In Northern Ireland, Pat Ryan reported the following anecdote:

> A storyteller recounted how he was visiting various schools around Castlederg. Two schools in the area shared the same bus route.

Although the children from the two schools rode the bus together every day, the groups never spoke to one another. Each viewed the children from the different school as being of the "other" side.

Around the end of the storyteller's residency, the principal of the school informed him that a "miracle" had occurred. Overhearing one of the children from the "other" school talking about a "surprise" visit from the storyteller who was to come that day, the eavesdropper and his friends began to regale their opposites, proclaiming that the storyteller was "brilliant." They even proceeded to reveal the teller's entire repertoire, performing all his stories, riddles, and songs. By the end of the bus journey no one could have stopped the two groups chattering to each other even if they wanted to! (1995, 24).

The fact that storytelling can be pleasurable and fascinating lends to its inclusivity because youth will want to be involved, to participate, and to collaborate in such projects. Further, this builds genuine bonds formed in the context of a shared pleasurable activity where people can be themselves rather than be required to meet specific performance standards, as is the case in many other activities.

STORYTELLING IS INTIMATE

Storytelling is an intimate experience that is shared simultaneously. Many storytellers emphasize the role of laughing together—or even being scared together during a scary story—to build bonds of community. As storyteller January Kiefer put it, "True laughter engages you. It's almost like a way of applauding. It's a spontaneous form of expression that comes out of being so fully engaged that you laugh or you applaud or you shout. All of those very spontaneous forms of expression, to me, come out of full engagement with something" (personal communication, 1996).

CO-CREATION

Storytelling is seen by tellers as co-creation because, without pictures and with the simplicity of the narrative, listeners have to visualize the story and fill in the details themselves. Also, much storytelling—including most traditional styles—involves forms of audience participation, which fulfills many functions, including keeping children engaged and delighted in the process. Some contemporary storytelling is highly participatory. When storytelling is conceived as an interaction between teller and audience, an element of unpredictability enters into the storytelling experiences as neither the teller nor the audience has total control. Youth recognize this dynamic in storytelling. They delight in these events, love storytellers, and talk about storytelling with great enthusiasm after an event.

ELICITIVE TEACHING

It is well established that stories encode meaning and that storytelling is a mode of teaching intellectual, cultural, and moral values. Because storytelling is collaborative, this educational process—especially as practiced by these storytellers—is elicitive and empowering. This kind of approach to teaching—whether that teaching is for general education or social transformation—is noncoercive.

Professional storyteller Judith Black, who creates stories and story-based workshops to teach a range of subjects, insists that storytelling involves a balance between the teller, the listener, and the story. She emphasizes that storytelling is not about "consciousness raising," framed in subject-object terms:

> I think if you go into it thinking you're gonna teach a lesson or raise a consciousness, you're gonna walk into a wall because it puts you here and puts your listeners there. And you have something you're going to give them. And that's bullshit. It's an equal relationship. . . .
>
> All you can do is share an experience and hope that everyone enters that experience, has it, and then leaves with a transformation, but you don't know what it's gonna be because people come to you with different things in their heads and different things in their hearts. And if you think you can dictate what they're gonna exit with, then you're God. And I don't think any of us have hit that place yet. (personal communication, 1996)

Many storytellers emphasize that they do not seek to be didactic or give prescriptive advice; they do not proselytize. While stories may bring up issues in an effort to create social change, the storytelling process remains collaborative and noncoercive. Rather, it is an invitation to change. In their story-based workshop on racism, "Face to Face," January Kiefer and Blake Travis perform a series of skits around the topic of racism, but as Travis emphasizes, they do not resolve issues for the audience:

> At the moments of the most high tension, we go "Freeze!" to let the audience make a decision about how they feel with what just happened rather than letting it come to some resolution. We don't resolve anything. We don't answer any questions.

We just put it out there: Bam! What do you think about
this? . . . Because this is what's goin' on around this question of
racism. This is what we do to ourselves. This is what we do to each
other around racism. (personal communication, 1996)

Their powerful and thought-provoking pieces create discussion and, Travis said,
"many minds shift."

Consistent with storytellers' commitment to a paradigm of shared power,
January Kiefer resisted the label of leader. When asked if she saw herself as a
leader, Keifer responded: "No not really. Maybe an inspirer. I don't know what
'a leader' means. A leader . . . what is a leader? Does a leader have an idea about
where they want to take people? 'A leader' is a hard word. Hard. I mean it's hard
like 'military leader.' I don't like the word leader. Inspirer is a better world."
Rather than leading people to a particular place, Kiefer and other tellers seek
to inspire people to begin their own self-directed journeys.

RE-STORY-ING SELF AND SOCIETY

In the aftermath of violence, both civilians and combatants often feel isolated
because the social fabric of society is weakened as a result of protracted conflict.
While a peace accord may have been reached, society may remain in a state that
is unstable, contested, and disorganized, with the future unclear. This is a "negative peace." What is required to achieve positive peace is not only political organization but also culture building and people envisioning the future, both individually and communally. This is a creative and collective process.

A constructive storytelling process helps communities to build inclusivity at
the grassroots, repair relationships, heal from trauma, and reduce prejudice. Public, but locally based, storytelling—easily organized, accessible, and able to take
many forms—provides a medium for a collaborative process of meaning making
and relationship building that is (1) grounded by persons' experiences and perspectives and therefore elicitive rather than proscriptive, and (2) grounded by real
one-on-one or relatively immediate interaction, which builds bonds of community
that can be a resource in good times and bad. This is a necessary first step for social
change that mediates between the personal and political. In particular, youth disaffected and alienated by war need to be integrated into the civic culture. Storytelling can engage the energy of youth as catalysts for change by meeting their
needs, addressing critical issues, and redefining relations through a process of
reconciliation built upon "truth, mercy, justice, and peace," as Lederach (1997)
puts it.

Storytelling has the potential to build real bonds of community between people. Such relationships are a critical resource in conflict resolution. In the context of a trusting relationship where there is a free flow of communication, shared problems can be addressed. Storytelling is one means of building a relationship that can transcend differences. Affective bonds and shared knowledge developed during storytelling can foster a shared identity and culture that may transcend particularities without erasing them.

Storytelling also involves the story. This is knowledge that is being proposed, examined, and reflected upon in a shared context. The story contains knowledge that may transcend the individuals as it speaks to a principle or idea that has been shared for a long time by a wider group. Or, the experience of the individual shared in that one story becomes representative of the experiences of a larger group or a broader set of human conditions, as did that of Rigoberto Menchu Tum.

A major concern in the field of conflict resolution and peace studies is to be especially sensitive to how various intervention approaches and models might translate across cultures (Avruch and Black 1994). Further, the importance of respecting indigenous knowledge systems and involving the participants in the design of programs and systems was discussed by Lederach (1996, 1997) and has been a major concern of many practitioners working globally in our field. Because story is used in all cultures and because story-based interventions are so flexible, they can be adapted to what is appropriate in different contexts.

Stories operate in the world and get results (Raheja and Gold 1994). But stories are also constrained (Chase 1995). We must find ways to create spaces where youth can participate more fully in defining themselves and their communities, often in the aftermath of violence, conflict, and tragedy.

For youth, being a part of this process is possible and extremely empowering. While anyone can participate in storytelling activities, skills in communication and listening improve with practice. As people hear more stories, their knowledge base increases. Importantly, students become engaged in a social and existential project of making sense of their world and creating a vision to shape the future.

Recommendations

Following are some special considerations for developing story-based projects to promote reconciliation, healing, and empowerment within and between communities:

DO WHAT IS APPROPRIATE. Storytelling is more a medium than a particular model. A constructive storytelling process may take shape in innumerable ways. Consider what is appropriate in a particular context as well as the objectives of the project.

ENSURE A BALANCE OF POWER. Empowering storytelling is storytelling that provides for power equality. Such storytelling must provide people with the space to speak. Empowering storytelling is about including stories rather than using stories dogmatically to promote a particular point of view. However, it might be appropriate to share stories that provide examples of reconciliation or successful non-violent approaches to conflict.[4] It is always important to provide for discussion of stories told.

BE COMFORTABLE WITH THE UNEXPECTED. While every project has objectives, those objectives must be broad. If the aim of the project is to get people to think a certain way, this is in the spirit of proscriptive teaching and objectifies the receiver of the story. This goes against the ethos of constructive storytelling, which is necessarily inclusive. Giving people the space to have their say always creates an element of unpredictability, which can make people uncomfortable, and critical voices may be discouraged. It is important to have a safe place to examine all perspectives respectfully.

ALLOW FOR CREATIVE POSSIBILITIES. Storytelling approaches to reconciliation may involve personal narratives or creative tales. Consider artistic or other story-based projects that allow for multiple perspectives and experiences to co-exist. For example, the stories of diverse persons in one community can be collected and woven together in one dramatic form. Also, storytelling can be combined with other artistic forms, such as dance, music, and art.

RECOGNIZE THAT PEOPLE DEVELOP THEIR IDEAS IN THE PROCESS. Previous research found that storytelling not only gave people the space to voice their perspectives, but given that space, people's perspectives began to develop (Senehi 2000). It is critical to provide the safety for people to take risks, to be themselves, and to develop their communication skills and their own viewpoints. Reconciliation, peace building, civic society, even peace itself is as much a process as an outcome.

RECOGNIZE THE SIGNIFICANCE OF ART EDUCATION. Art for art's sake is wonderful because it allows people to be themselves rather than focus on meeting some prescribed standard, as is usually the case in school, on the job, and in so many arenas of life. Meanwhile, through storytelling and other arts, students learn skills of creativity and objectivity that are necessary for problem-solving and envisioning alternatives to conflict and strife. Importantly, they learn communication skills that are critical for participating empathically and persuasively in social life.

Notes

1. Sometimes public education, such as in the United States, is a harsh means for resocializing indigenous persons and immigrants (Barman et al. 1986; Adams, 1999). In educational institutions, the silence of faculty and administration around issues such as drop-out rates, lack of job opportunities, and social inequality may confuse students and prevent a critical awareness (M. Fine 1989).

2. Stories told in childhood may be connected with intense bonds of love that the child has for her or his caregiver(s) during the time of life when she or he is most helpless.

3. De Palazzo facilitates prejudice reduction workshops for the National Conference of Community and Justice in south Florida. For more than five years, she has used story-based projects and strategies in her work with youth around issues of prejudice in schools. As part of a project where youth develop "Heritage Panels," youth are asked to relate an event where they were the object or witness of prejudice.

4. See, for example, the films developed or promoted by the Arts and Culture Section of the international nongovernmental organization Search for Common Ground.

FIGURE 1: THE MEANING OF STORIES

STORIES

	More Violent (characterized by "power over" and exclusionary practices)	More Peaceful (characterized by "power with" and mutual recognition)
IDENTITY	• Group knowledge and history exclude or misrepresent whole groups of people. • Collective trauma remains unacknowledged in historical narratives and unhealed. • Stories encode enemy images of the other. • Stories make social inequality appear natural.	• Stories are an accessible and flexible means of articulating alternative viewpoints. • All feel their story is told and heard. • Stories serve the interests of the listeners. • Stories express identity and dignity in the face of oppression. • People understand each other by hearing each other's stories.
EDUCATION AND SOCIALIZATION	• Prejudice and social inequality are taught to children through stories. • Stories normalize structural and/or direct violence. • Stories glorify war in order to recruit soldiers.	• Stories told in the homeplace and other local settings are a means for passing on history and knowledge for those excluded from the public transcript. • Stories teach without proselytizing. • People enjoy stories and are receptive to them.

EMOTION	• Stories tap into emotions (e.g., the love of family members who have died or feelings of humiliation) in order to foment fear and hatred and to incite actions of direct violence. • When collective trauma remains unacknowledged, fear and mistrust intensify.	• Stories offer comfort and hope during hardship. • Stories are joyful. • People share laughter and tears. • People remember and in this way reconnect with lost loved ones and their own past. • Stories are a part of healing from the trauma of violence.
MORALITY	• Moral community excludes identity groups. • Other party is demonized and devalued on moral grounds.	• Stories compellingly exert moral pressure on those in power. • Stories touch the heart and engender a shared identity that can humanize the enemy or re-humanize a demonized other.

FIGURE 2: THE STORYTELLING PROCESS

Empowerment (inclusion, shared power, accessibility to process)	Mutual Recognition (mutual respect, inclusion of culture, understanding)	Knowledge (awareness-of-self-in-context, honesty)
Storytelling Is Low Tech Storytelling requires little or no equipment, money, or personnel. *People can participate in cultural production regardless of financial circumstances.*	Safe Environment Empowering storytellers seek to create an environment where people feel safe to be who they are. They also seek a safe world by means of lessons of respect and inclusion. *Storytelling promotes an ethic of mutual recognition.*	Awareness-of-Self-in-Context Storytelling articulates identity and names problems and experiences. Stories encode wisdom. *Storytelling is a means for developing and articulating knowledge in a social context.*

Everybody Gets It
Storytelling is intellectually accessible. *Everybody can understand stories and participate with little performance anxiety regardless of age, cultural training, or special needs.*

Skills Are Easy to Acquire
Storytelling does not require a selective or costly training process. Empowering storytellers encourages everybody to be a storyteller. *All groups can participate in cultural production with minimal gatekeepers.*

Teller Is Accessible
Storytellers perform in person and are accessible after performance to talk with listeners. *Audience members are close to the sources of cultural production.*

Shared, Intimate Experience
Because it is an interpersonal interaction, storytelling is intimate for both listeners and tellers. *Storytelling creates bonds of community that are felt and sensed.*

Openness
Storytellers reveal their values with the stories they tell. Empowering storytellers are interested in listening to the stories of others. At an interpersonal level, storytellers seek to get to know each other beyond the surface level. *Storytelling promotes mutual understanding.*

Pleasurable
Storytellers and listeners share the pleasurable experience of the story together, and laugh and/or cry together. *Storytelling creates bonds.*

Co-Creation
Storytelling is highly participatory and interactive with the audience. The audience helps shape the storytelling experience. *Audience members participate in cultural production.*

Elicitive Teaching
Storytelling is not didactic or prescriptive but rather is an elicitive teaching style. Post-story discussion allows for a shared process of developing knowledge. *Storytelling is a teaching method that is empowering to participants.*

Contextually Driven
Because storytelling is so inexpensive and do-able, small inexpensive projects tailored to specific needs are possible. *People develop and shape their agendas and ideas through storytelling.*

JOHAN GALTUNG

Theoretical Challenges of Peace Building with and for Youth

A SHORT STORY FROM POST-ACCORD EUROPE

May 8, 1945, VJ Day, Victory in Europe, a ceasefire accord. Nazi-Germany had been defeated,[1] to be followed by Japan on August 15. Anglo-Saxon supremacy[2] was reinstated. To make sure everybody got the point they had tribunals in Nuremberg and Tokyo with themselves as judges, carefully controlling victors' justice, just as the winners did after the First World War through the Second Versailles Treaty of 1919.[3] The inner Anglo-Saxon balance had, however, shifted from the English to the American leg. The ambiguous France persisted in its ambiguity, and Italy tested the waters.

There had been much discussion of what to do with Germany, tempered by the concern of not repeating the mistakes of the Versailles Treaty. One formula was to punish, and severely so, the key leaders of evil Germany, assuming the people to be basically good after some political and cultural de-Nazification. As a military power Germany had to be cut down to a minimum but not as an economic power. Whatever the arguments, it all changed with what was seen as the other challenge to Anglo-American power, particularly Anglo-American capitalist supremacy: the Soviet Union and communism. Germany was enlisted in the anti-Soviet alliance; so were old Nazis. The Cold War took over.

Two French politicians, Jean Monnet and Robert Schuman, had already gone a significant step further, however. Nazi-Germany had been barbaric; for that reason a new Germany, de-Nazified, had to become a member of a European family to be created on that belligerent continent. A long process started, from the Coal and Steel Union of May 9, 1950, to the present European Union.

So much for the official text; at the same time an undertext was unfolding, more in action than in words. Young people from the resistance movements in Germany, Italy, and France had a very different perspective: not "what to do *with* Germany" but "what to do *together with* Germany." Because they were rooted in the resistance movement, they knew another reality underneath—a reality that was not Nazi, Fascist, or collaborationist but something human on which to build. Their reality was continental Europe rather than Anglo-American geopolitics. What they wanted was a European federation. They were unimpressed with Coudenhove-Kalergi's pan-Europeanism, which they saw as too much Charlemagne, authoritarian, top-down.

Out of this sentiment from the late 1940s and early 1950s came very concrete action that made history. Border posts were torn down between Germany and France at Hagenau near Strasbourg and between Italy and France at Ventimiglia and Modane. There was also an organization with a very meaningful name in the present context: *Jeunesse Européenne Federaliste* (JEF).[4]

So this was youth building peace by weaving youth together around a very concrete and very ambitious goal. It was "post-accord" in the sense of taking place after ceasefire agreements. But the whole discourse, expressed in action-speech-thought, was entirely different. And it was not merely critical.

Critique is usually "intra-paradigmatic," or within the same discourse. But these youth's discourse was extra-paradigmatic, if not exactly new, bringing in a very constructive perspective. Those youth did not want the French *Europe des patries*–the Europe of the fatherlands–but *Europe Patrie*–Europe as a fatherland. What remains to be said is a rather major point: "those youth" won. The European Union is in name not a federation because of Anglo-Saxon problems with the word "federation." But it comes very close. Their method was seen as anarchist and dangerous, expressing a yearning to come together in something solid and tight beyond the state system. The peace accords made by the generation ahead of them did not address their concerns. Possibly Monnet-Schuman was a compromise between the harshest Allied plans for Germany, with de-industrialization and permanent divisions as elements, and the borderless Europe, without any threat from these youth. But reality has so far turned out to be a compromise between Monnet-Schuman and them.

The basic lesson to be drawn from this story is that youth may have visions beyond accords arrived at by adults. Different nations and classes have different perspectives, as do genders and age cohorts. Dramatic events may impinge on a person directly or they may be mediated. But they leave traces. Those traces are integrated into paradigms inculcated through family, friends, and schools. Those paradigms harden. After some time new events have less impact; they are only confirming paradigms already established. Gestalts have been formed. Great drama, like wars, would be needed for new perspectives to break through, gestate, emerge, and be articulated.

When do gestalts harden, developing almost impenetrable crusts? Is this when certificates of "maturity" are issued? When does s/he becomes an adult? Is it in late puberty or in the early twenties? It can hardly be later than twenty-five. Rigidity sets in and the person becomes predictable. The Second World War was exactly that for adults—the second, to be understood like the first. For adolescents (like this author) it was *the* life-shaping event. With no firm, preexisting paradigms youth can develop their own paradigms and interpret things differently, including "peace accords." Rather than implementing them, they might even reject them.

A basic mechanism behind gestalt formation is the striving for cognitive consonance. The ideas included in the paradigm must harmonize with each other. For the gestalt to be a system, no basic contradiction, disharmony, or conflict is allowed. Or at least this is what Aristotelian/Cartesian logic, that pillar of Western thought, demands. Oriental yin/yang is more flexible.

By the late twenties the systems have had their dissonances ironed out, with clear friend/foe, good/evil borders. This means that for a new experience to enter and reshape a paradigm it must be strong like a war, an occupation, or a catastrophe at the personal level. This is why cohorts—people born in the same, say, five years who have been through experiences like Vietnam or the freedom of the Republic of South Africa on April 27, 1994—will share some paradigms defining what should/should not happen. If they were hit in early adulthood the paradigms may stay with them for life because their gestalts were not yet fully hardened. The world is seen, for better or for worse, as having a "New Beginning." And the hardening starts.

VIOLENCE, PEACE: ARE YOUTH DIFFERENT FROM ADULTS?

Do youth and adults approach violence and peace differently, as Carol Gilligan (1982) postulates for women and men? According to Gilligan women tend to react with more empathy,[5] trying to relieve suffering regardless of whether the sufferers are "worthy" or "unworthy," whereas men have to justify their actions in terms of some general principles like "national interest," "human rights," and "humanitarianism." The short formulation of what has just been said, vulgarizing but not entirely off the mark, would be that women are more emotionally steered by compassion and men more cognitively steered by deduction from general principles.

Is there a similar formula for youth versus adults? One is very well known, somewhat hackneyed, again vulgarizing but not entirely off the mark: youth are more idealist, adults more realist. And, as discussed above, youth may be more open, adults more closed. Are these two different points or two different ways of saying the same thing? Let us have a look. To be young is to have less past and more future, less trauma suffered and inflicted and more hope. That means a combination of less knowledge and less experience, in principle making youth more free to dream ideals and less impeded by useful knowledge and experience than adults. But knowledge can also harden into inflexible mind-sets, and experience can harden into inflexible habits. Moreover, adults may simply have given up, settling at a low level of ideas and ideals. Being less shaped by experience, youth are more open to ideas and ideals. But as we grow older generalizing from experience may gain the upper hand.

Ideas and ideals come from somewhere, such as from the traumas of being a victim and/or combatant; or from significant others like family and friends; or from the deep culture, or collective subconscious, through its many carriers like street names, monuments, museums, anthems, national parks and holidays, and school curricula. We should not assume "idealist" to mean that youth are necessarily pacifist or socialist. Rather, what we might assume, or hypothesize, would be that youth crave something new and different and see change as feasible, steered less by reality and more by ideals. Youth may be more revolutionary, wanting to change everything here and now, because reality falls so short of their ideals. This may make them pacifist or socialist but could also make them militaristic or fascist.[6] Either way, they would probably stand for a world negating that of their parents. They would often stand for an antithesis of what already is.[7]

Whereas gender perspectives tend to complement each other, generation/cohort perspectives may tend to exclude each other. Gender is more oriental, *yin/yang;* while generation is more occidental, *thesis/antithesis.* There may be a synthesis somewhere, to be arrived at later. But many youth may prefer a clear negation of adult positions to implementation or completion of them. But then there also may be those watersheds in history, *Achsenzeiten,* when all fault lines are activated, including class and nation. Lower classes will mobilize for negation of dominant society, not for inclusion. The same may apply to youth, like the European youth who rejected a post–World War II accord or, possibly, world youth today, faced with Anglo-American peace accords in the former Yugoslavia, the Middle East, and west/central Asia.[8]

The youth/adult divide is not sharp. Some youth seem to be born old; some adults remain young forever. But, following the reasoning above, those prematurely aged youngsters have probably closed their gestalt very early, for several reasons. Their deep culture may handle all questions that arise, including deep trauma, violence, and war.[9] The child's never-ending "why" tapers off: they already know the answer. They may have been so heavily punished from an early age for any new answer that closure is the best defense. Nothing may ever happen in their lives that calls for an extra-paradigmatic response.

The key word is *creativity*. The distinction between coming up with new answers to old questions and asking new questions points to a *Creativity I* versus the more advanced *Creativity II*. Creativity I locates the question, its raw material, inside the paradigm, strolling outside to process an answer. Creativity II is extra-paradigmatic in both questions and answers. Children may exhibit both types, having soft paradigms or none at all. If they harden early we get an aged youth, good at reciting old answers to old questions and gradually acquiring the habit of answering new questions with the same tired old answers. The secret of the ever young may be less overload of deep culture or life in zones of multicultural ambiguity.[10] The habit of asking "why" never ends. They have been rewarded early in life for new questions and new answers. Their environment is filled with challenges or they seek them, preferring excess creativity to a frozen life with lasting challenge deficit.

Much of the same can be said about the woman-man distinction. Girls and boys may to a large extent be rewarded for different types of intelligence—girls for emotional/social intelligence and boys for the cognitive aspects. The two types may, as mentioned, complement rather than exclude each other in the family and in the society at large—except at the top, where the ultimate power is located, one reason why the ubiquitous patriarchy will impose the male style. Lower down, parity and androgyny may bring out the rich synergy of complementarity.

Something similar may of course happen to the cohorts, but more as synthesis than as complementarity. The older generation may have opted for capitalism, the younger and revolutionary for socialism, or the other way round. They may meet in social democracy. But then they also may not. They may fight it out, and one of them may win and impose its vision of the good society.

The terms "idealist"/"realist" and "emotional"/"cognitive" have been avoided as being too general. "Idea-ist" and "reality-ist" might have captured the distinction better, but those words do not exist. Needless to say, we are talking about more versus less compassion and deductiveness and their implications. All traits are found in both genders and generations. There is no sharp dichotomy, only distributions with different averages and usually not even strong correlations. The hypotheses for the four quadrants of humanity would be the following:

YOUTH-WOMAN: open, seeking new approaches, avoiding violence
YOUTH-MEN: open, seeking new approaches, open for new violence
ADULT-WOMAN: closed to new approaches, avoiding violence
ADULT-MAN: closed to new approaches, ready for old violence (see figure 1)

A number of conclusions can be drawn from these hypotheses.

Figure 1

	WOMAN More compassionate	**MAN** More deductive
YOUTH More open-minded	More open-minded More compassionate	More open-minded More deductive
ADULT More closed-minded	More closed-minded More compassionate	More closed-minded More deductive

1. It makes little sense to talk about "youth" in general. Girls and boys are easily more different than youth and adults. Thus, girls would tend to be more nonviolent and boys less, and boys would tend to be less oriented toward alleviating suffering regardless of by whom it is inflicted and girls more. Both would search for new approaches, but boys might also be searching for new forms of violence.
2. The adult woman may be very peace oriented and against violence according to paradigms of earlier generations. The peace movement has been through several paradigms during the last century, such as before the Second World War, after the Second World War, and after the Cold War.[11] Youth and/or women have been paving the way for these shifts.
3. The problematic group from the point of view of peace by peaceful means is adult males. "Peace accords" carry the signature of their authors, generally adult, even old, and male. The accords are often short on creativity and long on violence, waiting for the parties to kill each other till they are ready for accords or imposing a ceasefire violently. There are better options, more compassionate and more open-minded, than what is usually produced by the adult male quadrant, however.

4. For peace to prevail, youth women, and youth and women, should meet often. *Older men should meet less.*

To this the older men may respond by asking for the evidence that the other three quadrants are that much better. And women can respond, with much justification, that they are living in a world governed by men. Youth can say that they have been born into a world governed by adults. Both can blame the Other for the calamities of the world and point to the way they have been excluded, by men and adults respectively, particularly by adult men, from any chance to set the world right.

Take as an example one of the best-confirmed hypotheses in social science, almost a truism: *violence breeds violence.* Some mechanisms are synchronic, like the *counterattack,* or by creating a context of a culture of violence where violence is normal and compassion for the bereaved and a search for nonviolent ways of solving the conflict are not. And some are diachronic, like revenge, *blowback,* a time bomb waiting to explode, or a vendetta between two clans. Or by creating a culture of violence in a reproductive system such as a family with father beating mother, mother beating the eldest child, and the eldest child beating the siblings, with the consequence that all children do the same as parents, thinking it is normal.

The more synchronic and diachronic violence, and the older the person, the more firmly anchored is violence in the person's paradigm. He, usually a he, will download wisdom like, for example, "History has taught us ____"; "If you want peace prepare for war." The younger a person is, unless living in an exceptionally violent context, the lower the probability of this violence/peace paradigm filled with a culture of violence becoming normal/natural. When hardened as a gestalt we may even talk of brain damage posing as realism.

But youth are, generally speaking, less inclined to see violence as normal and natural. The longer the remaining life span—life expectancy—the more vested one's interest is in creative and nonviolent ways of handling conflict at all levels—at the personal microlevel, the social mesolevel, the interstate and internation macrolevel, and the interregion and intercivilization megalevel. In an increasingly globalizing world, macro and mega conflicts will become increasingly familiar and significant to increasing numbers. And it will become increasingly important that coming generations—the coming youth cohorts—do not assume that violence at one level generalizes to other levels, or that nonviolence at one level *cannot* generalize to other levels.

U.S. culture has an unfortunate tendency to psychologize, reducing all conflicts to the microlevel, as seen in the conflict in the UN Security Council in February 2003 over the then-coming Iraq war. Speculations about the persons involved blocked any understanding of the real disagreements and conflicts. If the U.S. microlevel is already very violent, the idea that the problem will wither away if we substitute one person for the other comes easily. The name for person change in a democracy is *election,* hence the temptation to manipulate those elections and the temptation to capture or kill inconvenient leaders.

Correspondingly, U.S. culture takes the marvelous peace among the 50 states and the 2,500 municipalities for granted. There is much peace derived from the equality and equity with which states and municipalities relate to each other, which is not captured in the dualist paradigm of hierarchy versus anarchy. Federal stick and carrot power matter, but that peace is much more solid.

A Case: The Younger Generation, Adult Experts, and the Year 2000

At the end of the 1960s a comparative interview study was made of the images—what they thought would happen and what they hoped would happen—held by nine thousand persons in ten countries around the world of the Year 2000 (see Ornauer et al. 1976). For Year 2000 to be personally meaningful, only the younger generation was interviewed, the cutting-off point being the age of forty. At the same time numerous predictions by experts, all (well) above forty years of age, were collected. Then the Year 2000 came, and with it the time for the three obvious comparisons in the triangle stated above: the younger generation, adult experts, and the Year 2000 (Galtung 2003, 89).

The conclusion: *the younger generation was generally right.* Youth in the more developed countries were more so than those in the less developed countries, and the periphery in the more developed were more right than the center in those countries. Who was wrong, then? Blatantly wrong were the elites in the less developed countries, who probably more than any other group were carriers of official, Western, scientific, technological, and developmental optimism. But some were even more wrong: the experts in the more developed countries—possibly the master's voice for the elites in the less developed world.

We could put it this way: If at the end of the 1960s we had used younger nonelites in more developed countries as a guide to the future we would by and large have diagnosed it correctly, at least vastly more correctly than by using experts and their highly capital-intensive studies. *Learn from the people,* in other words. The wise politicians will take young people's predictions seriously; identify a problem syndrome and then attack that problem holistically. The less wise will ask their experts.

Moreover, a comparison suggests that the expert answers will reflect the following:

Narrowness, limited to the expert field of presumed competence

Macro-orientation (toward states, economies), not a human and social orientation such as attention to basic needs at unequal levels of satisfaction

General optimism, particularly about the intellectual and political paradigm of the agency employing the expert

A limited class perspective, to the class carried by and carrying that agency, like top civil servants/capitalists

An equally limited gender, race, and nation perspective, like predicting "more women in leading positions"

A special expert language, such as the modeling lingo

No surprises, trend rather than transcendence oriented

A general status quo discourse, assuming no major future changes but the same ends and means, only with efficiency problems—and we would also expect the expert models to be very costly.

Most points are specifications of a major concept above: *the closed mind,* with a narrow range of possible answers—and questions—built into the paradigms carried by that mind. We see immediately the distance to the younger generation. None of this would apply to them. Of course, "nonexperts" do not command a shared, specific niche of state-of-the-art knowledge. But they have the advantage of knowing where the shoe pinches. They can scan the whole horizon, holistically, and report any problem they sense. Living all over they can report from their gender, generation, race, class, and national perspectives. Together they see a lot. They do not stick to any niche or discourse they have struggled to conquer, nor do they suffer from excessive *déformation profesionelle.* They are not limited to trend analysis but can equip reality, past and future, with major jumps. They read their worlds without expensive studies. The "nonexperts" in the 1969 study saw the future in terms of mental illness and narcotics, more desire for success, more interest in material things—and in terms of more criminality and unemployment. Generally, *what people did not ask for (automation) they got; what they did ask for (peace) they did not get*—a bad deal.

The respondents were also given a list of twenty-five "strategies to obtain peace" and asked to pick their favorite peace theory. The five most popular strategies were "hunger and poverty must be abolished all over the world"; "increased trade, exchange and cooperation also between countries that are not on friendly terms"; "improve the United Nations so as to make it more efficient than it is today"; "the gap between poor and rich countries must disappear"; and "it must be possible for people all over the world to choose freely their governments."

But these are not the peace theories inspiring governments. Hunger and poverty are both increasing. When countries "are not on friendly terms" economic sanctions are used, killing hundreds of thousands of people. The UN is sabotaged, particularly by one country, the United States, who is very often in a UN minority with two or three countries, breaks international law, and does not even pay the UN dues. The gap between poor and rich countries is increasing. More people than ever can now freely choose their governments, but elections are a very narrow approach to democracy. And democracies are not necessarily peaceful, as witnessed by the joint attack on Yugoslavia in 1999 by nineteen of them.[12] What governments pursue is not peace but national interest, if possible backed by military power policies.

What do we make of this? The problem is not knowledge or intelligence but rather the narrowness of discourse and angles.

ENTERS CONFLICT

There is a very counter-productive tendency in Anglo-Saxon countries to confuse conflict with violence, and the absence of violence, before an outbreak or after a ceasefire, with peace. Conflict means that parties have incompatible, contradictory goals, with attitudinal and behavioral consequences like hatred-apathy-love and violence-apathy-peace. Love-peace is also found in conflict, like in Gandhi's love your adversary—you are parts of each other and have a conflict in common. The best approach to conflict is to identify legitimate goals and to find an acceptable and sustainable solution by bridging the gap. This is not the way the United States and Al-Qaeda approach conflict for the time being. A person grows up between drives/needs on the one hand and compelling norms, from the inside as internalized culture and from the outside as institutionalized structure, on the other. There is no biological need to be violent. But there is a biological need not to be hurt and harmed by somebody else's violence, and conflict carries a violence potential in its womb.

Violence has to be learned. Young people watch how adults handle conflicts, assuming that what they see is normal and natural. They grow up surrounded by the fear of evil forces. Young Americans, for example, are served stories of violence at all levels—micro, meso, macro, and mega—legitimized by a compliant, violent media. A very bad beginning.

So there is a need for another story. A peace story.

Conflict, War, and Peace: A Paradigm

The following paradigm for peace studies and action is presented as a standard history, with variations, of how conflict can lead to violence and to organized group violence in the form of war; it is also indicative of how violence can be avoided or reduced. The paradigm assumes two stages preceding violence, but it assumes no *need* for violence like that for air, water, food, sex, sleep. The first stage is an unresolved, untransformed *conflict*–a ubiquitous phenomenon in human reality, easily leading to frustration because of blocked goals, with a potential for aggression against parties perceived as standing in the way.

The second stage is *polarization*–reduction to two actors, Self and Other. Under extreme polarization the Other is dehumanized as Satan's chosen people and the Self exalted as God's Chosen People and as the carrier of supreme values, sacred or secular. Holders of such premodern imagery tend to enter conflicts prepolarized and project an inevitable final battle between God and Satan. Untransformed conflict plus low humanization leads to violence.

This paradigm is as much an image of human reality as exposure to pathogens plus low resistance (immunity) leads to disease. Like disease, violence is caused by the preceding stages; and like disease, violence can be prevented by removing those causes. Conflict is removed as a cause by bridging the gap through *transformation* so that the conflict can be handled by the parties nonviolently, creatively, and with empathy. Polarization is removed through *depolarization:* (re)linking the parties positively and flattening the gradient from Self to Other. That process humanizes both parties, giving them light as well as shadow.[13]

As violence is self-reinforcing through many mechanisms, including introducing new conflicts and by being polarizing, it should be minimized. Violence makes things worse. Conflict transformation should be by peaceful means. Conflict transformation *removes the bellogen* of frustration/aggression, and depolarization *adds a paxogen* of humanization corresponding to the immune system. (More generally, the peace homologue of the immune system is culture of peace plus structure of peace.)

In UN jargon these two activities are known generically as *peacemaking* and *peace building*. In medical jargon they are similar to primary and secondary prophylaxis, removing pathogens and strengthening the self-healing capacity of the body. Then there is *peacekeeping*–controlling the violence, reducing it, even removing it, like primary health care in a polyclinic removes the symptoms of disease. The fourth stage, *reconciliation* for healing and closure, corresponds to rehabilitation in health care. In peace as in health, the therapy is in the complete package, not in one part.

The basic paradigm for transformation of simple conflicts with only two incompatible goals would assume that neither party can prevail over the other by peaceful means. This leaves three possibilities: *compromise,* usually unsatisfactory to all; creating a new reality; or *transcendence,* so that both goals could come close to realization, or so that both goals are denied. Both positive and negative transcendence presuppose empathy with the parties, a high level of creativity, and the ability to work nonviolently. At the end of the tunnel is the light of genuine, not fake, conflict transformation (Galtung 2000).

What does peace look like in this paradigm? Peace includes the *absence of direct violence* engaged in by the military and others. But it also includes the *absence of structural violence:* the unintended slow but massive suffering caused by economic and political structures. And it includes the absence of the *cultural violence* that legitimizes direct and/or structural violence. All these absences add up to *negative peace,* and the simplest approach would be mutual isolation, no structure and no culture. This is better than violence but not peace because *positive peace* is missing (see figure 2).[14]

There are six tasks (numbered on figure 2). First, there is the task of eliminating the direct violence that causes suffering, then eliminating the structures that cause suffering through economic inequity (or walls placing Jews or much of Palestine in ghettos), and then eliminating cultural themes that justify one or the other. The task known as "ceasefire" is only one-sixth of a complete peace process; most peace processes are actually ceasefire processes.

Next emerge the three tasks of building direct, structural, and cultural peace. The parties exchange goods rather than "bads" or violence. The structural

Figure 2

Violence	Direct (harming, hurting)	Structural (harming, hurting)	Cultural (justifying violence)
Negative Peace	[1] absence of = ceasefire	[2] absence of = no exploitation; or structure = *atomie*	[3] absence of = no justification; or culture = *anomie*
Positive Peace	[4] presence of = cooperation	[5] presence of = equity, equality	[6] presence of = culture of peace and dialogue
Peace	negative + positive	negative + positive	negative + positive

version of this process builds cooperation into the structure as something sustainable under the heading of equity for the economy, equality for the polity, reciprocity, equal rights, benefits, and dignity: what you want for yourself you should also be willing to give the Other. It entails a culture of peace positively confirming and stimulating.

Let us have a deeper look at the culture of peace. The root of a conflict is by definition in goals that are incompatible—also known as a contradiction. But a conflict also has attitudinal and behavioral components. And those attitudes are conditioned by the collective subconscious—the deep culture, cosmology—of that nation, gender, generation, and so on. And the behavior is conditioned by acquired, learned patterns in conflict situations. The deep culture is a storehouse of assumptions,[15] also about conflict; conflicts are like that—defining what is normal/natural about them, without questioning.[16] Civilizations take a stand on such key issues as to whether history is basically linear and heading for a crisis with heaven or hell as the only outcomes, or relaxed, oscillating softly through time. Space may be defined for us as essentially dualistic—us or them, Self versus Other—or more diverse. If dualistic that Other can be seen as a Periphery to be dominated; as Barbarians to be kept at a distance, or as Evil, Satanic, lurking and lurching, just waiting to get at us. The deep culture may then see history basically as a struggle between God and Satan, among other things for our souls, focusing on wars and hoping for a hero who wins that war for us and/or a saint who ushers in peace. And in the still deeper culture there are views of knowledge: as atomistic, dividing reality into small parts, deductive and contradiction-free; or as holistic and dialectic, focusing on a contradictory totality.

The most *unfortunate* deep culture combination for peace building includes the following elements:

- A view of contradictions as absolute, true *or* false, good *or* evil
- A focus on a few actors and goals and a deductive approach
- Projecting Self on God and Other on Satan, with strong gradients
- Conflict decided by heroes or saints with strong Egos, not by ordinary people
- Seeing Other as Evil, Barbarian, Periphery—that is, dehumanized
- Seeing world space dualistically as Self vs (all) Other(s)
- Seeing time as moving toward crisis, then catharsis or apocalypse

This most unfortunate combination is a good guide to the *hard Occident (I)* (see Galtung 1996, part 4), with such expressions as (Hitlerite) Nazism, (Stalinist) Bolshevism, and U.S. and Islamic fundamentalism. Violence, even genocide (massive category killing of the Other), comes easily after exclusion and dehumanization: for example, September 11 and its aftermath.

The most *fortunate* deep culture combination for peace building contains the following elements:

- A view of contradictions as normal and mutable, like yin/yang
- A holistic, dialectic, and inclusive view of conflict formations
- A civilization with no Satan—no Principle of Evil
- A civilization with "conflict transformation by people" stories
- A civilization that sees all humans and life as parts of each other
- A civilization with Self and Other as parts of a higher totality[17]
- A civilization with an oscillating, relaxed time cosmology

This most fortunate combination is a good guide to the *soft Occident (II)* found in soft Christianity-Judaism-Islam-secularism, in (some) women's approaches, in soft Hinduism and nonritualized Buddhism, and in very many "indigenous" civilizations (like the Polynesian *ho'o pono pono*, or the Somalian *shir*). Sinic and Nipponic civilizations are in between these two extremes, with unfortunate views of the Other as Barbarian or Periphery. A culture of peace would have to build on the soft elements, wherever they are.

Peace development would have to combine *cultural development* and *structural development*. Some perspectives on those two:

- Is the culture endorsing the *basic needs* of oneself (I-culture)?
- Is the culture also endorsing the *basic needs* of others (We-culture)?
- Are there norms of *compassion, solidarity*?
- Are all these norms *compelling* (internalized/institutionalized)?
- How *multiple* is the structure? How many interaction systems?
- How *connected* is each system? How directly with each other?
- How *reciprocal* is the relation (equity, mutual benefit)?
- How *insubstitutable/thick* is the relation (primary versus secondary)?

Women often feel more at ease in such family-type peace structures. Zero cultural development means absence of norms (*culturelessness* = *anomie*) and zero structural development means absence of structure (*structurelessness* = *atomie*). Neither peace nor war. No good.

SEPTEMBER 11 AND THE PEACE PARADIGM

Actually, there are at least three recent 9/11s. On September 11, 1973, in Santiago, Chile, a U.S.-supported[18] state terrorist coup killed democracy and some

3,200 people, and many thousands were tortured. On September 11, 1990, in Guatemala City, anthropologist Myrna Mack, who was researching the fate of indigenous people who had been uprooted or were being repatriated, was stabbed to death (twenty-eight wounds) in the context of a Guatemalan civil war that left over 200,000 killed and tortured, mainly from state terrorism.[19] The beacon of hope was a young woman, Rigoberta Menchú. On September 11, 2001, in New York City and Washington, D.C., three planes hijacked by nineteen Arab youths, fifteen from Saudi Arabia, were used as flying bombs in a terrorist attack against the World Trade Center and the Pentagon, killing some 3,000 people.

Violence, indeed. Preceded by massive dehumanization, certainly. But how about the underlying conflicts? Who are the parties to the conflicts, what are their goals? Are those goals legitimate or not, or can we transcend them, bridging the gap between the legitimate goals? The first two 9/11s are internationalized class conflicts, pitting those who want political equality and economic equity against those who do not, with race added in the Guatemalan case. The solution may be a social democracy for equity and equality. Chile is coming close.[20] Guatemala, El Salvador, and Chiapas are not; they are as inequitable and unequal as ever. How about September 11, 2001? The Arab/Wahhabite goal was probably *justice* by executing two buildings in public space for alleged sins against Alla'h and lack of *respect* for Islam. The U.S. goal status quo, with *free trade*. Even to talk about bridging the gap is taboo today. And yet the key parties, let us call them Washington and Al Qaeda—not 1.4 billion Christians and 1.3 billion Muslims—will have to start doing exactly that, through secret negotiations and all that. They cannot go on eliminating each other in the search for the elusive "roots" of the Evil on the other side that would make them victorious. Wiser people on either side—probably some steps removed from the two overfocused, and very similar, top figures—may already have started feeling their way into negotiation, or even better, dialogue processes.

Task [1] (see figure 2 above) would already be a tremendous step forward from the present. "No attack on the United States in exchange for U.S. military withdrawal from Muslim countries that so want" could serve as an example of a possible deal. Another would be to explore the concept of "globalization-free zones." But the basic approach would be through mutual exploration to identify the legitimate elements in such goals as "free trade" and "respect."

Cultural violence stands massively in the way of positive structural peace in the other two cases, and in the case of September 11, 2001, even in the way of negative direct peace. In the Guatemalan case the white "Ladinos" still look at the red "indigenos" as animals. "Pagans" they are not, the cultural "integration" having been more successful than the political, economic, and military structures. The fault lines show up very clearly. In the case of September 11, 2001, the culture of violence goes beyond racial prejudice, bringing in such premodern, pre-Enlightenment, Puritan and Wahhabite figures of thought as Chosenness, by God for Self and by Satan for Other, with visions of glory as God's reward and trauma as punishment, and of the final battle, Armageddon, where whoever is not with us is against us. Maybe one day Enlightenment strikes in both cultures.[21] And one day even reconciliation.

ENTER YOUTH AGAIN, AND WOMEN

We now have a theory linking generation and gender to violence and peace and a paradigm of conflict, violence, and peace. We want hypotheses about likely contributions by youth and by women as a basis for comparison, comparing both with adult men. In this paradigm we started with the role of *conflict transformation,* and more particularly with *creativity* on the one hand and *empathy, nonviolence* on the other; and *transcendence* on the one hand and *compromise* on the other. The next step was the role of *peace building,* and more particularly of building *positive peace* on the one hand and *negative peace* on the other; and *structural-cultural peace* on the one hand and *direct peace* on the other. And then was introduced the role of *deep culture,* and the *least fortunate* deep culture on the one hand and the *most fortunate* on the other. As the reader may have guessed, the hypotheses will associate youth with "on the one hand" and women with "on the other." Adult males will be associated more with the violent option, using conflict to impose.

A very strong point for youth would be creativity coming from their less closed, more open mind. And true creativity would jump, transcend, go beyond, like that of the young federalists in postwar Europe. Women are then seen as more careful, more compromise oriented than "jumpy," with empathy and nonviolence as their very strong points. A second strong point for youth would be the focus on building peace, not only abstaining from war—in other words, on positive, not only negative, peace. This would spill over into peace architecture, building structures and cultures of peace. Women are seen as more focused on the direct acts of solidarity rooted in compassion and less on architecture, structures, cultures, abstractions.

A weak point for the youth, but then more for young men than for young women, would be in the deep culture. There is something male, not only hard Occident, and particularly young male, in the "least fortunate" combination. And there is something female, young, or more adult in the "most fortunate" combination, not only soft Occident. In other words, the images that emerge for youth are not unambiguous. The peace images are more unambiguous for women.

Let us try this out on Anglo-Saxon women. The role of Anglo-Saxon women in the struggle against slavery, against colonialism, and against war—three major recipes for human suffering—is undeniable. Men too were active, but women maybe even more massively so. One possible connection would be what many see as the strength of the Anglo-Saxon tradition—the "due process" and the "rule by rules, not by rulers." But rules are abstract. They can be combined into systems and theories and be taught, in schools of economics, law, and war. They make distinctions between "worthy and unworthy sufferers," and that is where women of any age may depart from men of any age. For older men that is no problem: they made the rules, or at least they believe in them. Younger men may want to make new rules. We get a triangle ("trialectics," "trialogue") of older men producing and upholding violent rules, women objecting and refusing, and younger men attracted by the challenge to build new systems with new rules.

But the miracle of peace still happens. Some youth and some women may refuse to be imprinted by older men and develop their own ways. How? Where? When? But it is obvious: *By youth and women all over the world uniting for peace* and having good dialogues with older men. They are not beyond redemption. They are not "Other." But they badly need the human impulse of women and the open mind of youth. As peace builders women have a major edge over youth, however. Women remain women throughout their lives, whereas young males are heading for that losing quadrant of adult, old males. Women may also be heading for some rigidity, for some closure of mind. But a woman's mind may stabilize and become static at a more beneficial point for peace, with higher levels of empathy and compassion and a generally nonviolent style, than the rigid male mind. If there is a relation between age and that higher level of knowledge known as wisdom, when experiences flow together into higher levels of insight, older women should be depositories of experiences from countless conflicts in families and networks and organizations related to school, neighborhood, and work. Each adult woman is a conflict resource.

How about young males? If they stabilize at some point around twenty-five years of age, then what happens next? They probably become even more so. Those leaning toward "peace by peaceful means" may become even more so inclined; so may those who go for the belligerent means. But males, and women also for that matter, are not steered by inner gestalts alone but also by rewards and punishment from the outside. Of the world's about two hundred countries, only thirty have no armies. That means that the "bellogenic" young male will have a career possibility in most of them. The "paxogenic" young or no-longer-so-young person will probably have to build his/her own niche.

Youth who are good at conflict transformation, peace building, and peace-making should be nursed, trained, encouraged, and rewarded. There should be prizes for the best conflict transformation proposals, for the best peace-building and peacekeeping practices for youth of both genders. Creativity, both types I and II, should be rewarded. Youth may well be our best protection against further deterioration toward total war.

NOTES

This chapter is a modified text of a keynote address given by Professor Galtung at the University of Notre Dame on September 11, 2003, as part of the Kroc Institute's Research Initiative on the Resolution of Ethnic Conflict [RIREC] conference on Peace Building after Peace Accords.

1. The moral defeat, the deep inner acknowledgment of evil perpetrated, came some twenty years later when a new generation was old enough to challenge the parent generation and most of the perpetrators had retired biologically or socially.

2. They were challenged by those countries in alliance with an Italy for all seasons—new arrivals in the interstate arena after reinventing themselves in 1870–71, 1868, and 1861.

3. The first treaty, very similar in form only opposite in content with the names of the two countries reversed, sealed the German victory over France in the 1870–71 war.

4. The first secretary general, Anna Anfossi (later professor of sociology at the University of Torino), was the source for the story.

5. The emotional, and indeed practical, drama of pregnancy, birth, lactation, feeding, and protecting infants might easily dispose for compassion with other women. Men probably relate to other men more in terms of their social position, which may dispose for subordination, domination, or competition rather than compassion, the relation to soldiers on the other side being the extreme case. Shorter on compassion, men would need some guiding principles to regulate the insubordination, domination, and competition, including violence in general.

6. Intifada youth come to mind. The first Intifada, begun in December 1987, was mainly nonviolent, and certainly so by Middle East standards. The stone throwing was mainly symbolic. The second, Al Aqsa Intifada, of September 2000 has been violent, including suicide by deploying an explosive device. What motivation prevails in that act, killing Self or Other, suicide or bombing, probably varies a lot. The difference between the two Intifadas may be partly or mainly due to a change from hope to despair as the Oslo "peace process" unfolded.

7. An interesting example is participation in elections. Thomas Geoghegan, in "Dems—Why Not Woo the Young?" (*Nation*, July 21/28, 2003, 10), makes

the point that "The dropoff in voting has been heaviest among the young." Thus, the turnout percentage of all twenty-one to twenty-four year olds at presidential elections was 51 percent in 1968 (Nixon-Humphrey, both for the war against Vietnam) and 35 percent in 2000 (Bush-Gore, both, it turned out, for the war against Iraq). As Geoghegan points out: "In 1968 half the kids voted: Now that's the rate nation-wide. In 2000, it was 35 percent of kids. So won't it, one day, also be 35 percent nationwide?"

8. The present author has worked for many years in the three regions, with extensive dialogues at all levels with all kinds of groups, including youth and women, mediating on behalf of TRANSCEND. The following are some conclusions about "peace accords," with the caveat that I myself am an adult male:

In the former Yugoslavia, the proposals by then-UN Secretary General Javier Pérez de Cuéllar—to withhold recognition until an acceptable solution has been found for the minorities, to work symmetrically on all parts of Yugoslavia, to have a policy for Yugoslavia as a whole—should have been followed. As it stands now only one problem has been solved: Slovenia. In all the other parts violence has made the situation worse and nothing has been solved. Self-determination should have been the guide, possibly leading to autonomy for the Serbian parts of Croatia, independence for Republika Srpska, the Croatian part of Bosnia and Herzegovina integrated into Croatia, a Bosniak independent city-state around Sarajevo, independence for Kosova but as a federation with two Serbian cantons, and similar arrangements for Macedonia and Montenegro. And then some kind of Yugoslav community, like the Nordic community, for cooperation among neighbors—with democracy, human rights, and reconciliation—should have been created. As it stands now Yugoslavia, particularly BiH under the Dayton Accords, is a ticking time bomb.

In the Middle East there have been some ceasefire efforts like the Oslo process or the efforts associated with Camp David II and the Roadmap, but no real "peace process." As minimum conditions Israel has to be willing to grant Palestine what they both want: a state, a capital in Jerusalem, the right of (some) return. Even so Israel is too big and Palestine too small to build a peace structure with equality and equity. A two-state solution is only a necessary condition; a Middle East community modeled to some extent after the European community, with Syria, Lebanon, Jordan, and Egypt, might be much more peace productive politically, economically, and culturally.

In west/central Asia, the attacks on Iraq and Afghanistan bear a colonial imprint: oil and/or pipelines, military bases, and efforts to rule directly or indirectly from one central point, Baghdad or Kabul. This will never succeed. The peoples in Iraq and Afghanistan share one deep sentiment: foreigners out! And they share a problem: the internal divisions are so deep that they call for a federation, possibly a confederation. Unitary states will not be peace productive, and even less so when under foreign control or their marionettes. Democracy without federalism in a multinational county leads to civil war.

For more about the possibilities of peace in these areas see www.transcend.org and Galtung and Jacobsen (2002) and Galtung (2004). In my view the major contribution of youth and women would be to approach these non–peace accords with an open mind, not to implement them, but to change them into peace accords.

9. Thus, as will be discussed later, if life and the world is seen in pre-Enlightenment terms as a stage for the perennial battle between God and Satan, the work of Satan will easily be identified and pre-polarization will find its concrete interpretation as signaled in expressions like "They are like that," or "Their true nature came out."

10. This is a strong argument for multiculturalism.

11. First generation of peace approaches, to the Second World War, included the following: *peace movements*—advocating, demonstrating; *war abolition*—eliminating war as a social institution; and *global governance*—globalizing conflict transformation. Their motto: *Peace is too important to leave to the generals.*

Second generation of peace approaches, after the Second World War, included the following: *peace education/journalism*—for knowledge/information; *nonviolence*—to be able to struggle nonviolently; *conflict transformation*—solving conflicts creatively. Their motto: *Peace is too important to leave to states.*

Third generation of peace approaches, after the Cold War, include the following: *peace cultures*—going into deep cultures if needed; *basic human needs*—as non-negotiable pillars; *peace structures*—repairing fault lines like gender. Their motto: *Peace is too important for shallow approaches.*

The first generation was *a reaction against war.* People demanded peace through governmental cooperation, above nations and states. The second generation is a *reaction against governments.* People became increasingly skeptical and wanted to work for peace themselves. In the third generation there is a reaction against simplistic peace approaches, realizing how deep rooted—*and linked to development and satisfaction of basic needs*—these problems are.

12. Dubbed "democratic totalitarianism" by Zinoviev (1999).

13. Carl Gustav Jung (1969) argued that those aspects of ourselves we do not recognize or reject may be projected unto others under polarization.

14. For more on this see part 1 of Galtung (1996).

15. For more about this see part 4 of Galtung (1996).

16. Thus, when asked, "How about conflict?" a typical U.S. answer runs as follows: you try to compromise, and if that does not work you fight it out and the winner decides. Missing are positive and negative transcendence, with (literally speaking) fatal consequences.

17. In Zulu this is known as *ubuntu,* an important concept in the South African Truth and Reconciliation process.

18. The expression comes from Larry Rohter, "Chile's Wound, 30 Years Later, Is Still Inflamed," *New York Times*, September 10, 2003. "And Washington's hands were not clean, either" is a mild understatement. The article in the German *Der Spiegel* ("Der andere 11. September," no. 37 [2003]) is considerably more explicit about the roles of Nixon and Kissinger.

19. I am indebted to Charles Reilly for making me aware of this 9/11.

20. Thus, on the occasion of the thirtieth anniversary, the present president of Chile, Ricardo Lagos, in an interview in *El País* (September 10, 2003) said: "Hemos logrado la subordinación del poder militar al civil" ("We have succeeded in making military power subordinate to civilian power"). Salvador Allende's niece, the author Isabel Allende, says "Allende is finally becoming a heroic figure in Chile" (*El País*, English edition, September 6, 2003).

21. But isn't the United States the first modern nation? It is and it is not. The Pilgrims were a capsule of premodernity transported across the Atlantic a good century before Enlightenment struck. The idea of the Covenant, defining relations to Self and to Other, has survived centuries of very energetic modernization and postmodernization in other fields.

Siobhán McEvoy-Levy

Conclusion

Youth and Post-Accord Peace Building

I get peace.
I always get peace.
Peace is quietness.
Peace is silence.[1]

It is only through our organization that we have the possibility of a future. Alone, only weapons await us.[2]

If we look beyond the barrel of the gun, it is our youth pointing the guns at us. We have to stand with our youth to support them. We must unite with them to stop the armed actors from taking them.[3]

How is it possible to extract meaning from the stunning and immobilizing tragedy of war that will help break cycles of violence? As this volume seeks to show, part of the answer lies in making youth visible and heard. The lived complexity of the social and political agency of youth is important to understand and engage if sustainable peace is sought after protracted armed conflict. Involved with various forms of violence, pre- and post-accord, youth may be labeled troublemakers. Yet others, as we have shown, are peacemakers in numerous ways. And many drift into a third space—apathy—or shape-shift through a variety of related social positions—victim, warrior, alienated youth, community activist—over time. It is a disturbing indication of the almost ideological antipathy to youth that this shape-shifting ability is accepted for leaders of armed groups—terrorists turned statesmen (Stephenson 1996–97, 105)—while war-affected children and youth soldiers are widely conceptualized and feared as "lost generations," even by sympathetic analysts.[4] To construct effective peace-building mechanisms, we need to develop a more nuanced portrait of youth in conflict.

To that end each of the chapters in this volume offers insights into the challenge of youth in particular contexts or explores theoretical issues relevant to youth and peace building; *context is important.* Identifying youth as a category for analysis and policy is complicated by the fact that youth are not a homogeneous entity either globally or locally. The experiences of young people in warfare around the world are highly variable and their pathways into violence different. The different contexts and different identities (both individual and collective) of the young people in question must be considered when making plans for postwar rehabilitation. This diversity necessitates conflict-specific and deeply ethnographic approaches to the study of youth in postwar situations, particularly where recommendations are to be made about rehabilitation and reconstruction. Depending on context, youth may be more or less directly influential on the dynamics of war and peace. But the differences in the experiences of youth do not completely resist generalization. People and their societies and cultures ought to be considered "as coessentially both unique and resonating with the human condition in myriad complex ways" (Nordstrom 1997, 6). This point is accented by the nature of contemporary warfare and peace processes, especially the globalization of war paraphernalia, strategies, and personnel and linked systems of humanitarian aid. As Nordstrom explains:

> Massive interlinked and very international war-related industries make war possible in any location in the world. I have seen the same weapons vendors, mercenaries, military advisors, supplies and military training manuals—both illicit and formal—circle the globe, moving from one war to the next. Politicians, military and paramilitary troops, and diplomats meet and talk across virtually all boundaries of nation and state. Business salespeople and blackmarketeers sell the items necessary to outfit troops and launch a battle. Media specialists create a cultural diaspora of every war-related ethos from the Rambo figure to BBC broadcasts reaching the farthest regions of the globe. Propagandists the world over exchange information on how to make casualties palatable to noncombatants and human rights organizations. Everything from development dollars to human rights organi-

zations, from covert operations specialists to illegal industries that gain from conflict, builds on the linkages of these networks that shape war and peace as we know it today. (1997, 5)

The globalization of contemporary armed conflict necessitates further attention to the shared condition of youth. One universal challenge in unraveling the relationship of youth to war and peace building is in the difficulties the nature of contemporary warfare pose for distinguishing between the "the deeds of those responsible" and the plight of the "rightless" (see Sanford following Arendt in chapter 2 of this volume), the voiceless, or victims of violence. This is because the youth soldier is both rightless and responsible at once. *Tidy analytical categories are impossible in contemporary war zones.* As many of the chapters in this volume show, often the categories of victim, perpetrator, and bystander are blurred. Additionally, experience of armed conflict may blur or recast such categories as childhood, adolescence, youth, and adulthood in ways that require us to reconsider the meaning of these terms in context (a difficulty that our new youth category helps address). This confusion has more than philosophical significance because the conflict between youth who committed violent acts and others in their communities who were not combatants continues after accords over the provision of aid and over positions of authority. The fracturing of social trust and cultural upheaval that the blurring of militant/civilian and child/adult roles creates is a major barrier to reconciliation.

Nordstrom's highlighting of the global network of vested interests that constitute war is important for this book in another way: it serves as a reminder that although many of the youth we have studied here are perpetrators of violence, they are not ultimately those Arendt (1973) meant when she referred to "those responsible." *Youth are the foot soldiers of war and shape its dynamics in crucial ways, but they are not the architects of war.* The architects remain states and political and economic elites. While youth do shape the dynamics of peace processes, *they are not the architects of peace processes,* either. In fact, although both troublemakers and peacemakers at the grass roots, youth are invariably marginalized from political and economic decision making. It is useful to consider what is lost as a result and whether youth political participation in peace processes could function as a peace-building mechanism. The second part of this conclusion argues a case for youth political participation but with some cautions. However, the first question addressed is what, if anything, a youth lens can contribute to building knowledge about conflict and peace building.

Viewing Conflict and Peace Processes Through a Youth Lens

A youth lens helps develop a more complete picture of the sources and dynamics of conflict reproduction and transformation and the challenge of reconciliation. It underlines how sustainable peace necessitates a culture shift that the peace process must facilitate. Since the culture of divided societies in transition is predominantly a culture of conflict, this requires attention to how processes of conflict reproduction and transformation (which is also cultural reproduction and transformation) occur and are affected by the peace process. It is recognized that women have various roles that contribute to cultural and conflict reproduction. They function "as biological reproducers of members of ethnic collectivities; as reproducers of the boundaries of ethnic and national groups; as actors in the ideological reproduction of the collectivity and as transmitters of its culture; as signifiers of ethnic and national difference; and as participants in national, economic, political and military struggles" (Porter, 1998, 42; see also Yuval-Davis and Anthias, 1989). We show how young people (both male and female), by virtue of their life stages and experiences in conflict, contribute to cultural reproduction in some of these same ways, as well as in their own ways. Measured by the extent to which youth are leaders in armed conflict and recognized as political factors, a strong youth influence is clear in the Palestinian-Israeli conflict, Rwanda, Sierra Leone, and South Africa, but only a weak youth influence is found in Bosnia and Northern Ireland. Measured in terms of conflict values or ideological reproduction, however, the effect of youth becomes strengthened in all contexts.

Youth and Conflict Reproduction

Youth, particularly children, are passive agents of conflict reproduction. When victimized they function as symbols of the inhumanity of "the other" and serve as justification for a variety of defensive and reactionary policies. But youth are also active agents of conflict reproduction when they are participants in armed conflict and when they act as transmitters of knowledge and creators of meaning and culture. No other group in society simultaneously interacts with school, home, the street, the workforce, cultural and social institutions like the church or voluntary and leisure organizations, and the "military" in the way youth do. Youth are shaped by numerous interactions between these institutions themselves embedded in conflict dynamics. In turn, youth have enormous impact on the dynamics of conflict. As we see in these chapters, conflict is reproduced through layers and memories of trauma; through stories and texts that transmit images of the other, perceptions of grievance, and evaluations of peace processes; and through experiences and retellings of oppression, violence, and lack of economic opportunity. Youth participate at the heart of these processes of meaning making. To a great extent youth are the shock absorbers of the societal change that accompanies war and peace processes. Out of this they create a variety of narratives that are transmitted to peers, to younger siblings, and also to adults.

As Sanford (chapter 2) shows in Guatemala, the young soldiers remember their recruitment experiences within the context of community boundaries transgressed, family sanctity violated, and bodily annihilation: "If his body had been more whole, I would have embraced my father. But all I could do was pick up the bones" (Gaspar, quoted in chapter 2). In their testimonies we see how memories of trauma translate into ideologies unrelated to a specific armed group or community. Gaspar claims he allowed himself to be recruited into the army because "I saw that the world was made up of abusers and abused and I didn't want to be abused anymore." In Northern Ireland youth contribute to the reproduction of ethnic or national boundaries through territorialism—helping to paint curbstones with national colors, erecting flags, throwing stones and bottles at ethnic interfaces, policing shopping or recreation areas to keep them "Taig-" or "Prod-free" zones, and building barricades. But like Gaspar, the ideology sustaining war is rooted in survival strategy. John evaluates an imperfect peace process saying, "I'd rather get a beatin', than get shot dead, you know. [As] long as you wake up" (quoted in chapter 6) and also lists a catalogue of intracommunal violence. Both Gaspar and John transmit a story of the inevitability of violence as a fact of their lives to be negotiated rather than transformed. Although ethnicity and group identification are central concepts, they are neither more or less salient in explaining how conflicts are reproduced in these cases than class, economic position, gender, actual experience of violence, memory, and discursive conventions that flow into constructions of a complex past.

Peace building occurs in dialogue with the past. Versions of history and inherited tradition that permeate the ecologies of children and youth signaled in art forms, cultural festivals, local storytelling and family chronicles, school textbooks and curricula, and political rhetoric often work against conflict resolution. Peace builders have to compete with the discourses and values that sustain war. To compete effectively they need to know how much and what kind of these discourses and values for war youth have inculcated and how they reproduce or transform them. It is important, then, to study further how youth think and feel about war and peace, peace processes, conflict and conflict resolution, politics and violence, themselves, the "other," and the future. As Boulding

(1988) has argued, for peace to be created it has to first be imagined. Predicting future behavior and designing structures for promoting and maintaining peace over the long term requires preparatory work at the most fundamental level of how people think and feel. It requires attention to how, from their own authentic experiences, young people conceptualize the problems that confront them.

When consulted in this volume, young people across the board conceptualize their greatest problem as a lack of "security." While different in each context, "security" is found to contain a common set of linkages. In Sierra Leone it is conceptualized as reacceptance into a community, and a sense of identity, purpose, and dignity. In other contexts the emphasis is on protection from interface street fighting or personal assaults, freedom of movement and belief, or quality of education and job opportunity (Northern Ireland, Bosnia). In others the effect of poverty, homelessness, police impunity (Angola), unemployment, social and economic inequality, and vigilante justice may be most tangible (Guatemala, South Africa); or security is tied to land ownership, which creates economic stability leading to the ability to establish marital bonds and families (Rwanda). In each case security is not viewed simply as freedom from physical violence/militarization but is also intertwined with economic survival and opportunity and with perceptions of positive self-worth. These findings underline the importance of holistic reintegration programs for ex-combatants and complex peace building addressing the multiple needs of war-affected youth in general. But they also underline how conflict reproduction is a function of insecurity defined more broadly than most peace processes allow, at least in their initial and perhaps most vulnerable stages.

Amplifying the voices of youth also underlines the need for attention to the whole conflict life cycle during peace processes and to the connections between prewar, war-related, and postwar trauma as part of a continuum of conflict experience. The experience of violence for the individual, and his/her family and community, who has survived armed conflict is made up of many more layers than attention only to the macrowar would suggest. Along with witnessing the humiliations, arbitrary arrests, and disappearances of loved ones, the structural violence of poverty, unemployment, displacement, domestic violence, generational and gender conflict, and subtle ethnic discrimination all influence entry into youth soldiering, and much of this continues after accords. Peace builders must address layers of trauma and acknowledge that experience of war is only one part of "a continuum of life experience" (chapter 2) involving different forms of violence and victimization. Again, the depth of this trauma is not usually accommodated by the focus on weapons, armies, demilitarization, and territory that characterizes early peace processes. But violence prevention after accords requires a broad understanding of the sources of violence.

As we show in this volume, youths' subjective experiences—the meaning they give to particular events—are important in understanding war and peace as social processes and reaching the center of violence. Ideas, beliefs, images, and myths contribute to the development and maintenance of imagined communities (B. Anderson 1991)—nations and ethnic or religious groups most obviously. However, armed forces, rebel bands, and criminal gangs also function according to structures of belief and value, sometimes overlapping with national or ethnic constructions. There is a complex composition, then, to the identifications of young people in post-accord contexts where armed groups; nation, ethnic, or religious groups; local community; family; and the emergent adult self are intertwined. Volkan underlines the depth and layers of such processes when he describes "the transgenerational transmission of injured selves infused with the memory of the ancestors' trauma" (1997, 48–90). But as Bar-On (1996) has found in studies of the intergenerational transmission of trauma in three generations of Holocaust survivors, the questions that successive generations ask, and the dialogues they instigate about the past, can have a healing effect for those involved. This is a contention borne out by the studies in this volume—the role of the next generation in asking critical questions is central to their role as conflict transformers.

CONFLICT TRANSFORMATION

Youth are passive agents of conflict transformation when they function symbolically as the raison d'être for peace processes. Politicians' rhetoric, such as "We're doing it for our children" and "They are our future," illustrates the use of children in this role. But youth are more powerful as active conflict transformers. This is demonstrated by the Angolan storm drain orphans, the involvement of youth in the Colombian Peace Communities and Guatemalan Communities of Population in Resistance, the compelling example from the midst of conflict in Sonnenschein's recounting of how youth from Neve Shalom/Wahat al Salam respond to their call to Israeli military service, and the activities and motivations of the young activists at peace centers in Gornji Vakuf/Uskoplje and the Spirit of Enniskillen in Northern Ireland, among others in this book. These youth are not only the carriers of conflict memory and trauma but also the creators of peaceful culture and contributors to conflict transformation. The foundation of any peace-building activity in the post-accord period will be the reserves of "moral imagination" (chapter 2), the small acts of resistance to the hegemony of war, and critical social thinking that pave the way for locally grounded activities that are authentic and workable. Despite their relative invisibility, these initiatives exist organically and need to be supported and fostered rather than created anew. Nordstrom's study, in particular, expands our notions of how communities are generated and sustained and shows us how important peace work is done through the loose, informal networks that people seem to instinctively forge under conditions of sociopolitical violence. They are perhaps proof of the existence of the innate human will to build justice and peace (see chapters 4 and 8). The dynamics leading to these formations, the values that sustain them even when all around conditions seem antithetical to humane and compassionate endeavor, are vital to identify. Thus, a further challenge for researchers is to find the nooks and enclaves where conflict is transformed unexpectedly—or perhaps more precisely, to find the places where peace forms without being named—and begin to devise means to support these organic processes.

A broader conceptualization of peace building and peace builders—one that highlights microlocal processes—will find the contributions of many other youth and provide a more complete view of the experience of war and of the sources of peace. In turn, it will help build more effective conflict transformation approaches. More ethnographic and psychological research is necessary on the motivations and life experiences that create peace activists (broadly defined) and the long-term effects of such activism as a complement to a growing literature on pathways into participation in armed conflict. Galtung endorses this view in his chapter (chapter 11) when, from the perspective of the post-9/11 conflict in the Middle East, he writes that youth must be trained and rewarded for creativity in conflict transformation, for "they may well be our best protection against further deterioration toward total war." And as Cairns et al. (chapter 5) emphasize, to "create a true culture of peace," much more research is needed on the "factors that mediate between the sociocultural context in which children find themselves and their ideas about peace."

Are not youth historically identified with radicalism and revolution, with idealism and visionary new paradigms? This is Galtung's contention, and he makes a persuasive case for the breadth and creativity of youth vision by drawing on the case of Federalist-minded youth in Europe after World War II. Does this make youth agents for reconciliation? Not necessarily, as he notes, because youth also tend toward "antithesis": negating adult positions. In the post-accord period in internal conflicts, the cross-generational coalitions typical of nationalist and self-determination struggles may fall apart. And radicalism and breaks with tradition may just as easily lead to a rejection of a peace accord. The potential of the next generations, pro- or antipeace, can be better understood through analysis of young people's values, attitudes, and strategic thinking, and through analysis of their subjective understandings of the losses, gains, and opportunities inherent to a peace process. At the same time, it is important to reiterate that youth who do become involved in political violence often do so because of a variety of non-choices related to survival and altruistic perceptions of themselves as community/nation defenders (see chapters 1, 2, and 6 in this volume). Some former militants are involved in peace work after accords and view this work as a continuation or renewal of their commitment to social change (see, for example, McEvoy-Levy 2001a). Attention to a conflict's life cycle reminds us that a person may move through a range of identities—victim, warrior, outsider, peace builder—over time. In this volume this is illustrated by the reintegrated youth in Sierra Leone and by the Guatemalan informants who as youth were combatants and as adults work in Mayan rights organizations. Thus, thinking constructively about peace and youth may require us to question the analytically pleasing but often fictitious bifurcation of violent youth and peaceful youth and to foster peace-building projects that actively seek out the variety of youth with different experiences. Such projects would be encased in a dialogue of different positions. They would accommodate diverse ethnic, religious, national, class, or gender positions and different psychological and intellectual positions in response to injustice and threat. Our findings also underline the importance of responding to youth desires to have positive social roles and make positive contributions to the task of reconciliation. And as Adwan and Bar-On (chapter 9) show, the pursuit of participant symmetry must be an intentional, regularly evaluated, and guarded aspect of a collaborative peace-building project.

Yet, as all of the young activists and "world builders" in this volume emphasize, it would be a mistake to exaggerate the strength of their presence in the face of youth apathy, low self-esteem and sense of powerlessness, the lack of media attention such activities often receive, and the powerful forces for war and violence they battle. As Helsing, introducing the young activists Kirlic, McMaster, and Sonnenschein, emphasizes, young peace activists such as these must be supported by the international community. This would seem to entail not only direct funds for youth projects but also the international community using its funds and moral persuasion to influence local elites to create contexts in which the next generation is enabled to work toward reconciliation rather than becoming accustomed to cemented divisions and conflict management (see chapter 7 in this volume). Helsing sees this as taking advantage of a narrow window of opportunity. He argues that "young people have less of an interest vested in the status quo than adults and thus have the greatest incentive to push for change." This is also Galtung's view. He makes a strong argument for the peace-building "wisdom" of youth (female youth in particular), who are not restricted by the insular "discourse and angles" of established "expertise." "Wise politicians," he says, will consult youth and foster their potential before "gestalts harden," before creative "dissonances" are "ironed out," and before visions narrow.

We know there are no simple road maps to reconciliation. Reconciliation[5] and healing are difficult concepts to define and even more difficult to operationalize. When operationalized, it is almost impossible to prove their success (Borer 2000). But the need for reconciliation and healing after war is indisputable. As Amadiume and An-Na'im write, "silence is not forgetting" (2000, 14). The task of reconciliation requires devices for dealing with the past that capture the imagination and approval of the young and that help make youth visible and heard in peace processes. However, the chapters in this volume suggest that conflict transformation efforts that only address memories and reveal truths (important and difficult as that might be) but are not elsewhere in the process of peace building linked with the creation of "institutional truth" (see Mamdani 2000) and with restitution, reparation, opportunity, and political voice are likely to be seen as frauds, and even causes for renewed violence. At the same time, while the direct line from healing to reconciliation or vice versa through (multiply defined) constructions such as justice, truth, and the past is unclear, the relationship between healing, reconciliation, and dealing with the past is clearly a constitutive and dynamic one. Within that process the role of story is central, and various forms of storytelling ought to be important components of peace education (see a discussion below).

When talking about a sustainable peace, we are talking not just in terms of the next generation but also of the succeeding generations. And, as Bar-On writes in relation to Holocaust survivors and their children and grandchildren, it may be that only "secondary reconciliation, decades later, is possible (1996, 168). No single generation can be made responsible for peace building. However, it is precisely because "the child lives on inside the adult" (Apfel and Simon 1996, 4), and because conflicts are transmitted transgenerationally, that healing work must begin as soon as accords are signed. As Adwan and Bar-On argue, even when accords fail and no new peace process is in sight, it is important to work with the next generations in mind. Yet, even with better understanding of the long-term conflict reproduction and transformation roles of youth, reconciliation will not be furthered unless the role of one key institution—the peace process itself—is recognized as a mechanism of socialization.

PEACE PROCESSES ARE EDUCATIONAL INSTITUTIONS

Peace processes are powerful educational institutions because they are artificial constructions extended in time that create expectations; restructure society, economy, and politics; and utilize a variety of discourses aimed at influencing opinion and values. Embedded in conflict history and prehistory, they shape memories and narratives of conflict (and affect conflict reproduction and transformation). But because of concern with the technicalities of transition and the jockeying for position of armed actors and political elites and states, the fact that peace processes become local institutions of the society undergoing transition, shaping values, expectations, and actions, may be underestimated. In the Northern Ireland case, the "peace process" is insinuated into almost all local media coverage and much popular discourse, and almost every aspect of politics caters to it—none of which has prevented localized sectarian violence and youth disillusionment. "Peace process" has become synonymous with contained, low-level, zero-sum sectarian politics and not with any other notion of a transformed society (see chapter 6 in this volume). In Bosnia the Dayton Accords are a distant construct imposed from outside but a social institution nonetheless reinforcing apathy (see chapter 7). As Sommers (chapter 3) points out, in Rwanda much attention has been given to war crimes and perpetrators and not enough to the original, economic structural causes of the genocide.

Youth are particularly influenced by the peace processes' socialization effects. The next generation in a post-accord setting are students both of conflict and of how conflicts are resolved. We show how lessons are learned from the everyday experience of life under a post-accord dispensation, from the political debates surrounding implementation of an accord, from the issues that the accord itself addresses and the values that structure new institutions, from the ways in which perpetrators are defined and treated, from who is elevated and who is left behind. In Sommer's chapter, one of the Rwandan youth whose economic opportunities are circumscribed by land shortage expresses his disillusionment clearly: "I don't understand what's happening in this world. The people who killed each other get assistance while we who lived peacefully do not."

As mentioned, lessons are also inherent to how the conflict is officially mediated, remembered, and reconstructed. A conscious "selling" of the benefits of peace through the strategic rhetoric of elites is one approach to taking control of the educating effects of the peace process. Leaders at all levels of society need to articulate "peace" as rewarding, complex, and relevant in youth-friendly formats. They need to make youth visible in elite political discourse not just as problem makers or recipients of aid but officially central to a repairing of society. But the real education for youth will lie in whether they remain objects of elite rhetoric and policy, whether they become participants in the transition process, and whether peace brings tangible benefits. Youth responses to peace processes that do not sufficiently integrate or answer their interests and needs, that do not use and develop their skills and experience, and that they perceive as unjust or illegitimate are likely to involve violence, falling at various points on a spectrum of social and political activity. As we show, lack of ownership and disillusionment may be expressed in self-destructive behavior such as alcohol and drug abuse, depression, or street fighting, rejectionist violence, and criminal activity. All of these responses negatively influence the development of sustainable peace. An important element, then, of any peace process would seem to be engaging youth as active participants and learning from them what "tangible benefits" would really mean. This is explored below in a section on political participation.

IMPORTANCE OF PEACE EDUCATION

These studies point to the importance of peace education as a formal requirement of peace processes. There are many modes of peace education (Harris 1999), but these studies suggest that an integrated peace education—involving conflict resolution training, intercultural understanding, empathy and human rights curricula, dialogue about contentious issues, and community-based service projects—should be as central to peace processes and their implementation as law and order measures, psychosocial work, infrastructural and economic development, and truth-telling processes. In fact, peace education may provide support to each of these areas. Briefly, peace education that provides employable skills—such as youth work certificates (as in the Spirit of Enniskillen project, discussed in chapter 8) or trade skills (see chapter 1)—supports economic development. Peace education that fosters political voice, empathy, identity security, and confidence in dialogue is a good foundation for psychosocial healing and for participation in and healing from formal truth-telling processes (see chapters 5, 6, 7, and 9 in this volume). Peace education that teaches conflict resolution skills and empowers youth is a bulwark against renewed violence.

Expanding access to general education is a vital part of postwar reconstruction and an essential protection measure in war-torn countries (Sommers 2002; Smith and Vaux 2003). Many youth, as we show in our studies, may be beyond school age or, for a variety of reasons, marginalized from mainstream education (see also Sommers 2002). So an important consideration will be how to provide access to peace education through informal venues. Peace education needs to be taken to the street and to the variety of places where youth live, work, learn, and struggle. For that to be successful, peace education has to be contextual and relevant. The roles that young people have in war suggest that peace education must be activist in nature, oriented toward social change, and involve skills building and community service if it is to appeal to youth. "Peace" is a vague and undertheorized concept, one with much less concrete meaning than war for children (Hakvoort and Oppenheimer 1993; Hall 1993; chapters 5 and 6 in this volume). And for peace education programs to be more effective, we need to build our knowledge about how children acquire knowledge about peace (see chapter 5).

In the meantime, Adwan and Bar-On have demonstrated the value of creating "real texts" through intergroup dialogue. The historical narratives that the Palestinian and Israeli teachers created together in the Sharing History project concretized the contentious issues and provided a basis for deeper discussion. The difficult conversations that ensue among the teachers once they are confronted with their students' reactions to the narratives show the power of young people to shape adult responses to peace-building efforts. As one Palestinian teacher explains, students want to know "'Why is this done now when many people are martyrs?'" This teacher expresses the pain and divided loyalties that such bridge building induces: "It is a tormenting experience. We have here a good time but when we go home we hear that something happened. There is a contradiction between meeting and trying to build some trust and the outside circumstances that definitely do not help. I have to go through humiliating experiences every day. I feel I have a split personality, I live two lives." Although almost leading to a collapse of the endeavor, the students' reactions spur the teachers to reconsider and rewrite the narratives. They use their hard-worn knowledge of their students' fears and resistance to authenticate the process. Although difficult, the narrative-sharing dialogue was at the same time empowering because the creation of parallel narratives contributed to identity security. Two still competing but converging counter-narratives to war emerged from a collaboration between change agents (the teachers) and some of their harshest local critics (their students).

All conflicts extend and expand through storytelling, but particularly where religious and ethnic conflicts are concerned the creation of texts promotes symmetry and legitimacy of deeply held beliefs, which, when transformed into narratives for wider consumption, are made more secure. In storytelling encounter groups, each participant's story is privileged for the length of its telling (the speaker and her experiences recognized by the group), and the pool of narratives collectively form a new history, still one of conflict where deep differences remain but one better understood, humanized, and with others' suffering made real. In general, these studies show how storytelling—including personal conflict narratives, group narratives, public storytelling, and story-based intergroup dialogue—may be a compelling counter-ritual to violence and demonizing narratives and a powerful mechanism for peace building. Overall, it is concluded that peace education programs that are implemented in schools and through informal education venues are a means to stabilize peace accords, foster reconciliation, and produce sustainable peace. Peace education should be a central commitment attached to any peace agreement.

Youth Political Participation as a Peace-Building Mechanism

One of the most glaring inadequacies of peace processes to date has been their failure to truly include and engage youth. As Helsing (chapter 8) points out, even in the most recent Track Two Israeli-Palestinian Geneva Accords (2003), there were only two references to youth (in terms of potential exchange programs) and a couple of minor references to education in a twenty-page document. Many of the chapters in this volume bring out both the desire and the ability of youth to be constructive participants in peace processes. During negotiations youth participation can be most easily fostered by creating consultation linkages between political elites and already existing community-based organizations involving youth. And measures to widen the base of engaged youth ought to be central to the implementation agenda after peace accords. Why is this desirable? How could youth involvement in the politics of peace processes contribute to the stability of peace accords and the success of peace building?

In summary, the studies in this volume suggest that youth political participation could be a peace-building mechanism in four ways. First, young people's militarized identities are potentially transformed through political participation, which may foster resilience. Political participation for youth may be a violence prevention mechanism in the post-accord period. Second, through consultation and linkages of youth with sites of power, economic and political institutions in particular, important and authentic information about young people's needs and the appropriate means to fulfill them can be transferred. Engaged youth have something to teach adults, particularly political elites encased in their roles as conflict brokers, about the root causes of conflict. Third, youth have rights to participation, the fulfillment of which is not only a good in itself but also a practical manifestation of a post-accord human rights culture in creation. Fourth, youth political participation provides actual practice in power sharing that facilitates the sustainability of peace accords.

Transforming Militarized Identities

Militarized youth who have been key actors in armed conflict often have strong desires for political participation in the transition but are overlooked. In South

Africa youth were central to the anti-apartheid struggle, but once negotiations began and the armed struggle was suspended, the young were instructed to stand down and return if possible to more normal pursuits for their age group while older leaders returned from prison and exile. This was, in part, a recognition by leaders that youth have special needs, particularly educational ones, but many of the youth themselves felt cheated of decision-making power (Straker et al. 1992; CSVR 1998; Marks 1999). In the long run, this marginalization of youth during transition has posed significant challenges to the post-apartheid governments as it is linked with the development of both criminal gangs and alternative youth policing bodies. Even though more than in other countries youth were included in the transition in South Africa—giving testimonies to the Truth and Reconciliation Commission and honored with the creation of National Youth Day, for example—militarized youth identities remained a challenge. Straker et al. (1992) make the point that common youth fantasies of "saving the world" are in peacetime or nonwar situations channeled into occupational choices, volunteerism, games, or politics. In war, and particularly in a protracted, anti-authoritarian movement, they are channeled into "the struggle." What happens in a postwar situation where youth who have developed strong identities based around protection of their communities, ethnic conflict, and resistance of state oppression find few contexts—vocational, political, or otherwise—within which to exert and expand these identities? The patterns of post-accord violence provide one answer. Full-scale rebellion in Palestine, self-defense units in South Africa, "recreational" rioting in Northern Ireland, the re-abduction of youth soldiers and renewed fighting following the Lome Accords in Sierra Leone, and, generally, crime and the emergence of dissident and "spoiler" groups are all recastings and re-experiences of "the struggle." Another answer comes in the shape of the structural violence of land shortage and economic stagnation that traps youth in poverty and manifests itself in "despair" and self-destructive acts in Rwanda and in the Bosnian "brain drain."

Most of the studies in this volume link that marginal status with resort to violence. Political participation may be a way to help transform militarized identities by moving youth from the margins to the centers of power, and power and peace processes may be transformed in the process. But it will not be a panacea. In Rwanda there are actual attempts to include youth, but they currently sit uneasily with dire economic realities. In Bosnia politics and politicians are subject to extreme distrust, and, in most of the cases at which we look, issues of future well being figure more prominently than political voice in young people's own analyses of the major challenges of post-accord periods. Clearly, our findings suggest that an integrated set of needs must be met (Maslow's [1987] hierarchy is continually relevant). But of all of these, political participation (a need that collapses Maslow's categories of belonging, esteem, and knowledge/understanding needs) has been awarded the least attention as a peace-building mechanism. This is shortsighted given recent findings and theory linking resilience with political activism.

FOSTERING RESILIENCE

Psychological resiliency or coping ability in young people may be positively linked with active participation in politics and political violence (Cairns 1996; Cairns and Dawes 1996; Barber 1999; Straker et al. 1992), at least in low-intensity conflicts (Jones 2000). Among youth who experienced and partici-pated in political violence in South Africa, for example, psychological resiliency and the ability to cope and be constructive citizens in the post-apartheid period was higher for those who had leadership roles in anti-apartheid militant groups (Straker et al. 1992). Similarly, an Israeli study's findings suggest that "political commitment" inoculates children against trauma (Ziv, Kruglanski, and Schul-man 1974). McWhirter's 1990 study in Northern Ireland found that being an "active protagonist" enhanced self-esteem for some young people. Cairns (1996) writes:

> As conflicts come to an end the fear is often expressed that as mem-
> bers of groups trained to kill or maim young people will not be able
> to be resocialized. Anecdotal evidence suggests that this is not neces-
> sarily true. One possible explanation that is yet to be tested empiri-
> cally, is that a key element in membership of paramilitary groups
> may be the development of a morality of loyalty which in turn is
> related to the development of a relevant situated social identity (137).

Some of the studies in this volume show how even where soldiering has been a survival tactic, or street fighting and rioting are expressions of a variety of youth interests, there is a strong connection between ethno-political loyalty and a more broadly conceived ethic of community service or altruism and to varying degrees of resilience and hope (see chapters 1, 4, and 6). Although these studies do not measure for psychological resilience, they lend support to Cairns' hypothesis. However, the findings on resilience emerge from periods of youth involvement in armed conflict, mostly national liberation struggles, when deep commitment, training, and discipline were the norm, and in kinds of conflicts, particularly guerrilla wars, where active, voluntary civilian participation in a vari-ety of ways was possible. In other types of conflict, where forced recruitment and genocide are factors, the resilience-participation link is uncertain.

Barber (1999) concluded that resilience is "conditional on future events." His work and the studies in this volume suggest that in post-accord periods in general, when certain forms of political violence may continue but "the struggle" is declared suspended or over and expectations are raised but change happens very slowly, the need for resilience-building opportunities for youth through community activism is great. A better understanding and theorizing of the links between participation in political violence, politics, and post-accord peace building is essential. At the very least, closer youth involvement in post-accord political processes is essential for the transfer of their knowledge of these dynamics and youth needs.

TRANSFER OF VITAL KNOWLEDGE

The marginalization of youth from politics reinforces structural inadequacies of peace processes because it leads to the loss of vital information. "War. War. Whoever hasn't experienced it doesn't know what it is," a twelve-year-old Bosnian refugee reminds us (Raymond 2000, 45). A complete picture of the effects of a conflict, and the specific reconstruction and reconciliation challenges, requires as detailed and inclusive conflict narratives as possible. And as key actors, youth must be consulted. Youth who have had active roles in violence (pre- and post-accord) are not "lost generation"(s), broken, brutalized, irredeemably disaffected from society, or lacking in political skill or insight. The coping strategies, survival techniques, and knowledge that youth develop under conditions of war or protracted political violence equip them for active roles in building their societies' futures and ought to be harnessed in official peace-building processes. As one of the young people from Northern Ireland states: "People don't listen to us. . . . But where do parents get all their information [about local violence] from? Kids" (chapter 6). A young Bosnian puts it this way: "Decisions are made for us by people who do not have an idea of what we are faced with on a daily basis" (chapter 7). Youth have vital knowledge of the real effects of war on the ground, the grassroots dynamics of the post-accord period, and also creative and critical responses to violence. The young people Nordstrom encounters developed egalitarian communities and "rich philosophical systems" and offered practical knowledge of how to negotiate a world of armed power and competition without being co-opted by its relentless narrowing of options. "That's just illusion," they tell us (see chapter 4).

Like youth, teachers are often also at the front lines of the transition to peace. Their local and microlocal knowledge is an invaluable indicator of the health of a peace process and a source of information about the evolving needs and interests of individual constituencies on the ground and about peace-building mechanisms that work. Yet teachers are often not consulted about the transformation of education institutions after accords, never mind included at other levels of the peace process (see chapter 5). Much more in-depth political consultation and ethnographic research on the experience of youth and teachers in peace processes needs to be done, along with sustained surveying of attitudes. As Kirlic's testimony reveals, teachers are not always sympathetic or supportive of young people's peace activism, a perhaps unsurprising fact given their own marginality from decision-making and change processes. This underlines the extent to which the dialogues that take place between youth and teachers in classrooms are sources of important information about what conflict resolution requires, as shown in Adwan and Bar-On's chapter.

CREATING A HUMAN RIGHTS CULTURE

Involving youth in the politics of peace processes will help create a human rights culture. Youth already have rights in international law to consultation and involvement in peace processes. Even children (under 18s) have rights of participation (under the Convention on the Rights of the Child, articles 12 and 13).[6] The United Nations and several other children's rights advocating agencies recognize that "war affected children, particularly adolescents, should be involved in peace processes and in developing policy and programming for their own rehabilitation, reintegration and education, as well as in the development of their communities" (International Tribunal for Children's Rights 2000). The Office of the Secretary-General for Children in Armed Conflict considers a core area of attention to be "systematically making children the priority in peace processes," seeing children as "subjects of rights and potential citizens, rather than objects of concern and victims" (Kumar 2000). In its recommendations the tribunal emphasized children's rights to be consulted and the potential usefulness of their "skills in danger management," as well as "their own knowledge and opinions about war and peace." While this is still a developing norm, it is more than simply rhetorical as the example of the representation of young people at the 2002 UN Special Session on Children illustrates. We share these aims based on the conclusions of our studies, but we argue that widening the view to take in people in their twenties is useful because it takes into consideration the population in war zones that is generally most active in armed conflict and has the greatest stake in future development, while also being marginalized from politics. It is a frame that can stand in complement to existing international legal norms providing full human rights for children and prohibiting child soldiering.

The development of a human rights culture is an often-trumpeted aim of peace accords, and one of the more tangible lessons of a peace process for the young will be the extent to which inclusion as a principle is a reality. Slye views a human rights culture as synonymous with "a reconciled society," defined as one "that strives to respect the dignity of all its members" (2000, 182), a process within which the next generation has constitutive roles. Furthermore, the complex, integrated definitions of security expounded by youth, as discussed earlier, suggest that young people's inclusion in debates about human rights provisions would help develop insights and policy as to how a fair and livable balance of civil, political, social, and economic rights may be best achieved. Young people live at the sharp end of some of the most difficult institutions to reform in post-accord situations—the police, the military, and the legal system. Marotta writes:

> In practical terms, integrating human rights in post-conflict reconstruction efforts means assisting war-torn countries in establishing a sound legal framework for the protection of human rights, backed up by adequate institutions with a sustainable capacity to ensure respect for those rights on a long-term basis. It also requires fostering human rights awareness among the general population so as to increase the level of accountability of government authorities and institutions. (2000, 69–70)

It is in this last capacity that young people can play important roles as human rights monitors and public reporters promoting accountability and justice. Yet, as Zartman argues, "justice has many referents and is ultimately subjective" (Zartman and Rasmussen 1997, 16). Consultation with young people expands the architecture of subjective positions that will ultimately be the foundation on which a human rights culture will stand or fall. Because although human rights engineering exemplifies the kind of text creation discussed earlier that concretizes and legitimizes people's needs and reduces fears, it relies upon a transformation of the conflict culture made up of multiple perspectives and multiple human rights compromises. Darby explains how this works in one relevant area: "The general population becomes accustomed, however reluctantly, to the need for more security searches, constant army patrols, increased surveillance, and the suspension of normal legal processes" (Darby and Mac Ginty 2000, 41). During protracted conflicts, youth are socialized to accept, if not overt abuses of human rights, a very constricted understanding of human rights as a social good and are, therefore, key actors to be engaged in breaking this barrier to a sustainable peace.

The marginalization of youth after war is often related to political expediency. In Mozambique, for example, children and youth were deliberately hidden by rebel leaders (fearing condemnation from national publics and international agencies) during the peace process and then simply "forgotten in the development and rebuilding process" (Sultan 2000, 45; see also Brett and McCallin 1996). One lesson for the future raised by this case is that the inclusion of youth could be considered as a test of good faith among parties to a peace agreement and even as restoration for the war crime of promoting child soldiering. While creating practical inclusion, the involvement of youth, therefore, could also symbolically contribute to reconciliation and set a precedent for human rights culture trumping political expediency. And again, a central role exists for youth in highlighting human rights abuses on the ground.

PRACTICE IN POWER SHARING

Political engagement of youth will provide the next generation with practice in power sharing, developing skills and values essential to a sustainable peace. After protracted political conflicts a major barrier to accommodation and power sharing between ethnic, religious, or political groups is mutual mistrust and distrust of systems of accommodation. Peace processes may be viewed as "normalization" of injustice or pacification processes and rejected (see chapter 9 in this volume). In many cases, because of divided towns and regions or segregated schools and workplaces, there has been little opportunity to meet and relate to "the other," reinforcing a lack of empathy and negative images. How can generations socialized by war be prepared to practice power sharing with an enemy so distant and demonized, or to recognize or respect politics as a means for change, self-expression, and protection? The architects of peace processes, whether internal elites or international brokers, seem to assume "a trickle-down-effect"; as people become accustomed to peace they will not want to go back to war. But although peace processes are socializing institutions, as was discussed earlier, the transaction is not only one way. And the paternalism and convenience politics of "top-down" processes that cement division and manage it, without addressing root injustices and misery, teach lessons that do not ultimately reinforce peace.

"Change occurs through politics" is the message peace process architects attempt to instill in the population. For disenfranchised and franchised but socially marginal youth such rhetoric will ring hollow unless politics entails an inclusion principle that extends deep as well as wide, including not only ethnic, national, or political opponents but also the variety of age, class, and gender cohorts within each group and that practically provides experience in power sharing. Real consultation with youth and the involvement of youth in discussions with decision makers about areas of peace accord implementation that affect them especially, such as policing/the security situation, education, human rights, and local economic development, will strengthen peace accords. We show how young women's restricted voice and continued marginality is both a symptom and a fuel for violence—direct and structural—and has still not received the attention it deserves in policy. The architects of peace processes ought to intentionally include youth and teachers into those processes and, using a gender sensitive lens, devise means to incorporate youth and educators into elite discussions and decision making. It should be a core task of peace processes to support the grassroots activities of youth in areas of community and youth development, particularly focused on youth-generated ideas and leadership structures. But an insincere or weak invitation to participation would likely be further politicizing and, in the end, destabilizing to a peace process. The adoption of political participation for youth as a peace-building mechanism requires careful, contextualized planning and the transfer of real power. The latter recognition involves confrontation with the vested interests of local and international elites, and change will be slow. But one contribution the studies in this volume can make to this process is in underlining the fact that currently youth are a wasted resource and that pragmatism alone should alert political elites to young people's destabilizing potential.

CONCLUSION

After accords youth are politically relevant because they have rights, because they have been combatants, because they affect peace processes, and because they are future voters, leaders, and reproducers of culture and conflict. Their interpretations of a peace process' success or failure, and how they conceptualize peace and war, will be immensely clarifying for those concerned with delivering a lasting peace. A fuller and more authoritative account of the effects of armed conflict and of peace processes is achieved by the use of multiple lenses, of which a youth lens is one important part, and will provide a basis upon which to develop more effective peace-building activities. This requires attention to the "positive" examples of youth engagement in peace-building processes, as well as their power as conflict reproducers and peace wreckers. The studies in this volume suggest that the most significant shared challenges facing youth organizing for peace and justice, interethnic dialogue, or simply to express themselves in besieged uninational settings are the vested interests of local elites, the narrow vision of peace process technocrats, and the memories and trauma of structural violence, displacement, and war, which combine to create and enforce limited opportunities for youth to be active social, economic, and political agents in the post-accord period. Resisting recruitment into renewed armed conflict, or new forms of post-accord violence, is made difficult by these dynamics of post-accord situations. It will be unfortunate if the dynamics of conflict resolution today reinforce in the next generation the psychological damage of war and its preceding traumas and injustices, but this is just what twenty-year-old Bosnian Namik Kirlic fears when he says that without improvement in young people's lives, "they will develop into adults who will not be able to take this country anywhere. Then, they will not be peacemakers or troublemakers; they will be passive, not-opinionated adults, who will be easily swayed by any political faction" (see chapter 8). Addressing this prospect not only in Bosnia but in numerous postwar situations is an enormous and urgent task for those who would be peace builders.

The evolution of international relations triggered by terrorism and preemptive war directly connects with the challenge of youth, armed conflict, and peace building. As Darby suggests, the U.S.-led "war on terror" changes the dynamics of internal conflicts around the world. States have greater freedom to abuse human rights against dissidents without sanction and to take a hard line in negotiating internal conflicts. Conversely, (non-Islamic) militants may be more likely to enter negotiations (at least as a stop-gap measure) as they face these state pressures and decreased support from their diasporas (Darby, 2006). While these forces may lead to more ceasefires in internal conflicts, it is dubious whether they can lead to sustainable peace. It seems unlikely that they will create a climate in which the trust and transparency necessary for hammering out workable agreements is present and where a human rights culture, peace education, and, eventually, genuine reconciliation can develop. The "war on terror" shifts the spotlight away from some of the most serious global challenges of poverty reduction, economic development, AIDS, and the environment, particularly in Africa, and this neglect sows the seeds of new conflicts. A move away from human rights and human security paradigms, and from diplomacy and negotiation as tools of statecraft, suggests that youth will receive less rather than more attention, even while they are increasingly relevant as armed actors. In the Middle East, under 15s make up 40 percent of the population generally. In Afghanistan alone, 50 percent of the population is under 18 (Khayat 1994 and UNICEF 2002). Youth are the foot soldiers in Afghanistan and Iraq, where recent wars have had enormous humanitarian impact on children and families (NGO Consortium 2002 and UNICEF et al. 2003).

The use of force to combat "terror," and monolithic, decontextualized images of the militant or terrorist, work against the kind of approaches to peace building that the studies in this volume recommend. We show how young people's militarized identities and the lure of redemptive violence are rooted in layers of trauma and in subjective understandings of the meaning of violence and the material and psychological benefits of peace; in complex loyalties to family, community, ethnic or religious group, and state; and in developmental and gendered responses to threats to survival and thriving. Force is not just a blunt instrument in response to these complexities; it is also inflammatory. It is educative, perversely invigorating, and likely reinforces resilience in the youth who are its recipients. It reinforces in the next generation a worldview of "abusers versus abused" and (re)creates grievance and hopelessness. The complexity and difficulty of post-accord peace building makes the case for avid war prevention work. In cases where war prevails, the urgent challenge is one of mitigating the damage as quickly and early as possible. The emerging lessons from internal conflicts are that this should be done through embracing holistic approaches to the reintegration of youth soldiers and to rebuilding their war-torn communities, through participatory, inclusive processes of reconstruction, and with truth processes and reparations that will reshape at a fundamental level the war-supporting ideologies of all the conflict parties.

NOTES

1. Excerpt from Northern Irish child's poem about peace, part of the study in this volume by Cairns et al. (chapter 5).

2. Peace activist youth in Colombia, quoted in Sanford (chapter 2) in this volume.

3. Mother of youth killed by paramilitaries in Colombia, quoted in Sanford (chapter 2) in this volume.

4. See, for example, Brendan O'Malley, "Lost Generation," *Times Education Supplement,* June 9, 2000, 13, about Chechen children; Mark Mathabane, "South Africa's Lost Generation," *New York Times,* June 4, 1999, A29; Jackson Kanneh, "Liberia: A Lost Generation," *Scholastic Update,* February 23, 1996, 5; Olivia Ward, "The Lost Generation," *New Internationalist,* July 1996, 3, about Chechen children; Tim Carrington, "Lost Generations," *Wall Street Journal (Eastern Edition),* December 29, 1994, A1, about Ugandan AIDS orphans; Brown, "The Lost Generation" (1994, 29), about children in Sudan; Sachs, "AIDS Orphans: Africa's Lost Generation" (1993, 10); Brook Larmer, "The Lost Generation," *Newsweek,* February 8, 1993, 39, about children of Argentina's disappeared; "Mozambique's Lost Generation," (1992, 27). A critical commentary on the media's use of these images is provided by Nancy Scheper-Hughes (1995).

5. Miall, Ramsbotham, and Woodhouse (1999) define "negative peace" as the absence of violence and "positive peace" as long-term reconciliation, and they conceive "pursuit of justice" (defined as truth/acknowledgement, reparation/rehabilitation, punishment/pardon) as the route between these states: "the

passage from negative to positive peace runs through justice" (208). Lederach defines "reconciliation" as "the redefinition and restoration of broken relationships" (1997, 84) and conceives of a meeting of truth, justice (which are distinct), mercy, and peace in the process. Assefa (2001) elaborates:

Reconciliation as a conflict handling mechanism entails the following core elements:

- Honest acknowledgement of the harm/injury each party has inflicted on the other.
- Sincere regrets and remorse for injury done.
- Readiness to apologize for one's role in inflicting the injury.
- Readiness of the conflicting parties to let go of the anger and bitterness caused by the conflict and the injury.
- Commitment by the offender not to repeat the injury.
- Sincere effort to redress past grievances that caused the conflict and compensate the damage caused to the extent possible.
- Entering into a new, mutually enriching relationship.

Reconciliation then refers to this new relationship that emerges as a consequence of these processes. What most people refer to as "healing" is the mending of deep emotional wounds (generated by the conflict) that follow the reconciliation process. (Assefa 2001, 340)

Assefa locates healing as the effect of reconciliation, while others would find healing to be more integral to the steps of a reconciliation process. For example, Boraine explains that "healing or restorative truth" was one kind of truth sought through the South African Truth and Reconciliation Commission, the others being "factual or forensic truth . . . personal and/or narrative truth [and] social or dialogical truth" (Boraine 2000, 151–52). Healing and reconciliation are bound up with each other too in various local reconciliation initiatives and community healing practices. On the different definitions of reconciliation, see also Borer (2000).

6. The Convention on the Rights of the Child states:

ARTICLE 12

1. States Parties shall assure to the child who is capable of forming his or her own views the right to express those views freely in all matters affecting the child, the views of the child being given due weight in accordance with the age and maturity of the child.

2. For this purpose, the child shall in particular be provided the opportunity to be heard in any judicial and administrative proceed-

ings affecting the child, either directly, or through a representative or an appropriate body, in a manner consistent with the procedural rules of national law.

ARTICLE 13

1. The child shall have the right to freedom of expression; this right shall include freedom to seek, receive and impart information and ideas of all kinds, regardless of frontiers, either orally, in writing or in print, in the form of art, or through any other media of the child's choice.

2. The exercise of this right may be subject to certain restrictions, but these shall only be such as are provided by law and are necessary:

(a) For respect of the rights or reputations of others; or

(b) For the protection of national security or of public order (order public), or of public health or morals.

See http://www.unicef.org/crc/fulltext.htm.

Abbott, Beth. 2000. "Child Soldiers: The Use of Children as Instruments of War." *Suffolk Transnational Law Review* 23 (2): 499–537.

Adams, Evelyn, ed. 1999. *At Home on Fidalgo.* Fidalgo Island, WA: Anacortes Community Forest Lands.

Adwan, Sami, and Ruth Firer. 1997. *The Narrative of Palestinian Refugees During the War of 1948 in Israeli and Palestinian History and Civic Education Textbooks.* Paris: UNESCO.

———. 1999. *The Narrative of the 1967 War in the Israeli and Palestinian History and Civics Textbooks and Curricula Statement.* Braunschwieg, Germany: Eckert Institute.

African Rights. 1995. *Rwanda: Death, Despair and Defiance.* London: African Rights.

Ahearn, F., ed. 2000. *Psychosocial Wellness of Refugees.* New York: Berghahn.

Albeck, Josef, Sami Adwan, and Dan Bar-On. 2002. "Dialogue Groups: TRT's Guidelines for Working Through Intractable Conflicts by Personal Storytelling in Encounter Groups." *Journal of Peace Psychology* 8 (4): 301–22.

Alfredson, Lisa. 2001. "Sexual Exploitation of Child Soldiers." *Child Soldiers Newsletter* (December): 1.

Amadiume, Ifi, and Abdullahi An-Na'im. 2000. *The Politics of Memory: Truth, Healing and Social Justice.* London: Zed.

American Academy of Pediatrics. 2000. "An Accord on Child Soldiers." *Pediatrics* 105 (5): 1045.

Amnesty International (AI). 1999. *Children's Rights: The Future Starts Here.* London: Amnesty International.

———. 2002. *Sierra Leone.* Retrieved September 14, 2002, from http://web.amnesty.org/web/ar2002.nsf/afr/sierra_leone!Open.

Anderson, Benedict. 1991. *Imagined Communities: Reflections on the Origin and Spread of Nationalism,* rev. ed. New York: Verso.

Anderson, Mary. 1999. *Do No Harm.* Boulder, CO: Lynne Rienner.

Andoni, Ghassan. 2001. "A Comparative Study of Intifada 1987 and Intifada 2000." In *The New Intifada: Resisting Israel's Apartheid,* ed. Roan Carey (pp. 209–18). New York: Verso.

Andripc, I., and Z. B. Juricipc et al. 1990. *The Development of Spiritual Life in Bosnia Under the Influence of Turkish Rule.* Durham, NC: Duke University Press.

Angvik, M., and B. von Borries, eds. 1997. *Youth and History: A Comparative European Survey on Historical Consciousness and Political Attitudes among Adolescents.* Hamburg: Koerber Foundation.

Ankerl, Guy. 1986. *Urbanization Overspeed in Tropical Africa, 1970-2000: Facts, Social Problems, and Policy.* INU Societal Research Series, ed. Dirk Pereboom. Geneva: INU Press, Interuniversity Institute.

Apfel, Roberta J., and Bennett Simon. 1996. *Minefields in the Hearts: The Mental Health of Children in War and Communal Violence*. New Haven, CT: Yale University Press.

Apple, M. W. 1979. *Ideology and Curriculum*. London: Routledge and Kegan Paul.

Arendt, Hannah. 1973. *The Origins of Totalitarianism*. New York: Harcourt Brace.

Arlow, Michael. 2003. "Conflict and Curriculum Change in Northern Ireland." In *Reframing Social Contracts: Curriculum Policy Reform in Societies Emerging from Civil Strife,* ed. Sobhi Tawil and Alexandra Harley. International Bureau of Education.

Assefa, Hizkias. 2001. "Reconcilation." In *Peacebuilding: A Field Guide,* ed. Luc Reycher and Thania Paffenholz (pp. 336–42). Boulder, CO: Lynne Rienner.

Avruch, Kevin, and Peter Black. 1994. "Conflict Resolution in Intercultural Settings: Problems and Perspectives." In *Conflict Resolution Theory and Practice: Integration and Application,* ed. Dennis Sandole and Hugo van der Merwe (pp. 131–45). Manchester: Manchester University Press.

Ball, Nicole. 1996. "The Challenge of Rebuilding War-Torn Societies." In *Turbulent Peace: The Challenges of Managing International Conflict,* ed. Chester Crocker, Fen Osler Hampson, and Pamela Aall (pp. 607–22). Washington, DC: United States Institute of Peace.

Baptista, Zezo. 2000. *A Contagem Regressiva.* Luanda, Angola: Ponto Um.

Barber, Brian K. 1999. "Political Violence, Family Relations, and Palestinian Youth Functioning." *Journal of Adolescent Research* 14 (2): 206–31.

Barman, Jean et al. 1986. *Indian Experience in Canada, Vol 1: The Legacy.* Vancouver: University of British Columbia Press.

Bar-On, Dan. 1996. "Attempting to Overcome the Transgenerational Transmission of Trauma: Dialogue Between Descendants and Victims of Perpetrators." In *Minefields in the Hearts: The Mental Health of Children in War and Communal Violence,* ed. Roberta J. Apfel and Bennett Simon (pp. 165–88). New Haven, CT: Yale University Press..

———. 1999. *The Others Within Us: Changes in the Israeli Collective Identity from a Social Psychological Perspective* [in Hebrew]. Jerusalem: Ben Gurion University Press and Mosad Bialik.

———, ed. 2000. *Bridging the Gap: Storytelling as a Way to Work through Political and Collective Hostilities.* Hamburg: Körber-Stiftung.

Bar-On, Dan, and Fatma Kassem. n.d. "Storytelling as a Way to Work Through Intractable Conflicts: The TRT German-Jewish Experience and Its Relevance to the Palestinian-Israeli Context." Unpublished paper.

Bender, L., and J. Frosch. 1942. "Children's Reactions to the War." *American Journal of Orthopsychiatry* 22: 571–86.

Berg, B. L. 1998. *Qualitative Research Methods for the Social Sciences.* Boston: Allyn and Bacon.

Berman, D. M. 2001. *The Heroes of Treca Gimnazija: A War School in Sarajevo, 1992–1995.* Boulder, CO: Rowman and Littlefield.

Berman, Sheldon. 1997. *Children's Consciousness and Development of Social Responsibility.* New York: State University of New York Press.

Bobo, Jacqueline. 1996. *Black Women as Cultural Readers.* New York: Columbia University Press.

Bonnerjea, Lucy, 1994. "Disasters, Family Tracing and Children's Rights: Some Questions about the Best Interests of Separated Children." *Disasters* 18 (3): 277–83.

Boothby, Neil, and C. Knudsen. 2000. "Children of the Gun." *Scientific American* 282 (6): 6–66.

Boraine, Alex. 2000. "Truth and Reconciliation in South Africa: The Third Way." In *Truth V. Justice: The Morality of Truth Commissions,* ed. Robert I. Rotberg and Dennis Thompson (pp. 141–57). Princeton, NJ: Princeton University Press.

Borer, Tristan Anne. 2000. "Debating Definitions." Occasional Paper, Joan B. Kroc Institute for International Peace Studies.

———. Forthcoming. *Telling the Truths: Truth Telling and Peace Building in Post-Conflict Societies.* Notre Dame, IN: University of Notre Dame Press.

Boulding, Elise. 1988. *Building a Global Civic Culture: Education for an Interdependent World.* New York: Teachers College Press.

———. 1990. *Building a Global Civic Culture: Education for an Interdependent World.* Syracuse, NY: Syracuse University Press.

———. 1997. "Introduction to Rethinking Peace Building." *Peace and Conflict Studies* 4 (1): 1–2.

Bourdieu, Pierre. 1973. "Cultural Reproduction and Social Reproduction." In *Knowledge, Education and Cultural Change,* ed. R. Brown (pp. 71–112). London: Tavistock.

Boutros-Ghali, Boutros, and United Nations Department of Public Information. 1992. *An Agenda for Peace: Preventive Diplomacy, Peacemaking and Peace-Keeping: Report of the Secretary-General Pursuant to the Statement Adopted by the Summit Meeting of the Security Council on 31 January 1992.* New York: United Nations.

Bracken, Patrick. 1996. "The Rehabilitation of Child Soldiers: Defining Needs and Appropriate Responses." *Medicine, Conflict and Survival* 12 (April/June): 1362–69.

Bracken, P., and C. Petty, eds. 1998. *Rethinking the Trauma of War.* London: Free Association.

Brett, Rachel, and Irma Specht. 2004. *Young Soldiers and Why They Choose to Fight.* Boulder: Lynne Rienner.

Brett, Rachel, and Margaret McCallin. 1996. *Children: The Invisible Soldiers.* Vaxjo, Sweden: Rädda Barnen.

Brock-Utne, Birgit. 1985. *Feminist Perspectives on Peace and Education.* New York: Pergamon Press.

Bronfenbrenner, Urie. 1979. *The Ecology of Human Development.* Cambridge, MA: Harvard University Press.

Brown, Charles R. 1994. "The Lost Generation." *Freedom Review* 25 (4): 29.

Burman, Erica. 1994. "Innocents Abroad: Western Fantasies of Childhood and the Iconography of Emergencies." *Disasters* 18 (3): 238–53.

Byrne, Sean. 1997a. *Growing Up in a Divided Society: The Influence of Conflict on Belfast Schoolchildren.* Cranbury, NJ: Associated University Presses.

———. 1997b. "The Politics of a New Era in Northern Ireland: Belfast Schoolchildren's Images of Political Conflict and Social Change." *Mind and Human Interaction* 7 (2): 52–71.

——. 2000. "Belfast Schoolchildren and Ethnoreligious Conflict in Northern Ireland." In *Social Conflict and Collective Identity*, ed. Pat Coy and Lynne Woehrle. Lanham, MD: Rowman and Littlefield.

CAIN. n.d. a. Conflict Archive on the Internet. Retrieved June 15, 2005, from http://cain.ulst.ac.uk/ni/popul.html.

——. n.d. b. Conflict Archive on the Internet. Retrieved June 15, 2005, from http://cain.ulst.ac.uk/othelem/incorepaper.

Cairns, Ed. 1987. *Caught in the Crossfire: Children and the Northern Ireland Conflict.* Belfast and Syracuse, NY: Appletree and Syracuse University Press.

——. 1991. "Is Northern Ireland a Conservative Society?" In *Social Attitudes in Northern Ireland*, vol. 1, ed. P. Stringer and G. Robinson (pp. 142–51). Belfast, Northern Ireland: Blackstaff.

——. 1996. *Children and Political Violence.* Oxford: Blackwell.

Cairns, Ed, and Alan Dawes. 1996. "Children: Ethnic and Political Violence— A Commentary." *Child Development* 67: 129–39.

Cairns, Ed, and John Darby. 1998. "The Conflict in Northern Ireland: Causes, Consequences and Controls." *American Psychologist* 53 (7): 754–60.

Cairns, Ed, Frances McLernon, and Ilse Hakvoort. 2003. "The Impact of the Peace Process in Northern Ireland on Adolescents' Ideas About War and Peace." Paper presented at the 8th International Symposium on the Contributions of Psychology to Peace, Sunne, Sweden, June.

Cameron, Sara. 2000. "The Role of Children as Peace-makers in Colombia." *Development* 43 (1): 40–45.

Campbell, Scott. 1999. *Democratic Republic of Congo: The Casualties of War–Civilians, Rule of Law and Democratic Freedoms.* New York: Human Rights Watch.

Castello-Branco, V. 1997. "Child Soldiers: The Experience of the Mozambican Association for Public Health." *Development in Practice* 7 (4): 494–97.

Center for the Study of Violence and Reconciliation (CSVR). 1998. "Into the Heart of Darkness: Journeys of the Amagents in Crime, Violence and Death." Paper prepared as part of research conducted by the Centre for the Study of Violence and Reconciliation for the Council for Scientific and Industrial Research (CSIR), Johannesburg.

Chase, Susan E. 1995. *Ambiguous Empowerment: The Work Narratives of Women School Superintendents.* Amherst: University of Massachusetts Press.

Chaudhry, Samena. 2001. "Rehabilitating Sudan's Child Soldiers." *British Medical Journal* (June): 179.

Cilliers, Jaco. 2001. "Local Reactions to Post-Conflict Peacebuilding Efforts in Bosnia-Herzegovina and South Africa." PhD diss., University of Michigan.

Clements, Kevin. P. 1997. "Peacebuilding and Conflict Transformation." *Peace and Conflict Studies* 4 (1): 3–13.

Coalition 2000: International Coalition to Stop the Use of Child Soldiers. n.d. "Girls with Guns: An Agenda on Child Soldiers for 'Beijing Plus Five.'" Retrieved June 5, 2001, from http://www.child-soldiers.org/.

Coalition to Stop the Use of Child Soldiers (CSUCS). 2001. *Child Soldiers: Global Report.* New York: CSUCS.

CODHES (Consultoria para los Derechos Humanos y el Desplazamiento). 2003. *Alto Naya: Un clamo que no cesa.* April. Bogota: CODHES.

Coffield, Frank. 1995. "Always the Trainee, Never the Employee? Increasingly Protracted Transitions in the UK." In *Youth in Europe: Social Change in Western Europe,* ed. A. Cavalli and O. Galland (pp. 45–62). London: Pinter.

Cohen, Roger, 2000. "The Hidden Revolution: The Serbian Students Who Brought Down Milosevic." *New York Times Magazine,* November 26, 43–47, 118, 148.

Cohn, Ilene, and Guy Goodwin-Gill. 1994. *Child Soldiers. The Role of Children in Armed Conflicts.* New York: Oxford Clarendon Press/Henry Dunant Institute.

Coles, Robert. 1986. *The Political Life of Children.* Boston: Houghton Mifflin.

———. 1989. *The Call of Stories: Teaching and the Moral Imagination.* Boston: Houghton Mifflin.

Colombian Commission of Jurists (CCJ). 1999a. *Derechos humanos en Colombia.* Bogota: CCJ.

———. 1999b. *Follow-up to Recommendations of the Representative of the Secretary General of the United Nations for Internal Displacements, 1996–1999.* Bogota: Support Group for Displaced Peoples Organizations (GAD).

Commission for Historical Clarification (CEH). 1999. *Guatemala Memoria del Silencio, vols. 1–12.* Guatemala City: CEH.

Communities of Populations in Resistance (CPR) Support Group. 1993. *Bulletin from the CPR Support Group* 1 (2).

Consentino, Donald. 1982. *Defiant Maids and Stubborn Farmers: Tradition and Innovation in Mende Story Performance.* Cambridge: Cambridge University Press.

Cooper, P. 1965. "The Development of the Concept of War." *Journal of Peace Research* 2 (1): 1–17.

Cote, James E., and Anton L. Allahar. 1996. *Generation on Hold: Coming of Age in the Late Twentieth Century.* New York: New York University Press.

Cousens, E. M., and Charles Cater. 2001. *Toward Peace in Bosnia: Implementing the Dayton Accords.* Boulder, CO: Lynne Rienner.

Crocker, Chester A., and Fen Osler Hampson. 1996. "Making Peace Settlements Work." *Foreign Policy* 104 (Fall): 54–71.

Curle, A. 1971. *Making Peace.* London: Tavistock.

Danieli, Y., N. Rodley, and L. Weisaeth, eds. 1996. *International Responses to Traumatic Stress.* Amytyville, NY: Baywood.

Danziger, K. 1963. "The Psychological Future of an Oppressed Group," *Social Forces* 42: 32–40.

Darby, John. 1986. *Intimidation and the Control of Conflict in Northern Ireland.* Dublin: Gill and MacMillan.

———. 1990. "Intimidation and Interaction in a Small Belfast Community: The Water and the Fish." In *Political Violence: Ireland in a Comparative Perspective,* ed. John Darby, Nicholas Dodge, and Anthony C. Hepburn (pp. 83–102). Belfast and Ottawa: Appletree Press and University of Ottawa Press.

———. 2001. *The Effects of Violence on Peace Processes.* Washington, DC: United States Institute of Peace Press.

———. 2006. *Violence and Reconstruction.* Notre Dame, IN: University of Notre Dame Press.

Darby, John, and Roger Mac Ginty, eds. 2000. *The Management of Peace Processes.* London: Macmillan/St. Martin's.

——. 2002. *Guns and Government: The Management of the Northern Ireland Peace Process.* Basingstoke: Palgrave.

Das, Veena. 2000. "The Act of Witnessing: Violence, Poisonous Knowledge and Subjectivity." In *Violence and Subjectivity,* ed. Veena Das and Arthur Kleinman (pp. 205–26). Berkeley: University of California Press.

Davis, G. S. 1996. *Religion and Justice in the War Over Bosnia.* New York: Routledge.

Dawes, Alan. 1994. "The Emotional Impact of Political Violence." In *Children and Adversity: Psychological Perspectives on South African Research,* ed. Alan Dawes and D. Donald. Cape Town: David Philip.

De Berry, Jo. 2001. "Child Soldiers and the Convention on the Rights of the Child." *Annals of the Academy of Political and Social Science* 575 (May): 92–105.

Defense for Children International Palestine Section. n.d. Retrieved on October 30, 2005, from http://www.dci-pal.org/.

Dennis, Michael. 1999. "The ILO Convention and the Worst Forms of Child Labor." *American Journal of International Law* 93 (4): 943–48.

——. 2000. "Newly Adopted Protocols to the Convention on the Rights of the Child." *American Journal of International Law* 94 (4): 789–96.

De Oliveiria, Walter, and Carmen Montecinos. 1998. "Social Pedagogy: Presence, Commitment, Identification, Availability." *Teaching Education Journal* 9 (Winter/Spring): 67–68.

Des Forges, Alison. 1999. *Leave None to Tell the Story: Genocide in Rwanda.* New York, Washington, London, Brussels: Human Rights Watch; and Paris: International Federation of Human Rights.

De Silva, Harendra. 2001. "Conscription of Children in Armed Conflict—A Form of Child Abuse." *Child Abuse Review* 10 (2): 125–34.

De Waal, Alex. 1996. "Contemporary Warfare in Africa: Changing Context, Changing Strategies." *IDS Bulletin* 27 (3): 6–16.

Dodge, C. P. 1990. "Health Implications of War in Uganda and Sudan." *Social Sciences and Medicine* 31 (6): 691–98.

Donia, R. J., and J. V. A. Fine. 1994. *Bosnia and Hercegovina: A Tradition Betrayed.* New York: Columbia University Press.

Dunn, S. 1995. *Facets of the Conflict in Northern Ireland.* New York: St. Martin's Press.

Economist Intelligence Unit. 2003. Rwanda: Country Report. Available online at http://www.eiu.com/.

Education for Pluralism, Human Rights and Democracy. 2002. *Annual Report.* University of Ulster, UNESCO Center.

Eggers. Ellen K. 1997. *Historical Dictionary of Burundi,* 2nd ed. Lanham, MD: Scarecrow Press.

Eisele, Kimi. 2001. "Documenting the Then and the Now." *Orion Afield* (Autumn): 16–20.

Fajardo-Montaña, Dario. 2001. "Los Circuitos de los Desplazamientos Forzados en Colombia." In *Exodo, Patrimonio e Identidad,* ed. Martha Segura Naranjo (pp. 68–75). Bogota: Museo Nacional de Colombia.

Falla, Ricardo. 1992. *Masacres de la Selva.* Guatemala City: Editorial Universitario.

Fanon, Franz. 1966. *The Wretched of the Earth.* New York: Grove Press.

Ferguson, M. 1980. *The Aquarian Conspiracy: Personal and Social Transformation in the 1980s.* Los Angeles: J. P. Tarcher.

Ferguson, N., F. McLernon, and E. Cairns. 1994. "The Sociomoral Reflection Measure—Short Form: An Examination of Its Reliability and Validity in a Northern Irish Setting." *British Journal of Educational Psychology* 64: 483–89.

Fernando, Jude, ed. 2001. "Children's Rights." Special issue, *Annals of the American Academy of Political and Social Science* 575 (May): 8–224.

Fine, Elizabeth, and Jean Haskell Speer. 1992. *Performance, Culture, and Identity.* Westport, CT: Praeger.

Fine, Michelle. 1989. "Silencing and Nurturing Voice in an Improbable Context: Urban Adolescents in Public School." In *Critical Pedagogy, the State, and Cultural Struggle,* ed. Henry Giroux and Peter McLaren (pp. 152–73). Albany: State University of New York Press.

Freire, Paulo. 2001. *Pedagogy of the Oppressed.* New York: Continuum.

Frost, J. M. 1997. "Strange and Extraordinary Feats of Indian Magic." In *The Magician's Tale,* by David Hunt. London: Hodder and Stoughton.

Galeano, Eduardo. 1989. *The Book of Embraces.* London: W.W. Norton.

Gallagher, Tony. 2004. "Interculturalism in a Divided School System." In *Interculturalism: Critical Issues,* ed. D. Powell and F. Sze (pp. 111–17). Oxford: Inter-Disciplinary Press.

Galtung, Johan. 1965. "Institutionalized Conflict Resolution." *Journal of Peace Research* 2 (4): 348–95.

———. 1975–88. *Essays in Peace Research.* Copenhagen: Christian Ejlers.

———. 1985. "Twenty-Five Years of Peace Research: Ten Challenges and Some Responses." *Journal of Peace Research* 22: 142–58.

———. 1990. "Cultural Violence." *Journal of Peace Research* 27 (3): 291–305.

———. 1996. *Peace by Peaceful Means.* Peace and Conflict, Development and Civilization. Oslo: International Peace Research Institute, Oslo (PRIO).

———. 2000. *Conflict Transformation by Peaceful Means.* Geneva: United Nations.

———. 2003. "What Did People Predict for the Year 2000—And What Happened?" and "What Did the Experts Predict?" in "Democracy Works: People, Experts and the Future," ed. with Håkan Wiberg. Special issue, *FUTURES* 89 (2): 107–22 and 123–46.

———. 2004. *Transcend and Transform.* London: PLUTO.

Galtung, Johan, and K. Jacobsen. 2002. *Searching for Peace.* 2nd ed. London: PLUTO.

Garbarino, James, and Kathleen Kostelny. 1997. "What Children Can Tell Us About Living in a War Zone. In *Children in a Violent Society,* ed. J. D. Osofsky (pp. 32–41). New York: Guilford Press.

Gasibirege, S., and S. Babalola. 2001. *Perceptions about the Gacaca Law in Rwanda: Evidence from a Multi-Method Study.* Special Publication no. 19. Baltimore: Center for Communication Programs, Johns Hopkins University School of Public Health.

Gellner, Ernst R. 1983. *Nations and Nationalism.* Cambridge: Blackwell.

Gillespie, J. M., and G. M. Allport. 1950. *Youth's Outlook on the Future: A Cross-National Study.* New York. Doubleday.

Gilligan, Carol. 1982. *In a Different Voice: Psychological Theory and Women's Development.* Cambridge, MA: Harvard University Press.

Goleman, Daniel. 1996. *Emotional Intelligence.* New York: Bantam.

Guide to the Optional Protocol on the Involvement of Children in Armed Conflict. 2003. New York: UNICEF.

Gurr, T. R. 1993. *Minorities at Risk: A Global View of Ethnopolitical Conflicts.* Washington, DC: United States Institute of Peace Press.

Haavelsrud, Magnus. 1987. "Peace Education: Operationalization of the Peace Concept." *Bulletin of Peace Proposals* 18 (3): 363–74.

Hakvoort, Ilse. 1995. "Children's Conceptions of Peace and War: A Longitudinal Study." *Peace and Conflict: Journal of Peace Psychology* 2: 1–15.

Hakvoort, Ilse, and Louis Oppenheimer. 1993. "Children and Adolescents: Conceptions of Peace, War, and Strategies to Attain Peace: A Dutch Case Study." *Journal of Peace Research* 30 (1): 65–77.

———. 1995. "Conceptualisation of Peace and War in Childhood and Adolescence." Poster session presented at the Sixth European Conference on Developmental Psychology, Krakow, August 22–26.

Hall, Robin. 1993. "How Children Think and Feel about War and Peace: An Australian Study." *Journal of Peace Research* 30 (2): 181–96.

Halsan, A. 2001. "Underage and Under Fire: An Enquiry into the Use of Child Soldiers, 1994–98." *Childhood* 8 (3): 340–62.

Hampson, Fen Osler. 1996a. *Nurturing Peace: Why Peace Settlements Succeed or Fail.* Washington, DC: United States Institute of Peace Press.

———. 1996b. "Why Orphaned Peace Settlements Are Prone to Failure." In *Managing Global Chaos: Sources of and Reponses to International Conflict,* ed. Chester A. Crocker, Fen Osler Hampson, and Pamela Aall (pp. 533–50). Washington, DC: United States Institute of Peace Press.

Haraway, Donna Jeanne. 1989. *Primate Visions.* New York: Routledge.

Hardt, Michael, and Antonio Negri. 2000. *Empire.* Cambridge, MA: Harvard University Press.

Harris, Ian. 1999. "Types of Peace Education." In *How Children Understand War and Peace: A Call for International Peace Education,* ed. Amiram Raviv, Louis Oppenheimer, and Daniel Bar-Tal (pp. 299–318). San Francisco: Jossey-Bass.

Harris, Ian, and Mary Lee Morrison. 2003. *Peace Education,* 2nd ed. Jefferson, NC: McFarland.

Heppner, Kevin. 2002. *"My gun was as tall as me": Child Soldiers in Burma.* New York: Human Rights Watch.

Herman, Judith. 1992. *Trauma and Recovery.* New York: Basic Books.

Hernandez-Hoyos, Diana. 1999. *Derecho Internacional Humanitario.* Bogota: Ediciones Juridicas Gustavon Ibanez.

Hoben, Susan J. 1989. *School, Work and Equity: Educational Reform in Rwanda.* African Research Studies No. 16. Boston: African Studies Center, Boston University.

Honwana, Alcinda. 1999a. "Non-western Concepts of Mental Health." In *The Refugee Experience, Vol. 1,* ed. M. Loughry and A. Ager (pp. 103–19). Oxford: Refugee Studies Programme.

———. 1999b. "Challenging Western Concepts of Trauma and Healing." *Track* 2 (8): 1. Available online at http://ccrweb.ccr.uct.ac.za/two/8_1/p30_collective_body.html.

hooks, bell. 1990. *Yearning: Race, Gender, and Cultural Politics.* Boston: South End Press.

Hosin, A., C. McClenahan, and E. Cairns. 1993. "The Impact of Political Violence in Northern Ireland on Children's Ideas about Their Country in 1980 and 1991."

Unpublished Paper. Coleraine, Northern Ireland: Centre for Study of Conflict, University of Ulster.

Hughes, Diane, and Kimberly DuMont. 1993. "Using Focus Groups to Facilitate Culturally Anchored Research." Special issue, *American Journal of Community Psychology* 21 (6): 775–806.

Human Rights Watch (HRW). 1994a. *Generation Under Fire: Children and Violence in Colombia.* New York: Human Rights Watch.

———. 1994b. *Easy Prey: Child Soldiers in Liberia.* New York: Human Rights Watch.

———. 1995. *Children of Sudan: Slaves, Street Children and Child Soldiers.* New York: Human Rights Watch.

———. 1998. *Sowing Terror: Atrocities Against Civilians in Sierra Leone.* New York: Human Rights Watch.

———. 2003. Introduction to *Rwanda's Lasting Wounds: Consequences of Genocide and War for Rwanda's Children.* New York: Human Rights Watch. Available online at http://www.hrw.org/reports/2003/rwanda0403/rwanda0403.htm.

Ilic, Vladimir. 2001. *"Otpor"–In or Beyond Politics.* Helsinki: Helsinki Committee for Human Rights in Serbia.

International Crisis Group (ICG). 2003. *Colombia's Humanitarian Crisis.* Brussels: ICG.

International Tribunal for Children's Rights. 2000. "Report from the First Hearings, Colchester, UK, April." Retrieved November 19, 2001, from http://www.ibcr. org/index_en.shtml.

IPCRI. 2003. "Analysis and Evaluation of the New Palestinian Curriculum." Report submitted to the USA Public Affairs Office, U.S. Consulate General, Jerusalem, March 2003.

IRIN (UN Office for the Coordination of Humanitarian Affairs). 2003. "Rwanda: US Official Pledges to Mobilise Resources in Fight against HIV/AIDS" December 3. Available online at http://www.plusnews.org/AIDSreport.asp? ReportID=2807andSelectRegion=Great_LakesandSelectCountry=RWANDA.

Ivic, I., and O. Perzic. 2002. "Yugoslavia: Divergent Tendencies–Centralization and Ethnification. In *Democracy in Textbooks and Student Minds,* ed. H. Daun. New York: Nova Science.

Jackson, Stevi, and Sue Scott. 2000. "Childhood." In *Social Divisions,* ed. Geoff Payne (pp. 152–84). New York: St Martin's.

Jagodic, G. K. 2000. "Is War a Good or a Bad Thing? The Attitudes of Croatian, Israeli and Palestinian Children Towards War." *International Journal of Psychology* 35 (6): 241–57.

Jarman, Neil. 2002. *Managing Disorder: Responding to Interface Violence in North Belfast.* Belfast: Research Branch, Office of First Minister and Deputy First Minister.

Jarman, Neil, and Chris O'Halloran. 2001. "Recreational Rioting: Young People, Interface Areas and Violence." *Child Care in Practice* 7 (1): 2–16.

Johnson, Alan. 1996. "'It's good to talk': The Focus Group and the Sociological Imagination." *Sociological Review* 44 (3): 517–39.

Jones, Lynne. 2000. "Adolescent Understandings of Political Violence and Their Relationship to Mental Health: A Qualitative Study of Bosnia-Herzegovina." Paper submitted to International Conference on War-Affected Children, Winnipeg, Canada, September 11–17. Retrieved November 19, 2001, from http://www.waraffectedchildren.gc.ca/socscimedpaper-e.asp.

Jung, Carl Gustav. 1969. *Archetypes and the Collective Unconscious: The Collected Works of C. G. Jung, Vol. 9, Pt. 1,* ed. William McGuire. Bollingen.

Kalshoven, Frits. 1995. "Child Soldiers: The Role of Children in Armed Conflicts." *American Journal of International Law* 89 (4): 849–52.

Kaplan, Robert D. 1994. "The Coming Anarchy." *Atlantic Monthly* (February): 44–76.

Keane, John. 1996. *Reflections on Violence.* London: Verso.

Keairns, Yvonne. 2003. *The Voices of Girl Child Soldiers–Colombia.* New York: Quaker United Nations Office.

Kelly, Paddy. 2000. Testimony to the First Hearings of the International Tribunal for Children's Rights, Colchester, UK, April 2000. Retrieved November 19, 2001, from http://www.ibcr.org/index_en.shtml.

Khayat, Abdullah. 1994. "A Problem for Palestine: Gaza's Birthrate Highest in Middle East." Washington Report on Middle East Affairs, January. Retrieved November 19, 2001, from http://www.washington-report.org/backissues/0194/9401035.htm.

Klare, Michael. 1999. "The Kalashnikov Age." *Bulletin of Atomic Scientists* 55 (1): 18–22.

Kolouh-Westin, L. 2002. "Bosnia and Herzegovina and Its Tripartite Education Systems." In *Democracy in Textbooks and Student Minds,* ed. H. Daun. New York: Nova Science.

Kolucki, B. 1993. *Circo da Paz.* New York: UNICEF.

Kosovar Youth Council. 2000. "Promoting Kosovar Adolescent/Youth Protection and Capacities: Youth Identified Problems and Solutions." Paper submitted to International Conference on War-Affected Children, Winnipeg, Canada, September 11–17. Retrieved November 19, 2001, from http://www.waraffectedchildren.gc.ca/kosovo-e.asp.

Kriesberg, L. 1998. *Constructive Conflicts: From Escalation to Resolution.* Lanham, MD: Rowman and Littlefield.

Kritz, Neil. J., ed. 1995. *Transitional Justice: How Emerging Democracies Reckon with Former Regimes.* Washington, DC: United States Institute for Peace Press.

Kumar, Chetan. 2000. Testimony to the First Hearings of the International Tribunal for Children's Rights, Colchester, UK, April 2000. Available online at http://www.ibcr.org/index_en.shtml.

Kundera, Milan. 1982. *The Joke.* Trans. Michael Henry Heim. New York: Harper and Row.

Kuperman, Alan J. 2001. *The Limits of Humanitarian Intervention: Genocide in Rwanda.* Washington, DC: Brookings Institution Press.

Lampe, J. R. 1996. *Yugoslavia as History: Twice There Was a Country.* New York: Cambridge University Press.

Lantieri, Linda, and Janet Patti. 1996. *Waging Peace in Our Schools.* Boston: Beacon.

Lasswell, Harold. [1972] 1990. *Politics: Who Gets What, When and How.* New York: Peter Smith.

Lederach, John Paul. 1995. "Conflict Transformation in Protracted Internal Conflicts: The Case for a Comprehensive Framework." In *Conflict Transformation,* ed. K. Rupesinghe (pp. 201–22). New York: St. Martin's Press.

———. 1996. *Preparing for Peace: Conflict Transformation across Cultures.* Syracuse, NY: Syracuse University Press.

———. 1997. *Building Peace: Sustainable Reconciliation in Divided Societies.* Washington, DC: United States Institute of Peace.

———. 1998. "Remember and Change." In *Transforming Violence: Linking Local and Global Peacemaking,* ed. Judy Zimmerman Herr and Robert Herr (pp. 177–89). Scottsdale, PA: Herald.

———. 2003. "The Horizon of Peacebuilding: The Strategic Challenges of Post Agreement Change." *Peace Colloquy* 3 (Summer). Available online at http://www.nd.edu/~krocinst/colloquy/issue%203/highlights_horizons.htm.

Lévinas, E. [1961] 1990. *Totalité et infini. Essai sur l'extériorité.* Den Haag; dt.: Totalität und Unendlichkeit. Versuch über Exteriorität. Freiburg: Alber. English trans. *Totality and Infinity: An Essay on Exteriority.* Pittsburgh: Duquesne University Press.

Liddell, C., J. Kemp, and M. Moema. 1993. "The Young Lions—South African Children and Youth in Political Struggle." In *The Psychological Effects of War and Violence on Children,* ed. L. Leavitt and N. Fox (pp. 199–214). Hillsdale, NJ: Lawrence Erlbaum.

Lovell, Erin, and E. Mark Cummings. 2001. "Conflict, Conflict Resolution and the Children of Northern Ireland: Towards Understanding the Impact on Children and Families." Joan B. Kroc Institute Working Papers Series, University of Notre Dame.

Lowicki, Jane, and Allison Pillsbury. 2000. "Recognizing War-affected Adolescents: Frameworks for Action." *Development* 43 (1): 73–84.

Luke, A. 1988. *Literacy, Booklet, and Ideology.* London: Falmer Press.

MacDonald, Margaret Read. 1992. *Peace Tales: World Folktales to Talk About.* North Haven, CT: Shoe String Press.

Mac Ginty, Roger. 2003. *What Our Politicians Should Know.* Retrieved June 10, 2004, from http://www.ark.ac.uk/publications/updates/update18.pdf.

Mach, Zdzislaw. 1993. *Symbols, Conflict, and Identity: Essays in Political Anthropology.* New York: State University of New York Press.

Machel, Graça. 1996. "Impact of Armed Conflict on Children." Report of the Expert of the Secretary-General, Ms. Graca Machel (Document A/51/306). United Nations: New York. Available online at http://www.unicef.org/graca/.

———. 2001. *The Impact of War on Children.* London: Hurst and Company.

MacManus, Sarah. 1996. *Young v. Old.* Boulder, CO: Westview.

Maier, K. 1998. "The Universal Soldier." *Yale Review* 86 (1): 70–93.

Malcolm, N. 1996. *Bosnia: A Short History.* Washington Square: New York University Press.

Malinowski, Bronislaw. 1922. *Argonauts of the Western Pacific.* London: G. Routledge and Sons.

Malkki, Liisa. 1995. *Purity and Exile: Violence, Memory and National Cosmology Among Hutu Refugees in Tanzania.* Chicago: University of Chicago Press.

Mamdani, Mahmood. 2000. "The Truth According to the TRC." In *The Politics of Memory: Truth, Healing and Social Justice,* ed. Ifi Amadiume and Abdullahi An-Na'im (pp. 176–83). London: Zed.

———. 2001. *When Victims Become Killers: Colonialism, Nativism, and the Genocide in Rwanda.* Princeton: Princeton University Press.

Manz, Beatriz. 1988. *Refugees of a Hidden War–The Aftermath of Counterinsurgency in Guatemala.* Albany: State University of New York Press.

Maoz, I. 2000a. "Power Relations in Inter-group Encounters: A Case Study of Jewish-Arab Encounters in Israel." *International Journal of Intercultural Relations* 24: 259–77.

———. 2000b. "Multiple Conflicts and Competing Agendas: A Framework for Conceptualizing Structured Encounters between Groups in Conflict: The Case of a Coexistence Project between Jews and Palestinians in Israel." *Journal of Peace Psychology* 6: 135–56.

———. 2000c. "An Experiment in Peace: Reconciliation-aimed Dialogues of Israeli and Palestinian Youth." *Journal of Peace Research* 37: 721–36.

———. Forthcoming. "Peace Building in Violent Conflict: Israeli-Palestinian Post Oslo People to People Activities." *International Journal of Politics, Culture and Society.*

———. 1999. "South Africa's Transition and the Emergence of New Roles and Identities." Paper written for NICVA Conference, June 24.

Marotta, Francesa. 2000. "The Blue Flame and the Gold Shield: Methodology, Challenges and Lessons Learned on Human Rights Training for Police." In *Peacebuilding and Police Reform,* ed. Tor Tanke Holm and Espen Barthe Eide (pp. 69–92). Portland, OR: Frank Cass.

Marsella, A., T. Bornemann, S. Ekblad, and J. Orley, eds. 1994. *Amidst Peril and Pain: The Mental Health and Well-being of the World's Refugees.* Washington, DC: American Psychological Association.

Maslen, S., and S. Islamshah. 2000. "Revolution Not Evolution: Protecting the Rights of Children in Armed Conflicts in the New Millennium." *Development* 43 (1): 28.

Maslow, Abraham H. 1987. *Motivation and Personality,* 3rd ed. New York: Harper-Collins Publishers

Matar, Haggai. 2004. Testimonial posted on Gush Shalom (Peace Bloc) Web site. Retrieved September 15, 2004, from www.gush-shalom.org/archives/haggai_eng.html.

Mazurana, D., S. McKay, K. Carlson, and J. Kasper. 2002. "Girls in Fighting Forces and Groups: Their Recruitment, Participation, Demobilization, and Reintegration." *Peace and Conflict: Journal of Peace Psychology* 8 (2): 99–123.

McBeth, John. 2002. "Children of War." *Far Eastern Economic Review* 165 (17): 44–45.

McCallin, M. 1998. "Community Involvement in the Social Reintegration of Child Soldiers." In *Rethinking the Trauma of War,* ed. P. Bracken and C. Petty. London: Free Association.

McKay, Susan, and Dyan Mazurana. 2000. "Girls in Militaries, Paramilitaries, and Armed Opposition Groups." *Selected Proceedings from the International Conference on War-Affected Children.* Ottawa: UNICEF and Department of Foreign Affairs and International Trade.

McClenahan, C., and E. Cairns. 1993. "Children's Values in Northern Ireland: 1980–1990." Unpublished paper. Centre for Study of Conflict, University of Ulster, Coleraine.

McEvoy, Siobhán. 2000. "Communities and Peace: Young Catholics in Northern Ireland." *Journal of Peace Research* 37 (1): 89–96.

——. 2001a. "Youth, Violence and Conflict Transformation." *Peace Review: A Transnational Quarterly* 13 (1): 89–96.

——. 2001b. "Youth as Social and Political Agents: Issues in Post-Settlement Peace Building." Occasional Paper no. 21, Joan B. Kroc Institute for International Peace, University of Notre Dame.

McKay, Susan. 2000. *Northern Protestants: An Unsettled People.* Belfast: Blackstaff Press.

McKay, Susan, and Dyan Mazurana. 2000. "Girls in Militaries, Paramilitaries, and Armed Opposition Groups." Paper submitted to International Conference on War-Affected Children, Winnipeg, Canada, September 11–17. Available online at http://www.waraffectedchildren.gc.ca/girls-e.asp.

McKernan, J. 1980. "Pupil Values as Indicators of Intergroup Differences in Northern Ireland." In *A Society under Stress: Children and Young People in Northern Ireland,* ed. J. Harbinson and J. Harbinson (pp. 128–40). London: Open Books.

McLernon, F. 1998. "Northern Irish Children's Understanding of Peace, War and Strategies to Attain Peace." PhD diss., University of Ulster at Coleraine.

McLernon, F., and E. Cairns. 1999. "Children, Peace and War in Northern Ireland." In *How Children Understand War and Peace: A Call for International Peace Education,* ed. A. Raviv, L. Oppenheimer, and D. Bar-Tal (pp. 145–60). San Francisco: Jossey-Bass.

——. 2001. "The Impact of Political Violence on Images of War and Peace in the Drawings of Primary School Children." *Peace and Conflict: Journal of Peace Psychology* 7 (1): 45–57.

McLernon, F., N. Ferguson, and E. Cairns. 1997. "Comparison of Northern Irish Children's Attitudes to War and Peace before and after the Paramilitary Ceasefires." *International Journal of Behavioral Development* 20 (4): 715–30.

McLernon, F., R. Smith, and E. Cairns. 2002. "Concepts of Peace in the Poems of Northern Irish Schoolchildren." Unpublished manuscript. University of Ulster, Coleraine.

McWhirter, L. 1982. "Northern Irish Children's Conceptions of Violent Crime." *Howard Journal* 21: 167–77.

——. 1990. "How Do Children Cope with the Chronic Troubles in Northern Ireland." Paper presented at the conference Children and War, Jerusalem.

Mees, Ludger. 2000. "Basque Peace Process." In *The Management of Peace Processes,* ed. John Darby and Roger Mac Ginty (pp. 154–94). London: MacMillan/St. Martins.

Menkhaus, Ken. 1999. "Children of War." *New Routes* 4 (4): 4–7.

Mertus, Julie. 1999. *Kosovo: How Myths and Truths Started a War.* Berkeley: University of California Press.

Miall, Hugh, Oliver Ramsbotham, and Tom Woodhouse. 1999. *Contemporary Conflict Resolution: The Prevention, Management and Transformation of Deadly Conflicts.* Cambridge: Polity Press.

Millard, Ananda. 2001. "Children in Armed Conflict: Transcending Legal Responses." *Security Dialogue* 32 (2): 187–200.

Millett, Kate. 1994. *The Politics of Cruelty.* New York: W.W. Norton.

Minnow, Martha. 1998. *Between Vengeance and Forgiveness: Facing History after Genocide and Mass Violence.* Boston: Beacon Press.

Mitchell, C. R. 1981. *The Structure of International Conflict.* New York: St. Martin's Press.

Montell, F. B. 1995. "Focus Group Interviews: A New Feminist Method." Paper presented at the Annual Meeting of the American Sociological Association, Washington DC.

Montessori, Maria. 1972. *Education and Peace.* Chicago: Regency.

Montville, J. V. 1993. "The Healing Function of Political Conflict Resolution." In *Conflict Resolution Theory and Practice: Integration and Application,* ed. D. J. D. Sandole and H. Van der Merwe (pp. 112–27). Manchester: Manchester University Press.

Morgan, David L. 1996. "Focus Groups." *Annual Review of Sociology* 22: 129–52.

Morgan, David L., and Richard A. Krueger, eds. 1993. *Successful Focus Groups: Advancing the State of the Art.* London: Sage.

"Mozambique's Lost Generation" 1992. *World Press Review* 39 (11): 27.

Murison, Katharine, ed. 2003. *Africa South of the Sahara 2003.* London and New York: Europa Publications.

Myerhoff, Barbara. 1992. *Remembered Lives: The Work of Ritual, Storytelling and Growing Older.* Athens: University of Georgia Press.

National Poverty Reduction Programme and Ministry of Local Government and Social Affairs, Republic of Rwanda. n.d. *Ubudehe mu Kurwanya Ubukene: Ubudehe to Fight Poverty.* Available online at http://www.worldbank.org/wbi/attacking-poverty/programs/rwanda-nprp.pdf.

Nave, E., and E. Yogev. 2002. *Histories: Towards a Dialogue with Yesterday* [in Hebrew]. Tel-Aviv: Bavel.

NGO Consortium for the Care and Protection of Children in Emergencies (CCF International/Child Fund Afghanistan, International Rescue Committee, and Save the Children Federation). 2002. *The Situation of Children in Afghanistan, 2002: A Collaborative Assessment Report.* NGO Consortium.

Nichols-Casebolt, A., and P. Spakes. 1995. "Policy Research and the Voices of Women." *Social Work Research* 19: 49–55.

Nordstrom, Carolyn. 1997. *A Different Kind of War Story.* Philadelphia: University of Pennsylvania Press.

Northern Ireland Statistics and Research Agency (NISRA). 1998. *Annual Abstract of Statistics* 16. Belfast: NISRA.

Northrup, Terrell. 1989. "The Dynamic of Identity in Personal and Social Conflicts." In *Intractable Conflicts and Their Transformation,* ed. Louis Kriesberg, Stuart Thorson, and Terrell Northrup (pp. 55–82). Syracuse, NY: Syracuse University Press.

Notter, J. 1995. *Trust and Conflict Transformation.* Washington, DC: Institute for Multi-Track Diplomacy.

Ofcansky, Thomas. 2003. "Rwanda: Recent History." In *Africa South of the Sahara 2003,* ed. Katharine Murison. London and New York: Europa Publications.

Optow, S. 2001. "Moral Inclusion and the Process of Social Reconciliation." *Social Justice Research* 14 (2): 149–70.

Oppenheimer, L. 1996. "War as an Institution, but What about Peace? Developmental Perspectives." *International Journal of Behavioural Development* 19 (1): 201–18.

Ornauer, H. et al., eds. 1976. *Images of the World in the Year 2000.* Paris and New York: Mouton and Humanities Press.

Osorio, Flor Edilma, and Fabio Lozano. 1995. *Desplazamiento Rural: Violencia y Pobres.* Bogota: Consejeria Presidencial de Derechos Humanos.

Ould-Abdallah, Ahmedou. 2000. *Burundi on the Brink, 1993–95: A UN Special Envoy Reflects on Preventive Diplomacy.* Washington, DC: United States Institute of Peace Press.

Paez, Erika. 2003. "Child Soldiers in Colombia, South America." *Enabling Education Network* (7): 1–2.

Pearn, J. 2003. "Children and War." *Journal of Pediatrics and Child Health* 39 (3): 166.

Pecaut, Daniel. 2001. *Guerra contra la sociedad.* Bogota: Espasa e Hoy.

Peters, K., and P. Richards. 1998. "Why We Fight: Voices of Youth Combatants in Sierra Leone." *Africa* 8 (2): 183–210.

Peterson, Scott. 2000. *Me Against My Brother: At War in Somalia, Sudan, and Rwanda: A Journalist Reports from the Battlefields of Africa.* New York: Routledge.

Pinnock, Patricia. 2000. *Skyline.* Cape Town: David Philip.

Pinson, M. 1994. *The Muslims of Bosnia-Herzegovina: Their Historic Development from the Middle Ages to the Dissolution of Yugoslavia.* Cambridge, MA: Distributed for the Center for Middle Eastern Studies of Harvard University by Harvard University Press.

Porter, Elizabeth. 1998. "Identity, Location, Plurality: Women, Nationalism and Northern Ireland." In *Women, Ethnicity and Nationalism: The Politics of Transition,* ed. Rick Wilford and Robert L. Miller (pp. 36–61). London: Routledge.

Profamilia. 2001. *Salud Sexual y Reproductiva en Zonas Marginales, Situacion de las Mujeres Desplazadas.* Bogota: Profamilia.

Prunier, Gérard. 1995. *The Rwanda Crisis: History of a Genocide.* New York: Columbia University Press.

Punamaki, R. L. 1987. *Childhood under Conflict: The Attitudes and Emotional Life of Israeli and Palestinian Children.* Research Report No. 32. Finland: Tamere Peace Research Institute.

Quzmar, Khaled. 2000. Testimony to the First Hearings of the International Tribunal for Children's Rights, Colchester, UK, April. Retrieved November 19, 2001, from http://www.ibcr.org/index_en.shtml.

Raheja, Gloria Goodwin, and Ann Grodzins Gold. 1994. *Listen to the Heron's Words: Reimagining Gender and Kinship in North India.* Berkeley: University of California Press.

Rakita, Sara. 1999. *Forgotten Children of War: Sierra Leonean Refugee Children in Guinea.* New York: Human Rights Watch.

Rakodi, Carole. 1997. Introduction to *The Urban Challenge in Africa: Growth and Management of Its Large Cities,* ed. C. Rakodi. New York: United Nations University Press.

Ramgoolie, Monique. 2001. "Prosecution of Sierra Leone's Child Soldiers: What Message Is the UN Trying to Send?" *Journal of Public Affairs* 12 (Spring): 145–62.

Ramirez, Maria Clemencia. 2001. *Entre el estado y la guerrilla: Identidad y ciudadania en el movimiento de los campesinos cocaleros del Putumayo.* Bogota: Instituto Colombiano de Antropologia e Historia.

Rashied, Ahmed. 2000. *Taliban: Militant Islam, Oil and Fundamentalism in Central Asia.* New Haven, CT: Yale University Press/Nota Bene.

Raviv, R., Louis Oppenheimer, and Daniel Bar-Tal, eds. 1999. *How Children Understand War and Peace: A Call for International Peace Education.* San Francisco: Jossey-Bass.

Raymond, Alan, and Susan Raymond. 2000. *Children in War.* New York: TV Books.

Reardon, Betty Ann. 1993. *Women and Peace.* Albany: State University of New York Press.

Reitan, Ruth. 2000. "Strategic Nonviolent Conflict in Kosovo." *Peace and Change* 25 (1): 71–101.

Reychler, Luc. 2001. "Conceptual Framework." In *Peacebuilding: A Field Guide,* ed. Luc Reychler and Thania Paffenholz (pp. 3–15). Boulder, CO: Lynne Rienner.

Reychler, Luc, and Thania Paffenholz. 2001. *Peacebuilding: A Field Guide.* Boulder, CO: Lynne Rienner.

Richards, Paul. 1996. *Fighting for the Rain Forest: War, Youth and Resources in Sierra Leone.* Oxford: James Currey.

———. 2002. "Militia Conscription in Sierra Leone: Recruitment of Young Fighters in an African War." In *The Comparative Study of Conscription in the Armed Forces,* ed. L. Mjoset and S. Van Holde (pp. 255–76). Comparative Social Research, vol. 20. Amsterdam: Elsevier.

Rigby, Andrew. 2001. *Justice and Reconciliation: After the Violence.* Boulder, CO: Lynne Rienner.

Roldan, Mary. 2002. *Blood and Fire–La Violencia in Antioquia.* Durham, NC: Duke University Press.

Rone, Jemera. 1994. *The Lost Boys: Child Soldiers and Unaccompanied Boys in Southern Sudan.* New York: Human Rights Watch.

Ronen, D. 1995. "Ethnic Conflict and Self-Rule: On a New Approach to the Study of Conflict Transformation." In *Conflict Transformation,* ed. K. Rupesinghe. New York: St. Martin's Press.

Rose, R. 1976. *Northern Ireland: A Time for Choice.* London: MacMillan.

Rothstein, R. L. 1999. *After the Peace: Resistance and Reconciliation.* Boulder, CO: Lynne Rienner.

Roy, Sara. 2001. "Decline and Disfigurement: The Palestinian Economy after Olso." In *The New Intifada: Resisting Israel's Apartheid,* ed. Roane Carey (pp. 91–105). New York: Verso.

Rupesinghe, K. 1995. *Conflict Transformation.* New York: St. Martin's Press.

Ryan, Pat. 1995. *Storytelling in Ireland: A Re-awakening.* Londonderry: Verbal Arts Centre.

Sachs, Aaron. 1993. "AIDS Orphans: Africa's Lost Generation." *World Watch* 6 (5): 10.

Said, Edward. 2001. "Palestinians Under Seige." In *The New Intifada: Resisting Israel's Apartheid,* ed. Roane Carey (pp. 27–42). New York: Verso.

Salem, Richard, ed. 2000. *Witness to Genocide: The Children of Rwanda.* New York: Friendship Press.

Salomon, Gavriel. 2004. "Does Peace Education Make a Difference in the Context of an Intractable Conflict?" *Peace and Conflict: Journal of Peace Psychology* 10 (3): 257–274.

Samary, C. 1995. *Yugoslavia Dismembered.* New York: Monthly Review Press.

Sanford, Victoria. 2003a. *Buried Secrets: Truth and Human Rights in Guatemala.* London: Palgrave Macmillan.

——. 2003b. *Violencia y Genocidio en Guatemala.* Guatemala City: FandG Editores.

——. 2003c. "Peacebuilding in the War Zone: The Case of Colombian Peace Communities." *International Journal of Peacekeeping* 10 (2).

——. 2004. *Mothers, Widows and Guerrilleras: Anonymous Conversations with Survivors of State Terror.* Uppsala: Peace and Life Institute.

Scheper-Hughes, Nancy. 1995. "Who's the killer? Popular Justice and Human Rights and in a South African Squatter Camp." *Social Justice* 22 (3): 143–64.

Scheub, Harold. 1996. *The Tongue Is Fire: South African Storytellers and Apartheid.* Madison: University of Wisconsin Press.

Schwerin, Edward. 1995. *Mediation, Citizen Empowerment, and Transformational Politics.* Westport, CT: Praeger.

Scott, James C. 1990. *Domination and the Arts of Resistance: Hidden Transcripts.* New Haven, CT: Yale University Press.

Senehi, Jessica. 1996. "Storytelling and Conflict—A Matter of Life and Death." *Mind and Human Interaction* 7 (3): 150–64.

——. 2000. "Constructive Storytelling: Building Community, Building Peace." PhD diss., Syracuse University.

——. 2003. "Constructive Storytelling: A Peace Process." *Peace and Conflict Studies* 9 (2): 41–63.

Sherif, M., O. Harvey, B. White, W. Hood, and C. Sherif. 1961. *Intergroup Cooperation and Competition: The Robbers Cave Experiment.* Norman, OK: University Book Exchange.

Shirlow, Peter. 2002. "The Geography and Politics of Fear in Belfast." Lecture presented to Royal Geographic Society in Belfast, January 4.

Shor, Ira. 1996. *When Students Have Power: Negotiating Authority in a Critical Pedagogy.* Chicago: University of Chicago Press.

Simms, Laura. 2002. *Stories to Nourish Our Children in a Time of Crisis.* Tampa, FL: Holland and Knight Charitable Fund.

Skinner, Elliott. 1999. "Child Soldiers in Africa: A Disaster for Future Families." *International Journal on World Peace* 16 (2): 7–22.

Slye, Ronald C. 2000. "Amnesty, Truth, and Reconciliation: Reflections on the South African Amnesty Process." In *Truth v. Justice: The Morality of Truth Commissions,* ed. Robert I. Rotberg and Dennis Thompson (pp. 170–88). Princeton, NJ: Princeton University Press.

Smillie, I., and L. Gberie 2000. "Diamonds, Children and the Political Economy of Conflict: The Experience of Sierra Leone." Background paper for the International Conference on War-Affected Children, Winnipeg, September.

Smith, Alan, and Tony Vaux. 2003. "Education, Conflict and International Development." UK Department for International Development.

Smith, Anthony. 1986. *The Ethnic Origins of Nations.* Oxford: Basil Blackwell.

Somasundaram, Daya. 2002. "Child Soldiers: Understanding the Context." *British Medical Journal* 324 (73): 1268–72.

Sommers, Marc. 2001a. *Fear in Bongoland: Burundi Refugees in Urban Tanzania.* Refugee and Forced Migration Studies, vol. 8. New York and Oxford: Berghahn Books.

——. 2001b. "Young, Male and Pentecostal: Urban Refugees in Dar es Salaam, Tanzania." *Journal of Refugee Studies* 14 (4): 1–24.

——. 2002. "Children, Education and War: Reaching Education for All (EFA) Objectives in Countries Affected by Conflict." Working Paper 1, World Bank Conflict Prevention and Reconstruction Unit.

——. 2003. *Urbanization, War, and Africa's Youth at Risk: Towards Understanding and Addressing Future Challenges.* Washington, DC: Basic Education and Support Policy (BEPS) Activity, U.S. Agency for International Support.

Sommers, Marc, and Liz McClintock. 2003. "On Hidden Ground: One Coexistence Strategy in Central Africa." In *Imagine Coexistence: Restoring Humanity after Violent Ethnic Conflict,* ed. Antonia Chayes and Martha Minow (pp. 35–41). San Francisco: Jossey-Bass.

Spencer, D., and W. Spencer. 1995. "Third-Party Mediation and Conflict Transformation: Experiences in Ethiopia, Sudan, and Liberia." In *Conflict Transformation,* ed. K. Rupesinghe (pp. 162–200). New York: St. Martin's Press.

Spergel, Irving A. 1995. *The Youth Gang Problem: A Community Approach.* New York: Oxford University Press.

Spielmann, M. 1986. "If Peace Comes: Future Expectations of Israeli Children and Youth." *Journal of Peace Research* 23 (1): 51–67.

Spivak, Gayatri. 1988. "Can the Subaltern Speak?" In *Marxism and the Interpretation of Culture,* ed. Carl Nelson and Lawrence Grossberg (pp. 271–313). Urbana: University of Illinois Press.

Staub, Ervin. 1989. *Roots of Evil.* New York: Cambridge University Press.

Stedman, Stephen. 1997. "Spoiler Problems in Peace Processes." *International Security* 22 (2): 5–53.

Stedman, Stephen John, Donald Rothchild, and Elizabeth M. Cousens, eds. 2002. *Ending Civil Wars: The Implementation of Peace Agreements.* Boulder, CO: Lynne Rienner.

Steinberg, S., and D. Bar-On. 2002. "An Analysis of the Group Process in Encounters between Jews and Palestinians Using a Typology for Discourse Classification." *International Journal of Intercultural Relations* 26: 199–214.

Stephenson, Jonathan. 1996–97. "Northern Ireland: Treating Terrorists as Statesmen." *Foreign Policy* (Winter): 125–41.

Straker, Gillian, with Fatima Moosa, Rise Becker, and Madiyoyo Nkwale. 1992. *Faces in the Revolution: The Psychological Effect of Violence on Township Youth in South Africa.* Athens: Ohio University Press.

Sultan, Abubacar. 2000. "Testimony." In *The Protection of War-Affected Children: Securing Children's Rights in the Context of Armed Conflict.* Report of the First Hearings of the International Tribunal for Children's Rights, Colchester, UK, April 3–6. Retrieved March 2004 from http://www.ibcr.org/.

Summerfield, D. 1999. "The Nature of Conflict and the Implications for Appropriate Psychosocial Responses." In *The Refugee Experience, Vol. 1,* ed. M. Loughry and A. Ager. Oxford: Refugee Studies Programme. Available online at http://earlybird.qeh.ox.ac.uk/rfgexp/rsp_tre/student/natconf/toc.htm.

Svirsky, Gila. 2001. "The Israeli Peace Movement Since the Al-Aqsa Intifada." In *The New Intifada: Resisting Israel's Apartheid,* ed. Roane Carey (pp. 323–30). New York: Verso.

Tassara, Carlos, Dalia Maria Jimenez Castrillon, and Luigi Grando et al., eds. 1999. *El desplazamiento por la violencia en Colombia.* Bogota: UNHCR.

Tawil, S., A. Harley, and L. Porteous. 2003. *Curriculum Change and Social Cohesion in Conflict-Affected Societies.* Geneva: UNESCO.

Thompson, Carol. 1999. "Beyond Civil Society: Child Soldiers as Citizens in Mozambique." *Review of African Political Economy* 26 (80): 191–206.

Tolley, H. 1973. *Children and War: Political Socialisation to International Conflict.* New York: Teachers College Press.

Tonkin, Elizabeth. 1992. *Narrating Our Pasts: The Social Construction of Oral History.* Cambridge: Cambridge University Press.

Torrey, Barbara Boyle. 1998. "We Need More Research on the Impact of Rapid Urban Growth." *Chronicle of Higher Education* (October 23): B6.

Udovicki, J., and J. Ridgeway. 1995. *Yugoslavia's Ethnic Nightmare: The Inside Story of Europe's Unfolding Ordeal.* New York: Lawrence Hill Books.

UNESCO. 1995. *UNESCO and a Culture of Peace.* Paris: UNESCO Publishing.

UNICEF. 1995. *The State of the World's Children 1995.* Oxford: Oxford University Press.

——. 1996. *The State of the World's Children 1996.* Oxford: Oxford University Press.

——. 2002. *State of the World's Children 2002.* New York: UNICEF.

UNICEF and Partner INGOs. 2003. "Key Issues Emerging from Inter-Agency Child Protection Assessment." Advocacy Points. Unpublished.

UNICEF statistics. 2002. Available online at http://www.unicef.org/statistics/index-countrystats.html.

United Nations. 2000. Statistics on Youth. Retrieved June 24, 2002, from http://www.un.org/esa/socdev/unyin/wywatch/country.htm.

United Nations Development Program (UNDP). 2001. *Human Development Report 2001: Making New Technologies Work for Human Development.* New York and Oxford: Oxford University Press.

United Nations Development Program and International Council on National Youth Policy. 2003. Government of Rwanda National Youth Policy: Youth Policy in Rwanda. Available online at http://www.ceasurf.org/icnyp/rwanda.doc.

United States Institute of Peace (USIP). 2000. "Strategic Nonviolent Action Key to Serbia's Revolution." *Peace Watch* 7 (1): 1–3.

Unsworth, Sue, and Peter Uvin. 2002. "A New Look at Civil Society Support in Rwanda?" Unpublished paper.

Urban, Greg. 1991. *A Discourse-Centered Approach to Culture: Native South American Myths and Rituals.* Austin: University of Texas Press.

——. 1996. *Metaphysical Community.* Austin: University of Texas Press.

Uvin, Peter. 1998. *Aiding Violence: The Development Enterprise in Rwanda.* West Hartford, CT: Kumarian Press.

Van der Merwe, H. W. 1989. *Pursuing Justice and Peace in South Africa.* London: Routledge.

van Eden, Karen. n.d. "Synergy for a New System in South Africa." Retrieved November 19, 2001, from http://www.uct.ac.za/depts/criminology/articles/trad1.htm.

Vayrynen, R. 1991. "To Settle or to Transform? Perspectives on the Resolution of National and International Conflicts." In *New Directions in Conflict Theory: Conflict*

Resolution and Conflict Transformation, ed. R. Vayrynen (pp. 1–25). London: Sage.

Vayrynen, Raimo, ed. 1991. *New Directions in Conflict Theory: Conflict Resolution and Conflict Transformation.* London: Sage.

Volkan, Vamik D. 1988. *The Need to Have Enemies and Allies: From Clinical Practice to International Relationships.* Northvale, NJ: J. Aronson.

———. 1997. *Bloodlines: From Ethnic Pride to Ethnic Terrorism.* New York: Farrar, Straus and Giroux.

Volkan, Vamik D., and D. A. Julius et al. 1990. *The Psychodynamics of International Relationships.* Lexington, MA: Lexington Books.

Von Arnim, Gabriele, ed. 2000. *Yearbook of Human Rights, 2000.* Frankfurt: Suhrkamp Taschenbuch.

Wallach, John. 2000. *The Enemy Has a Face: The Seeds of Peace Experience.* Washington, DC: United States Institute of Peace.

Wallensteen, P. 1991. "The Resolution and Transformation of International Conflicts: A Structural Perspective." In *New Directions in Conflict Theory: Conflict Resolution and Conflict Transformation,* ed. Raimo Vayrynen (pp. 129–54). London: Sage.

Waller, David. 1996. *Rwanda: Which Way Now?* UK and Ireland: Oxfam UK and Ireland.

Weis, A., and A. Nazarenko. 1998. *Strategies and Needs of NGO's: Dealing with Ethno-Political Conflicts in the New Eastern Democracies.* Berlin: Berghof Research Center for Constructive Conflict.

Wessells, Michael G. 1997. "Child Soldiers." *Bulletin of the Atomic Scientists* 53 (6): 32–39.

———. 1998. "Children, Armed Conflict, and Peace." *Journal of Peace Research* 35 (5): 635–46.

———. 1999. "Culture, Power, and Community: Intercultural Approaches to Psychosocial Assistance and Healing." In *Honoring Differences: Cultural Issues in the Treatment of Trauma and Loss,* ed. K. Nader, N. Dubrow, and B. Stamm (pp. 276–82). New York: Taylor and Francis.

———. 2000. "How We Can Prevent Child Soldiering." *Peace Review: A Transnational Quarterly* 12 (3): 407–13.

———. 2002. "Recruitment of Children as Soldiers in Sub-Saharan Africa: An Ecological Analysis." In *The Comparative Study of Conscription in the Armed Forces,* ed. L. Mjoset and S. Van Holde (pp. 237–55). Comparative Social Research, Vol. 20. Amsterdam: Elsevier.

Wessells, Michael G., and C. Monteiro. 2001. "Psychosocial Interventions and Postwar Reconstruction in Angola: Interweaving Western and Traditional Approaches." In *Peace, Conflict, and Violence: Peace Psychology for the 21st Century,* ed. D. Christie, R. V. Wagner, and D. Winter (pp. 262–75). Upper Saddle River, NJ: Prentice-Hall.

West, Harry. 2000. "Girls with Guns: Narrating the Experience of War of FRELIMO's 'Female Detachment,'" *Anthropological Quarterly* 73 (4): 180.

Winnipeg Agenda for War-Affected Children. 2000. Home page. Retrieved November 19, 2001, from http://www.waraffectedchildren.gc.ca/Final_Agenda-e.asp.

Women's Commission for Refugee Women and Children (WCRWC). 2002. *Unseen Millions: The Catastrophe of Internal Displacement in Colombia–Children and Adolescents At-Risk.* New York: WCRWC.

Yin, R. K. 1982. "Studying the Implementation of Public Programs." In *Studying Implementation: Methodological and Administrative Issues,* ed. W. Williams (pp. 36–72). Chatham, NJ: Chatham House.

Young, Wendy. 2002. "The Protection of Refugee Women and Children." *Refugees* (Winter/Spring): 37–44.

Youth at the United Nations. 2002. Country Profiles on the Situation of Youth: Rwanda: Statistics on Youth Educational Indicators. Available online at http://esa.un.org/socdev/unyin/country3b.asp?countrycode=rw.

Yuval-Davis, Nira, and Flora Anthias. 1989. *Women-Nation-State.* Basingstoke: Macmillan.

Zack-Williams, A. B. 2001. "Child Soldiers in the Civil War in Sierra Leone." *Review of African Political Economy* 28 (87): 73–82.

Zartman, William I., and J. Lewis Rasmussen, eds. 1997. *Peacemaking in International Conflict: Methods and Techniques.* Washington, DC: United States Institute of Peace Press.

Zinoviev, Alexandre. 1999. *La Grande Rupture: Sociologies d'un Monde Boulversé* [The Great Rupture: Sociology of a World Turned Upside Down: Where is the New World Order Headed?]. Lausanne: L'Age d'Homme.

Zipes, Jack, ed. and trans. 1989. *Fairy Tales and Fables from the Weimar Days.* Hanover, NH: University Press of New England.

Ziv, A., A. W. Kruglanski, and S. Schulman. 1974. "Children's Psychological Reactions to Wartime Stress." *Journal of Personality and Social Psychology* 30: 24–30.

About the Contributors

SAMI ADWAN is associate professor of education at Bethlehem University, Palestine National Authority. He has published widely on the role of education in peace building and is co-author (with Daniel Bar-On) of *The Role of Non-Government Organizations in Peacebuilding Between Palestinians and Israelis* (PRIME, 2000). With Dan Bar-On he is co-director of the Peace Research Institute in the Middle East (PRIME), and in 2005, along with Dan Bar-On, he was awarded the IIE Goldberg Prize for Peace in the Middle East.

DAN BAR-ON is a professor at the Ben Gurion University in Israel. He has numerous publications, including a pioneering study of the children of Holocaust perpetrators entitled *Legacy of Silence: Encounters with Children of the Third Reich* (Harvard University Press, 1989) and is co-author (with Sami Adwan) of *Victimhood and Beyond* (PRIME, 2001). With Sami Adwan he is co-director of the Peace Research Institute in the Middle East (PRIME), and in 2005, along with Sami Adwan, he was awarded the IIE Goldberg Prize for Peace in the Middle East.

SEAN BYRNE is professor and director of the Arthur V. Mauro Centre for Peace and Justice at St. Paul's College, University of Manitoba, Canada. Previously, he was director of the doctoral program in the Department of Conflict Analysis and Resolution at Nova Southeastern University, Ft. Lauderdale. Byrne has many publications in the areas of third-party intervention, ethnic conflict analysis and resolution, and children and conflict. His books include *Growing Up in a Divided Society: The Influence of Conflict on Belfast Schoolchildren* (Associated University Press, 1997), and with Cynthia Irvin, *Reconcilable Differences: Turning Points in Ethnopolitical Conflicts* (Kumarian Press, 2000). With Cynthia Irvin, he has received research grants from the United States Institute for Peace and the Social Science and Humanities Research Council (SSHRC) to explore the role of economic assistance in building the peace dividend in Northern Ireland.

ED CAIRNS is professor of psychology in the School of Psychology at the University of Ulster in Coleraine. He has spent the last thirty years studying the psychological aspects of political violence in relation to the conflict in Northern Ireland. During this time he has been a visiting scholar at the Universities of

Florida, Cape Town, and Melbourne. He is a Fellow of the British Psychological Society and past president of the Division of Peace Psychology of the American Psychological Association. His most recent book (edited with Michael Roe in 2003) is *The Role of Memory in Ethnic Conflict,* published by Palgrave Macmillan.

JACO CILLIERS is deputy regional director for Catholic Relief Services in southern Africa. He has lived and worked in numerous conflict societies. His research focuses on post-conflict peace building in divided societies. His publications include "Building Bridges for Interfaith Dialogue" in *Interfaith Dialogue and Peacebuilding,* ed. D. R. Smock (United States Institute of Peace Press, 2002) and "Organizing Conflict Resolution Interventions in Situations of Rapid Change" in *Theory and Practice in Ethnic Conflict Management: Conceptualizing Successes and Failure,* ed. M. H. Ros and J. Rothman (Macmillan, 1999).

JOHAN GALTUNG is professor of peace studies and founder and co-director of TRANSCEND: A Peace and Development Network, Norway. He has written numerous publications, including *Conflict Resolution by Peaceful Means (The TRANSCEND Method)* (United Nations, 2000).

ILSE HAKVOORT is a professor in the Department of Education at Goteborg University, Sweden. She has been co-coordinator of the Cross-cultural Research Program on Children and Peace since its establishment in 1996. Her research interests focus on the development of children's conceptualization of peace and war, learning and development in different sociocultural contexts, peace education, and storytelling. She teaches courses on communication and conflict resolution.

JEFFREY W. HELSING is a program officer in the United States Institute of Peace's Education Program, where he is responsible for many of the institute's faculty and teacher workshops and develops teaching curricula on international conflict analysis and management. Helsing has written "The American Shadow: United States Foreign Policy in the Middle East," in *The International Relations of the Middle East in the 21st Century: Patterns of Continuity and Change,* and recently completed a chapter on "Regionalization, Internationalization, and Perpetuation of Conflict in the Middle East" for a book entitled *The Internationalization of Ethnic Conflict.* Helsing is currently co-editing, with Julie Mertus of American University, *Human Rights and Conflict: New Actors, Strategies and Ethical Dilemmas,* a book on the relationship between human rights, peace, and conflict to be published by the United States Institute of Peace Press. In addition, Helsing is the author of *Johnson's War/Johnson's Great Society: The Guns and Butter Trap.*

DAVIDSON JONAH is a field-based emergency team leader and child protection specialist with the Christian Children's Fund and has worked recently in Chad, Sudan, Sierra Leone, and Indonesia. For over a decade, he served as National Director of CCF/Sierra Leone, and he has also served as chair of the national child protection committee.

SIOBHÁN MCEVOY-LEVY is assistant professor of political science at Butler University in Indianapolis, Indiana, where she teaches courses on Peace and Conflict Studies, U.S. Foreign Policy, Political Communication, and Children and Youth, and where she coordinates an undergraduate minor program in Peace Studies. She is the author of *American Exceptionalism and US Foreign Policy* (Palgrave, 2001). Since 2001 McEvoy-Levy has published a number of articles and book chapters on war-affected children and youth, peace processes, and post-conflict peace building. Between 2002 and 2003 she was co-director of the Research Initiative on the Resolution of Ethnic Conflict (RIREC) Project of the Joan B. Kroc Institute for International Peace Studies at the University of Notre Dame. McEvoy-Levy's current research projects are on youth narratives, children born of wartime rape, and post-conflict education.

FRANCES MCLERNON is a lecturer in social and abnormal psychology at the University of Ulster in Northern Ireland. Her PhD research was based on Northern Irish children's attitudes toward war and peace before and after the paramilitary ceasefires, and it was published in the *International Journal of Behavioral Development* in 1997. Her more recent work, carried out in the Centre for the Study of Conflict at University of Ulster, Coleraine, involved a three-year research project investigating the role of intergroup contact in the processes of forgiveness and reconciliation in Northern Ireland.

WENDY MOORE is a graduate in psychology from the University of Ulster. She is now a doctoral student in the UNESCO Centre at the University of Ulster where she is researching the role of forgiveness and reconciliation in education.

CAROLYN NORDSTROM is professor of anthropology at the University of Notre Dame and fellow of the Kellogg Institute. She has undertaken extensive field research on the front lines of wars in many regions around the world, including southern Africa, southeast Asia, and central Europe. Her recent publications include *Shadows of War: Violence, Power and International Profiteering in the 21st Century* (University of California Press 2004), *A Different Kind of War Story* (University of Pennsylvania Press, 1997), and *Fieldwork Under Fire,* coedited with

Antonius Robben (University of California Press, 1995). Her work has been funded by the Macarthur Foundation and John Simon Guggenheim Foundation.

VICTORIA SANFORD is assistant professor of anthropology at Lehman College/ City University of New York and senior research fellow at the Institute on Violence and Survival, Virginia Foundation for the Humanities. She is the author of *Buried Secrets: Truth and Human Rights in Guatemala* (Palgrave Macmillan, 2003) and *Violencia y Genocidio en Guatemala* (FyG Editores, 2003). She has just completed *La Masacre de Panzos: Etnicidad, tierra y violencia en Guatemala* (FyG Editores) and *Engaged Observer: Anthropology, Advocacy and Activism,* coedited with Asale Angel-Ajani (Rutgers University Press). She is currently writing *Morality and Survival: Child Soldiers and Displacement in Guatemala and Colombia.*

JESSICA SENEHI is associate director of the Arthur V. Mauro Centre for Peace and Justice at St. Paul's College, University of Manitoba, Canada. Previously she was assistant professor of conflict analysis and resolution at Nova Southeastern University, where she taught master's- and doctoral-level courses in international, cross-cultural, and community conflict resolution for four years. Her research and writing focuses on the role of culture and storytelling in social movements and interethnic peace building, violence against children, youth activism, and peace education. She has served as a community mediator and conflict resolution trainer and taught youth leadership. She holds an MS in psychology and PhD in social science from Syracuse University. Her research was supported by a 2003–04 University of Manitoba research project grant for research on peace building and popular expressive traditions.

MARC SOMMERS is an associate research professor of humanitarian studies at the Fletcher School of Law and Diplomacy and a research fellow with Boston University's African Studies Center. He has carried out research in twenty war-affected countries and regularly writes and consults on youth, education, peace education, conflict negotiation, child soldiers, urbanization, human rights, and security issues in war and postwar contexts. His book, *Fear in Bongoland: Burundi Refugees in Urban Tanzania* (2001), received the 2003 Margaret Mead Award from the American Anthropological Association and the Society for Applied Anthropology.

MICHAEL WESSELLS is Senior Child Protection Specialist for Christian Children's Fund, professor of clinical population and family health in the Program on Forced Migration and Health at Columbia University, and professor of psychology at Randolph-Macon College. He has served as president of the American Psychological Association Division of Peace Psychology and Psychologists for Social Responsibility. He is a core member of the Mellon Foundation Psychosocial Working Group on Refugees, which defines a global framework and research agenda on refugee assistance, and of the UN research network on Children and Armed Conflict. Author of three books and over sixty published papers and chapters, his current research on children and armed conflict examines child soldiers, displaced children, psychosocial assistance in emergencies, and post-conflict reconstruction for peace. In countries such as Angola, Afghanistan, Sierra Leone, East Timor, Uganda, Kosova, and Sri Lanka, he helps to develop community-based, culturally grounded programs of psychosocial support that link relief and development assistance to war-affected children, families, and communities.